# JAZZ WEST
## 1945-1985

### THE A-Z GUIDE TO
### WEST COAST JAZZ MUSIC

## BY K. O. ECKLAND

## PHOTOGRAPHS BY ED LAWLESS

**CYPRESS**
Carmel-by-the-Sea, California

ISBN 0 938995 03 0 hardbound
ISBN 0 938995 04 9 softbound

Library of Congress Catalog Card Number 86-071431

Printed in the United States of America

Published by Cypress
P. O. Box 223179, Carmel CA 93922

*Laissez les bon temps rouler...*

To Lu Watters, for starting the good times again.
To Turk Murphy, for keeping them rolling.

# CONTENTS

PREFACE   9
ALPHABETICAL LISTINGS   17
YOUTH GROUPS   225
ADDENDA   228
THE ORGANIZATIONS   231
THE CELEBRATIONS   239
FAMILY ALBUM   255
REFERENCES   285

That jazz is cyclical by nature is generally conceded, but this most recent cycle is somewhat of a phenomenon. For one thing, the current cycle of jazz has had a longer lifespan than did the original and, for another, the number of people touched by the music is many times the size it was back at the beginning.

To understand this cycle approach better, we must first mark a starting point. We might consider the year 1900, at the peak of a ragtime craze, which was about when the squalling infant jazz began to make its presence known under that title in the black community, where its primitive rhythms and uncomplicated structures were readily understood and repeated, where the music itself was a means of communication among the people who created it.

The word, originally "jass" (and sometimes "jas"), came right out of the bordellos of New Orleans, a sobriquet for the sex act. Eventually the word would shed its original connotation but at first there was this blatancy which kept it from being a popular topic in polite company, in black as well as white households. The music itself was officially condemned by hierarchs of the Baptist church, who championed their own spirituals (although they swayed a lot more than they used to), but a fallacy lying therein was that jazz actually concerned itself with sanctity as much as it did sin. Religion and gospel were tap roots and even as missionaries campaigned to convert slaves to Christianity, they were adding to their own hymnals African rhythms and lyrics. Black bands, however, were quick to develop the sounds as they played their dances and street concerts, yet the name "jazz" was never used openly. Buddy Bolden featured a "ragtime" band, as did others.

By 1910, Bolden had been put away in an insane asylum but jazz music had established its beachhead, principally in the Storyville district. Ragtime had already made it to the neat parlors of white America since its beginnings in the 1880s — hardly a piano went by that didn't have a dogeared copy of "Alexander's Ragtime Band" or "Maple Leaf" on it — but jazz music itself was yet unpublished and quite unaccepted anywhere but in its own back yard. It wasn't until 1922 that King Oliver was recorded with his Creole Jazz Band.

Touring minstrel shows openly performed jazz tunes under every title but that. The all-white Jack Laine Ragtime Band in 1915, training grounds for many members of the Original Dixieland Jass Band (ODJB) to come, was popular in the minstrel show circuit with its "improvisations" on Negro music (which was actually scored note for note), sometimes lightly alluded to in programs as "those songs from the Dixie's land."

Apparently the first group to use the title outside of the local area was Bert Kelly's Jass Band (spelled thusly) in Chicago, March 1916. Prior to that, the first white group in New Orleans, Tom Brown's Band, began toying with the new sounds in 1915, later changing its title first to Brown's Dixieland Jass Band for touring, and subsequently The Louisiana Five. Brown, a product of Laine's Band, and like the ODJB in 1917, took on the "Dixieland" label in order to downplay "Jass," as well as to disavow any connection with black jazz. In order to understand this oblique approach, one must take into consideration the existing social conditions. Except for New Orleans, a more cosmopolitan, tolerant city by virtue of its being a homogenous port of trade, our nation wallowed in an era of deep-rooted bigotry where blacks had even less than second-class status (for musicians, traceries of Jim Crow would reach well into the forties). Not long removed from slavery, they were objects of burlesque, openly referred to in popular songs as "darkies" and "pickaninnies" and certainly not to be taken seriously. There was, therefore, understandable shock that they should be responsible for a music form with such immense and catholic appeal.

But jazz was finally unleashed and our initial cycle really begins about 1915. It hit big, especially after the Great War, when people needed something different, something lively and expressive to take their minds off their troubles. Before it gained respectability, it was treated as the bastard child of music, not too unlike rock-and-roll in the mid-fifties. References to the "Jazz Age" brought about mental pictures of flaming youth, kids lashing out at the propriety of their elders, smoky speakeasies and low-life musicians. It represented a sinful, daring fling to all who dared to roll their stockings down and embrace its frantic rhythms.

But it was the new wave and as such it thrived for two decades before it was gradually absorbed into the encroaching big band sounds. The end of the cycle was not abrupt, nor even final for that matter, but one could circle 1935 as the end of the "pure" jazz era. The brassy sweetness of orchestral music was what audiences then craved.

So that accounts for some 20 years of activity. Certainly there were jazz bands around after 1935, and audiences always willing to listen, but the heyday of the small jazz club was gone. Red Nichols, Eddie Condon, Fats Waller, Louis Amstrong, were all still going but perhaps not so steadily as in the old days. Some, like Kid Ory, dropped out of music completely in order to make a living; others joined or formed big bands.

Of importance to consider is that the Midwest and the East Coast were at all times throughout the first cycle of jazz the focal point, the breeding ground. Any town worth its salt boasted of at least one jazz joint. Beyond the Rockies, however, Westerners in general displayed a shallow interest in the new music and only Hollywood's silver screen offered any idea of what it was all about as pit orchestras played the curious, syncopated rhythms. Jazzmen like Jelly Roll Morton and King Oliver and Kid Ory made forays into the wild west but soon went back to New Orleans, Chicago or New York, where work was steady. Although many former New Orleans musicians did remain in the West to form bands, work was sporadic at best and usually popular only in the black-owned clubs. The real influx of jazz-oriented musicians didn't come west until the advent of the big bands in the thirties.

In contrast, the recent cycle — more of a cycle within a cycle — which could be said to have started at the end of the Second World War, is still very much alive and apparently still growing at this writing. This accounts for nearly 40 years!

Perhaps more than any one person, the blame for this cycle's upsweep, especially in the West, can be placed on Lu Watters. Before the appearance of his Yerba Buena Jazz Band in San Francisco (more accurately the second appearance, considering the pre-war *Dawn Club*), the West Coast was a desert where jazz was concerned. West of the Rockies and from border to border, only one active social jazz club existed and that one primarily focused on record collecting. Then came the formative get-togethers at Berkeley's *Big Bear* from which the YBJB grew, and as it gained popularity, so did jazz. By 1950, kids began taking up banjos and trombones to have a go at this "new" sound. In Los Angeles, places like the *Hangover Club* and the *Beverly Cavern* became meccas for jazz devotees. They were new hot spots for old jazz bands, some of them brought out of early retirements. New groups like the Firehouse Five Plus Two and the Castle Jazz Band popped up. From the East they came, as well — Pete Daily and his Chicagoans were suddenly household words on the Coast. Records began reappearing on jukeboxes and radio and in record stores.

However, referring to that cycle within a cycle, there was a head-to-head confrontation with a splinter form of jazz — bebop, or progressive. Audiences, especially young ones, were confronted by peer pressure, hard and fast options of choosing between the loose, fast-paced, gut-level traditional jazz or the more cerebral progressive jazz. They were either "mods" or "moldy figs," there was no in-between. Then into the fray came the stranger to our shore, rock 'n' roll! During this period, the jazz cycle-within-a-cycle began a downward turn and it looked as if the second coming would be short-lived.

But instead of bottoming out, the curve started up again. It's difficult to fix the exact time or find any one cause, but jazz took a second breath — a big one this time. Perhaps it was a rebellion against rock and its insistent clamoring, perhaps it was a desire to return to the less complicated times of yesteryear. I can't say with authority, so I leave that subject to more learned minds.

It was in the late sixties that I became aware of the cycle effect, one which has continued in force to this date. In order to judge accurately where the peak of any cycle is, one must first plot both ends. We can mark point A at 1945, but since there isn't any point B in sight, it's hard to say where the apogee is or just how long the good times will roll.

There are perhaps more successful jazz bands presently extant than were during the original cycle. The captive audience is much larger, and by "captive" I refer to that audience which actively seeks out jazz as a source of entertainment and therapy. To the audiences of the '20s, jazz was "pop" music, that society's background music. It was just there and hardly deserving of special treatment like jazz clubs or festivals.

Remarkably, this cycle's growth has taken place with scant media support and none from recording companies, whose backing makes millionaires overnight from those playing the commercially acceptable stuff aimed at a mass youth market. In contemporary recordings, there have been a few experimental forays by rock groups looking for "new" material and by vocalists — Leon Redbone, for example — who have demonstrated a successful, if curious, blending of old and new, but the burden of jazz record production and distribution still lies with the individual bands and a few independent producers. Mass-media "jazz critics" in the main focus upon exponents of fusion and avant-garde musicians, managing to overlook the talents of traditional jazz artists; a notable exception is Phil Elwood of the *San Francisco Examiner*, who retains a more broad-based attitude about his subject matter.

Oases bloom here and there, however. See's Candies found it commercially rewarding enough to support a regular, live radio show featuring Turk Murphy (although, in that case, it didn't hurt that See's president, Charles Huggins, was a jazz aficionado). Other radio stations, primarily FM, offer regular jazz programs with erudite hosts like Richard Hadlock, Jim Hodges, Vince Marino, Dave Richoux and Bob Ringwald, but their reach is limited. Commercial stations stick to commercial music, away from art and into business. Dave Dexter Jr, a Capitol Records producer, in his book *Playback*, said that jazz and big-band would be back in 30 days if they had broadcast time and that "the wretched Top 40 domination of the airwaves today precludes anything artistically laudable being heard by American youth..."

Concern is expressed by many who watch with wonder the proliferation of jazz festivals and the apparently never-ending echelons of new jazz bands. "Anything this good can't last," one person told me. There is a lot of climbing on the bandwagon on the parts of merchants and cabaret owners who eye with envy — and a wee touch of cupidity — the swarming crowds of "footstompers." However, this borderline acceptance of jazz brings up a curious contradiction. There are fewer jazz joints now than there were at the beginning of the present cycle. With the exception of pizza parlors and beer bars and such, jazz bands don't seem to last in regular night clubs. Jazz is still not supported by the multitudes and, except for the perennial Turk Murphy Jazz Band, hardly a single group on the West Coast has a

11

place to play that is enduring or fully supported by those footstompers. Yet, many jubilees and festivals are early sell-outs.

## WHAT IS JAZZ, DADDY?

This is not meant to be a definitive work on the physical or mental psychology of jazz — that subject will be left for more competent hands to juggle. It is, rather, a record of those who have maintained the fine art of jazz music.

Jazz itself is enigmatic, suffering from misconceptions, half-truths and fable. Like the beach, it is neither land nor sea. Essentially, jazz is considered to be purely improvised, syncopated and for the most part uncomposed, none of which is true. That it is an intuitive and acquired music *is* true, for there were initially no schools to train musicians, and there are presently precious few educational programs available which stress formal training in grass-roots jazz — one notable exception is Fullerton State College. Another truism is that jazz is an experience of the moment; a musical snowflake. Any particular tune played five times by a competent musician will five times be different and, without orchestrations, cannot be duplicated. Jazz, therefore, might appropriately be described as playing the music, as opposed to playing the composer.

There will be those who understandably take exception to my use of such an all-encompassing title for this book, but I remain defensive in my position. I accept the word "jazz" in its original value, signifying that music with roots in New Orleans or which is consonant. Everything after that should rightfully be considered an amendment — bop, cool jazz, mainstream, progressive. They who embrace these titles are merely stacking their blocks on an existing foundation and should in all fairness give due tribute to their roots. So, what then should I title a book?

"Traditional jazz" is universally accepted, but allusive at best in light of the varied sounds of jazz bands today. Very few play in the original, traditional New Orleans idiom.

"Dixieland" is a description universally despised by jazz musicians and has come to represent a verbal parody on all that is meaningful in their music — straw hats, beer bars and repertoires limited to "Tiger Rag" and "The Saints." The word originally was a geographic description of that area where the "Dixie" could be found — a ten-dollar bill with DIX printed on it — and only secondarily as the country below the Mason-Dixon Line, which is far removed from the deep South as we know it. The word was adopted by white bands to camouflage the fact that the music they played was originated by the blacks. It was felt a title other than "jazz" was necessary to remove the stigma of those Storyville bordellos and to bring a touch of social acceptability. "Dixieland" thereby became suitable for a culture which thrives on descriptive titles. More recently, we've seen the word "rock" (white) take over from "rhythm and blues" and "race music" (black), broadened even more to embrace "country rock" and "punk rock," both demanding of subclassification.

"Classic jazz" appears with regularity, yet that phrase seems to cloak earthy rhythms in a somber tuxedo. However, it's at least closer to fact.

How about "West Coast" jazz? There isn't any such thing. That's a geographical arabesque coined by someone desperate for an adjective. If this is indicative of the Watters/Murphy sound, then it would best be called just that, and there would then be an unfair implication of mimicry. Listen to a recording of Gene Mayl's Dixieland Rhythm Kings (Ohio) from the mid-fifties, with their "West Coast" sound, and judge how much validity that title would have.

"Hot jazz," as opposed to "cool jazz," is getting close but is "Storyville Blues" really "hot?" What happened to the middleground of "tepid" and "lukewarm?" I still claim there is no bill to be filled.

So we come back to plain old "jazz," the one word that best signifies the matrix from which all else would come. I will aggressively use that word descriptively, with neither subclassifications nor attendant adjectives, and those who take exception to this posture will have to serve me a more suitable replacement.

## ABOUT THE CONTENTS

This was the hard row to hoe. Who would be included and who would I offend by exclusion? Why would Lawrence Welk be listed and Benny Goodman not? And where is good old Louis Armstrong or Pete Fountain? In approaching this project, I had to first set up some guidelines, rather severe ones.

First, the musicians or groups of musicians had to be predominately performers with traditional orientation. That automatically scratched Theolonius Monk and a few thousand others. Welk made it only because he had a great little jazz combo buried under that barrage of bubbles. Goodman didn't make it because he abandoned this form of jazz in the thirties.

Secondly, they had to be West Coast, or West Coast-ish, musicians. There went Pete and Satchmo. There were many bands during the time frame of this book which were popular on the West Coast, but they were principally touring bands with the East or Midwest their base of operations. Even their records were foreign to us — Commodore, Blue Note, and the likes. George Wettling and Sharkey Bonano were favorites but we couldn't catch their acts, except for occasional concerts. The same goes for the New Black Eagles and the Preservation Hall bunch. Turk Murphy and Dixie Flyers and Uptown Lowdown were here, they were our own. We could not only buy their records, we could have them autographed.

Thirdly, and with no small amount of anguish, I decided to omit the big bands, even those which played "some Dixie." The specialty at which they excelled, and obviously felt more comfortable with, was in recreating yet another great cyclical age.

One might argue here about where the fine line was drawn between Jazz Formula playing "Chicago" and High Sierra doing the same song. There didn't appear to be any real one, except when it came down to the question: could Jazz Formula extemporize on "Big Bear Stomp?" The same held true for High Sierra and "A String Of Pearls." Either group was quite capable of playing either song, but would they want to? The fine line then became basic tune selection.

Some groups, like Chicago Six and Fulton Street, made a fluid transition between two worlds and this was quite acceptable to their audiences. Another band stands out as a curious exception to Rule Three — Royal Society Jazz Orchestra. The group was formed from primarily jazz-oriented musicians, they played a lot of what could be called jazz (at least by titles) and were actively sought out by jazz fans at festivals. In this case, the ayes had it.

Data may appear conspicuously brief in cases of more renown musicians. Here I felt that previous publications have devoted much space to them and it was my desire to avoid redundancy. Serious researchers should consult the reference appendix. With space a consideration, musicians may not have to their credit all the bands they ever played with. It's easy for someone to say he "played with Kid Ory" when in fact he only sat in a set or, in some cases, may have been a temporary replacement for a regular band member. Were I to embrace an all-inclusive line of thinking, the end product would require a couple of strong men to lift it!

Missing are "invisible" jazz bands — those which were temporary creations, such as all-star or special occasion bands with blue-sky names. Many bands had the lifespan of a mayfly and are not listed. Omitted are what might be regarded non-derogatorily as "Elks

13

Club bands," perhaps playing credible jazz, but to a limited audience only and never appearing out of their bailiwick.

Some bands represented a real can of worms when it came to sorting out personnel and dates. Incompleteness was rampant on the part of band historians, and there's one instance where it was a game of musical chairs between three bands. One musician even admitted that at one period in time he was playing with no less than five different groups! At best I could only generalize subject matter and time references.

Any exclusion is not out of prejudice. Carelessness, perhaps, but not because of any personal or hearsay bias. Yet there is a certain incompleteness to this book and I didn't want it that way, but I bit off quite a chunk. Some musicians who had passed on left no legacy of information for me to rummage through; some were unlocatable; others had aged and memories had become dim, especially where specific dates and places were concerned. Some with egos or interest down around the zero mark couldn't have cared less about being listed. The geographic area being what it is, personal contact was impossible, and stringers — those who volunteered to gather information in areas remote to me — began dropping like flies once they realized the scope of the task they would face.

Vital statistics are included where known, as are vocations in the case of non-professional musicians. That doesn't sound right, I know, but I mean so few in the present milieu of jazz can earn a living from music alone. The greatest cornetist around may find that driving a taxi during the day helps keep bread on the table.

Whether or not this book has specific worth and serves a valid purpose stands to be judged in future light. If more than any one thing, it is a tribute to some 2500 regional performers who have continued to breathe life into America's only native art form and at least deserve mention for their efforts.

## A LITTLE APPLAUSE

Most instrumental in providing information contained in this book were countless musicians and band leaders and, in some instances, their friends and followers. However, in light of assistance above and beyond the call of duty, it is my wish to give deserved credit to some who share a dedicated love for the beast, who made the monumental task of information gathering a bit less arduous.

Heading this cadre were Jim Goggin, Dottie and Ed Lawless, and Mamie Russell, who never put me on hold, no matter what time I called. Others who provided sizeable chunks of valuable reference were Doris Belleque, Jim Borkenhagen, Dave Bourne, Dick Hadlock, Stephen Joseph, Bob Mielke, Bill Mitchell, Witt Mueller, Bill Napier, Gene Norman, Ron Ortmann, Hal Smith, and Harriet Vogel.

As for the other half of this book, my very special thanks goes to Ed Lawless, who just "happened to have his camera with him" at all the right times. His ability to capture fleeting moments on film accounts for the preservation of fragile images for some 30 years, all methodically catalogued in an impressive rank of filing cabinets. There just may be artier photographers around, but I guarantee you there are none more dedicated. Ed, or "Doc," as a lot of us know him, spends countless hours in his darkroom, grinding out countless enlargements for countless musicians, and I don't know any who has ever received a bill from him.

The other half of the team is his wife, Dottie. Both are welcomed everywhere jazz is played and, although recognized by bandleaders and sidemen alike, they still insist on paying door tabs and cover charges as gestures of support. A strange breed.

Because of the Lawless files, photographs which would have otherwise been a major hurdle were easy to come by. A simple phone call to Ed with a few requirements and he'd call the hospital, tell them something important just came up and would they hold off the operation for a few hours, and the packet would be in my mailbox a day or two later. Although the majority of photographs is the end result of one man's dedication and devotion to jazz musicians, in a few instances pictures came from other sources and are identified as such, with appropriate thanks due to Jack Boppel, Marlene Bruhn, Al Douglas, Wayne Nicholls, and even my son, Dan Eckland, who followed the Firehouse Five around for a while until he discovered girls were almost as much fun.

## THE LISTINGS

Band listings indicate, where known, popular title of the group; original locale; years of existence; general information; personnel of the original group and periods of involvement; subsequent personnel (ADD:) and periods of involvement; recording data. *Italics are recording groups only.*

Individual listings indicate, where known, full name; instrument(s); year of birth (and death, if so); place of birth; trade or vocation, if not a professional musician or if avocational in nature; other band affiliations, with titles shortened logically and [brackets] used to signify frequent or special involvement, such as recording or regular sub; incidental information; recording data.

In date references, the arrow symbol (→) indicates that those groups or personnel were extant at the time of publication.

Recording data are not meant to compete with professional discographies and serve only to indicate a cross-section of the recorded works of specific bands or musicians. An equal sign in album numbers ( = L12000) indicates a continuation of the preceding manufacturer. Listings consist for the most part of LPs, with 78s and 45s added only in cases of certain relevance, and may contain no reference to foreign labels or re-pressings of duplicate information under other labels — as in the case of "supermarket" albums. Dates usually refer to the year of release but, sometimes, as in anthologies, may include recording dates much earlier than album release date. The waters become murky here and the suggestion is for serious discographers to consult more specific references.

Method of listing all entries is logical, using the American Library Association system. Bands are generally alphabetized by their principal title with subordinated personal names — i.e.: **CHICAGOANS (PETE DAILY'S)**, but **PETE DAILY'S RHYTHM KINGS**, since there are other Rhythm Kings — except in the case of created titles, like **EMPEROR NORTON'S JAZZ BAND**, which is listed under E. **DR JON** is treated as **DOCTOR JON, 32nd STREET** as **THIRTY-SECOND STREET**. First names are treated informally — **Bill** takes precedence over **William**.

Within the listings, certain abbreviations are used to conserve space:

| | | | |
|---|---|---|---|
| acc | accordian | DB | Dixieland Band |
| alt | alternate | dir | director |
| arr | arranger | DJB | Dixieland Jazz Band |
| asax | alto sax | do. | ditto previous entry |
| bjo | banjo | eb | electric bass |
| bsax | bass sax | eg | electric guitar |
| bro | brother | fdr | founder |
| CHI | Chicago | flug | flugelhorn |
| cl | clarinet | g | guitar |
| comp | composer, -ed | JB | Jazz Band |
| cor | cornet | LA | Los Angeles |
| d | drums | ldr | leader |

15

| marr | married (to) | SEA | Seattle |
|------|-------------|-----|---------|
| mello | mellophone | SF | San Francisco |
| NO | New Orleans | sis | sister |
| NY | Ney York | SJ | San Jose |
| o | organ | ssax | soprano sax |
| org | organizer | tbn | trombone |
| orig | original | tpt | trumpet |
| p | piano | tsax | tenor sax |
| perc | percussion | tu | tuba |
| PTL | Portland | v | vocal |
| rec | record, -ed, -ing | vib | vibraphone |
| SAC | Sacramento | viol | violin |
| sb | string bass | wb | washboard |
| SD | San Diego | xyl | xylophone |

States are indicated by postal code (ZIP)

## Recordings:

| | |
|------|-----|
| *BR* | *Berkeley Rhythm* |
| *CAP* | *Capitol* |
| *cass* | *cassette* |
| *DC* | *Dawn Club* |
| *DJ* | *Dixieland Jubilee* |
| *EUPH* | *Euphonic* |
| *GHB* | *George H Buck* |
| *GTJ* | *Good Time Jazz* |
| *JM* | *Jazz Man* |
| *MMRC* | *Merrymakers* |
| *RIV* | *Riverside* |
| *SS* | *Shoestring* |
| *SJS* | *Sacramento Jazz Society* |
| *SOS* | *Stomp Off* |
| *VIC* | *Victor* |
| *WB* | *Warner Brothers* |

Other abbreviations indicate uncertain manufacturer or are the band's own labels.

# A

## ABALONE STOMPERS Monterey 1958→

Although "Papa" Jake Stock had a band since 40, the title came in 58 from a remark by a drummer that the music "sounded like a lonely abalone calling its mate at three in the morning." The group at the time featured the Stock family with whatever additional sidemen were necessary. One of the most laid-back groups ever to appear anywhere since its initial appearance at the first Monterey Jazz Festival (58), personnel included practically every local musician at one time or another, and listing is random with some of the more enduring members.

Ned Brundage, d (75,77,84); Jackie Coon, tpt (75→); Eddie Erickson, bjo (64-74,83→); Al Hays, tu (70); Joe Ingram, tpt (70-75); Mary Ingram, p (70-74); Buddy Jones, sb (75); Lew Keizer, tpt (78); Jack Mathis, tpt (-60); Bill Newman, g (75); Eric Nicoll, d (80→); Dudley Nix, d (-60); Alan O'Dea, tu (→); Bob Phillips, p (→); Eddie Smith, tpt (70-72); Grace Stock, p (-60); JAKE STOCK, cl; Jackson Stock, tbn (78→); Barney Watson, tbn (-60).

*cass "With Love from Jake and the Boys" (85)*

**Bill Abbott, d** *(1918 Medford OR) insurance* - Capital City; Emerald

**Calvin "Cal" Abbott, reeds** *(1934 Springfield MO) aircraft maintenance* - Apex; [Delta Jazz]; Euphonic; Euphoria; Jubilee; King Riverbottom; Magnolia; Prof Plum

**Jerry Abernathy, p** - Crown City

**Don "Abe" Abrahamson, d** *postal service* - Hume St

**Steve Abrams, wbd, d** *(1933 Hamburg GERMANY) pharmacist* - Churchill St; Jubilee; King Riverbottom

**Bob Adamowecz, reeds** *(Phoenix AZ)* - Desert City

**Alan Adams, tbn** - Jazzbo

**Dick Adams, reeds** *(Seattle WA)* - Great Excelsior

**Jim Adams, tpt** *(1932 Los Angeles CA) real estate* - Mardi Gras-LA; Rosy McHargue

**Steve Adams, d** - Apex

**Dom Addario, tpt** - Yankee Air Pirates

**Marie Addario, bjo** - Yankee Air Pirates

**Grace Ades, v** - Marin Jazz

**Charley Ahrens, bass, tbn** *(1926 Manitowoc WI) mechanical engr* - Oregon; Pussyfoot

**Charley Aimo, tpt** - New Bull Moose; Outcast

## AIN'T NO HEAVEN SEVEN SEA 1983→

John Gibson, tpt; Dave Gilbert, p; Ward Kennedy, tbn; Karl May, bjo; John Mazzarella, d; TERRY ROGERS, reeds; Al Rustad, tu.

**Steve Alaniz, reeds** - Lemon St; Riverboat Ramblers

**Jerry Albert, tpt** *optometrist* - Jelly Roll Jazz Society

**Dave Albertson, bass** - Emperor Norton

**Gary Aleshire, tbn** *(Tacoma WA) humane society* - ldr Destiny; Oregon; Traffic Jammers

**Cindy Alexander, tbn** - Headliners

**Patrick Alexander, tbn** - ldr Riverboat Ramblers

**William "Aud" Alexander, bjo** *(1895 Cherokee IA)* - solo; led own groups

**Manuel Alcantar, cor** *(1948 Palo Alto CA) sales* - Royal Society; led own groups

## ALEXANDER'S JAZZ BAND SF 1951

Ostensibly SCOBEY'S FRISCO BAND but retitled for a short while when Scobey took over *Hambone Kelly's* after Watters' YERBA BUENA JB disbanded, renaming it *Alexander's.*

Jack Buck, tbn; Squire Girsback, sb/tu; Clancy Hayes, bjo/v; Fred Higuera, d; George Probert, ssax; BOB SCOBEY, tpt; Wally Rose, p. ADD: Burt Bales, p; Jack Crook, cl; Bill Dart, d; Gordon Edwards, d; Darnell Howard, cl; Harry Mordecai, bjo; Bill Newman, bjo/g; Hotz O'Casey, cl.

*GTJ 53-54 (50); JM 33-34 (50); TRILON 220-222, 242-243 (47)*

**Danny Alguire, tpt** *(1912 Chicksha OK) animation dir* - Jim Beatty; Firehouse 5 + 2; Bob Wills

DANNY ALGUIRE
October 1964

Dan Eckland

**Lorraine Alkire, bjo** *optometrics* - Hume St

**Bob Allen, bass, tpt** *attorney* - ldr Chris Kelly; Jelly Roll JB-LA; NO Creole Gumbo; Reno Charlie; So Bay Zephyr; Southern Stompers

**Jay Allen, bass** - Silver Dollar-SAC

**Pete Allen, bass** *(1921 Kentfield CA) radio tech* - Bearcats; Burp Hollow; Casa Bonita; Funky NOJB; Golden Age; Golden Gate Stompers; Lionel Hampton; [Magnolia]; New Washboard Rhythm Kings; Oakland Hot Babies; Kid Ory-SF; Polecats; Muggsy Spanier; Silicon; Stone Age; Joe Sullivan

**Rex Allen, tbn** *(1952 San Leandro CA)* - [Delta Jazz]; [Oregon]; Phrisco; SF Swing Express; Tappers; World's Greatest JB

**Vernon Alley, bass** *(1915 Winnemucca NV)* - Lionel Hampton; Turk Murphy; Jack Sheedy; [Ralph Sutton]; led own groups

## ALLIGATOR JAZZ QUINTET LA 1985→

SHELLY LORD-HOWE, tpt; Jack Keister, reeds; Chuck Rimmer, tu; Jeff Stein, tbn; Dee Trent, bjo.

**Mark Allin, reeds** - Jazzin' Jrs

**Dave Allison, bjo** - ldr Party Peppers

**Hugh Allison, d** *(1924 Salina KS)* - Pete Daily; Rosy McHargue

**Bill Allred, tbn** *(Davenport IA)* - [Fulton St]; ldr Golden State; ldr Rosie O'Grady (FL); led own groups; music dir Disney World (FL)

**John Allred, tbn** *(1963)* - Jazz Minors; son of Bill Allred

**Wayne Allwine, d, eb, reeds** *(1947 Glendale CA) sound engr* - Monrovia; had 9-piece folk group during mid '60s; is present voice of Mickey Mouse

**Ed Alsman, d** - Great Excelsior

**Harry Alto, bass, bjo, g** *(1920 Walnut Creek CA)* - Sam Donahue; Emperor Norton

## AMBULANCE CHASERS LA 1982

Assembled to replace SOUTH FRISCO JB during their European tour. Comprised of Disney musicians, subsequently evolved into MONROVIA OLD STYLE JB.

Norm Carlisle, bjo; Jack Faul, bjo; Ralph Hall, tu; Ward Kimball, d; Joe Parker, cor; GEORGE PROBERT, ssax; Frank Thomas, p; Jack Wadsworth, bsax/ssax.

**Frank Amoss, d** - Jazz Inc; King Zulu; ldr Mississippi

**Clyde Amsler, reeds** - Blueblowers; Cats 'n' Jammers

**John Anagnostou, d** - Dixieland Delinquents

**C. J. "Speed" Anderson** *AFM official* - Conductors

**Chuck Anderson, tbn** *(1932 Omaha NB)* - Tex Beneke; Les Elgart; Dixie Katz; Harry James; Jazz Inc; Miss-Behavin'; Orange Blossom; Paradise; led own groups

**Diane Anderson, v** - Dixieland Inc

**Don Anderson, tbn, tpt** *(1928 Two Harbors MN)* - Island City; Shakey City; led own group

VINNIE ARMSTRONG
October 1984

REX ALLEN
April 1983

## DON ANDERSON'S DIXIELAND BAND SEA 1960

*Lake City Tavern* SEA (60). See SHAKEY CITY SEVEN.
DON ANDERSON, tpt; Dave Coleman, d; Mike Hobi, tbn; Red Kelly, sb; Rollie Morehouse, cl; Johnny Wittwer, p.

**Ed Anderson, tbn** *(1922 Superior WI) aerospace engr* - Dick Cary; Bob Crosby; Elaine Mitchell; Red Nichols

**Ernie Anderson, bjo** - Banjo Kings

**George Anderson, reeds** - Nightblooming

**Johnny Anderson, p** *(1909 Goldfield NV)* - [Bunk Johnson]; blind SF pianist played mostly cocktail lounges into the late '40s; devotee and exponent of Jelly Roll Morton and other early pianists; intermission entertainer at *Hambone Kelly's* (c48).

**.Walter "Skippy" Anderson, p** *(19—19—)* - Blueblowers; Pete Daily; Phil Harris; Turk Murphy; Jack Teagarden

**Carol Andreen, v** - Crown City; San Diego DJB; marr Phil Andreen

**Phil Andreen, tbn** - ldr Crown City; ldr San Diego DJB; co-fdr America's Finest City Dixieland Jazz Club

**George Andrus, d** - Dixie Katz; Monarch

## AND THAT'S JAZZ Alameda 1979→

Ed Blanchard, tu (-84); Bob Franklin, p (-83); Barrie Luttge, bjo (-84); GENE R MAURICE, cor; Phil Stiers, cl (-84); Bert Thompson, d (-84); Wayne Torkelson, tbn (-84). ADD: Bob Brennen, tbn (84→); Leonard Dixon, cl (84→); Griff Harries, p (83→); Bob Hinman, sb; Bud Lyons, d (84→); Dave Richoux, tu (84→); Al Villaire, cl; Jack Wiecks, bjo (84→).

**Pete Andreadis, d** - Kansas City; Outcast; Thee Saints

## ANGEL CITY JAZZ BAND LA 1975→

Originally formed to perform at Sacramento Dixieland Jubilee, have remained extant since. House band of Jazz Forum 75-80.
Ike Candioti, d (-79); CHUCK CONKLIN, cor; Elaine Mitchell, p/v; Gordon Mitchell, tbn (-77); Dolph Morris, sb (75-79,85→); Jimmy Shivnan, reeds (-76,78); Dan Snyder, tbn (-79,82→). ADD: Joe Ashworth, ssax (76-77); Ham Carson, reeds (83-84); Joe Darensbourg, cl (76-84); Phil Gray, tbn (80); Bill Hadnott, sb (83-84); Ted Higgins, d (84→); Steve King, g (83→); Jerry McKenzie, d (80); Marge Murphy, v (76-82); Red Murphy, g (76-81); Wayne Songer, reeds (alt); Dave Stone, sb (80); Chuck Thomas, sax (84→); Jeffery Walker, cl (83→).
*ANGEL CITY "South By Southwest"* (76)

**Mike Angelos, bass** - ldr 32nd St

**Scott Anthony, bjo** *(1948 Summit NJ) artist* - ldr Golden Gate Rhythm Machine; solo; long-term intermission entertainer at *Earthquake McGoon's*
*DAWSON & CHAMBERS 001 "Rags and Other Old Tunes"* (82)

**Phil Antonaides, d** - UC Jazz

## APEX JASS BAND SJ 1976-82

Formed at a South Bay Trad Jazz Society Christmas Party. Scott started on trombone, switched to cornet after Kirk and Swanson left to form PROF PLUM; Abbott left to join EUPHORIA.

Cal Abbott, cl (-77); Bill Armstrong, bjo (-78); Jeff Bender, p; Phil Kirk, tpt (-78); JOHN SCOTT, tbn/cor; Bob Hinman, sb (-77). ADD: Steve Adams, d (77); Derek Brown, tu (78-); Don Hartburg, tbn (79); Rick Holzgrafe, tbn (80-82); Marc Marcus, cl (77-78); Gary Milliken, cl (79-82); Dick Speer, bjo (79-81); John Stringer, cl (78-79); Mike Swanson, tu (77-78); Joyce Taylor, bjo (80-82).

**Steve Apple, d** *(1961 Palo Alto CA) shipping clerk* - Churchill St; Royal Society

**Moise "Moe" Arellano, p** *(19—19—)* - Wild Bill Davison

## ARISTOCRATS OF JAZZ Santa Barbara 1952→

House band of Santa Barbara Dixieland Society.

Cay Eckmier, p; Al Moyle, tpt; JOHNNY MOYLE, tbn; Bob Noren, tsax; Johnny Palif, cl; J B Penney, bjo; Jack Waller, d.

**Bill Armstrong, bjo** *(1930 Chester PA)* - Apex; ldr Bay Flats; ldr Churchill St; Emperor Norton; Hot Jazz Stompers; Jubilee; ldr King Riverbottom; Magnolia; Prof Plum

**Jim Armstrong, cor, tbn** *(1939 Belfast IRELAND) teacher* - Grand Dominion; Hot Jazz Hot Shots; Phoenix

**Norvin "Vinnie" Armstrong, p** *(1942 Pasadena CA) computer programmer* - Fine Time; French Qtr; Southland; Sunset Music; Wilmington; Yankee Wailers

**Art Arnett, bass, tbn** - Blue Fox; Headliners

**"Buddy" Arnold, reeds** *(1926 New York NY) therapist* - [Calif Ramblers]

**Mike Arnold, reeds** - Fink St; Silver Cornet

**Leif Arntzen, tpt** - Lloyd Arntzen; son of Lloyd Arntzen

**Lloyd Arntzen, reeds** - Dixieland Express; ldr St Valentine; led own groups

## LLOYD ARNTZEN CLASSIC JAZZ BAND Vancouver BC

Leif Arntzen, tpt; LLOYD ARNTZEN, cl/ssax; Mickey Earnshaw, d; Doug Parker, p; Dave Robbins, tbn; Peter Trill, sb.

**Marvin Ash (Ashbaugh), p** *(1914-1974 Lamar CO)* - Levee Loungers; Wingy Manone; Rosy McHargue; Joe Rushton; Muggsy Spanier; Jack Teagarden; led own groups; solo; co-fdr Poor Angel Jazz Society
*CAP 885; = 15435; = H321 "Classics In Jazz" (50 1 cut); DECCA DL8346 "New Orleans At Midnight"; FAIRMONT F104 "Jazz Piano of Marvin Ash"; JM 335; JUMP J12-9 "Marvin Ash" (82); MIRROR 48-50; VELTONE 208, 209*

## MARVIN ASH JAZZ BAND LA 1946

*(Hangover Club):* MARVIN ASH, p; John Freeland, d; Bob Higgins, tpt; Matty Matlock, cl; Lou McGarrity, tbn.

**Joe Ashworth, reeds** *(1938 Newark NJ)* Angel City; co-org Hot Frogs; Jelly Roll Jazz Soc

**Joe Ashworth, reeds** *(1938 Newark NJ)* - Angel City; co-org Hot Frogs; Jelly Roll Jazz Society

**Everett Atchison, bass** *(1926 Surrey BC) health professional* - Grand Dominion; Hot Jazz Hot Shots; Phoenix

**Jim Atlas, bass** - Fine Time

**Ariana Attie, v** - So Bay Zephyr

**Joe Audino, p** *chemist* - Cats 'n' Jammers; Old Sacramento; Oregon; dir and arr Andrews Sisters

**Chuck Austin, d** - Reno Charlie

**Augusta "Claire" Austin, v** *(1918 Yakima WA)* - blues singer in the Bessie Smith tradition; appeared with numerous bands, two years with Bill Napier at *Pier 23* SF; rec with Dixieland Rhythm Kings (OH), Great Excelsior, Turk Murphy, Kid Ory, Bob Scobey, as well as her own combos

*CONTEMPORARY C5002 "When Your Lover Has Gone" w/Bob Scobey; GHB 22 "Claire Austin and Great Excelsior JB"; JAZZOLOGY J52*

**Tom Avants, bass** - Uptown Lowdown

**Arte Azenzer, p** - Beverly Hills

MARVIN ASH August 1965

# B

Ted Babcock, bjo *(1934 WA)* - Desert City; Frank Yankovic

## BACK BAY JAZZ BAND Newport Beach 1974-77

Organized from a group performing casuals since 71. *Zubie's* Costa Mesa (74-75), *French Quarter* Anaheim (75-76), *Tropiano's* Garden Grove (76-77).

Mike Baird, cl/sax; DAN BARRETT, tbn; Dan Comins, cor (74-77); Vince Saunders, bjo; Bryan Shaw, cor (74); Paul Woltz, tu; Laurence Wright, bjo/p.

Chuck Bailey, reeds - Desert City

Stanley "Bud" Baird, p, tpt *(1919 Bandon OR)* construction - Oregon

Mike Baird, reeds *(1933 Pasadena CA)* social worker - Back Bay; [Calif Ramblers]; Chris Kelly; Dawn on Century; Down Home; El Dorado-LA; Golden Eagle; Roger Jamieson; Jelly Roll JB-LA; Resurrection; Rhythm Kings; [Royal Gardens]; Smog City; So Frisco; Southern Stompers

Bill Baker, bass - Sutterville

George Baker, bjo - Spike Jones; Turk Murphy; Sinners

Rick Baker, tpt - Camellia; Dixiecrats; Easy Winners

## BALBOA BAY JAZZ BAND Coos Bay

BOB DOWNER, bjo; others unknown.

## BALBOA BLUES BAND Costa Mesa

JIM GREEN, bjo; others unknown.

## BALBOA JAZZ BAND SD c1976

Bill Campbell, p; Herb Harper, tbn; Ted Hawke, d; Jack Lesberg, sb; Tom Mullinix, tpt; CHARLIE ROMERO, cl.

Burton "Burt" Bales, p *(1916 Stevenson MT)* electronic tech - Alexander's; Sidney Bechet; [Delta Jazz]; Estuary; *Frisco Footwarmers*; ldr *Gin Bottle 4*; Jelly Roll JB-SF; Bunk Johnson; Marty Marsala; Wingy Manone; Turk Murphy; co-ldr Rose & Thistle; Bob Scobey; Yerba Buena; solo; led own groups; *Pier 23* (54-66), *Washington St Bar & Grill* (83→); retired from performing 68-75

ABC 181 *"Jazz From the SF Waterfront"* (58); EUPH ESR2010 *"New Orleans Ragtime"* (75); GTJ L19 *"After Hours"* (53); = 9-10, 35-36; = L12025 *"They Tore My Playhouse Down"* (1 side)

## BURT BALES' DIXIELAND JAZZ BAND SF 1944-49, 1950-indef

*Victor's & Roxie's* Oakland (50-51).

1949: BURT BALES, p; Bill Bardin, tbn; Vince Cattolica, cl; Al Guerra, d. ADD: Bill Dart, d (51); Jack Minger, tpt (50-51); Hotz O'Casey, cl (50-51). 1955: BALES; Bunky Colman, cl; Don Marchant, d; Bob Mielke, tbn; Dick Oxtot, bjo.

## BURT BALES TRIO SF 1948-indef

Many variations under this title, starting at SF's *Players' Club* and leading to his *Pier 23* groups; sometimes augmented into larger groups (as the above listing) when occasioned.
BURT BALES, p; Jack Minger, tpt; Billy Newman, g.

**George Ball, d** - Rosy McHargue

**Ralph "Zulu" Ball, bass** *(1926 Boston MA)* - [Castle]; Firehouse 5 + 2; Good Time; Goose Island; Wingy Manone; ldr Milneburg; [Turk Murphy]; Tailgate; Thee Saints; Workingman; known perhaps as well for his black tuba as for his music. To CA 40

K O Eckland

BURT BALES (with Clancy Hayes), Victor's & Roxie's, c1950

MONTE BALLOU May 1978

**Monte Ballou, bjo, g** *(1902 Waterport NY)* - ldr Castle; Firehouse 5 + 2; Turk Murphy; Rose City Stompers; led own groups

**George Ballantyne, d** - Gem City

**Dani Balschweid, v** - Dr Jon

**Jon Balschweid, cor** - ldr Dr Jon

**Dannie Balser, p** *(1954 Chicago Heights IL) bartender* - Tuleburg

**Keith Baltz, bass** - Cell Block; Headliners

## BANJO KINGS, THE LA 1950-55

Ernie Anderson, bjo; George Bruns, tu; Jerry Hamm, d; Monte Mountjoy, d; DICK ROBERTS, bjo; Frank Thomas, p.

*GTJ L12015 "The Banjo Kings"; = L12029 "do. Vol 2"; = M12036 "Go West"*

**Jack Baran, p** *(Detroit MI)* - Hiz Honor; Jazz Beaux; Purple Gang

## BARBARY COAST STOMPERS East SF Bay 1951

Bill Dart, d; Norman Klehm, tpt; Dick Lammi, tu/sb; BOB MIELKE, tbn; Bill Napier, cl; Jerry Stanton, p.

**Dick Barber, reeds** *(1928 Corvallis OR) circuit court judge* - Capital City; Portland Rose

**Hugh Barclay, tpt** - Dixieland Express

**Bill Bardin, tbn** *(1929 San Bernardino CA) warehouseman* - [Bay City]; Burt Bales; Casa Bonita; [Delta Jazz]; Fine Time; Funky NOJB; Golden Age; Golden Gate Stompers; Earl Hines; Bunk Johnson; NO Syncopators; [Oakland A]; Oakland Hot Babies; Stone Age; Benny Strickler

**Ed Barksdale, bjo, g** *(1909 Detroit MI)* - Louisiana Gents

**Denny Barnard, bjo** *(1930 Oxnard CA) avocado grover* - Riverbank; ldr Last Chance; WFDJE&MKRB

**Tom Barnebey, cor, p** - Down Home; Jelly Roll JB-LA; Jubilee; Smog City

**Paul "Polo" Barnes, reeds** *(1902-1981 New Orleans LA)* - Papa Celestin; King Oliver; Resurrection; orig Tuxedo Band; Young Men From NO

**Bert Barr, cor** *(1944 Vallejo CA) upholstery shop owner* - ldr Chicago Ramblers; ldr Emerald; ldr Uptown Lowdown

**Rose Marie (Sparks) Barr, p** *(1932 Seattle WA) music teacher* - Uptown Lowdown; marr Bert Barr

## BARRELHOUSE JAZZ BAND Oakland 1973-?

Donna Corrigan, p; Al Flood, cl/ssax; Mike Harryman, tu; Chuck McLain, tbn; Ernie Peterson Jr, tpt; Ed Rentner, d. ADD: Jean Cole, p; Jim Gammon, tpt; Cork Larson, bjo; Walter Lee, d; John Parker, cor; Joe Roberts, bjo; Earl Scheelar, cl.

**Dan Barrett, cor, tbn** *(1955 Pasadena CA)* - Back Bay ldr; Down Home; Fink St; Golden Eagle; Golden West; Bob Neighbor; Port Costa; Resurrection; Silver Cornet; Stomp Aces; Sunset Music; Wilmington

**Ben Barrow, g** - Hiz Honor; Jazz Beaux

**Allen Barrows, bass, tbn** *(1920 Billings MT) sales* - Conductors; Rainier

**Hank Bartels, bass** *(1931 New Orleans LA)* - Dukes of Dixieland; Gas House; Golden State; Gramercy

**Vince Bartels, d** *(1957 Baton Rouge LA) construction* - Fulton St; Sutterville

**Perry Barth, d** - Duwamish; Rainy City; Saints

**Jim Bartolotto, bjo, tbn** - Camellia; Old Sacramento

## BASIN STREET TRIO SF 1979-?

DEVON HARKINS, p; Freddie Higuera, d; Phil Howe, cl/ssax. ADD at times: Ellis Horne, cl; Bobby Stowell, cl/sax.

**Bob Bashor, tbn** *(Kelso WA)* - Gold Standard; Gramercy; [Oregon]; Riverbank; Bobby Sherwood; Sinners

**Bill Bassen, reeds** *(1923 Everett WA) food distributor* - Island City

**Tom Bassen, p** *(1918 Everett WA) aircraft painting* - Island City

## BATHTUB GIN PARTY BAND Bellingham WA

George Delrich, cor; Ernie Marshall, sb; Larry Micheau, bjo; Duane Sammons, d; Ian Smith, p; BOB STORMS, cl; Norm Storms, tbn.

**Bob Bates, bass** *(1923 Pocatello ID)* - Dave Brubeck; Marty Marsala; Jack Sheedy

**Jim Bates, bass** *(1930 Boise ID)* - Page Cavanaugh; Freddy Martin; Note-ables

**Norm Bates, p, bass** *(1927 Boise ID) computer science* - Dave Brubeck; [Oakland A]; Wally Rose; Jack Sheedy; led own groups; bro of Bob Bates

**Ray Bauduc, d** *(1906 or 1909 New Orleans LA)* - co-ldr Bauduc-Lamare; Bob Crosby; Jimmy Dorsey; Levee Loungers; Ben Pollack; co-ldr Riverboat Dandies; Jack Teagarden; Joe Venuti; led own groups. Comp *South Rampart St Parade*; to CA 48, TX 71

## BAUDUC-LAMARE JAZZ BAND LA c1955

RAY BAUDUC, d; Gene Bolen, cl; Jack Coon, mel; Rolly Furnas, tbn; Manny Klein, tpt; NAPPY LAMARE, g; Ray Leatherwood, sb; Eddie Miller, tsax; Stan Wrightsman, p.
*CAP 919, 15131; =T887 "Riverboat Dandies"; =T1198 "Two-Beat Generation" (55)*

**E. S. "Scotty" Baughman, d** *(1920 Kansas City MO)* - Good Time Levee

**Wilda Baughn, p** *(Half Moon Bay CA)* - Swanee's Swingers; Wilda's Easy Winners. Blind from birth, learned piano at Berkeley School for Blind; BA in music at SJ State. Popular around SAC area as club soloist, and performed with many groups in the West
*SJS 16 "Wilda Entertains the Hired Help" (81)*

**Fred Baumberger, g** *(1934 Washington PA) journalist* - Jazz Formula; Jazz Forum; Note-ables

**Ted Bavin, bass** - Fink St

## BAY CITY JAZZ BAND SF 1955-59

Then a youth group, possibly the best duplication of Watters' YBJB at the time; formed out of CANAL STREET JB; Farey assumed leadership upon Newbauer's departure. *Sail'N* SF (55-57).

Lloyd Byassee, d; Al Cavallin, tpt (-57); EV FAREY, cor; Roy Giomi, cl; Don Keeler, p (-57); SANFORD NEWBAUER, tbn (-57); Tito Patri, bjo (-57); Walt Yost, tu/cor. ADD: Jack Beecher, sb (56-); Bill Carter, cl; Pete Clute, p; Barry Durkee, bjo (56); Al Nortier, p; Ray Skjelbred, p (81-83); Bob Storm, d; Lee Valencia, bjo (57-59); Jack Vastine, bjo (57); Randy Wilkerson, d. 75 SACRAMENTO JUBILEE: Bill Bardin, tbn; Tom Buck, tpt; FAREY; Tony Jackson, d; Bill Napier, cl; Skjelbred; Ed Turner, bjo/g; Yost.
*GTJ L12017 "The Bay City JB" (56)*

## BAY CITY MUSIC COMPANY SF 1975-76

Began as BAY CITY FIVE and BAY CITY SIX. *The Warehouse* Port Costa (75), subbed at *Earthquake McGoon's* (75-76). Title was revived for a short time with personnel from GOLDEN STATE JB (85), but most of the original members went into SUNSET MUSIC COMPANY (76).

RAY BAUDUC
February 1977

WILDA BAUGHN
February 1973

Jim Cumming, sb; EV FAREY, cor; Tony Johnson, d; Jack Knox, g; Bob Mielke, tbn; Bill Napier, cl; Ray Skjelbred, p. SUBS: Bill Bardin, tbn; Devon Harkins, p; Bill Maginnis, d; Thad Vandon, d.

## BAY CITY STOMPERS see TURK MURPHY JB

## BAY FLATS JAZZ BAND SF
BILL ARMSTRONG, bjo; others unknown.

## BAYSIDE JAZZ BAND Oakland 1950
Second place winners *Record Changer* magazine contest in 50.
Bob Brennan, tbn; Herb Ehlenburg, p; Jerry Good, sb; PETE JACK, d; Gardiner McCauley, bjo; Bill Rohr, tpt; Lenny Stevens, cl.
*REC CHANGER 104 (50)*

**Don Beam, d** *hotel mgr* - Impossible

**Floyd Bean, p** - Bob Crosby

## BEARCATS (BOB MIELKE'S) SF 1953-indef
Long-lived group which was the breeding ground for many Bay Area musicians; formed from the nucleus of SUPERIOR STOMPERS (52-53). *Pioneer Club* San Leandro, *El Rancho* Lafayette (53-54); *Lark's Club* Berkeley (55), *Reno's* Oakland (56), *Tin Angel* (54) and *Burp Hollow* (57-60) SF.
Pete Allen, sb; Bunky Colman, cl; Bill Dart, d (-54); BOB MIELKE, tbn; Dick Oxtot, bjo; P T Stanton, tpt. ADD: Bill Erickson, tpt; Don Fay, d (54-55); Frank Goudie, cl; Mel Lieberman, cl; Don Marchant, d (55-?).

GORDON BENNETT
January 1976

**Cliff Beard, p** *(1906-1985)* - Wild Bill Davison; Nightblooming

**Jim Beatty, reeds** *(1934 Jamestown NY)* - Wild Bill Davison; Jazz Saints (NO); Oregon; Salt City 6 (UT); led own groups

## JIM BEATTY JAZZ BAND Lake Oswego OR 1967→

Group began in Jamestown NY 63, continued with new personnel upon Beatty's move to OR. *Barbary Coast Room, Barry's Tavern, Godfather Club, Harvey's* PTL, much concert and festival work. Influenced formation of Oregon City Traditional Jazz Society.

JIM BEATTY, c/ssax; Norm Domreis, p; Edwin Fountaine, sb; Jim Goodwin, cor; John Picardi, d; Archie Thomas, tbn. 1975: Danny Alguire, cor; BEATTY; George Bruns, tbn; Domreis; Delane Guild, d; Bill Stauffer, tu; Dave Wierbach, bjo/bsax. 1985: BEATTY; Vince Carey, d; Domreis; Goodwin; Jim Maihack, tbn; Dick Monsey, bjo/g; Hugo Schulz, sb. ADD: Wild Bill Davison.

*LN CP6555; NORTHWESTERN 2773 "In Portland" (70); TRIAD 501 "Salutes the Bicentennial" (75); =906 "The Joys of Jazz" (77); =915 "Jim Beatty-Will Bill Davison 1978 Tour" (78); VECTOR VR005 "Live At Harvey's" (81)*

**Heinrich "Heinie" Beau, reeds** *(1911 Calvary WI)* *arr* - Tommy Dorsey; Benny Goodman; Gordon Jenkins; Red Nichols; Resurrection; Paul Weston; led own groups; studios; to CA 43; Jazz Forum "Jazzman Of the Year" 85

## *HEINIE BEAU AND HIS HOLLYWOOD JAZZ QUARTET* LA

Rec group which expanded to sextet, in the form of an All-Star jazz band.

HEINIE BEAU, cl; Morty Corb, sb; Arnold Ross, p; Alvin Stoller, d. ADD QUINTET: Nick Fatool, d; Ray Leatherwood, sb; Eddie Miller, tsax; Ray Sherman, p. ADD SEXTET: Corb; Gene Estes, vib; Bob Havens, tbn; Jack Sperling, d; Johnny Varro, p.

*CORAL CRL57247 "Heinie Beau Jazz All-Stars"; HENRI "Heinie Beau & Hollywood Jazz Quartet" (80); = "Heinie Beau & Hollywood Jazz Quintet w/Eddie Miller"; = "Heinie Beau & Hollywood Sextet"*

**Jeff Beaumonte, reeds, cor** *(1949 Hollywood CA) antique auto restoration* - British Connection; Down Home; co-ldr Fink St; Orange Blossom; San Juan; ldr Silver Cornet

**Wayne Bedrosian, p** - ldr Bourbon St 5

**Jack Beecher, bass** - Bay City

**Dave Beeman, tpt, bass** - ldr Dixiecrats; Gas House; Shakey's Inferior; Sutterville

**Joe Belardino, d** - Fulton St; Gas House; Gramercy; Grand Republic

**Al Bell, tpt** - Feather Riverboat

**Hugh Bell, flug, tpt** *(1920 Beaumont TX) school bus driver* - Louisiana Gents; Resurrection

**Check Belt, bjo** - Boondockers

**Tom Belton, d** - Jubilee

**Bud Benadom, d** - Do-Do-Wah

**Jeff Bender, p** *(1934 Boston MA) investments* - Apex; Jubilee; Hot Jazz Stompers; Magnolia; led own groups

**Bob Bennett, bjo** *(1961 Fresno CA)* - Blue St

**Cyril Bennett, p** - Jazz Cardinals; Jelly Roll JB-SF; Pier 23; Rose & Thistle

31

**Don Bennett, bass** - Marin Jazz; Swing Fever; Norma Teagarden

**Gordon Bennett, bass** *(1933 Auburn ME)* - Casa Bonita; Jazz Cardinals; Rose & Thistle

**John Bennett, p** - [Capital City]; ldr Swipesy

**Russ Bennett, bjo** *auto sales* - Frisco JB; Yerba Buena; led own dance orch ('30s), popular during summers at Russian River resorts

**John Benson, p** *computer electronics* - Royal Society

**Howard Berg, reeds** - Gold Standard; Swanee's

**Pete Berg, g** - Bob Neighbor; Stone Age

**Jack Berka, reeds** - Dixie Jazz Bravos; Jamboree Hal

## BERKELEY RHYTHM Berkeley 1971-80

Formed from original duo of Skjelbred and a sideman (originally Goodwin) which played long-term engagement at *Bull Valley Inn* (73-80), then *Earthquake McGoon's* (72) and *Berkeley Square*, other Bay Area locations. Leadership was taken over by Hadlock in 1980.

Dave Clarkson, tsax; Jim Cumming, sb; Jim Goodwin, tpt (-76); DICK HADLOCK, ssax; Jack Knox, g; Oz Ramsey, d; RAY SKJELBRED, p. ADD: Ev Farey, tpt (76); Burt Noah, tsax; Bob Mielke, tbn.

*BR 1 "Berkeley Rhythm, Vol 1" (71)*

**Byron Berry, tpt** - Conspiracy; Jazz Cardinals; Kid Ory; [Ray Skjelbred]; Joe Sullivan

**Howard Berry, reeds** - Cell Block; Mudville; Red Hot Peppers

**Gene Berthelsen, tpt** - Camellia; ldr Cats 'n' Jammers; dir Jazzin' Jrs; Old Sacramento

**Maren Berthelsen, v** - Cats 'n' Jammers; Jazzin' Jrs

**Vic Berton, d** *(1896-1951 Chicago IL)* - LA Philharmonic; Red Nichols. Comp *Sobbin' Blues*

**Bert Bertram, tbn** - Uptown Lowdown

**John Best, tpt** *(1913 Shelby NC)* - Charlie Barnet; Les Brown; Bob Crosby; Benny Goodman; Levee Loungers; Billy May; Rampart St; Artie Shaw; Sounds of Dixieland; studios; led own groups; to CA 48
*MERCURY PPS2009 "Dixieland Left and Right"*

## BEVERLY HILLS UNLISTED JAZZ BAND LA 1979→

Arte Azenzer, p; Allen Goodman, d; CONRAD JANIS, tbn; Sheldon Keller, tu/sb/bjo; Paul Mazlansky, tpt; Russ Reinberg, cl; George Segal, bjo; Rex Schull, bjo; Bill Vogel, tpt. ADD: Pete Keir, tu; Arnold Ross, p; Mike Silverman, tpt.

## BIENVILLE JAZZ BAND LA 1967→

Bill Mitchell, p; Ed Chapin, cl; Chuck Greening, tu; Vic Loring, bjo; Ken Smith, cor; BURT TAYLOR, tbn. ADD: Ron Going, cl (75→).

**Ken Bielman, p** - Oregon

**Albany Leon "Barney" Bigard, reeds** *(1906-1980 New Orleans LA)* - Louis Armstrong; Crown City; Duke Ellington; Jelly Roll Morton; King Oliver; Kid Ory; Ben Pollack; Jack Teagarden; Young Men From NO; led own groups, most notable of which, the Jazzopators,

BARNEY BIGARD  September 1974

came from within the Ellington band; to CA 42-72 occasional residences
*DELMARK DS211 "Bucket's Got a Hole In It"; LIBERTY 3072 "Barney Bigard"*

**Bernie Billings, reeds** - Pete Daily

**Bill Bird, reeds** - King Riverbottom

**John Bishop, g** - City of Industry; Jamboree Hal; New Bull Moose; Triple RRR

**Dave Bishow, wb, reeds** *(19—19—)* - ldr Plum Forest

**Bob Bissonnette, bjo** - Polecats

**Ida Bithell, p** - Silicon; marr Joe Bithell

**Joe Bithell, bass** *(1929 Oakland CA)* - Buena Vista; Mud Flat; ldr Silicon

**Roy Bjanes, bass** *artist* - Jelly Roll Jazz Society

**Art Bjork, d** - Oversextette

**Fred Bjork, tbn** - Original Inferior

**Dave Black, d** *(1928 Philadelphia PA)* - Georgie Auld; [Delta Jazz]; Duke Ellington; Charlie Parker; SF Swing Express; Bob Scobey; Zoot Sims

**Lou Black, tpt** - co-ldr Grand Republic; bro of Stan Black

**Stan Black, bass, tbn** - Boondockers; Fulton St; co-ldr Grand Republic

## BLACK DIAMOND JAZZ BAND Stockton 1982→

Tom Downs, tu; Bill Gunter, wb; John Howard, cl (-84); Bill Jeffries, tbn; GEORGE KNOBLAUCH, bjo; FRED SPITZER, cor (-84). ADD: Marty Eggers, p (83→); Wes Grant, tpt (84→); Phil Stiers, cl (84→).

**Bill Blackson, d** - Traffic Jammers

**Charlie Blackwell, d** - Blueblowers; Resurrection

**Larry Blair, bjo** - Jazz-a-Ma-Tass

**Ben Blakeman, bjo** - Jazz Beaux; Hiz Honor; Purple Gang; Riverbank

**Andy Blakeney, tpt** *(1898 Quitman MS) board of educ* - Crown City; Lionel Hampton; Roger Jamieson; Legends; King Oliver; Kid Ory; Preservation Hall (NO); Resurrection; Reb Spikes; So Frisco; Tuxedo; led own groups; to CA 28-35, HI 35-40, CA 40

## ANDY BLAKENEY JAZZ BAND LA 1949-50, 1956

Into *Beverly Cavern* after Ory left (49), *400 Club* (50), other venues in So Calif.

ANDY BLAKENEY, tpt; L Z Cooper, p; Reginald Jones, sb; Albert Nicholas, cl; Alton Redd, d; William Woodman, tbn. ADD: Streamline Ewing, sb; Phil Gomez, cl; Bob McCracken, cl; Warren Smith, tbn.

**Ed Blanchard, bass** *(1926 Oakland CA) graphic designer* - And That's Jazz; [Oakland A]

**Kay Blanchard, reeds** *teacher* - Nightblooming; Satin Dolls

**Seaton Blanco, bass** - Oversextette

**Sammy Blank, reeds** *(19—1973)* - Ted Lewis; Nob Hill

**Orrin "Fess" Blattner, tbn** *(1917 PA) music teacher* - ldr Gem City; Freddy Slack

**Dolph Bleiler, d** *(19—1955 Seattle WA)* - Rainy City

**Eric Bleumke, tbn** - Happy JB

**Hal Blevins, tbn** - Jazz-a-Ma-Tass; Merrymakers

**Barry Block, reeds** - Golden Age

**Tom Blodgett, p** - Dixieland Express

**Ken Blood, tbn** *(1921 Albert Lea MN)* - Bye Bye Blues; Dixieland Inc

## BLUEBLOWERS (JOHNNY LUCAS') LA 1949-82

Long-lived group underwent many metamorphoses during its lifetime after beginning as a trio playing at *The Track* Pasadena, and its members were numerous. Played various locations ranging from LA to CHI, *Beverly Cavern* (52,64), *Zucca's* Pasadena (58), even an extended stay at the *Napoleon Club* Patpong, Bangkok (72-74). Was still occasionally active at this writing.

Ray Evans, d; George Kleinberg, p; JOHNNY LUCAS, tpt. ADD: Charlie Blackwell, d (58); Gene Bolen, cl (54-56,58); Dick Braxhoofden, bjo/g (79-81); Bill Campbell, p (55); Norm Coles, p (58-64); Lee Countryman, p (55,57); Lou Diamond, d (53-55); Len Esterdahl, bjo/g (52,55); Jerry Fuller, cl (53); Tommy Geckler, tbn (64); Chuck Hamilton, sb (58); Mike Hobi, tbn (52-53); Mario Ibanez, tbn (74-75); Willie Martinez, cl (56-57); Matty Matlock, cl (52,57); Mel McCoy, g (74); Dolph Morris, sb (64-79); Monty Mountjoy, d (52,56-57); Max Murray, reeds (65); Bill Newman, g (77-79); Don Owens, p (52,55); Syl Rice, d (64); Warren Smith, tbn (66); Bruce Squires, tbn (58); Jess Stacy, p (52); Bob Stone, sb (52); Floyd Stone, cl/sax (66); Cajun Verret, tbn (57); Gene Washington, d (65-81); Bill Wood, cl (64-66).

*JM LJ333*

## BLUE FOX JAZZ BAND Turlock CA 1984→

Founded by Talbert in Mexicali, Mexico, where he met Gibson. The band performed around Yuma AZ before relocating in CA.

Art Arnett, tbn/tu; Ken Brock, tpt; Harry the Hipster Gibson; p; Dutch Mills, cl/sax (-84); Joe Runnels, d; DAN TALBERT, tbn/tpt. ADD: Brad Zank, bjo (85→).

## BLUE STREET JAZZ BAND Fresno 1983→

House band of Fresno Dixieland Society.

Bob Bennett, bjo; FORREST HELMICK, tpt; Mark Marin, tu; John Martin, cl/ssax; Dave Ruffner, tbn; Larry Widener, d. ADD: Sherri Colby, v (85→); Dan Sensano, p (84→).

**Paul Boberg, bjo, g** - Casa Bonita; Stone Age

## BOB CATS see CROSBY BOB CATS

**Ed Bock, d** - Saints

**Jim Bodrero, bass** - Knights of Camelot

**Friedhelm Boeckh, bass** - Good Time Levee

**Will Boemer, perc** *(1945 TX) office worker* - Chrysanthemum

**Chet Bogan, cor** - Desert City

**Jim Bogan, reeds** - Cottonmouth; Orange Empire; Storyville Stompers

**John Boland, reeds** *(1936 Decatur IL) real estate* - Ray Bauduc; [Bay City]; Jelly Roll JB-SF; Original Inferior; Tri-City; Dave Weirbach

**Gene Bolen, reeds** - Bauduc-Lamare; Blueblowers; Pete Daily; Dukes of Dixieland; Wingy Manone

**Charley Bonner, tpt** *(1919 Boston MA) piano tech* - Dixie Unltd; WFDJE&MKRB

**Benny Booker, bass** - Roger Jamieson; Resurrection

## BOONDOCKERS SAC 1960-70

Named after first venue at Hotel Boondock in Walnut Grove; later into pizza parlors in SAC.

Check Belt, bjo; Bill Gunter, d/wbd; BILL RICHARDS, p; Frank Owen, sb. ADD: Stan Black, sb; Bob Ringwald, p; Don Shumacher, bjo.

**Paul Boore, reeds** *(1925 St Joseph MO) insurance* - John Simon orch; Tuleburg; led own dance orch

**Jack Booth, tbn** *(1924 Youngstown OH)* - Dixie Rhythm Ramblers; Jazz-a-Ma-Tass; King Zulu; OC Dixiecats

**Jack Boppel, bjo** *photography* - Jazzin' Babies; Smogville

**Bill Borcher, tpt** *(1919 International Falls MN) college adm* - ldr Oregon; long-time jazz activist, org Sacramento Jubilee

**Jim Borkenhagen, tpt** *(1924 Hutchinson MN) teacher* - El Dorado-SJ; King Riverbottom; Magnolia

**Rod Borrie, tbn** *(NJ) prof of psychology* - Phoenix; St Valentine; ldr Westside Feetwarmers

**Sterling Bose, tpt** - Bob Crosby

**Vince Bosco, bass** - Jazz-a-Ma-Tass

**John Boskovich Jr, reeds** - ldr Louisiana Purchase; ldr River Rats; ldr UC Jazz

**Eric Bouchard, reeds** - Bourbon St DJB

## BOURBON STREET DIXIELAND JAZZ BAND Monterey 1975

Eric Bouchard, cl; Tim Byers, tbn; Phil Jenkins, tu; Jim Oerman, d; BOBBY ORLANDO, p; Bill Powell, tsax.

## BOURBON STREET 5 + 1 Fresno 1965-68

WAYNE BEDROSIAN, p; Al Nersesian, d; Bob Russell, cl; Ray Sasaki, tpt; others unknown.

## BOURBON STREET JAZZ BAND Tucson AZ

Len Ferrone, sb; Ken Hawk, d; Jim Hockings, tbn; Red Sather, cl; Neal Spaulding, p; MANNY TREUMANN, cor (-84). ADD: Bill Eagle, cor (84-); EDDY LAIN.

**V. J. Bourgeois, d** *(TX)* - Al Donahue; Will Osborne; Silver Stope

**"Professor" Dave Bourne, p, brass** *(1939 Santa Maria CA)* - ldr Dawn of Century; ldr Resurrection; co-fdr Maple Leaf Club; ragtime exponent; *Casey's Bar* LA (72→); bachelor of music USC
*ARCANE AR602 "Silks and Rags"; = AR603 "This One's For Art"; EUPH "Eight on Eighty-Eight" w/Knocky Parker*

**Jim Bouska, tbn** - Cell Block; Pier 100; Tuleburg

**Norm Bowden, tpt** *(1915 Victoria BC)* - Resurrection

**Chuck Bowers, tpt** - King Zulu

**Gil Bowers, p** - Bob Crosby

**Dave Bowman, p** - Bob Crosby

**Dick Bowman, tbn** - Cider City

**Lance Boyce, tpt** - MDJB

**George Boyd, reeds** - Cats 'n' Jammers; Easy Winners; Riverbank

**Bob Boyer, reeds** *teacher* - Royal Bourbon St

**Les Boynton, bass** - High Society JB

VINCE BARTELS
October 1985

ANDY BLAKENEY
May 1974

HARVEY O BROOKS, 400 Club, 1962

**Steve Bradbury, bass** - Sticks Strings

**Gary Bradski, tpt** *(1958)* - Churchill St

**Jon Brand, bass** - Jazz Minors

**Phil Brandt Jr, tbn** *(1915 Columbia MO) banker* - Capital City; co-fdr Oregon

**Wellman Braud (Breaux), d** *(1891-1966 New Orleans LA)* - Barbara Dane; Joe Darensbourg; Duke Ellington; Kid Ory; to CA 56

**Dick Braxhoofden, bjo, g** - Blueblowers; Tailgate Ramblers

**Chris Braymen, tbn** *(1959)* - Churchill St; Maynard Ferguson

**Doug Bray, tbn** *(1922 New Haven CT) high school principal* - Over the Hill

**Don Brayton, bass** *(1940 Cambridge MA)* - Euphonic; Euphoria

**McNeal Breaux, bass** *(1916 New Orleans LA)* - Paul Barbarin; Papa Celestin; La Honda; St Peter; cousin of Wellman Braud

**Tom Brenkwitz, tpt** - Golden Gate JB; Gutbucket

**Bob Brennan, tbn** *(1931 Oakland CA) contractor* - And That's Jazz; Bayside; Golden Gate JB; Gutbucket; Knights of Camelot

**Herb Brennan, d** - Dr Jon

**Johnny Brent, d** - Turk Murphy

**Bob Brewer, bass, tbn** *(1924 Artesia NM) teacher* - Conductors

**Roy Brewer, tbn** *(1930 Grand Island NB) film editor* - Delta Rhythm Kings; Great Pacific-LA; ldr Knights; So Frisco; ldr Tailgate Ramblers

**Hollis Bridwell, reeds** - King Zulu

**Bill Bright, p** - Pete Kelly

## BRITISH CONNECTION Corona del Mar 1980→

Traditionally oriented group. *Plaza de Cafes* Newport Beach (80→).

Jeff Beaumonte, cor; STAN CHAPMAN, tbn; Mike Fay, sb; Ron Going, cl; Vic Loring, bjo; Laurence Wright, asax/d (-81), cor (81-85). ADD: Brian Sherick, d (83-85); Ed Slauson, d (81-83).

*JRW 2000 "The British Connection" (82)*

**Dick Broadie, reeds** - Jazz Ramblers; Workingman

**Ken Brock, tpt** - Blue Fox; Headliners; ldr San Diego Chargers JB

**Matt Brodie, reeds** *stock broker* - Port City

**Delourde Brooks, v** - Dixieland Inc

**Harvey Brooks, reeds** *(1925 OR) teacher* - Stumptown

**Harvey O Brooks, p** *(1898-1968 Philadelphia PA)* - Teddy Buckner; Dixie Flyers; Kid Ory; Young Men From NO; comp *A Little Bird Told Me, I'm No Angel*, others

**Albert "Pud" Brown, reeds, tpt** *(1917 Wilmington DE)* - Teddy Buckner; Chicagoans; Pete Daily; Jimmy Dorsey; Levee Loungers; Rosy McHargue; Kid Ory; [Bob Scobey]; Jack Teagarden; led own groups; to CA 49, NO 73

*NO JAZZ 1 "Pud Brown's Tenor for Two" (77); =2 "Then and Now" (79); =3 "Pud Does It Again!" (82)*

**Charley Brown, d** - St Valentine

**Dave Brown, bjo** *(1946 Seattle WA) professional clown* - Duwamish; Uptown Lowdown

**Derek Brown, bass** - Apex; WFDJE&MKRB

**Joe Brown, p** - Mudville; Red Hot Peppers

**Lance Brown, tbn** - co-ldr Happy JB

**Tom Brozene, cor** *(1954)* - Churchill St; Royal Society

**Gene Bruhjell, d** *(1936 ND) economics* - June Christy; Desert City; Mel Torme

**Ned Brundage, d** - Abalone; Dixieland Inc; ldr Monterey Bay Stompers

**Ross Brunett, reeds** - Jazz-a-Ma-Tass

**George Bruno, reeds** - ldr Old Sacramento; ldr River City; led own big band

**George Bruns, bass, tbn** *(1914-1983 Sandy OR) comp, arr* - Banjo Kings; Jim Beatty; Castle; Firehouse 5 + 2; *Gin Bottle 4*; Turk Murphy; Rose City Stompers. Comp *Davy Crockett, Zorro*, others

**Clora Bryant, tpt** *(Denison TX)* - Roger Jamieson

**Ernie Bucio, tpt** - Headliners

**Maynard "Jim" Buchmann, reeds** *music teacher* - [Castle]; Conductors; Muddy River

**Herb Buck, p** *(1929-1977)* - ldr Buena Vista; ldr Golden Gate JB; ldr Gutbucket; Monterey Bay; ldr Mud Flat

**Jack Buck, tbn, p** *(1911 Keokuk IA)* - Alexander's; *Frisco Footwarmers*; Frisco JB; Great Pacific-SF; Clancy Hayes; Bob Scobey; Yerba Buena; led own groups

## JACK BUCK JAZZ BAND SF 1977→

JACK BUCK, p; Charlie Clark, cl; John Cook, vibes; John Farkas, tbn; Bob Hinman, sb; Bob Neighbor, tpt; Bob Ulsh, d.

## JACK BUCK'S FRISCO JAZZ BAND SF 1979-83

JACK BUCK, p; John Cook, vib; Jim Cumming, sb; John Farkas, tbn; Bill Napier, cl; Bob Neighbor, tpt; Bob Ulsh, d.

**Tom Buck, tpt** - [Bay City]; ldr Delta JB; Jubilee

**Sheri Buckles, reeds** - Dixie Darlings

**John Edward "Teddy" Buckner, tpt** *(1909 Sherman TX)* - Sidney Bechet; Lionel Hampton; Kid Ory; led own groups. With his Louis-like horn sound, still made occasional appearances at this writing and his band, while far removed from the original, retained Buckner's traditional flavor; to CA 35. Featured in film *Pete Kelly's Blues* (55)

## TEDDY BUCKNER JAZZ BAND LA c1954→

*Beverly Cavern, 400 Club*; Disneyland for many years during summers '60s-'70s.

TEDDY BUCKNER, tpt; Harvey O Brooks, p; Joe Darensbourg, cl; Arthur Edwards, sb; Jessie Sales, d; William Woodman, tbn. ADD: Teddy Edwards, d; John Ewing, tbn; Chester Lane, p; Al Riemen, tbn; Caughey Roberts, cl; Chuck Thomas, sax.

*CRESCENDO "Midnight In Moscow"; DJ 503 "In Concert at the Dixieland Jubilee" (55); = 504 "And His Dixieland Band" (54); = 505 "Salute To Louis Armstrong" (54); = 507 "Teddy Buckner and the All-Stars" (56); = "On the Sunset Strip"*

NED BRUNDAGE January 1979

**Lloyd Bucks, bjo** - Dixieland Inc

## BUENA VISTA JAZZ BAND Berkeley 1954-55

Formed from MUD FLAT FIVE.
Joe Bithell, tu; HERB BUCK, p; Gene Maurice, cor; Dudley Stone, d; Al Villaire, ssax. ADD:
Bob Coblenz, cl.

**Jeff Buenz, g** *(1956 Castro Valley CA)* - [Magnolia]

**Jim Buettner, p** - Rainier; Traffic Jammers

**Don Bull, p** - Jubilee; Knights of Camelot

## BULL MOOSE PARTY BAND see NEW BULL MOOSE

**Lance Buller, tbn, tpt** *computers* - Jazz Forum; Jelly Roll Jazz Society; ldr Monarch;
Resurrection

**Bob Burdick, bjo** - Prof Plum

**Joe Burger, d** - Coos Bay

**Bill Burgess, tpt** *(1926 Evanston IL)* - ldr Dixieland Inc

**Earl Burgess, tbn** - Natural Gas

**Dick Burley, tbn** - Emerald City; Oregon

**Jim Burlingame, p** *insurance* - Churchill St

41

JERRY BUTZEN  March 1977

**Norm Burnham, p** *(1926 Portland ME) service mgr* - Downey; Jamboree Hal; Jazz-a-Ma-Tass; Little Big Band; Milneburg; New Bull Moose; Outcast

**Buddy Burns, bass** *(1900 New Orleans LA)* - Papa Celestin; Crescent Bay; Chris Kelly; George Lewis; ldr NO Creole Gumbo

**Bob Burns, bjo** - Tailgate JB

## BURP HOLLOW JAZZ BAND SF 1958-?

Pete Allen, sb; Bill Erickson, tpt; Wally Floyd, d; Bill Napier, cl; Bob Mielke, tbn; Bruce Paulson, p.

**Russell Burt, reeds** *(1964 Bellflower CA) student* - Lemon St

**Tom Butke, tbn** - UC Jazz

**Jim Butler, tbn** - Cats 'n' Jammers

**Roy "Smedley" Butler, d** *(1920 San Bernardino CA)* - Emperor Norton; Gas House; Claude Thornhill

**Carl Butte, bass** *(1924 Salem OR) engr* - Capital City; Oregon

**George Butterfield, bass** - Nob Hill

**Ted Butterman, tpt** - Golden Gate Stompers

**Jerry Butzen, tbn** *(1926-1984 Sheboygan WI) longshoreman* - [Delta Jazz]; Golden Age; Nob Hill; Wally Rose; Seaside Synco; Sweet & Hot

**Harry Buyukian, tpt** - Live Steam

**Lloyd Byassee, d** *(1935)* - Bay City; Canal St; Great Pacific-SF

## BYE BYE BLUES BOYS' BAND Monterey 1984→

Ken Blood, tbn; Johnny Carlin, tpt; Dick Dotts, p; Bucky McGeoghegan, sb; Bob Meek, tsax; DON PELLERIN, cl; Newell Strayer, d.

**Tim Byers, tbn** - Bourbon St DJB

**Norm Bylin, reeds** - Capitol City; Dr Mix

# C

**Greg Cabibi, d** *(1935 San Jose CA)* - El Dorado-SJ

**Tommy Cain, reeds** - Casa Bonita

**Ed Cairns, p** - Dixie Unltd

**Allen Caldiera, bjo** - Do-Do-Wah St

**Roy Calhoun, d** *(AZ) music store owner* - Desert City

## CALIFORNIA EXPRESS Stockton 1983→

Formed to play *Great America Hotel* Santa Clara.

John Fehd, bjo; John Herby, d; VAL HERBY, p; DAVE JOHNSON, tpt; Ken O'Brien, tbn; Reuben Smith, tu; Eric van Nice, reeds.

## CALIFORNIA RAMBLERS LA 1984→

Originally titled NEW RHYTHM KINGS.

Mike Baird, reeds; Ham Carson, reeds (-84); Wayland Chester, bjo (-84); Richard Cruz, tpt (-84, alt 85); Buster Fitzpatrick, sb (-84); DAVID HUTSON, reeds; Brad Kay, p; Dick Randolph, cor; Bill Schreiber, d; Bill Vogel, tpt; Robert Young, bsax. ADD: Buddy Arnold, reeds (alt 85→); Joe Farrell, reeds (85→); John S Reynolds, bjo/g (85→); Dan Weinstein, tbn/viol (85→).

**Glenn Calkins, tbn** *(1945 Alhambra CA) soil chemist* - Golden Eagle; Resurrection; Rhythm Kings; Triple RRR

**George "Red" Callender, bass** *(1918 Richmond VA)* - Joe Alexander; Louis Armstrong; Nat Cole; Errol Garner; Lionel Hampton; JATP; Art Tatum; studios and recs; led own combos; to CA 35
  *CROWN CLP5012 "Callender Speaks Low"; MODERN LMP1207 "Swingin' Suite"*

## CAMELLIA CITY HOT SIX SAC 1976→

Gene Berthelsen, tpt (-79); TOM DAWSON, d; Dick Leupp, tbn (-81); Jean Levinson, tu/sb (-81); Bob Rutherford, p (-81); Bill Wise, cl. ADD: Rick Baker, tpt (82); Jim Bartolotto, bjo (81→); Jay Dewald, tbn (84→); Mark Gotwalt, d (84); Mike Hudson, tbn (82-84); Mark Johnson, tpt (73); Richard Karch, sb (82); Robin Lanbie, tu (73); Gene Lancelle, tpt (79); John Landers, p (81); John Landes, tbn (84→); Bob Nash, bjo (82); Emmett O'Sullivan, p/cl (82→); Ken Pearsall, p (84); Kurt Pearsall, tpt (80-82); Roy Pierce, tbn (81); Dave Rybski, tu.

DICK CARY May 1976

**Bill Campbell, p** - Balboa JB; Blueblowers; Excelsior; solo

**Harry Campbell, bjo** *(1905 MO) CPA* - Monterey Bay Classic

## CANAL STREET JAZZ BAND SF 1953-55

The origins of BAY CITY JB. *Lark's Club* Berkeley (53-54).

Lloyd Byassee, d; Ev Farey, cor; Dean Fraser, tu; Roy Giomi, cl; Bill Mulhern, p; SANFORD NEWBAUER, tbn; Kent Stow, bjo.

## CANAL STREET STOMPERS see TAILGATE JB

**Ike Candioti, d** *(1921-1986 New York NY)* - Angel City; Roger Jamieson; Jazz Formula; Jazz Forum

**Pat Canosa, tpt** - Old Sacramento

**Tom Cantrell, cor** *(1945 Sacramento CA) teacher* - Devil Mtn

**Dave Caparone, tbn** *(1939 Pittsburgh PA) vintner* - WFDJE&MKRB

## CAPITAL CITY JAZZ BAND Salem 1975→

Formed principally from personnel of OREGON JB.

Bill Abbott, d; Philip Brandt, tbn; Dave Gentry, sb (-82); Charlie Hawkes, cl (-77); BLAKE MADDOX, tpt; Charles Ruff, p. ADD: Dick Barber, ssax (77→); John Bennett, p (83-84 alt); Carl Butte, tu/sb (82-85); John Lesch, p (76-80 alt); Jim Maihack, bjo/tbn/tu (82→ alt).

## CAPITOL CITY JAZZ BAND SAC 1975-78

Jack Crook, cl; Droops Earnhart, p; Frank Haggerty, bjo/g; TOM KING, tpt; Bill Spreter, sb; Hal Swan, tbn; Cliff Swesey, d. ADD: Norm Bylin, cl/sax; Jack Gumbiner, p; Dee Hendricks, sb; Elton Lewis, vib; John Parker, sb; Mike Pittsley, tbn; Jerry Walcott, tbn.

**Frankie Capp, d** *(1931 Worcester MA)* - Fine Time; Stan Kenton; Billy May; studios

**Brian Cardello, tbn** *(1958 Santa Barbara CA) tv news photog* - Sticks Strings

**Bob Cardoza, p** - Old Sacramento

**Julius Cardoza, tbn** *(1923 Gustine CA)* - ldr Feather Riverboat; Ponca City; co-fdr Feather River Jazz Society

**Thomas "Papa Mutt" Carey, tpt** *(1891-1948 Hahnville LA)* - Johnny Dodds; Ed Hall; orig Chris Kelly Band; Kid Ory; led own groups. To CA 21; took over remnants of Ory's touring band; led film studio group playing "mood music;" retired in 41 to become a train porter until Ory recalled him in 44. Appeared in film *New Orleans* (47)
    *CENTURY 4007, 4008, 4013, 4017, 4018*

**Vince Carey, d** *(1954 Portland OR)* - Jim Beatty

**Johnny Carlin, tpt** - Bye Bye Blues; Cypress

**Norm Carlisle, bjo** *(1928 Inglewood CA) film ed* - Ambulance

**John Carlson, bass** *(1912 ND)* - Hi7 Honor; Mardi Gras-SAC

**Ron Carpani, reeds** - Coos Bay

**John Carpenter, bjo** *(1941 Elkhart IN) sales* - Hyperion

**George Carr, bass** - Jazz-a-Ma-Tass

**Bernard Carrere, bass** *(New Orleans LA)* - Roger Jamieson; Resurrection; Young Men From NO

**Bill Carroll, bass, tbn** *(1934 San Rafael CA)* - El Dorado-SJ; [Jazz Cardinals]; Turk Murphy; Original Inferior; Sinners

**Jack Carroll, tpt** - Turk Murphy

**Janet Carroll, v** *actress* - Hot Frogs

**Bill Carson, tbn** *(1933 Bridgeton NJ)* *medical consultant* - Hot Jazz Stompers; Prof Plum

**Ernie Carson, cor** - Ray Bauduc; Turk Murphy; Sinners; Smokey Stover (NV); Dave Weirbach

**Hamilton "Ham" Carson, reeds** - Angel City; Calif Ramblers; Great Excelsior; Monrovia; Rhythm Kings

**Bill Carter, reeds** *(1935 Los Angeles CA)* - Bay City; Crescent Bay; El Dorado-SJ; Euphoria; Magnolia; Turk Murphy; Sunset Music

**Bill Carter, tpt** - Portland Rose

**"Birdie" Carter, reeds** - Charlie's

**Jimmy Carter, d** - Pier 23

**Waldo Carter, tpt** - Harry James; [Nob Hill]; Tony Pastor; Sweet & Hot

**Dick Cary, alto horn, p, tpt** *(1916 Hartford CT)* *arr, comp* - Louis Armstrong; Eddie Condon; Bob Crosby; Crown City; Dawn of Century; Jimmy Dorsey; Matty Matlock; Ben Pollack; led own groups; studios and recs; to CA 59; auth *Brass Quintets*
   *CIRCLE CLP18 "The Amazing Dick Cary" (81); COLUMBIA CL1425 "And the Dixieland Doodlers"; STEREOCRAFT RTN106 "Hot and Cool"*

## CASA BONITA GARDEN ORCHESTRA East SF Bay 1975-78

A large swing oriented band evolving from Funk's smaller jazz group. *Berkeley Square* (75-58), involving those listed.

Pete Allen, sb; Bill Bardin, tbn; Paul Boberg, g; Tommy Cain, sax; MANNY FUNK, d; Dick Hadlock, sax; Alan Hall, p; Mike Marcus, sb; Jack Minger, tpt; Lloyd Rice, sax; P T Stanton, g; Lloyd Stark, p.

**Janed Casady, p** - Yankee Air Pirates

**Jack Caskey, tpt** - Shakey City

## CASTLE JAZZ BAND PTL 1943-51

Actually formed for a short time in 40, then re-formed under the leadership of Ballou three years later and named for their night club venue. To all intents and purposes, CSJB really came into being after the war (47).

1940: Skoot Hoskins, g; Bill Pavia, cl; George Phillips, tbn; Al Puderbaugh, p; Dick Sheurman, cor; Axel Tyle, d; Hank Wales, sb.

1943: MONTE BALLOU, bjo; Bob Johnson, p (-47); Pavia (-48); Phillips (-47,50); Sheurman (-44); Tyle (-48). ADD: George Bruns, tbn (47-48); Freddie Crewes, p (50-51); Ned Dodson, cor (44, 50); Larry Dufresne, p (47-50); Hi Gates, tbn (50-51); Bob Gilbert, cl (50-51); Bob Helm, cl (51); Don Kinch, tpt (47-50); Myron Shepler, sb (44-47); Bob Short, tu (47-50), tu (50-51); Don Tooley, p (47); Blackie Webster, tu (50-51); Homer Welch, d (47-50).

*CASTLE 2-15 (47-50); GTJ L12030 "The Famous Castle JB in Hi-Fi" (57); =M12037 "The Five Pennies" (59). Notable occasion when Bob Scobey, stationed at Ft Lewis WA in 44, was called to play with CJB, cutting one side of a record (Muskrat Ramble) never commercially issued.*

**Tom Castle, bjo** - Hogin's; co-fdr San Joaquin Dixieland Jazz Society

**Charlie Castro, d** *(1934 Yosemite Park CA) natl park ranger* - High Sierra; Jazzberry

**Lori Catania, v** *(1932 Los Berros CA)* - Napa Valley

**Dick Cathcart, tpt** *(1924 Michigan City IN)* - Bob Crosby; Ray Noble; Ben Pollack; Lawrence Welk; many others; led own groups; studios and recs. Music dir/tpt for film *Pete Kelly's Blues* (55)

*WB WS1275 "Bix MCMLIX" (59)*

**Larry Catlin, d** - Rainier

**Vince Cattolica, reeds** *(1923 San Francisco CA)* - Alexander's; Burt Bales; Conspiracy; Earl Hines; Marty Marsala; Bob Neighbor; Nob Hill; Wally Rose; Jack Sheedy; Joe Sullivan; Sweet & Hot; led own groups. Blind from birth, retired from playing 84

VINCE CATTOLICA March 1977

## CATS 'N' JAMMERS SAC 1980→

Joe Audino, p (-84); GENE BERTHELSEN, cor; Maren Berthelsen, v (-84); George Boyd, cl (-83); Kent Dunavent, tbn (-83); Scott Gordon, d (-82); Mark Thomas, tu (-81). ADD: Clyde Amsler, cl (85); Jim Butler, tbn (84→); Leonard Dixon, cl (84); Gerry Garner, d (82→); John Landes, tbn (83); Jean Levinson, tu (81-83); Don Lewis, bjo (81→); Tom Lopes, sb (84→); Brian Richardson, tbn (85); Frank Silva, cl (83); Roger Snell, p (85); Ken Wood, p (84→).

**Frank Caughman, tbn** - Old Sacramento

**Al Cavallin, tpt** - Bay City

**Dave Cavanaugh, reeds** *arr, A&R Capitol Records* - ldr Curbstone Cops; Bobby Sherwood; led own groups

**Maggie Cavanaugh, v** - Gold Standard

**Ken Cave, bass** - Hiz Honor

**George Cecil, d** - Hangtown

**Kevin Celey, tpt** - Raisin City

## CELL BLOCK SEVEN Stockton 1981→

No relation to Dallas TX band of that name.

Frankie Gale, sb (-84); Bill Hannaford, tbn; Earl Miller, cl (-84); Keith Randles, d; BOB ROMANS, cor; John Simon, bjo; Johnny Wilder, p. ADD: Keith Baltz, tu (85→); Howard Berry, cl (84); Jim Bouska, tbn (81); Dave Radmore, sb (84-85); Mike Reilly, d (-86); Beth Sanders, cl/ssax (84→); Rich Simmons, d (86→).

**Frank Chaddock, tpt** *(1929 South Haven MI)* - Chicago 6; Cottonmouth; Jewel City

**Milt Chambers, bjo** - Jubilee

**Hal Champness, bass** - Shakey City

**Dave Chaney, tpt** *(Springfield OH)* - Desert City; Stan Kenton; Gene· Krupa

**Larry Channave, tpt** - ldr High Society JB

**Richard Chapman, bjo** - Happy JB

**Stan Chapman, tbn** *(1932 Fullerton CA)* - ldr British Connection; Down Home; ldr Royal Gardens

**Scott Chapman, p** - British Connection; ldr Newport Summit; son of Stan Chapman

**Al Chappel, p** - Carse Sneddon

**Marvin Chappell, bass** - Purple Gang

## CHARLIE'S GOOD TIME BAND SD c1982

Birdie Carter, cl/sax; BILL DENDLE, bjo; Ken Donica, tu/sb; Jerry Fenwick, tpt; Dick Lopez, d; Larry Okmin, cl; Dale Saare, tbn.

**Ernie Chavez, reeds** *(1927 San Juan Bautista CA)* - Emperor Norton

**John Chessell, bjo** *(1943 Los Angeles CA) deputy DA* - Miss-Behavin'

**Weyland Chester, bjo** *banjo maker* - Calif Ramblers; Rhythm Kings

## CHICAGOANS (PETE DAILY'S) LA 1945-indef

*Royal Room* Hollywood (49-51), *Cliff House, Club Hangover, Say When* SF (early '50s), *Astor's, White Way Inn* San Fernando Valley (late '50s), many others plus national tours.

Skippy Anderson, p (45-49,50-55); PETE DAILY, cor; Sleepy Kaplan, d (45); Rosy McHargue, cl (45-49); Warren Smith, tbn (45-54,52-55). ADD: Hugh Allison, d (50-55); Bernie Billings, sax (49); Pud Brown, cl/tsax (50-52); Red Cooper, d (46); George Defebaugh, d (45-50); Barrett Deems, d; Len Esterdahl, g/bjo (49,50-55); Dick Fisher, bjo (45); Jerry Fuller, cl (54-55); Rolly Furnas, tbn; Budd Hatch, tu/sb (50-54); Buddy Hayes, tu; Burt Johnson, tbn (50-52); Nappy Lamare, bjo/g (49-50); Matty Matlock, cl; Bernie Miller, tu (54); Don Owens, p (49-50); Joe Rushton, bsax (45); Phil Stephens, sb; Stan Story, cl (49-50); Jimmy Stutz, sb (48-50); Country Washburne, tu (49); Bud Wilson, tbn (45).

76-77 SACRAMENTO JUBILEES: Allison; Brown; DAILY; Hayes; Al Jenkins, tbn; Lamare; Owens.

*CAP 15095, 15315 (47); =942, 15432, 15433, 15434, 57728, 57760, 576008 (49); =1588; JUMP 12, 14, 24 (46); =JL2 (46); =J12-5 "Pete Daily and His Chicagoans" (67); SUNSET 7559, 7556 (45)*

## CHICAGO SIX SD 1980→

*Belly Up Tavern* Solana Beach (80→).

Frank Chaddock, tpt; BOB FINCH, bs; John Hall, d; Bob Long, p (80); Bill Reinhart, cl (80). ADD: Mark Dresser, sb (80 alt); Billy Hawkins, tbn (80→); Bill Hunter, p (80→); Ed Reed, cl (80→).

*FAN AB005 "Live At the Belly Up Tavern" (82)*

DAVE CAPARONE (with Dennis Jackman, Charlie Bonner) April 1979

## CHICAGO LOOPERS (CHARLIE LAVERE'S) LA 1944-indef

Nick Fatool, d; CHARLIE LAVERE, p; Matty Matlock, cl; Billy May, tpt; Floyd O'Brien, tbn; Artie Shapiro, sb. ADD: Chuck Mackey, tpt; Rosy McHargue, cl; Joe Rushton, bsax; Andy Secrest, cor; Jack Teagarden, tbn; Rico Vallese, cor; George van Eps, g; Joe Venuti, viol; Country Washburne, sb; Joe Yukl, tbn.

*DAWN DC12006 "Charlie Lavere's Chicago Loopers" (72); JUMP 1-3, 5, 6 (44); =26, 32 (50). Also recorded several sides under the title of BILLY MAY'S JB.*

## CHICAGO RAMBLERS Vallejo CA c1960

Formed while members were in high school.

BERT BARR, cor; Tom Jacobus, tu; Frank Jamison, p; Mark Krunosky, cor/sax; Jerry MacKenzie, cl/ssax; Larry Risner, bjo; Jim Snoke, tbn. ADD: Loren Koravec, cor; Rich Raskin, sb; Aaron Wheeler, tbn.

*MMRC 103 "The Chicago Ramblers"*

## CHICAGO STOMPERS LA c1973

RAY LINN, tpt; others unknown.

## CHRIS KELLY'S BLACK AND WHITE NEW ORLEANS JAZZ BAND LA 1983→

Perhaps the last of the mixed-race bands to feature original NO musicians (Burns, Edwards, Ewing and Purnell). Group was reportedly named after a cat, which in turn was named after a jazz band of the '20s.

BOB ALLEN, tpt; Mike Baird, cl; Buddy Burns, sb; Teddy Edwards, d; Streamline Ewing, tbn; Ron Ortman, bjo; Alton Purnell, p.

**Bob Christy, bass** - ldr Jazz-a-Ma-Tass; Little Big Band

BILL CARSON May 1985

## CHRYSANTHEMUM RAGTIME BAND SF 1978→

Young musicians with varied backgrounds in classical and jazz organized for political fundraisings, remained together to concentrate on music of the 1890-1920 period, rags in particular. Had regular FM radio program since 83, which won Broadcast Media Award 84. Monthly concerts at Hotel Utah (79-81), *Valencia Rose Cafe* (81-85). Personnel changed considerably with only Delorier, Groody and Vermazen remaining from the original.

Will Boemer, perc; Pat Crossen, tbn; Larry Delorier, flute; Myrriah Ellis, viola; Scott Fogelsong, p; Philip Groody, cello; Deborah Persellin, viol; Bob Phillips, tu; Bill Tull, cl; BRUCE VERMAZEN, cor; Susan Wong, viol. OTHERS: India Cooke, viol; Marcia Ellard, tu; Bill Ganz, p; Mike Green, cl; Tom Gschwind, viol; Hokum Jeebs, tu; Sabra Jones, cl; David LaMarche, p; Alan Lornie, viol; Robert Morris, p; Lulu van Heusen, viol; Chuck Ward, p; Lisa Weiner, cl; Jerome Weingart, viola.

*SOS 1047 "Bringing 'em Back Alive" (83); = 1079 "Come On and Hear"*

**Gary Church, tpt** - Desert City

## CHURCHILL STREET JAZZ BAND Palo Alto 1975→

First organized in 74 and named after street on which Palo Alto High School was located, CSJB was Armstrong's pet project wherein young musicians would be exposed to the sounds of traditional jazz. *Flying Lady* Morgan Hill (82→).

Steve Apple, d (-79); BILL ARMSTRONG, bjo; Gary Bradski, tpt (-79); John Hallesy, tbn (-79); Paul Jacqua, tpt (-82); Paul Price, p (-79); Tom Small, tbn (-83); John Stringer, cl (-82); Jeff Wells, tu (-79). ADD: Steve Abrams, d (79-82); Chris Braymen, tbn (83→); Tom Brozene, cor (82→); Jim Burlingame, p (79-80); Frederick Hodges, p; Joe Hopkins, reeds (83→); Art Juncker, p (83→); Jack Mangan, d (82-83); Kent Mikasa, tpt (79-83); Don Neely, cl/sax (82-83); Dave Richoux, tu (79-82); Rick Siverson, tu/bsax (82-83), cor/reeds (83→); Bruce Vermazen, cor; John Walling, tu (83→).

*ALPHA 2001 "Churchill St JB" (77)*

## CIDER CITY JAZZ BAND Santa Cruz 1979

Dick Bowman, tbn; Bob Fischbeck, cl; LEW KEIZER, tpt; Moe Isaac, tbn; Paul Mehling, g; Newell Strayer, d.

## CITY OF INDUSTRY CHAMBER ENSEMBLE San Pedro 1984

John Bishop, g; Luster Hite, d; Alex Hunter, sax; Bob Kennerson, p; Dick Randolph, cor; Jim Sheldon, tbn; Russ Weathers, sb; JACK WIDMARK, cl/sax.

**Bob Claire, d** - Phoenix

**Charlie Clark, p** - Jazzbo; Pearl Pacific; San Diego DJB

**Charlie Clark, reeds** *(1919 Webster Grove MO) graphic designer* - And That's Jazz; Jack Buck; Burp Hollow; Jubilee

**Don Clark, tbn** *(1933 Vancouver BC)* - Gas Town; Lance Harrison

**Mahlon Clark, reeds** *(1923 Portsmouth VA)* - Will Bradley; Peewee Hunt; Ray McKinley; Lawrence Welk; Louis Prima; studios

*JEWEL 5000, 5001*

**Peter Clark, tpt** - St Valentine

**Tom Clark, bass** *(1945 Lafayette IN) telephone tech* - Jubilee

**Dave Clarkson, reeds** *(19—1971)* - Berkeley Rhythm

**Ben Cleall, d** - Dixie Jazz Bravos

**Elbert "Peewee" Claybrook, reeds** *(1912 Halls TN)* - Vernon Alley; Fate Marable; [Oakland A]; Dick Oxtot

**Tim Cline, p** - Jazz Minors

**Pete Clute, p** - Bay City; Turk Murphy; Original Inferior; Rhythm Wizards

**Mike Coates, tbn** *(1958 Pittsburgh PA) investments* - Tri-City

**Curt Cobb, d** *(1959 San Jose CA)* - Emperor Norton

**Ira Cobb, tpt** - ldr Jazzbo

## IRA COBB'S JAZZBO NODB see JAZZBO

**Bob Coblentz, reeds** - Buena Vista; Gutbucket; [Jewel City]

**Nick Cochrane, tpt** - *Dixieboppers*; Rosy McHargue; Joe Rushton

**Ernie Cockayne, bjo** - Dixieland Express

**Jeremy Cohen, viol** - Rhythm Kings

**Henry Coker, tbn** *(1919 Dallas TX)* - Count Basie; Benny Carter; Eddie Heywood; Louisiana Gents

**Alex Colchak, d** - Pier 23

**Jean Cole, p** *(1948 Lawrence KS) employment mgr* - Barrelhouse

**Dave Coleman, d** - Don Anderson

**Preston Coleman, bass** - San Juan

**Norm Coles, p** - Blueblowers

**Jim Collins, bjo** - Triple RRR

**Arnold "Bunky" Colman, reeds** *(1931-1983 San Francisco CA) physician* - Burt Bales; Bearcats; Golden State; [Gutbucket]; Marin Jazz; Marty Marsala; Polecats; Rose & Thistle; [Silver Stope]

**Al Colter, tpt** - Crescent Bay; Pepper

**Steve Comber, bass** - [Fulton St]; Toot Suite

**Joe Comfort, sb** - Louisiana Gents

**Dan Comins, cor** *tax consultant* - Down Home; Golden Eagle; Milneburg; Orange Blossom; Resurrection; Royal Gardens; So Frisco; Wilmington

## CONDOR JAZZ BAND Del Mar

Allan Crowne, tpt; Bob Finch, sb; Vic Loring, bjo; Walt Sereth, cl; John Valley, tbn; Lee Wedberg, d; GORDON WILSON, p.

## CONDUCTORS RAGTIME BAND PTL 1972-81

Grew from a jam group held in Kinch's instrument shop; went on to steady engagement at *Old Town Strutters Hall* (76-79), civic events and casuals until Kinch disbanded the group upon Tyle's death. The two, plus Dufresne, were members of orig CASTLE JB.

Patti Bagan (Kinch), v; Al Barrows, tu (-77); Bob Brewer, tbn; Maynard Buchmann, reeds

BILL CARROLL November 1978

BILL CAMPBELL
April 1967

(-76); Jerry Heermans, p (-77); DON KINCH, cor; John McKinley, bjo (-76); Axel Tyle, d.
ADD: Speed Anderson, p (77); Ted des Plantes, p (78-80); Larry Dufresne, p (77-78); Bud Gerlach, cl (76-80); Jim Goodwin, cor (80-81); Myron La Hood, cl (80-81); Hal Smith, d/tu (76); Chris Tyle, cor (77-79); Mark Vehrencamp, tu (80-81); Dave Weirbach, bjo/bsax (75-78 alt).

REX RL5123 *"Don Kinch and the Conductors"* (75)

**Al Conger, tuba** - Turk Murphy

**Larry Conger, tpt** - Turk Murphy; bro of Al Conger

**Meryl Conger, cor** *(1935 OR) insurance* - Jim Beatty; ldr Rose City JB; Stumptown

**Chuck Conklin, cor** *(1932 Pitman NJ) film sound engr* - ldr Angel City; fdr Jazz Forum; exec dir LA Classic Jazz Festival

**Ray Conniff, tbn** *(1916 Attleboro MA) arr* - Bunny Berigan; Curbstone Cops; Harry James; Artie Shaw; ABC staff orch; first US jazz artist to be recorded in USSR (74)

**Vern Conrad, d** *(1934 Touchet WA) construction* - Peewee Hunt; Island City; Shakey City; ex-Chicago Bears footballer

**Ray Conseur, d** - Jazzbo; Pearl Pacific; San Diego DJB

## THE CONSPIRACY East SF Bay 1967

So titled because the group was an attempt to merge a jazz front line with a rock rhythm section but the novelty never caught on. Appeared around the Bay Area for a short time before disbanding. Made one 45rpm single rec.

Byron Berry, tpt; Vince Cattolica, cl (alt); John Lowrey, eg; Bob Mielke, tbn; Bill Napier, cl (alt); DICK OXTOT, sb; Jack Taylor, d.

**Dick Conte, p** - solo

**Bill Contente, tpt** - Jazz Unltd

**John Cook, vibes** - Jack Buck

**Paul Cooke, tbn** - Gold Standard

**Jackie Coon, cor, flug, mello** *(1929 Beatrice NB)* - Abalone; Charlie Barnet; Bauduc-Lamare; Pete Fountain; Pete Lofthouse; Red Nichols; Louis Prima; Pearly Band; Jack Teagarden; led own groups

**Bill Cooper, bass** - Pete Lofthouse; Monarch; Pearly Band

**L. Z. Cooper, pno** - Andy Blakeney

**"Red" Cooper, d** *(19—19—)* - Pete Daily

## COOS BAY CLAMBAKE Coos Bay OR

Joe Burger, d; Ron Carpani, cl; Harry Douglas, p; Bob Downer, bjo; Chet Fors, tbn; Buddy Hayes, sb; Marge Jensen, v; Judy Jordan, p; Don Loftus, tu; FROSTY WEST, cor; Dave Willis, d.

**Gene Copelan, d** - Gas House

**Morty Corb, bass, tbn** *(1917 San Antonio TX)* - Louis Armstrong; [Heinie Beau]; Bob

JACKIE COON October 1985

Crosby; Benny Goodman; [Pete Kelly Big 7]; Jack Teagarden; Ted Vesely; studios and rec; led own groups
  TOPS "Strictly From Dixie"; TIME S2118 "We Like Dixieland"

**Dale Corliss, v** - Duwamish

**Carl Cornell, tpt** *(19—1978)* - Milneburg; Riverbank; Workingman

**Richie Cornell, d** - Sextet From Hunger

**Ed Cornett, tpt** - Crown City

**Donna Corrigan, p** - Barrelhouse

**Tom Corth, reeds** - Southland

**Bruce Cossachi, cor** - Duwamish

**Dave Cotter, bjo** *(1940 Los Angeles CA) sales rep* - Monterey Bay Classic

## COTTONMOUTH D'ARCY'S JAZZ VIPERS SD 1974→

David Crowne, cor; Jack Curtiss, bjo/g; Ralph Diana, bjo; Stan Kling, tbn; Jimmy Noone, reeds; Chris Norris, v; Winifred Stewart, sb; Eric van Nice, reeds; GORDON WILSON, p. ADD: Jim Bogen, cl (77-); Frank Chaddock, tpt (77); Bruce Dexter, tpt (78); Bob Finch, sb; Dennis Gilmore, cor; Harry Lyons, bjo; Lee Wedberg, d.

**Bill Coulson, tbn** - Coulson Family; Doc Olson; Sounds of Dixieland

## COULSON FAMILY JAZZ BAND La Jolla CA 1977-80
Comprised entirely of members of one family. Also titled DOC OLSON'S CONVICTION.
Bill, tbn; Dan, tu; David, tbn; Gail, bjo; Jean, wbd; Lainey, g; Monica, reeds; Nancy, tu;
Tom, d.

**Chuck Coulter, tbn** - Jazzbo; Milneburg; Nightblooming; Yankee Air Pirates

**Lee Countryman, p** - Blueblowers; Ted Vesely; Vine St

**Robert "Cus" Cousineau, d** *(1923 CA)* - Jimmy Dorsey; Errol Garner; Charlie Parker;
Marty Marsala; Wally Rose; Jack Sheedy

**Don Cox, tbn** - [Mardi Gras-LA]

**Mike Cox, bjo** *(1940 Newport WALES) teacher* - ldr Grand Dominion; ldr Phoenix

**Leon Crabbe, bjo** *(1929 McPherson KS) school principal* - Golden Eagle; Royal Gardens;
Southland

**Ron Cradit, reeds** - Sounds of Dixieland

**Ralph Craig, d** - Jazz-a-Ma-Tass; So Bay Zephyr

**Wally Craig, tbn** *(1927 Oakland CA) YMCA dir* - Hot Frogs; Jelly Roll JB; Jelly Roll Jazz
Society; Smogville; co-fdr Santa Clarita Dixieland Jazz Club

## *CREOLE SUNSHINE ORCHESTRA (HAL SMITH'S)* LA 1984
Mike Duffy, sb; Mike Fay, g; Bob Jackson, tpt; Roger Jamieson, tbn; Jimmy Noone Jr, cl;
Dick Shooshan, p; HAL SMITH, d.
*SOS 1078 "Do What Ory Say" (84)*

JACK CROOK
May 1984

## CRESCENT BAY JAZZ BAND LA 1955-60, 1970-71

Fdr Glenn Hildebrand dropped out and made only occasional appearances thereafter; *Guys & Dolls* (56-57), frat houses (55-60), sometimes appearing under titles The Saints JB and Mouldy Fygges. Personnel were also used by Ortmann and Onderwyzer for casuals under titles of KING JB and NIGHTBLOOMING JAZZMEN (59).

1955: Buddy Burns, sb; Al Coulter, tpt; Glenn Hildebrand, v (-55); John Jewett, cl; Pete O'Leary, bjo; RON ORTMANN, bjo; Norm Shacker, tbn; Lee Wedberg, d. ADD: Bill Carter, cl; Frank Demond, tbn; Bruce Dexter, tpt; Rudy Onderwyzer, tbn; Ray Ronnei, cor; Walt Sereth, d; Tom Sharpsteen, cl; Johnny St Cyr, bjo.

1970: Burns; RON GOING, cl; Sam Greer, d; Roger Jamieson, tbn; Doug Parker, bjo; ORTMANN; Ronnei.

**Freddie Crewes, bass, p** *(1922 Seattle WA)* - Castle; Turk Murphy; Original Inferior; solo

**Jack Crook, reeds** *(1906-1985 Lincoln CA)* - Alexander's; Capitol City; Delta JB; Frisco JB; Turk Murphy; Napa Valley; Bob Scobey; Sinners

## BOB CROSBY'S BOB CATS LA 1937-42, c1955, 1966-68

Ostensibly became popular under that title because of Decca recs, although Crosby's big band was notable for featuring numerous jazzmen. The group as such was taken over in 42 by Eddie Miller and performed under his name. A "reunion band" made several appearances in mid '50s, again in '60s, and sporadic appearances as late as 85 with a few original sidemen. Personnel shifted considerably, so listing has no date references.

Ray Bauduc, d; Bob Haggart, sb; Nappy Lamare, bjo/g; Yank Lawson, tpt; Matty Matlock, cl; Eddie Miller, sax; Warren Smith, tbn; Bob Zurke, p. ADD: Floyd Bean, p; Sterling Bose, tpt; Gil Bowers, p; Dave Bowman, p; Billy Butterfield, tpt; Cutty Cutshall, tbn; Hank D'Amico, cl; Irving Fazola, cl; Artie Foster, tbn; Bob Goodrich, tpt; Bob Havens, tbn; Rosy McHargue, cl; Fred Pfaff, tu; Ward Silloway, tbn; Muggsy Spanier, tpt; Jess Stacy, p; Haig Stephens, sb; Joe Sullivan, p; George Wettling, d; Bob Wilber, cl; Zeke Zarchy, tpt; many others. 84 SACRAMENTO JUBILEE: Dick Cary, tpt; CROSBY; Gene Estes, d; Havens; Haggart; Lamare; Yank Lawson, tpt; Miller; Abe Most, cl.

*DECCA 8061 "Bob Cats"; CORAL 56003 "Dixieland Jazz, Vol 1" (50); = 57005 "Bob Cats Ball"; = 57060 "Bob Cats Blues"; = 57061 "On Parade"; = 57062 "In Hi-Fi"; = 57089 "Bob Cats 1936-1956"; DOT 3136 "South Pacific Blows Warm"; MCA "Big Nose From Winnetka"; = "South Rampart St Parade"*

**Lee "Hambone" Crosby, bass** - ldr Estuary

**Patricia Crossen, tbn** *(1946 PA) music teacher* - Chrysanthemum

**Ron Crotty, bass** - Bob Neighbor

**Bill Crow, tpt** *(1927 Cloverdale CA) insurance* - Good Time Levee; Hangtown

**Van Crowell, cor** *(1938 CA)* - Stumptown

## CROWN CITY DIXIELAND BAND Pasadena

Carol Andreen, v; PHIL ANDREEN, tbn; Ed Cornett, tpt; Art Cutliff, cl; Bob Gobrecht, tu; Harry Gross, bjo; Bill Mitchell, p; Tad Wolicki, d.

## CROWN CITY JAZZ BAND Pasadena c1950s-60s

Barney Bigard, cl; Andy Blakeney, tpt; Dick Cary, tpt; Joe Darensbourg, cl/ssax; Mike

JIM CUMMING
June 1977

DeLay, tpt; Ed Garland, sb; Sammy Lee, sax; Bill Mitchell, p; GORDON MITCHELL, tbn; Max Murray, bsax; Johnny St Cyr, bjo; Floyd Stone, cl; Gene Washington, d.

**Allan Crowne, cor, tbn** *(1934 Santa Monica CA) stockbroker* - Condor; El Dorado-LA; Faultless; Goose Island; Impossible; Pepper; Reno Charlie; Resurrection; San Juan; So Bay Zephyr; Storyville

**David Crowne, cor** - Cottonmouth

**Phil Crumley, cor** *(1932 Des Moines IA) periodontist* - ldr Natural Gas

**Jesse "Tiny" Crump, p** *(1906 Paris TX)* - Marty Marsala; Bob Scobey; solo; to SF 1945

**Richard Cruz, tpt** *(1929 Rice TX) music teacher* - Calif Ramblers; ldr Dixie Jazz Bravos; Dixie Katz; ldr Fullertowne; ldr Jamboree Hal; Jazz Forum; dir Lemon St; Rhythm Kings; WFDJEMKRB

**George Cuddy, tbn** - Saints

**Henry Cuesta, reeds** *(1935 Corpus Christi TX)* - Jack Teagarden; Lawrence Welk

**Mike Culbert, cor** - Feather Riverboat

**Jim Cumming, bass** - *(1925 Saskatoon CANADA)* Berkeley Rhythm; Jack Buck; Jazz Cardinals; Fulton St; Red Gillham; Golden Age; Golden State; Good Time Levee; Jelly Roll-SF; Bob Neighbor; Port Costa; Silicon Gulch; Tappers; Mike Tilles JB; Tom Kats

## CURBSTONE COPS LA 1950-51

Novelty band included many credible studio musicians featured on a nightly national radio program (CBS) from Catalina Island Casino; later *Paris Inn* San Diego and other southland venues.

DAVE CAVANAUGH, sax; Ray Conniff, tbn; Stumpy Stumph, cor; others unknown.

**Mark Curry, reeds** *(1960 OR) student* - Golden West; Jazz Minors; Stumptown

**Benson Curtis** - jazz activist of long standing, had several radio programs in the LA area specializing in jazz; still active in occasional radio appearances. Honored many times by jazz clubs for his dedication and support. Grand Jubilator Sacramento Jubilee 78

**Doug Curtis, tbn** - Cypress; Dixieland Inc

**Jack Curtiss, bjo, g** - Cottonmouth

## CUSTER'S LAST BAND Stockton 1985→

Stanley Jarnolowez, sb; JERRY McKENZIE, cl; Renard Perry, tpt; Larry Salerno, d; Tom Shove, p; Sam Smith, tbn; Jan Sutherland, v.

**Art Cutliff, reeds** - Crown City

## CYPRESS SAND PEBBLES Monterey 1978

Johnny Carlin, tpt; Doug Curtis, tbn; Al Frobe, p; Greg Janusz, d; Bucky McGeoghegan, sb; Don Pellerin, cl; Stan Schuman, tsax.

# D

**"Duke" d'Alessio, reeds** - La Honda

**Thaman Pierce "Pete" Daily, cor** *(1911 Portland IN)* - ldr Chicagoans; Ozzie Nelson; Smokey Stover; led own groups. To CA 41, entered Merchant Marine, organized Chicagoans upon returning to CA in 45 and became instrumental in sparking a new national popular interest in jazz. Role model for Jack Webb in film *Pete Kelly's Blues* (55). Suffered incapacitating stroke in 79 as a final episode in a series of misfortunes, becoming partially paralyzed and confined to a wheelchair. Grand Jubilator Pismo Beach Jubilee 77 (unable to attend due to an auto accident) and 81, Sacramento Jubilee 81; Jazz Forum "Jazzman Of the Year" 83

*ECLECTIC E71 "Pete Daily" (78)*

## PETE DAILY'S CHICAGOANS see CHICAGOANS

Much confusion and inaccuracy lurks in data about earlier bands, especially those before 1960. Time has thrown a veil over everything. Most groups during that period considered were unworthy of documentation, so it was up to the bandleaders and sidemen to store facts and figures, if they so cared. In the case of Pete Daily, vital records were consumed in the fire that almost cost him his own life, as it did his wife's. It then became incumbent upon sidemen to provide essential years and locations, and therein problems loomed large. In the words of one researcher, "Those who spoke with the greatest authority soon painted themselves into a corner with lack of continuity."

Daily, the most authentic source of information, whose mind was bright and clear, was unable to speak because of a paralyzing stroke. Time had eroded the memory of others who were there, so there is a painful apparency of loss in the documentation of Daily's movements through the '40s and '50s. With these conditions in mind, data may be considered accurate but year references should be construed as having a "circa" preceding them.

---

## PETE DAILY JAZZ BAND LA 1952-76

Also performed under title of Pete Daily's Ragtime Band.

Skippy Anderson, p; PETE DAILY, cor; Lou Diamond, d; Len Esterdahl, bjo; Budd Hatch, sb; Burt Johnson, tbn; Willie Martinez, cl. ADD: Gene Bolen, cl; Bill Dart, d; Al Jenkins, tbn; Rosy McHargue, cl; Burr Middleton, d; Warren Smith, tbn.

*CAP H183 "Pete Daily's DJB"*

### *PETE DAILY'S RHYTHM KINGS* LA 1947-52

Essentially CHICAGOANS but title changed for rec purposes to avoid contractual confliction.

Skippy Anderson, p; PETE DAILY, cor; George Defebaugh, d; Len Esterdahl, bjo; Rosy McHargue, cl; Warren Smith, tbn; Jimmy Stutz, sb. ADD: Lou Diamond, d; Budd Hatch, sb; Burt Johnson, tbn.

*CAMAY CA3035 "The Bob Cats and Pete Daily"; CAP 728, 760, 1055, 1370, 1486, 1588, 2041, 15315, 15433, 15434, 60008, T35 "Dixie By Daily"; DECCA DL5261 "Dixieland Jazz Battle"; JM 14, 29, 30 (47); GTJ 61, 68; JUMP 12, 24*

**John Dale, bass** - Hiz Honor

**Ernie Dalleske, tpt** *(1939 Oxford NB)* - Emperor Norton; Saints

PETE DAILY RAGTIME BAND, White Way Inn, 1967
Gene Boien, Daily, Don Owens, Warren Smith, Roger Stillman, Lou Diamond

Wayne Nicholls

**Barbara Dane, g, v,** *(1927 Detroit MI)* - Turk Murphy; Jack Teagarden; guest work; gained popularity as folk singer on SF radio in early '50s, eventually had own tv program

**Rich Daneker, d** *radio dj* - Royal Bourbon St

**Dave Daniels, tbn** *(1939 Huntington WV) journalist* - Miss-Behavin'

**Joe Darensbourg, reeds** *(1906-1985 Baton Rouge LA)* - Angel City; Louis Armstrong; Teddy Buckner; Mutt Carey; Crown City; ldr Dixie Flyers; [Firehouse 5 + 2]; [Gin Bottle 4]; Legends; Liggins Honeydrippers; Wingy Manone; Fate Marable; Jelly Roll Morton; Kid Ory; Johnny Wittwer Trio; Young Men From NO; led own groups. To WA c40, CA 44. Suffered incapacitating stroke early in 85 which ended a long and illustrious career. Honored by LA Mayor Tom Bradley proclaiming 17 Jul 83 as "Joe Darensbourg Day." Grand Jubilator Pismo Beach Jubilee 78, Sacramento Jubilee 80; Jazz Forum "Jazzman Of the Year" 82. Comp *Lou-easy-an-i-a, Sacramento Jubilee* (theme)

    *GHB 90 "Barrelhousin' With Joe"; ANGEL CITY "From Old Sacramento to New Orleans" w/Angel City JB*

**JOE DARENSBOURG'S DIXIE FLYERS** see DIXIE FLYERS

**Bill Dart, d** - Alexander's; Barbary Coast; Bearcats; Pete Daily; Bunk Johnson; Turk Murphy; Jack Sheedy; Washboard 5; Yerba Buena

**Sammy Daulong, tpt** - ldr Pearl Pacific

**Julian Davidson, g** - Kid Ory

**Art Davis, tpt** - ldr Jazz-a-Ma-Tass

**Danny Davis, vib** *(1914 San Francisco CA)* - ldr Jazz Formula; ldr Jazz Forum

**Eddie Davis, d** *(Seattle WA)* - Rainy City

**Frances Davis, bass** *(1919 Enid OK)* - Jazz Formula; marr Danny Davis

**Frank Davis, cor** *(1955)* - Royal Society

**Joe Davis, reeds** - Headliners

**Ray Davis, bjo** *mill production engr* - Royal Bourbon St

**Ron Davis, bjo** - 32nd St

**William "Wild Bill" Davison, tpt** *(1906 Defiance OH)* - Barney Bigard; Eddie Condon; Salt City 6; led own groups; guested and toured with many more. Usually associated more with East Coast groups and clubs but moved to CA 60. Active at this writing only in All-Star groups. Jazz Forum "Jazzman Of the Year" 80. Numerous recs

## DAWN OF THE CENTURY RAGTIME ORCHESTRA LA 1967-?

One of the most authentic ragtime groups; featured at 72 St Louis Ragtime Festival. Began as a quartet, (2p/horn/tu), expanding by 70 with two viols and a tpt, subsequently adding instrumentation as required by the 1400 arrangements (c1910) which Bourne uncovered.

Mike Baird, cl; DAVE BOURNE, cor/tenor horn; Dave Kennedy, tbn; Jack Langlos, tpt; Art Levin, tu; Jack Malek, viol; Donna McClure, viol; Roy Roten, perc; Dick Zimmerman, p. ADD: Dick Cary, tpt; Victor de Veritch, viol; John Jewett, flute; Bill Stumpp, tpt; Holly Ulvate, flute.

*ARCANE AR601 "The Dawn of the Century Ragtime Orch"*

**Tom Dawson, d** - ldr Camellia

**Jim d'Amicis, d** *(1923 Raton NM)* - Emperor Norton

**Bob Dean, tbn** - King Zulu

**Al Deemer, tpt** *(1961 Los Angeles CA)* - Lemon St

**Ron Deeter, reeds** *electronics* - Royal Society; Silicon

**Pete Deetken, bjo** *(1936 Ross CA)* - Natural Gas

**George Defebaugh, d** - Pete Daily; Bob Higgins; Rosy McHargue

**John Dehler, bjo** - ldr San Diego Hysterical Dixieland Banjo Soc; co-fdr America's Finest City Dixieland Jazz Society

**Leo Dejan, tpt** - Resurrection

**Mike DeLay, tpt** *(1909-1975 New Orleans LA)* - Paul Barbarin; Papa Celestin; Crown City; Dixie Flyers; Roger Jamieson; Resurrection; Young Men From NO

**Lynn Delmerico, tpt** - Satin Dolls

**Hollis DeLoach, p** *(1915 Middleton MI)* *training specialist* - Dixie Unltd

**Larry Delorier, flute** *(1944 NH)* *office worker* - Chrysanthemum

**George Delrich, cor** - Bathtub Gin

## DELTA JAZZ BAND (TOM BUCK'S) SF 1973-74

*Henry VIII* Concord (73-74).

Jack Buck, p; TOM BUCK, tpt; Jack Crook, cl; John Farkas, tbn; Red Honore, sb; Bob Ulsh, d.

## DELTA JAZZ IRREGULARS Concord CA 1973-indef

Title came from the idea that the lineup was not fixed but rather was comprised of any of a number of Bay Area musicians; only ldr Bob Hinman was a "regular." *Henry VIII* Concord (73-79). Band was somewhat extant at this writing, appearing at special occasions.

## DELTA KING DERELICTS SAC 1974

Assembled specially for Sacramento Jubilee.

Ford Erfert, p; Bob Johnson, d; JOHN KNURR, sb; Jean Levinson, bjo/g; Emmett O'Sullivan, cl; Mike Pittsley, tbn; Al Smith, cor.

## DELTA RAMBLERS Disneyland

Charlie Romero, cl; others unknown.

## DELTA RHYTHM KINGS LA 1961-63

*Harbor Inn* LA (60-61), *Limelight* Pacific Ocean Park (61).

K O Eckland, p (-62); JIM HUBBART, cl; Clark Huddleston, bjo; Bill Pietsch, d; Hugh Polley, tpt; Jim Sheldon, tbn (61). ADD: Roy Brewer, tbn (61-63); Bert Grant, p (62-63).

*FILM TONE DRK-EP58 (63)*

**Frank Demond, tbn** - Crescent Bay; Preservation Hall (NO); Storyville; Tuxedo

**George "Jud" De Naut, bass** - Pete Kelly Big 7; Artie Shaw

**Bill Dendle; bjo** - ldr Charlie's; ldr So Market St

**Max Denning, viol** *Dept of Motor Vehicles* - Jazzberry

**James "Big Jim" DeNoon, bass, viol** *(19—1979)* - Monterey Bay Stompers

## DESERT CITY SIX Phoenix 1960→

Bob Adamowecz, cor (60); Edd Dickerman, bjo (60); Ed Johnson, cl (-61); DICK KNUTSON, tbn; John Mallot, d; Wally Wallace, tu (-61). ADD: Ted Babcock, bjo (80→); Chet Bogan, cor (77); Gene Bruhjell, d (79→); Roy Calhoun, d (69-71); Dave Chaney, tpt (78); Gary Church, tpt (79); Rick Felix, tu (79-84); Bob Haygood, p (83→); Ken Kennedy, d (68-71); Vern Kiel, cor (66-80); Ralph Milling, bjo (65-79); Steve Morris, d (78); Ray Nutaitis, tu (84→); Dick O'Dette, d (78-79); Dick Robinson, d (72); Bob Schroeder, cl (85→); Dan Shannon, eb (84-85); Lin Shoemaker, tu (64-79); Cheryl Stephens, v (79→); Jan Stiers, p (78-83); Bob Wardlaw, cl (65-85); Dick Williams, cor (82-84).

*DESERT CITY "That's a-Plenty" (75); = "Down In Honky Tonk Town" (75); = "Was I Drunk?" (80); = "Robert E Lee" (80)*

**Paul Desmond (Breitenfeld), reeds** *(1924-1982 San Francisco CA)* - Dave Brubeck; Jack Sheedy; led own progressive groups

## DESOLATION JAZZ ENSEMBLE see WORLD FAMOUS DESOLATION JAZZ ENSEMBLE

**Ted des Plantes, bass, p** - Conductors; Down Home; Portland Rose; ldr Stomp Aces

## DESTINY CITY JAZZ BAND Tacoma WA 1982→

Formed after TRAFFIC JAMMERS was abandoned due to the death of co-fder Wayne Simon.

GARY ALESHIRE, tbn; Bill Hobart, cor; Bob Holder, cl/sax; Al LaTourette, bjo; Keith Purvis, d; Cliff Rawnsley, p; Al Wied, tu; Peggy Wied, v.

**Franz "Dutch" Deutsch, reeds** *(1934 Sacramento CA)* - [Delta Jazz]; ldr Gas House; Golden State; ldr Gramercy; ldr Shakey's Inferior; Silver Dollar-SAC

DUTCH DEUTSCH Jan 1978

**Les Deutsch, bass, p, tpt** *(1955 Inglewood CA) mathematician* - New Bull Moose; Triple RRR

**Alice Deveau, p** - Raisin City

## DEVIL MOUNTAIN JAZZ BAND Oakley CA 1982→

Tom Cantrell, cor; Mark Giannini, d; Jean Keeler, p; KEN KEELER, bjo; Marty Main, sb; Pete Main, cl; Bruce Stuart, tbn. ADD: Bob Enos, tpt (83→); Pat Main, p; Dave Radmore, tu (83-84); Phil Stiers, bsax (84→).

*DMJB "Devil Mountain JB" (84)*

**Jay Dewald, tbn** - Camellia

**Reggie Dewar, tbn** - Goose Island; Jelly Roll Jazz Soc

## DEW DROP INN DIXIELAND JAZZ BAND Fresno 1984→

Ken Farnsworth, bjo; Bob Kennedy, cl; KEN KENNEDY, p; Carl Schmitt, tbn; Cal Sorensen, tpt; Elmer Tuschoff, tu; Howard Weber, d.

**Bruce Dexter, tpt** - Cottonmouth; Crescent Bay; El Dorado-LA

**Dale Dial, d** - Jazz Minors

**Jimmy Diamond, p** *(1921 Oakland CA)* - Charlie Barnet; ldr Jimmy Diamond Orch; Red Nichols; ldr Nob Hill Gang; Muggsy Spanier; Kid Ory

**Joe Diamond, tpt** - Ponca City

**Lou Diamond, d** *(19—19—)* - Blueblowers; Pete Daily; Rosy McHargue

**Ralph Diana, bjo** - Cottonmouth; Party Peppers; Pepper; ldr Red Pepper; San Juan; Smog City; Southern Stompers

**Dick Dice, p** - Storyville

**Edd Dickerman, bjo, g** - Desert City; *Flaming Deuces*; Jelly Roll JB-SF

**Jim Diven, d** - Dixie 6

**Ron Divincenzi, bass** - UC Jazz

## DIXIE BELLES LA c1980

Karen Donley, sb; PEGGY GILBERT, sax; Feather Johnson, sb; Peewee Preble, tbn; Natalie Robin, cl; Georgia Shilling, p; Jerrie Thill, d; Marion Wells, tpt.

## *DIXIEBOPPERS* LA 1947

Principally a rec group stemming from a radio show; also known as LEIGH AND VIRGINIA CROSBY DIXIEBOPPERS.

Nick Cochrane, tpt; Nick Fatool, d; Milt Golden, p; Rosy McHargue, cl; Joe Rushton, bsax; Gus van Camp, sb; Paul Wiegand, tbn.

*C&F 1-5 (47)*

## DIXIECRATS SAC 1978

Rick Baker, tpt; DAVE BEEMAN, tbn; Jerry Lopes, sb/tu; Ken Murphy, d; Eddie Smith, p; Don Spindler, cl.

**DIXIE FIVE** Pacific Grove CA

DOUG CURTIS, tbn; others unknown.

## DIXIE FLYERS (JOE DARENSBOURG'S) LA 1956-61

It was with this group that the rec of *Yellog Dog Blues* made the national best-seller list in 57.

Harvey Brooks, p (56-60); JOE DARENSBOURG, cl/ssax; Mike DeLay, tpt; Al Morgan, sb; Warren Smith, tbn; George Vann, d (-60). ADD: Wellman Braud, d (60-61); Bill Newman, bjo/g.

*GNP CRESCENDO DJ514 "Yellow Dog Blues" (75); LARK 782, LP331 "On a Lark"; =LS452; HOT ROD 1001; RED STICK LP5080 "Joe Darensbourg Remembers His Dixie Flyers"*

## DIXIE KATZ UNLIMITED Corona CA 1980→

Original lineup unknown. Chuck Anderson, tbn; George Andrus, d; Lance Buller, tpt (85); Richard Cruz, tpt (79,81,83); Art Dragon, tbn; Bill Grovesnor, p (85); Bill Hill, p; Jack Martin, bjo (-84); John Nelson, viol; Jim Ogden, tpt; Gene O'Neill, d; Scotty Plummer, bjo (85); Paul Reid, p; Charlie Romero, cl; John Whited, d; DEE WOOLEM, sb.

## DIXIELAND DISSONANTS SAC 1975

Kent Dunavent, tbn; John Fulwider, bjo; Tom Gorin, p; Jeff Karl, d; Emmett O'Sullivan, cl; KURT PEARSALL, tpt; Gary Stein, sb.

## DIXIELAND EXPRESS JAZZ BAND Victoria BC 1982→

Ernie Cockayne, bjo; Ron Draper, d; Keith Fraser, tu; NORRIE MacFARLANE, tpt; Al Pease, sl/ssax; Alf Sleigh, tbn. ADD: Lloyd Arntzen, cl/sax; Hugh Barclay, tbn; Tom Blodgett, p; Paul Mascioli, d.

## DIXIELAND FIVE see TRI-CITIES JB

## DIXIELAND INC Salinas 1978-85

Also titled MONTEREY BAY HOT JB.

Diane Anderson, v; Delourde Brooks, v; Lloyd Bucks, bjo; Ned Brundage, d; BILL BURGESS, tpt; Doug Curtis, tbn; Lorene Keltner, p; Edna Lewis, sax; Don Pellerin, cl; Bill van der Burg, sb.

## DIXIELAND JAZZ BRAVOS Fullerton 1980-81

Jack Berka, cl/sax; Ben Cleall, d; RICHARD CRUZ, tpt; Hal Groody, bjo; Gil Kraus, p; Ginny Osburn, p; Ed Slauson, d; Bob Smith, tbn; Ira Westley, sb; Dave Wright, tu/sb.

*CDJB 1 "Dixieland Jazz Bravos" (81)*

## DIXIELAND SYNCOPATORS Stockton

Bill Hannaford, tbn; George Knoblauch, tpt; GENE LANCELLE, tpt; Jody Lancelle, p; Earl Miller, cl; Johnny Strangio, d; Ray Walters, tu.

## DIXIE RHYTHM RAMBLERS Los Angeles 1978-indef

Jack Booth, tbn; Elmer Hess, sb; Robbie James, p; MOREY LEVANG, bjo/g; Wayne Schmus, cl; Dave Surtees, d; Ray Williams, tpt. ADD: Tommy Mann, cl; Bill Mitchell, p; Fred Montgomery, d; Shirley Pennington, sb.

JOHN DODGSHON
October 1981

DESERT CITY 6
October 1979

## DIXIE SIX SD 1981→

Jim Diven, d; Jeff Finch, v; Vince Greco, p; Eric Johnson, sb; David Richards, tpt; JIM WEISS, cl/sax; Tim Weiss, tbn.

## DIXIE UNLIMITED Atascadero CA 1979-83

Charlie Bonner, tpt (-82); JACK GODDARD, cl/ssax; Shirley Goddard, sb; Dick Johnson, p (-81); Bob Sloan, tbn (-81); Dick Young, d (-82). ADD: Hollis DeLoach, p (81-83); Oscar Perez, tpt (82); Ernie Paul, d (82-83); Peggy Rose, v (83); Gerald Shuester, tbn (81-83).

**Lee Dixon, reeds** - Sausalito

**Leonard Dixon, reeds** *(1924 Jackson MI) traffic mgr* - And That's Jazz; Cats 'n' Jammers; ldr Jazz Beaux; ldr Purple Gang; Riverbank

## DR JON'S MEDICINE SHOW & JAZZ BAND Astoria 1983→

Originally titled NEW RAGTIME 3 + 2 + 1.

JON BALSCHWEID, cor; Herb Brennan, d; Bill Langdon, p; Steve Matthes, cl; Bill Miller, tbn; Eric Peterson, tu; Bob Tarrant, bjo. ADD: Deni Balschweid, v; Manfred Johnson, tu; Steve Todd, tbn.

## DR MIX'S MAGIC ELIXIR JAZZ BAND SAC 1977-81

Original lineup unknown. Norm Bylin, cl (78); Chuck Heggli, bjo (78-81); Honorene Heggli, p; Tom Kenny, cl (79-80); Ed LaFranchi, tpt (79); Roger Mendez, d (79-81); DICK MIX, tbn; Dick Neary, g (80-81); John Olbrich, tbn; Emmett O'Sullivan, cl/tsax (77); Jim Painter, cl (81); Doug Parker, bjo (77); Bill Tharp, tpt (77-78,80-81); George Walker, d (77-78).

**Bob Dodds, tpt** - Swanee's

**John Dodgshon, cor, tbn, reeds** - [Delta Jazz]; 52nd St; Jubilee; Marin Jazz ldr; Rose & Thistle

## DO-DO-WAH STREET IRREGULARS Monterey

Bud Benadom, d; Allen Caldiera, bjo; Ed Greco, reeds; Joe Ingram, tpt; Jake Jacobsen, cor; John Keller, sb; Al Ring, tbn; Keith Rubrecht, tbn; Sal Russo, p.

**Bill Dods, bass, p** - [Spencer Quinn]; Rosy McHargue

**Ned Dodson, cor** - Castle

**Vince Dodson, cor** - Rose City Stompers; bro Ned Dodson

**Bob Doerschuk, p** - Churchill St; 52nd St

## DO-IT-YOURSELF DIXIE South SF Bay 1971-76

Not an extant group so much as a format for a structured jam set giving area jazz musicians opportunities to experiment together. Locations varied from *The Bold Knight* SJ to *The Country Store* Sunnyvale. Concept and management by Norton Fredlund and Jack Mangan.

**Ed Dolby, d** - Orange Pealers

**Ted Dolce, reeds** - Gold Standard

**Dave Dolson, reeds** *(1949 Santa Monica CA) Captain LAPD* - Good Time; ldr Jazzin' Babies; ldr Smogville

**Norm Domreis, p** *(1925 Los Angeles CA)* - Jim Beatty; Portland Rose

**Dick Doner, tbn** *(1936 Toledo OH) drafting service* - Good Time; Milneburg; Nightblooming; Workingman

**Ken Donica, bass** - Charlie's; So Market St

**Karen Donley, bass** - Dixie Belles

**John Doolittle, reeds** - Toot Suite

**Dick Dotts, p** *(1917 Garnett KS)* - Bye Bye Blues; ldr Jazz Otters; Monterey Bay Stompers

**Hank Dougherty, bjo** *(1936 OR) county commissioner* - Portland Rose; Stumptown

**Harry Douglas, p** - Coos Bay

**Dick Douty, tuba** - ldr Live Steam

**Bob Downer, bjo** - Coos Bay

## DOWNEY DIXIE DRIVERS Downey 1983→

Norm Burnham, p; Wally Geil, d; Dick Greenly, tbn; Jack Keister, cl; RAY LYON, bjo; Bill Maher, tpt; Vince Pescatore, sb.

## DOWN HOME JAZZ BAND Santa Ana 1972-76

Formed from FINK ST FIVE personnel; *Handlebars* Santa Ana (74), *Old Chicago Gaslighter* Newport Beach (75-76).

Mike Baird, cl (-72); Dan Barrett, cor (-72); Bill Mitchell, p (-75); Doug Parker, bjo (-74); HAL SMITH, d/wb; Paul Woltz, tu (-74). ADD: Tom Barnebey, cor (72); Jeff Beaumonte, tu (72-76); Stan Chapman, tbn (76); Ted DesPlantes, tu (73-74); Mike Fay, bjo (74); Larry Helm, cl (alt); Dave Kennedy, tbn (74); Vic Loring, bjo (76); Steve Resnick, bjo (alt); John Reynolds, bjo (alt); Robbie Rhodes, p (72-76); Bryan Shaw, cor (72); Ken Smith, cor (alt); Laurence Wright, cl (72-76); Bill Vogel, tpt (74-76).

**Leigh Downs, v** - Mississippi

**Tom Downs, bass** *(1937 San Francisco CA)* - Black Diamond; Emperor Norton; So Bay 7

**Art Dragon, tbn** - Dixie Katz

**Ron Draper, d** - Dixieland Express

**Mark Dresser, bass** - [Chicago 6]

**Dave Driver, g** *(Seattle WA) student* - Rainy City

**Steven Drivon, tbn** - Hangtown; Port City

## DROOP'S DIXIELAND DIGNITARIES SAC

DROOPS EARNHART, p; others unknown.

**Gina Drury, wb** *(1951 Hollywood CA) artist, writer* - Fink St; sis of Paul and Randy Woltz

**Mike Duffy, bass** *(1941 Seattle WA) English teacher* - Berkeley Rhythm; *Creole Sunshine, Flaming Deuces*; Golden Age; Golden State; co-org Grand Dominion; ldr Great Excelsior;

Jazz Cardinals; Lakeshore; Lake Spanaway; Magnolia; Port Costa; [Rainier]; Rhythmakers; Stone Age; Tom Kats; [Uptown Lowdown]

**Larry Dufresne, p** *(1914 Chicago IL)* - Castle; Conductors

**Bob Duggan, bjo** - Mardi Gras-LA

**Jack Duke, p** - Silver Dollar-SAC

**Larry Duke, tpt** - Happy JB

**Kent Dunavent, tbn** - Cats 'n' Jammers; Dixie Dissonants; Hangtown; Sutterville

**Dick Duncan, bjo** - Powerhouse

**Bob Dunn, p** *neurosurgeon* - Uptown Lowdown

**Don Dupree, reeds** *(1935 Lanesboro MN) librarian* - Jazz Formula; Jelly Roll Jazz Society; Note-ables

**Carlos Duran, bass** - Jack Sheedy

**Ray Durand, bass** - Pier 23

**Barry Durkee, bjo** *(19—1980)* - Bay City; Gas House; Original Inferior; ldr Rainier; Shakey's Inferior

**Eunice Duroe, tbn** - Satin Dolls

**Tom Dutart, bass** *(1935 Stockton CA) teacher* - Pete Dust; Tuleburg

**Pat Dutrow, bjo** *(1958 Richmond CA) inventory mgmt* - Prof Plum; Royal Society; Seaside Syncopators

## DUWAMISH DIXIELAND BAND SEA 1980→

Perry Barth, d (-84); Dave Brown, bjo (-82); Bruce Cosacchi, cor; Bruce Keck, tu; Kevin Johnston, bjo (-84); RAY JOHNSTON, bjo/tbn; Chuck Myrick, cl (-84); Elroy Pettyjohn, p (-84). ADD: Lynn Brown (Kronk), bjo; Dale Corliss, v (83-84); Dan Grinstead, p (84→); Al LaTourette, bjo (84→); Ken Miller, tbn; Mike Sheppard, cl (84→); Dick Walker, d (84→).

# E

**Bill Eagle, cor** - Bourbon St JB

**Adolphus "Droops" Earnhart, p** - Capitol City; Golden State; Gold Standard

**Mickey Earnshaw, d** - Lloyd Arntzen

**Chuck Eastman, bjo** *(1941 West Union IA) baker* - Headliners; Tuleburg

**Ed Easton, reeds** *(1936 York PA)* - Harry James; Big Tiny Little

## EASY WINNERS (WILDA'S) SAC 1977-79

Rick Baker, tpt (77); WILDA BAUGHN, p; George Boyd, cl (78); Henry Hogan, tpt (77); Tom King, tpt; Les Jasper, tbn (77-78); Eddie Macedo, bjo (77); Don McDonald, tpt; Frank Myers, sb (77-78); Bill Owens, d (78); John Picardi, d; Frank Silva, cl; Ted Thompson, tsax (78); Buddy Trumbo, d (77); Jerry Walcott, tbn.

**Charles Eberle, reeds** - ldr Knights of Camelot

**Dick Eckhardt, bass** - Monterey Bay Classic

**Kenneth "K.O." Eckland, p** *(1926 Cleveland OH) artist, writer* - Delta Rhythm Kings; Firehouse 5 + 2; Kansas City; Knights; ldr Pismo; org Polecats; Rex Stewart; Tailgate Ramblers; Thee Saints; ldr WFDJE&MKRB; co-fdr Basin St Regulars (CCHJS); comp *Sundown Mama*, others

**Cay Eckmier, p** - Aristocrats

**Bob Edson, tbn** *(1935 Bismark ND) chemical engr* - Pete Dust; Tuleburg

**Arthur Edwards, bass** *(1914 Ft Worth TX)* - Teddy Buckner; Horace Henderson; Bud Scott

**Gordon "Gramps" Edwards, d** - Alexander's; *Frisco Footwarmers*; Frisco JB; [Turk Murphy]; Bob Scobey

GORDON EDWARDS undated

**Teddy Edwards, d** *(New Orleans LA)* - Teddy Buckner; Papa Celestin; Chris Kelly; George Lewis; Resurrection; Silver Dollar-LA; Tuxedo

**Marty Eggers, p** *(1966 Los Angeles CA)* - Black Diamond

**Herb Ehlenburg, p** - Bayside

**Jim Eichel, bass** - Jazzbo

**Gene Eidy, d** *artist* - Mardi Gras-LA

**Art Eissinger, tbn** *municipal court judge* - ldr Hiz Honor

## EL DORADO JAZZ BAND SJ 1953-61

*Kerosene Club* (56-58), later named *K Club* (59-60); *Pete's Chicago Club* Sunnyvale (60-61) as a quartet during the week (Cabibi; Carroll; Reudger; Goudie or Horne) and a full band on Sundays. Sub for Turk Murphy at *Italian Village* SF (54). Ruedger assumed leadership after Leigh left to join Ev Farey; group folded when his regular job took him to OH.

Pete Fay, p; Frank Goulette, cor (-53); JIM LEIGH, tbn (-56,59-61); DAN RUEDGER, bjo; Roland Working, cl (-58). ADD: Jim Borkenhagen, tpt (53-61); Greg Cabibi, d (60-61); Bill Carroll, sb/tbn (57-61); Bill Carter, cl (57-61 alt); Squire Girsback, sb (55-58,60); Frank Goudie, cl (59-61); Ellis Horne, cl (60-61 alt); Carol Leigh, v (-56,59-61).

## EL DORADO JAZZ BAND LA 1963-67

On returning from OH, Ruedger formed a second version of his SF group out of one organized by Larry Marvin and Bob Raggio. *Ted's Grill* Santa Monica (63-64) and *Can-Can* Anaheim (64-65), *Leaping Liz's*, *McGoo's* Hollywood (65-66). Ruedger moved back to SF in 64 but band continued under Raggio's leadership.

Mike Baird, cl/asax; Alan Crowne, tbn; Bruce Dexter, tpt (-64 alt); Mike Fay, sb; BOB RAGGIO, wb; Ray Ronnei, cor; DAN RUEDGER, bjo (-65); Walt Sereth, cl (-64 alt). ADD: Clark Huddleston, bjo (64); Pete Keir, tu (rec); Vic Loring, bjo (64-66 alt); Bill Mitchell, p (67); Tom Sharpsteen, cl (64-67 alt); Dick Shooshan, p (rec).

*EPITAPH 4 "The El Dorado JB" (64)*

**Rudy Eleff, bass** - Tailgate Ramblers

**Myrriah Ellis, viola** *(1951) computer repair* - Chrysanthemum

**Rollie Ellis, bjo** - Shakey City

**Pat Ellison, tpt** - UC Jazz

## EMERALD CITY JAZZ BAND Eugene OR 1969-77

Bill Abbott, d; BERT BARR, cor (-71); Dick Burley, tbn; TOM JACOBUS, tu; Darrell Langevin, bjo; Jan Stiers, p; Phil Stiers, ssax. ADD: Wilbur Jensen, tpt (71-77).

## EMPEROR NORTON'S JAZZ BAND SJ 1963→

Fredlund started on valve trombone, switched to piano in 70. Notable is the number of sidemen who went on to lead their own groups (Armstrong, Marcus, Mangan, Scott, Vermazen).

NORTON FREDLUND, p, tbn; Don Frolich, p (-70); Barry Mallagh, tu (-67); Tom Rudy, bjo (-67); John Scott, cor (-67); Paul Widdess, cl (-67). ADD: Dave Albertson, tu (67); Harry Alto, g/bjo (76→); Bill Armstrong, bjo (61-65); Roy Butler, d (70-81); Ernie Chavez, tsax (82→); Curt Cobb, d (82→); Ernie Dalleske, tpt (80-81); Jim d'Amici, d (67-69); Al Hall, tbn (67); Sam Hernandez, tpt (82→); El Hubbard, tbn (76-77); Bob Keely, sb (82→); John Maloney, reeds (67→); Jack Mangan, cl (67, 70-75); Marc Marcus, cl (65-68); Phil Olander, sb (68-69); Dick Randolph, cor/tbn (68-69); Sandy Sandstrom, tpt (76-77); Joe Trubic, eb (76-77); Bruce Vermazen, tpt (67-69).

**Bob Enos, tpt** *(1925 Oakland CA) public utilities* - Devil Mtn

**Ford Erfert, p** - Delta King

**Bill Erickson, tpt, p** *(19—1967)* - Bearcats; Burp Hollow; Estuary; Bill Napier; Kid Ory-SF; Pier 23 ldr; Jack Sheedy; Stone Age; solo; led own groups

**Edward "Fast Eddie" Erickson, bjo** *(1949 San Francisco CA)* - Abalone; Disneyland; Disney World (FL); Mickey Finn (NV); solo

**Willie Erickson, p** - ldr Sugar Willie

**Phil Erlich, d** *(1964 Hempstead NY)* - Lemon St

**Eugean Ermel, d** *(1966 Salem OR) student* - Lemon St

**Len Esterdahl, bjo, g** - Blueblowers; Pete Daily

**Gene Estes, d, vib** - [Heinie Beau]; Bob Crosby

## ESTUARY JAZZ BAND Oakland c1959

Short-lived group formed by "Hambone" Crosby, host of a trad jazz program on a local radio station.

Burt Bales, p; LEE CROSBY, sb; Bill Erickson, tpt; Frank Goudie, cl; Don Marchant, d; Bob Mielke, tbn; Dick Oxtot, g.

**David Etterbeek, tpt** - ldr Jazzin' Jrs

**Jon Etterbeek, tbn** - Jazzin' Jrs

## EUPHONIC JAZZ BAND Palo Alto 1977-79

Formed from personnel of EUPHORIA JAZZ BAND.

Cal Abbott, cl; Don Brayton, tu/sb; Al McDearmon, p; BRIAN RICHARDSON, tbn; BIRCH SMITH, tpt; Karl Walterskirchen, bjo; unknown, d.

## EUPHORIA JAZZ BAND SJ 1973-77

Formed, according to Mangan, by "some guys with a common distaste for *Indiana*," embracing the Louis' Hot 5-Watters-Morton idiom. First exposure at SBTJS Session, Feb 73; *Country Store* Mountain View (74-75).

Don Brayton, tu/sb; Bill Carter, cl (73,75-76); Al McDearmon, p; Brian Richardson, tbn; JACK MANGAN, d; Birch Smith, tpt; Karl Walterkirschen, bjo. ADD: Cal Abbott, cl (77); Marc Marcus, cl (74).

*EUPHORIA "Messin' Around" (75)*

**Bob Evans, tpt** - Napa Valley

**Carl Evans, reeds** - Doc Olson; Pearl Pacific

**Ray Evans, d** - Blueblowers

**Tom Evans, reeds** - 32nd St

**Don Ewell, p** *(1916-1983 Baltimore MD)* - Doc Evans; Bunk Johnson; [Kid Ory]; Muggsy Spanier; [Turk Murphy]; Jack Teagarden; solo; led own groups principally in the East and Canada

*AUDIO FIDELITY CR130 "Don Ewell"; GTJ L12021 "Music to Listen to Don Ewell By" (57); =S10043 "Man Here Plays Fine Piano!" (61); =M12046 "Free 'n' Easy" (62); JAZZOLOGY J29 "And His All-Stars" (82); NO R7209 "Don Ewell/Herb Hall Quintet" (82); WINDIN' BALL 103 "Kid Ory's Creole Band Tunes" (75)*

**John "Streamline" Ewing, tbn** *(1917 Topeka KS)* - Teddy Buckner; Cab Calloway; Lionel Hampton; Chris Kelly; Jimmy Lunceford; Cootie Williams; Young Men From NO

**Tom Ewing, d** - New Bull Moose

## EXCELSIOR BANJO BAND LA 1960

*Rosey's Red Banjo* Westwood, Mapes Hotel Reno, Desert Inn Las Vegas.

Fred Hoeptner, p; ART LEVIN, tu; Spencer Vaughn, bjo; Vic Wahlmier, bjo; Maurey Walker, bjo. ADD: Bill Campbell, p.

NICK FATOOL (with Jim Cumming) May 1975

# F

John Fanning, vib *(19—19—)* - Monterey Bay Stompers

Ev Farey, tpt *(1930)* - co-ldr Bay City; Berkeley Rhythm; Canal St; ldr Golden State; Bob Helm; Jazz Cardinals; Jelly Roll JB-SF; Marin Jazz; Turk Murphy; [New Washboard Rhythm Kings]; [Oakland A]; Port City; *Riverside Roustabouts*; Tappers; Young Audiences

John Farkas, tbn *(1928 Glens Falls NY) manufacturer rep* - Jack Buck; Delta JB; Frisco JB; Red Gillham; Jubilee

Ken Farnsworth, bjo - Dew Drop

Joe Farrell, reeds *(1937 Chicago Heights IL)* - Calif Ramblers

Nick Fatool, d *(1915 Milbury MA)* - Dave Barbour; [Heinie Beau]; Billy Butterfield; Hoagy Carmichael; Chicago Loopers; *Dixieboppers*; Pete Fountain; Benny Goodman; Artie Shaw Gramercy 5; Glen Gray; Bobby Hackett; Matty Matlock; Pete Kelly Big 7; Rampart St; [Silver Stope]; studios and rec; led own groups

Jack Faul, bjo - Ambulance; Monrovia

Curt Faulkner, d - Over the Hill

## FAULTLESS JAZZ BAND San Pedro
Al Crowne, tpt; PAT GOGERTY, p; Luster Hite, d; Dave Kennedy, tbn; Pete Keir, tu; Rex Schull, bjo; Jack Widmark, reeds.

Don Fay, d - Bearcats

Mike Fay, bass, bjo *(1935 Los Angeles CA) packaging* - British Connection; Costa del Oro; *Creole Sunshine*; Down Home; El Dorado-LA; Golden Eagle; Orange Empire; Royal Gardens; Storyville Stompers; Sunset Music; Tuxedo

Rick Fay, reeds - [Back Bay]; [Firehouse 5 + 2]; Mardi Gras-LA

Pete Fay, p *(1930-1975 San Jose CA)* - El Dorado-SJ

## FEATHER RIVERBOAT JAZZ BAND Graeagle CA 1984→
JULIE CARDOZA, tbn; Mike Culbert, cor; Bob Greene, cor´ (-84); John Lasrieu, tu; John Malarkey, p; Herb Newell, cl; Mike Schooler, d (-84); Vern van Lone, bjo. ADD: Al Bell, tpt (84→); Jack Taylor, d (84→).

John Fehd, bjo - Calif Express; Headliners

Carol Fehr, bjo - Pearl Pacific; San Diego DJB

Bob Feldman, d - Headliners

Rick Felix, bass *(CA) music teacher* - Desert City

Jerry Fenwick, tpt - Charlie's; So Market St

Lonny Ferguson, reeds - King Zulu

Len Ferrone, bass - Bourbon St JB

Andrew Fielding, p - Monarch

**Dave Fields, tbn** - Fink St

**Dick Fields, d** - Portland Rose

## 52ND STREET REVIVAL SF 1984→

Named after NY street which was in the '30s and '40s the location of most small-group jazz bands, the group specialized in playing everything from NO classics to contemporary songs which could be interpreted in the framework of jazz.

John Dodgshon, tpt (-84); Bob Doerschuk, p; Dave Peters, d (-84); Brian Richardson, tbn; JOHN STRINGER, cl; Al Tobey, sb. ADD: Sam Hernandez, tpt (84→); Henk Wagner, d (84→).

**Ernie Figeroa, bass, tbn, tpt** *(1918 San Diego CA)* - Charlie Barnet; Stan Kenton; Marty Marsala; [Nob Hill]; [Oakland A]; Muggsy Spanier; [Ralph Sutton]; Sweet & Hot

**Bob Finch, bass** *(1925 San Diego CA)* - ldr Chicago 6; Condor; Cottonmouth; San Juan

**Jeff Finch, v** - Dixie 6

## FINE TIME BAND LA 1979-83

Group was assembled primarily to play European festivals, but played considerably on the West Coast, as well.

Norvin Armstrong, p; Jim Atlas, sb; Bill Bardin, tbn; Frankie Capp, d; GEORGE PROBERT, ssax; John Smith, ssax; Al Weber; boombass.

## FINK STREET FIVE LA 1969-81

Originally titled KEYSTONE KOPS BAND, the name changed a few months later, after the street in Hollywood on which Arnold lived.

Mike Arnold, cl (-71); Ted Bavin, sb (-69); JEFF BEAUMONTE, cl/sax; Dave Fields, tbn (-70); Steve Resnick, bjo. ADD: Dan Barrett, tbn (70-74); Rick Holzgrafe, tbn (74-81); Brian Shaw, cor (71-73); Hal Smith, d (71-73); Ted Thomas, d (79-81); Charlie Warren, tu (78-81); Gina Woltz, wbd (76-79); Paul Woltz, bjo, reeds, tu (69-73,77-81); LAURENCE WRIGHT, cor/sax (69-81); Hironobu Yoshikawa, cl (71-73).

**Bill Finke, p** - Natural Gas

**John Finley, tpt** - Alamo City (TX); French Qtr; Unquenchables

**Fred Finn, p** - co-ldr Mickey Finn

**Mickey Finn, bjo** - co-ldr Mickey Finn; marr Fred Finn

## MICKEY FINN SHOW SD c1955-indef

Popular high-energy show band appearing first in their own club in SD, later on tour, finally to Las Vegas. Featured on national tv.

FRED FINN, p; MICKEY FINN, bjo; Bob Jensen, tpt; Owen Lienhard, tu/sb; Richard Lopez, d; Cougar Nelson, tbn; Don Paltha, bjo.

## FIREHOUSE FIVE PLUS TWO LA 1949-52, 1953-71

Formed by Ward Kimball primarily from Walt Disney studio animators and production people, originally titled HUGAJEEDY 8 (48), then SAN GABRIEL VALLEY BLUE BLOWERS (49). The band was an immediate hit with its irreverent attitude toward music and was hard

JOHN FINLEY January 1968

pressed to keep up with the deluge of engagements, so much so that adherence to the
original idea of playing strictly for fun precipitated their dropping out of action for more
than a year (52-53) just to rest and catch up with other avocations. Lucas quit early on,
reluctant to maintain the frantic schedule and wanting to start BLUEBLOWERS; MacDonald
dropped due to studio workload, but rejoined the band later for a time; Penner and Roberts
died; Mallery left Disney and formed own band; however, the group was unusually stable in
personnel for such a long and strenuous career, perhaps testimony to the enjoyment and
camaraderie felt by its members.

Harper Goff, bjo (-51,54); WARD KIMBALL, tbn; Johnny Lucas, tpt (49); Jim MacDonald,
d (49,55-58); Clarke Mallery, cl (-54); Ed Penner, bsax/tu (-56); Frank Thomas, p (-64).
ADD: Danny Alguire, tpt (49-71); Ralph Ball, tu (56); George Bruns, tu (56-58,67-71); K O
Eckland, p (62-71); Eddie Forrest, d (57-71); Don Kinch, tu/tpt (58-68); Monte Mountjoy,
d (49-55); Billy Newman, bjo (64-71); George Probert, ssax (55-71); Dick Roberts, bjo
(51-54,55-64). OTHER (periodic subs): Rick Fay, cl/ssax; John Smith, cl/ssax; Ira Wesley,
tu.

*CALLIOPE 3033, 3017 "The Firehouse 5 + 2" (57-58) w/Jeannie Gayle and Barbara Dane; GTJ 1,
2, 5, 6 (49); = 13, 14, 23, 24, 29, 30 (50); = 12010 "Firehouse 5 Story, Vol 1" (55); = 12011 "do.
Vol 2" (55); = 12012 "do. Vol 3" (55); = 12014 "Plays For Lovers" (56); = 12018 "Goes South"
(56); = S10028 "Goes To Sea" (57); = S10038 "Crashes a Party!" (60); = S10040 "Dixieland
Favorites" (60); = S10044 "Around the World!" (61); = S10049 "At Disneyland" (62); = M12052
"Goes To a Fire!" (64); = S10054 "Twenty Years Later" (69)*

**Bob Fischbeck, reeds** - Cider City

**Dick Fisher, bjo** - Pete Daily

**Larry Fisher, d** *(1944 Los Angeles CA) sheriff dept* - Jazzin' Babies

**Jim Fitzgerald, tbn** *(Mason City IA)* - Royal Dixie

**"Buster" Fitzpatrick, bass** - Rhythm Kings

### FIVE GUYS NAMED MOE Vancouver BC 1983→

Named after a song of that title.

ERNIE KING, tbn; Chuck Logan, d; Jimmy Johnson, tsax; Chris Noel, sb; Joe Poppe, p. ADD: Liston Pickering, d; Scott Watson, sb.

### *FLAMING DEUCES (LEON OAKLEY'S)* Berkeley 1978

Edd Dickerman, g; Mike Duffy, sb; Richard Hadlock, asax/ssax; LEON OAKLEY, cor; Ray Skjelbred, p; Hal Smith, d.

*GHB 153 "Leon Oakley's Flaming Deuces" (82)*

**Jay Fleming, v** *(1939 OR) clerical* - Portland Rose; Stumptown

**Bill Fletcher, d** - Portland Rose

**Al Flood, reeds** *(1939 San Francisco CA) pharmacist* - Barrelhouse

**Wally Floyd, d** - Burp Hollow; Pier 23

**Scott Fogelsong, p** *(1951 TX) music teacher* - Chrysanthemum

**Bert Forbes, bjo** *(1964 Seattle WA)* - Lemon St

**Eddie Forrest, d** - Firehouse 5 + 2

**Lew Forrest, d** *(Brooklyn NY)* - Hot Frogs; Jazzin' Babies; New Bull Moose

**Chet Fors, tbn** - Coos Bay

**Ollie Fosback, reeds** *(1923 Cushman OR) financial consultant* - Oregon; Pussyfoot; Stumptown

**Artie Foster, tbn** - Bob Crosby

**George "Pops" Foster** *(1892-1969 McCall LA)* - Henry Red Allen; Louis Armstrong; Sidney Bechet; Don Ewell; Earl Hines; Fate Marable; King Oliver; Kid Ory; Sinners; Muggsy Spanier; Bob Wilber; led own combos; subject of *Pops Foster, New Orleans Jazzman* (Tom Stoddard 71)

**Elwin Fountaine, bass** *(1914 Danville AR)* - Jim Beatty

**Joanne Fox, p** - Over the Hill

**Don Francisconi, tpt** *teacher* - Jazzberry

**Bob Franklin, p** *(1923 Fresno CA)* - And That's Jazz; Jubilee; Natural Gas

**Doug Franks, p** - Joyful Noise

**Don Franzioni, tpt** - Royal Valley

**Dean Frazer, bass** - Canal St

**Keith Fraser, bass** - Dixieland Express

**John Fratis, d** - Hiz Honor

**Meredith "Marty" Frazier, cor** *(1943 Hutchison KS) social worker* - WFDJE&MKRB

**Alfred Frechette, tpt** *(19—1983 Kalamazoo MI)* - Purple Gang; Swanee's

**Gene Frechette, d** - Purple Gang

**Chris Frederickson, bass** - Razzamajazz

**Norton Fredlund, p, tbn** *(1934 Minneapolis MN) chemical engr* - co-org Do-It-Yourself; ldr Emperor Norton; King Riverbottom; Powerhouse

**John Freeland, d** - Marvin Ash

**Dave Freeman, bass** *(1940 Syracuse NY) test engr* - Hyperion

**Fran Freeman, wbd** *(1934 Yonkers NY) teacher* - Hyperion

**Jack Freeman, tbn** *(1930 Syracuse NY) cabinetmaker* - Hyperion

**Dick Fregulia, p** - solo

**Mike French, d** - Jazzin' Jrs

## FRENCH QUARTER JAZZ BAND LA c1964-65

John Finley, tpt; Jimmy Grey, cl; Jim Matheson, bsax; Bill Mitchell, p; Ken Peterson, sb; Jim Sheldon, tbn; WALT VENTRE, d. ADD: Vinnie Armstrong, p.

## FRISCO BAND see SCOBEY'S FRISCO BAND

## *FRISCO FOOTWARMERS* SF 1950

Burt Bales, p; Jack Buck, tbn; Gordon Edwards, d; Squire Girsback, tu/sb; Clancy Hayes, bjo/v; DARNELL HOWARD, cl; Bob Scobey, tpt.

*JM 33, 34 (50)*

## FRISCO JAZZ BAND SF 1946-49

Jack Buck, tbn; Jack Crook, cl; Gordon Edwards, d; Red Gillham, tpt; Clancy Hayes, v; Ray Jahnigen, p; PAT PATTON, bjo/sb. ADD: Russ Bennett, bjo; Stan Hall, g (47); Dave Smith, sb (47); Eddie Smith, tpt; Neal Spaulding, p (47).

*DC 12005 "The Frisco JB, 1946" (72); PACIFIC 606, 611, 614, 615, 616, 620, 631, 639 (46)*

**Al Frobe, p** - Cypress

**Don Froelich, p** *(1928 Ely NV)* - Emperor Norton; Jubilee; King Riverbottom; Storyville

**Bob Froeschle, bass** - High Society JB

**Jack Frost, bass, bjo, g, p** *(1939 Chicago IL)* - Golden Gate Rhythm Machine; [Turk Murphy]; Bob Neighbor; [Oakland A]; Phrisco; Sinners; combos

**Robin Frost, g, p** - orig King Riverbottom; [Spencer Quinn]; Rosy McHargue

**Ben Fuller, tbn** - Sausalito

**Jerry Fuller, reeds** *(Santa Maria CA)* - Blueblowers; Pete Daily; Dukes of Dixieland; Knights; Ben Pollack; Jack Teagarden

## FULLERTOWNE STRUTTERS Fullerton 1984→

*Sunset Pub* Sunset Beach, Meadowlark Country Club.

RICHARD CRUZ, tpt; Hal Groody, bjo/g; Jon Lundgren, d; Jorge Mirkin, reeds; Jerry Rothschild, p; Bob Smith, tbn; Dave Wright, tu/sb.

TUDIE GARLAND May 1974

**Jack Fulton, tpt** - Gas Town

## FULTON STREET JAZZ BAND SAC 1970→

Organized by Ringwald as an informal Chicago-style group to play *Capone's* pizza parlor on Fulton Avenue in Sacramento, thereby the name (changed to Street); became structured in 74 to play Sacramento Jubilee. When Ringwald left for LA in 79, Nelson assumed leadership and for a short while they were titled NEW FULTON STREET JB.

Stan Black, tu (74-76); Bob Johnson, d (74); Bob Newman, cl; BOB RINGWALD, p (-79); Tony Rossi, tbn (74); Al Smith, cor (74-75). ADD: Vince Bartels, d (79→); Joe Belardino, d (75-76); Jim Cumming, sb (77); Jack Gumbiner, p (80-81); Dee Hendricks, sb (75); Bob Hinman, sb (76); Bob Hirsch, p (81→); Roger Krum, sb (80→); Walt Kunnecke, cl/ssax (78-81); DEAN NELSON, tpt (75→); Mike Pittsley, tbn (77); Dennis Rasmussen, d (77); Jimmy Rivers, g (79-83); Dennis Sacco, d (78); Mike Starr, tbn (75→).

*SJS 11 "Diggin' Gold" (78); =12 "Sterling" (79); =14 "Good Clean Fun" (80) w/Wild Bill Davison; =18 "High on Hoagy" (81); =23 "Live!" (83); =27 "Jumpin' Jubilee Jazz" (84 1 cut); =29 "Just Friends" (Newman and Quartet 85)*

**John Fulwider, bjo** - Dixie Dissonants

**Jack Fulton, tbn** *(1934 Vancouver BC)* - Lance Harrison

**Jay Fung, bjo** - Live Steam; Raisin City

**Manny Funk, d** - ldr Casa Bonita; New Washboard RK; Oakland Hot Babies; led own groups

## FUNKY NEW ORLEANS JAZZ BAND SF c1971-74

Began as NEW ORLEANS HOUSE JB, titled after the club of that name in Berkeley owned by Scheelar (65), consisting of varied formats and personnel until FNOJB came into being.

Pete Allen, sb; Bill Bardin, tbn; Bob Helm, cl; Don Marchant, d; Dick Oxtot, bjo; EARL SCHEELAR, cor. ADD: John Smith, ssax; Karl Walterskirchen, bjo.

*HERWIN 301 "Make Me a Pallet On the Floor" (71)*

**Rolly Furnas, tbn** - Bauduc-Lamare; Pete Daily

---

# G

**Frankie Gale, bass** - Cell Block

**Jeff Gamberutti, reeds** - Sticks Strings

**Jim Gammon, tpt** *(1948 Berkeley CA)* student affairs - Barrelhouse; Jubilee

**Ed "Montudi" Garland, bass** *(1885-1980 New Orleans LA)* - Burt Bales; Andy Blakeney; Crown City; Joe Darensbourg; Earl Hines; Roger Jamieson; Knights; Legends; Turk Murphy; King Oliver; Kid Ory; [Tuxedo]; Young Men From NO

**Gerry Garner, d** - Cats 'n' Jammers

**Jim "Pinky" Garner, p** *(1951)* - Happy JB

**Norm Gary, reeds** - Riverbank

## GAS HOUSE GANG SAC 1974-78

The name comes from their origin as house band for *Big Al's Gas House* SAC; evolved into GRAMERCY 6.

Dave Beeman, tu (-76); Roy Butler, d (74); DUTCH DEUTSCH, cl; Tom Landino, bjo (74); Al Smith, tpt (76); Burt Wilson, tbn/p (74-75). ADD: Hank Bartels, sb/tu (77-78); Joe Belardino, d (77-78); Gene Copelan, d (74-76); Barry Durkee, bjo (74); Jack Gumbiner, p (74-78); Frank Haggerty, bjo/g (78); Tom King, tpt (76-78); Dick Mix, tbn (75); Renard Perry, tpt (75-76); Hal Swan, tbn;Will Tallacksen, bjo (74-76); Jerry Walcott, tbn (77-78).

## GAS TOWN JAZZ BAND Vancouver BC 1980

Don Clark, tbn; Jack Fulton, tpt; LANCE HARRISON, bjo/cl; Stan Johnson, sb; Blaine Wickford, d; Al Wold, p.

**Hiram "Hi" Gates, tbn** - Castle

**Abe Geban, d** - Hiz Honor

**Tommy Geckler, tbn** - Blueblowers

**Wally Geil, d** - Downey; Jamboree Hal; Triple RRR

## GEM CITY JAZZ BAND Los Gatos 1977→

Formed by Blattner upon his retirement from teaching.

George Ballantyne, d; FESS BLATTNER, tbn; Bill Helper, p; Brent Herhold, tu; Lila Lloyd, v; Ray Nordahl, tpt; Mike Passarelli, cl. ADD: Dennis Goes, d; Hal Moreno, p; Nile Norton, d (alt).

**Dave Gentry, bass** *(Sterling CO) studio artist* - Jim Beatty; Capital City; Oregon

**Dave Geolecke, tpt** - Mudville

**Don Geraci, d** - Charlie Barnet; Gramercy; Billy May

**Fabio Gerhardi, tbn** *(19—1985)* - Jazz-a-Ma-Tass

**Albert "Bud" Gerlach, reeds** *(1922 Chicago IL) stained glassmaker* - Conductors

**Dave Giampietro, reeds** *(1949 San Jose CA)* - Hot Jazz Stompers; Magnolia; ldr St Peter; degree in music

**Mark Giannini, d** *(1964 Antioch CA) student* - Devil Mtn

**George Gibbs, tbn** - Banjo Kings; Mississippi

**Harry "The Hipster" Gibson, p** - Blue Fox ldr; [Eddie Condon]; much road show work, mostly solo

**John Gibson, tpt** *neurosurgeon* - Ain't No Heaven

**Bruce Gifford, reeds** *(1931 Flint MI) teacher* - Jazz-a-Ma-Tass; ldr Jazz Generation

**Joe Gifford, bass** - Portland Rose

**Bob Gilbert, reeds** *(1922 Coos Bay OR) advertising* - Monte Ballou; Castle; Rex Stewart

**Dave Gilbert, p** *gastroenterologist* - Ain't No Heaven

**Howard Gilbert, d** - Great Excelsior; Uptown Lowdown; symphony orchs

**Peggy Gilbert, reeds** - ldr Dixie Belles

**Arthur "Red" Gillham, tpt** *(1910-1971 Oakland CA)* - Frisco JB; Golden Gate; Valley JB

**John Gill, bjo, reeds** *(1951 Bronx NY)* - [Jazz Cardinals]; Lakeshore; Turk Murphy

**Bob Gilman, p** *(Seattle WA) school counselor* - Great Excelsior; Rainy City; Shakey City; Sinners

**Russ Gilman, p** - Tailgate JB; Dave Weirbach

**Dennis Gilmore, cor** *(1933 Manchester ENGLAND) electronic engr* - Cottonmouth; Orange Blossom; Paradise; San Juan

**Bob Gimber, reeds** - Merrymakers

### *GIN BOTTLE FOUR* SF 1949
BURT BALES, p; George Bruns, sb; Joe Darensbourg, cl; Minor Hall, d.
*GTJ 35, 36 (49)*

**Roy Giomi, reeds** *(1930) teacher* - Bay City; Canal St; Great Pacific-SF

**Eino "Squire" Girsback, bass** *(1913-1983 Astoria OR)* - Alexander's; El Dorado-SJ; *Frisco Footwarmers*; Jelly Roll JB-SF; Bunk Johnson; Magnolia; Turk Murphy; Oakland A; Kid Ory; Bob Scobey; Yerba Buena

**Lloyd Glenn, p** *(1909-1985 San Antonio TX) A&R Down Beat records* - Teddy Buckner; Roger Jamieson; Kid Ory; solo; led own combos; to CA 42

**Jim Glitch, d** - King Zulu

**Mary Lou Gnoza, v** *(1941 Superior WI)* - Tri-City

**Bob Gobrecht, bass** - Crown City; San Diego DJB; father of Carol Andreen

SQUIRE GIRSBACK
May 1969

DENNIS GILMORE October 1985

**Dudley "Jack" Goddard, reeds** *(1920 Lincoln NB) general services mgr* - ldr Dixie Unltd; led other groups

**Shirley Goddard, bass** *(1925 Rossie IO) exec secretary* - Dixie Unltd; marr Jack Goddard

**Don Goe, bass** *(Seattle WA)* - ldr Saints

**Dennis Goes, d** *(1932 KS) educator* - Gem City

**Harper Goff, bjo** *(1911 Fort Collins CO) animator* - Firehouse 5 + 2; art dir for film *Pete Kelly's Blues* and Disneyland

**Pat Gogerty, p** - ldr Faultless

**Ron Going, reeds** *(1931 Madison CT) electrical engr* - Bienville; British Connection; co-ldr Crescent Bay; Roger Jamieson; Orange Empire; Resurrection; San Juan; ldr Tuxedo

**Bob Golden, cor** - orig King Riverbottom

**Fay Golden, p** *(1932 Palo Alto CA)* - Jubilee

**Milt Golden, p** *(19—19—)* - *Dixieboppers*

## GOLDEN AGE JAZZ BAND SF Bay 1970→

*Mandrake's* Berkeley, *The Point* Richmond.

Pete Allen, sb; Bill Bardin, tbn; Jane McGarrigle, p; DICK OXTOT, bjo; Walt Yost, tu. ADD: Barry Block, cl/sax (82); Jerry Butzen, tbn (83); Jim Goodwin, tpt (75-77); Barbara Higbie, p (79); Laurie Lewis, sb (78); Don Marchant, d; Bill Maginnis, d; Bob Mielke, tbn (75);

Jack Minger, tpt (78→); Bill Napier, cl (75); Bob Neighbor, tpt (78-79); Terry Rodriguez, p (82); Jim Rothermel, cl/sax (80→); Ray Skjelbred, p; Sharon Swenson, p (76); Linda Wiggins, p (82).

*ARHOOLIE "Golden Age JB"; = 4010 "Down In Honky Tonk Town" (80); COL "It Looks Like Snow" w/Phoebe Snow, v; "Live At the Point"*

## GOLDEN EAGLE JAZZ BAND Pasadena 1980→

Traditional sounding group was the house band at *The Depot* San Juan Capistrano, having re-formed from ROYAL GARDENS JB.

Dan Barrett, tbn (-82); Leon Crabbe, bjo; Mike Fay, sb; Walt Sereth, cl/ssax; DICK SHOOSHAN, p; Ken Smith, cor; Lee Wedberg, d; Paul Woltz, asax/bsax (-85). ADD: Glenn Calkins, tbn (82→); Chris Norris, v (82→); Bob Young, asax/bsax (85→).

*DR JAZZ 101 "Sunday At the Depot"; = 102 "Live At the Depot" (83); SOS 1080 "Oh, My Babe" (84)*

## GOLDEN GATE JAZZ BAND Berkeley 1949-50

Name changed to GUTBUCKET FIVE in 50.

Tom Brenkwitz, tpt; Bob Brennan, tbn; HERB BUCK, p; Bob Coblentz, cl; Verne Gordon, d.

## GOLDEN GATE STOMPERS SF 1960-63

Pete Allen, sb; Bill Bardin, tbn (-62); Ted Butterman, tpt; Frank Goudie, cl; Dick Oxtot, bjo; P T Stanton, tpt; Bill Young, d. ADD: Red Gillham, tpt; Jim Leigh, tbn (62-63).

## GOLDEN STATE JAZZ BAND SAC, SF 1978-85

Formed by Allred, Farey assumed leadership after Allred left for FL. Senator Hotel SAC (78), SF's *Rathskellar, Vic's Place* (78-80) and *Earthquake McGoon's* (as regular subs for Turk Murphy) (78-80), other venues in SF Bay Area and SAC. Name changed to BAY CITY MUSIC COMPANY in 85.

BILL ALLRED, tbn (-78); Hank Bartels, sb (-78 alt); Dutch Deutsch, cl (-78); Mike Duffy, sb (-80); Droops Earnhart, p (-78 alt); EV FAREY, cor; Dennis Rassmussen, d (-78 alt); Bill Richards, p (-78 alt); Hal Smith, d (-80). ADD: Bunky Colman, cl (80); Bob Helm, cl (78); Carl Lunsford, bjo (78-81); Bill Maginnis, d (80); Jim Maihack, tbn (84-85); Jack Mangan, d (80-81); Bob Mielke, tbn (78-84); Bill Napier, cl (78-85); Ray Skjelbred, p (81-83); Jack Stewart, p (83-85); Steve Strauss, sb (81).

*SOS 1006 "Alive and At Bay" (81)*

**George Goldsberry, reeds** *(1923 Galesburg IL) aeronautical engr* - Rainier; Uptown Lowdown

## GOLD STANDARD MUSIC COMPANY SAC 1980→

Bob Bashor, tbn (80); Ted Dolce, sax; Frank Myers, sb (-82); Renard Perry, tpt (80); PETE SALERNO, d; Roger Snell, p (-82). ADD: Howard Berg, cl (85→); Maggie Cavanaugh, v (85→); Paul Cooke, tbn (81); Droops Ernhart, p (83); Wes Grant, tpt (81); Les Jasper, tbn (83→); Tom King, tpt (82→); Jerry MacKenzie, cl (82-85); Paul Sarmento, sb (82→); Tom Shove, p (84→); Jan Sutherland, v (83-85); Tom Tucker, p (85→).

**Phil Gomez, reeds** - Andy Blakeney; Kid Ory

**Jerry Good, bass** - Bayside; SF Swing Express

**Allen Goodman, d** - Beverly Hills

**John Goodrich, reeds** *(1935 Spokane WA) music teacher* - Uptown Lowdown

## GOOD TIME GROUP LA 1978-indef

Formed from MILNEBURG CHAMBER ENSEMBLE, band is occasionally active, playing infrequently at Magic Mountain and Los Alamitos racetrack.

Zulu Ball, tu; Dave Dolson, ssax; Dick Donor, tbn; Dave Kennedy, tbn; Vic Loring, bjo; Dick Williams, cor (-80). ADD: Dick Miller, cor (80→).

## GOOD TIME LEVEE STOMPERS Shingle Springs CA 1976→

Re-formed by Kaehele in 78 into a more traditional sound when Crow and McCartney left to form HANGTOWN JAZZ COMPANY.

Scotty Baughman, d; Bill Crow, tpt (-78); JERRY KAEHELE, tbn; Dave McCartney, sb (-78); Ned Poffinbarger, bjo; Tom Sharpsteen, cl. ADD: Friedhelm Boeckh, sb (82-83); Jim Cumming, sb (84→); Wes Grant, tpt; Val Herby, bjo (alt 84→); Scott Jenkins, sb (84).

*MMRC 117 "Good Time Levee Stompers" (85)*

**Jim Goodwin, cor, p** *(1944 Portland OR)* - Jim Beatty; Berkeley Rhythm; [Delta Jazz]; Golden Age; Jelly Roll JB-SF; Muddy River; Oakland A; Pier 23; Port Costa; *SF Blues Serenaders*; Sunset Music

*BR 4 "Jim Goodwin and Friends" (81)*

## GOOSE ISLAND JAZZ BAND LA 1982→

Zulu Ball, tu; Al Crowne, tpt; Reggie Dewar, tbn; DEAN HONEY, cl; Rex Schull, bjo; Scott Webster, p. ADD: Norm Logan, tu (84); Freddie Throop, d (84); Burt Wilson, tbn (83).

**Bobby Gordon, reeds** - San Diego DJB

**Scott Gordon, d** - Cats 'n' Jammers

**Vern Gordon, d** - Golden Gate JB

**Herbert Gordy, bass** - Royal St

**Tom Gorin, p** - Dixie Dissonants; River City

**Mark Gotwalt, d** - Camellia

**Frank "Big Boy" Goudie, reeds** *(1898-1964 Royville LA)* - Bearcats; Sidney Bechet; El Dorado-SJ; Estuary; Golden Gate Stompers; Django Reinhart; Stone Age; orig Tuxedo Band (NO); to CA 57

**Frank Goulette, cor** *(1925 Manila PI) civil engr* - El Dorado-SF; Great Pacific-SF; ldr Monterey Bay Classic; ldr Originial Inferior; Plum Forest

**Bill Gould, p** - Jelly Roll JB-SF

**Brian Gould, tbn** - ldr Swing Fever

**Len Goulis, reeds** - Jazzbo

**Brad Gowans, tbn** - Rosy McHargue; Joe Rushton

**Eddie Graham, d** - Billy Butterfield; Earl Hines; Trummy Young

**Byron Graff, reeds** - Toot Suite

**Lloyd Grafton, d** *(19—19—)* - Jamboree Hal; ldr Merrymakers

## GRAMERCY SIX (DUTCH'S) Shingle Springs CA 1979→

Originated from GAS HOUSE GANG.

Hank Bartels, sb; Joe Belardino, p (-83); DUTCH DEUTSCH, cl; Jack Gumbiner, p (79); Frank Haggerty, bjo/g; Tom King, tpt (-82); Jerry Walcott, tbn (-82). ADD: Bob Bashor, tbn (82→); Don Geraci, d (83→); John Nelson, p (79→); Renard Perry, tpt (82→).

*SJS 27 "Jumpin' Jubilee Jazz" (81 1 cut)*

## GRAND DOMINION JAZZ BAND SEA 1982→

A special group composed of members of other Pacific Northwest bands in the manner of an "All-Star" group.

Jim Armstrong, tbn; MIKE COX, bjo; Mike Duffy, sb; Gerry Green, cl; Bob Jackson, tpt; Stephen Joseph, d; Bob Pelland, p.

## GRAND REPUBLIC JAZZ BAND SAC

Joe Belardino, d; LOU BLACK, tpt; Stan Black, tbn; Roger Snell, p; Jim Snoke, tu; Jim Valentine, cl. ADD: Jerry MacKenzie, reeds/bjo; Tom Shove, p.

**Russ Granger, tpt** *(1919 New Orleans LA)* - Jazz Generation

**Bert Grant, p** *(1922 Lansing MI)* - Delta Rhythm Kings; Jelly Roll JB-LA; bro of Wes Grant

**Harold Grant, bjo** - Royal St

**Larry Grant, tpt** *(1936 Vancouver BC) auditor* - Razzamajazz

**Wesley Grant, tpt** *(1935 Lansing MI)* - Black Diamond; Gold Standard; Good Time Levee; New Imperial; Resurrection; Swanee's

**Ted Gravance, d** - La Honda

**Phil Gray, tbn** - Angel City

## GREAT AMERICAN DIXIELAND JAZZ BAND Antioch CA ?→

Randy Johnson, bjo/g; Bill Langlois, sb; Kevin Porter, tbn; Bob Secor, p/tpt; Greg Sudmeier, d; MIKE VAX, tpt; Harvey Wainapel, sax. ADD: Bob Kaufman, d (85); Ray Loeckle, sax (85→).

## GREAT EXCELSIOR JAZZ BAND SEA 1961→

Organized by Duffy and Skjelbred. Duffy assumed leadership when Skjelbred left for SF (69); POWEL took over when Duffy left for SF (77).

Dick Adams, cl/ssax; Ed Alsman, d (-61); MIKE DUFFY, sb (-77); Bob Jackson, tpt; Bob McAllister, tbn; RAY SKJELBRED, p (-69). ADD: Ham Carson, reeds; Howard Gilbert, d (61-66); Bob Gilman, p (69-); Greg Kiplinger, d (81-); Joe Loughmiller, d (66-81); Bill Lovy, bjo/g (61-69); JAKE POWEL, bjo/g (69→); Ken Wiley, tbn.

*ASP 22 "Summer Sessions" (69); CHASTITY (68); GHB 22 "Claire Austin and GEJB"; STINGER 1-3 (72-75); NIELSEN RSRM1272 "Great Excelsior JB" (65); VOYAGER VLP2025 "Hot Jazz From the Territory" (76); = VLP2035 "Roast Chestnuts"; = VLP2045 "Remembering Joe" (82)*

## GREAT PACIFIC JAZZ BAND North Hollywood CA 1980→

Formed by Ringwald shortly after his move to LA from SAC. No relationship to the orig SF group.

Roy Brewer, tbn (-85); Don Nelson, ssax; BOB RINGWALD, bjo/p; Molly Ringwald, v; Ray

RED GILLHAM March 1969

JIM GOODWIN and BOB NEIGHBOR February 1973

Templin, d (-82); Jack Wadsworth, bsax; Zeke Zarchy, tpt. ADD: Bob Havens, tbn (85→); Burr Middleton, d (82→); Jim Turner, p (83→).

**GREAT PACIFIC JAZZ BAND** SF CA 1958-61
Organized by Sonnanstine and Wetterau after leaving Dixieland Rhythm Kings (OH) from BAY CITY JB personnel; featured two cornets and two banjos. Muir Beach, Stinson Beach, *Monkey Inn* Berkeley. Arrangements (by Sonnanstine and Wetterau) later served as basis for Shafer's JELLY ROLL JB.

Lloyd Byassee, d (-60); Roy Giomi, cl; Frank Goulette, cor (-60); Dick Lammi, tu/viol; Sanford Newbauer, tbn; Tito Patri, bjo (-60); CHARLES SONNANSTINE, cor; ROBIN WETTERAU, p. ADD: Bob Hodes, tpt; Phil Howe, cl; Bret Runkle, d (60); Bob Short, tbn; Birch Smith, cor (59-60); Lee Valencia, bjo (60-61); Walt Yost, tu.

**Ed Greco, reeds** - Do-Do-Wah

**Vince Greco, p** - Dixie 6

**Cecil Gregg, p** - OC Dixiecats

**Bob Green, cor** - Feather Riverboat

**Gerry Green, reeds** *(London ENGLAND) graphic artist* - Grand Dominion; Phoenix

**Jerry Green, p** - Jazzin' Babies

**Jim Green, bjo** *(1928 Fullerton CA) mechanical engr* - Hyperion; San Juan

**Walt Greenawald, bass** *(1928 Bethlehem PA)* - Hot Frogs; Jazzin' Babies; Powerhouse; Smogville

**Dick Greene, bass, reeds, tbn, tpt** *(1932 Westwood CA)* - Tex Beneke; Big Tiny Little; studios

**Dick Greenly, tbn** - Downey Dixie

**Ira Greenstein, tbn, tpt** - Riverbank

**Cheryl Greenwood, v** - Monrovia

**Gordon Greimes, reeds** *(1922 Seattle WA) tire distr* - Rainier; ldr Rainy City

**Jimmy Grey, reeds** - French Qtr; Tailgate Ramblers; Thee Saints

**Gus Griffin, p** - High Society JB

**Earl Griffiths, reeds** - King Zulu

**Dan Grinstead, p** - Duwamish

**Hal Groody, bjo, g** *(1922 Philadelphia PA)* - Dixie Jazz Bravos; Fullertowne; Jazz-a-MaTass; King Zulu; OC Dixiecats; So Bay Zephyr

**Philip Groody, cello** *(1946) printer* - Chrysanthemum

**Harry Gross, bjo** - Crown City

**Bill Grosvenor, p** - Dixie Katz; Jazz-a-Ma-Tass

**Johnny Guarnieri, p** *(1917-1985 New York NY)* - Louis Armstrong; Barney Bigard; Billy Butterfield; Jimmy Dorsey; Benny Goodman; Artie Shaw Gramercy 5; solo; studios; reportedly over 6000 rec titles; to CA 62

**Al Guerra, d** - Burt Bales

**Delane Guild, d** *(1948 Portland OR)* - Jim Beatty

89

**Frank Gulseth, reeds** - Saints

**Jack Gumbiner, p** *(1915 Chicago IL)* - Capitol City; Gas House; Gramercy; Mardi Gras-SAC

**Bill Gunter, d** *(1927 San Francisco CA)* - Black Diamond; Boondockers

**Barry Gurney, d** *(1959 Vancouver BC) steel fabrication* - Razzamajazz

### GUTBUCKET FIVE Berkeley 1950-51

*Larry Blake's Rathskellar* Berkeley.
Tom Brenkwitz, tpt; Bob Brennan, tbn; HERB BUCK, p; Al Villaire, ssax; Bob Witham, d.
ADD (as subs): Bunky Colman, cl; Red Honore, sb; Walt Lee, d; Gene Maurice, tpt; Dick Oxtot, cor; George Probert, ssax; Earl Scheelar, cl.

**Truett Guthrey, bjo** - Tuleburg

**Jean Gwinn, p** - ldr Jazz Ramblers; marr Phil Gwinn

**Phil Gwinn, tbn** *(1924 Los Angeles CA) illustrator* - Jazz Ramblers; Levee Loungers; Barry Martyn; New Bull Moose; Resurrection; Sunset

# H

**Roger Haapenen, tbn** - Uptown Lowdown

**"Skip" Hadden, d** - MDJB

**Richard Hadlock, reeds** - Berkeley Rhythm; Casa Bonita; [Delta Jazz Irreg]; *Flaming Deuces*; Jazz Cardinals; Marin Jazz; Turk Murphy; ldr Mystery Pacific; Bob Neighbor; New Washboard RK; [Oakland A]; Oakland Hot Babies; Rhythmakers; Speakeasy. Auth *Jazz Masters of the '20s*; former jazz writer for SF *Examiner*; had radio show "The Annals of Jazz" since 59

**Bill Hadnott, bass** - Angel City; Blueblowers; Illinois Jacquet; JATP; Resurrection

**Frank Haggerty, bjo, g** *(1918 San Mateo CA)* - Capitol City; Gas House; Gramercy; Turk Murphy; Kid Ory

**Marty Hagopian, bass** *(1925 Providence RI) USAF historian* - Ponca City

**Al Hall, tbn** - Emperor Norton; Oakland Hot Babies; Silicon

**Alan Hall, p** - Casa Bonita; Jazz Cardinals

**Harry Hall, p** - Rosy McHargue; Milneburg; Workingman

**Jackie Hall, v** *(1927 New York NY) secy* - Jubilee; marr Lynn Hall

**John Hall, d** *(1950 Escondido CA)* - Chicago 6; Ernie Hughes; Skeets Hurfurt

**Lynn Hall, p, tbn** *(1927 Great Falls MT) physical chemist* - ldr Jubilee; King Riverbottom

**Minor "Ram" Hall, d** *(1897-1959 Sellies LA)* - Don Ewell; *Gin Bottle 4*; King Oliver; Kid Ory; Knights; Johnny Wittwer

**Ralph Hall, bass, tbn** - Ambulance; Monrovia

**Ray Hall, d** - Jazz Ramblers

**Stan Hall, g** - Frisco JB

**Tom Hall, d** - Powerhouse

**John Hallesy, tbn** - Churchill St

**Ed Halsey, d** - Jewel City

**Chuck Hamilton, bass** - Blueblowers

**Jeff Hamilton, d** - Magnolia; Bob Neighbor; Port Costa; Sunset Music

**Jerry Hamm, d** - Banjo Kings; [Firehouse 5 + 2]

**Mark Hammond, bjo** *(1909 Wapato WA) air traffic control* - NOJB Hawaii

**Ted Hammond, bass** - Levee Loungers

## HANGTOWN JAZZ COMPANY Placerville CA 1978→

Formed from Jerry Kaehele's original group, which was the forerunner of GOOD TIME LEVEE STOMPERS.

Bill Crow, tpt; Steve Drivon, tbn (-81); DAVID McCARTNEY, sb; John Robinson, bjo/g; Larry Salerno, d (-81); Brian Shanley, cl (-80). ADD: George Cecil, d (84→); Kent Dunavent, tbn (83-?); Norm Headley, d; Charlie Hull, cl/sax (80→); Sam Smith, tbn (→).

*SJS 27 "Jumpin' Jubilee Jazz" (81 1 cut)*

BOB HAVENS 1967

**HANGTOWN SYNCOPATORS** see LAKE SPANAWAY JB

**Bill Hannaford, tbn** - Cell Block; Dixieland Syncopators

**Bob Hanscom, bjo, p** *(1935 CA) industrial engr* - Bay City; Monterey Bay Classic

## HAPPY JAZZ BAND Newport Beach CA 1966-70

Eric Bleumke, tbn (66-67); LANCE BROWN, tbn; Richard Chapman, bjo; Pinky Garner, p (-67); Howard Struble, tpt (66-67); Tat Thomas, cl; Bill Wolfe, sax (66-67); LAURENCE WRIGHT, d/cor/sax. ADD: Larry Duke, tpt (69-70); Terry Levitt, p (69-70); Vern Stracenner, cor (68); Paul Woltz, bsax (68-70); Randy Woltz, p (68-70).

## HAPPY SYNCOPATORS Stockton 1950-?

GENE LANCELLE, tpt; Jo Lancelle, p; Harry Penny, cl; Buddy Walters, tbn; Ray Walters, tu.

**Ralph Harden, tpt** - Jamboree Hal; Jazz-a-Ma-Tass ldr; Ted Vesely

**Jim Hardesty, d** - Jamboree Hal; Silver Dollar-SAC

**Devon Harkins, p** *(1927 Oakland CA)* - ldr Basin St Trio; Jazz Cardinals; Bob Neighbor; Phrisco; Pier 23; Speakeasy; solo and led own groups; accompanist for Janis Joplin, Helen Forrest. Long-term at Hotel Stewart, also *Pier 23, Jack London Inn, Gold St, Roaring '20s,* Hotel Fairmont, Palace Hotel SF

**Herb Harper, tbn** - Balboa JB

**Roy Harper, d** - co-ldr Riverbank

**"Buddy" Harpham, reeds** - River City

**Griff Harries, p** *animal feed* - And That's Jazz

**George Harris, bjo** - Yankee Air Pirates

**"Hap" Harris, bjo** - Shakey City

**Leonard Harris, reeds** *(1929 OR) accountant* - Portland Rose; Stumptown

**Brad Harrison, reeds** - Jazz Forum

**Lance Harrison, bjo, reeds** *(1915 Vancouver BC)* - Jim Beatty; ldr Gas Town; Carse Sneddon; led own groups

## LANCE HARRISON'S DIXIELAND JAZZ BAND Vancouver BC

Don Clark, tpt; Jack Fulton, tbn; LANCE HARRISON, bjo/reeds; Gavin Hussey, bass/reeds; Frank Mansell, p; Blain Wilkjord, d. ADD: Dave Robbins, tbn; Carse Sneddon, tpt.

**Mike Harryman, bass** *(1938 Glendale CA) personnel managment* - Barrelhouse

**Joe Hart, bjo** - ldr Oversextette

**Neil Hart, d** *(1922 Texola OK) genl store owner* - Oregon

**Don Hartburg, tbn** - Apex

**John Hartman, tbn** *dentist* - Natural Gas

**Steve Hartwell, d** *(1945 Oakland CA) employee recruitment* - Prof Plum; various rock groups

**Virgil Harwood, reeds** - Traffic Jammers

NEIL HART  May 1976

**Budd "Goat" Hatch, bass** - Pete Daily; Levee Loungers

**Bob Havens, tbn** *(1930 Quincy IL)* - [Heinie Beau]; Bob Crosby; Al Hirt; Ralph Flanagan; Pete Fountain; Great Pacific-LA; New Orleans 5 (NO); Lawrence Welk; led own groups

**Ken Hawk, d** - Bourbon St JB

**Ted Hawke, d** - Balboa JB

**Charley Hawkes, reeds** *architect* - Capital City; Oregon

**Billy Hawkins, tbn** - Chicago 6

**"Buddy" Hayes, bass** - Coos Bay; Pete Daily; Lawrence Welk

**Clarence "Clancy" Hayes, bjo, v** *(1908-1972 Caney KS)* - Alexander's; *Frisco Footwarmers*; Frisco JB; Bunk Johnson; Turk Murphy; Bob Scobey; ldr *Washboard 5*; World's Greatest JB; Yerba Buena; led own combos. To SF 26; popular for his distinctive vocal styling; featured on own radio show in the Bay Area for many years. Winner of *Down Beat* New Star Singer 54. Honored by SF Mayor Joseph Alioto proclamation of "Clancy Hayes Day" 31 May 70. Comp *Huggin' and a-Chalkin'*, others

    ABC 591 *"Live at Earthquake McGoon's"* (66); CALIF M1501 *"Scobey & Clancy Raid the Juke Box"* (58); DH 11-13; GTJ 12050 *"Swingin' Minstrel"*; VERVE V1003 *"Clancy Hayes Sings"*

**"Red" Hayes, bjo, g** - Hiz Honor

**Bob Haygood, p** *prof of psychology* - Desert City

**Al Hays, bass** - Abalone

**Cedric Haywood, p** *(1915-1968 Houston TX)* - Sidney Bechet; Lionel Hampton; Illinois Jacquet; Kid Ory; Sinners; led own groups

**Don Hayworth, reeds** - Raisin City

**Bob Hazen, tbn** - Orange Pealers

**Norm Headley, d** - Hangtown

## HEADLINERS JAZZ BAND Modesto CA 1981-84

Original lineup unknown. Cindy Alexander, tbn (81); Art Arnett, tbn (82); Keith Baltz, tu; Ken Brock, tpt (81); Ernie Bucio, tpt (81); Joe Davis, cl (81); Chuck Eastman, p/bjo (81); John Fehd, bjo; Bob Feldman, d; Nancy Fish, v; AL ROSET, reeds (-84); Joe Runnells, d (-82); Lance Silva, tbn; Dan Talbert, tbn (-82); John Wyatt, p (82); Stuart Zank, bjo (82-83); Vasile Znaco, tpt; Bob Romans, cor (82-83).

**Tommy Hearn, bjo, o** *(1902 Youngstown OH)* - Nightblooming. As organist, arr and played theme *Sweet Georgia Brown* used by the Harlem Globetrotters basketball group

**Ray Heath, tbn** - Chicago 6

**Donald "Jerry" Heermans, p** *(1925 Olympia WA) piano tech* - Conductors; John McKinley

**Chuck Heggli, bjo** - Dr Mix

**Honorene Heggli, p** - Dr Mix

**Loren Helberg, reeds** - Little Big Band

**Bob Heller, tbn** *(1963 Hemet CA)* - Lemon St

**Bob Helm, reeds** *(1914 Fairmead CA)* - Castle; Funky NOJB; Golden State; [Jazz Cardinals]; Jelly Roll JB-SF; Bunk Johnson; Turk Murphy; Oakland A; ldr *Riverside Roustabouts*; Rhythm Wizards; *SF Blues Serenaders*; [So Frisco]; Washboard 5; Yerba Buena; Young Audiences; led own groups
*RIV RLP2510 "Bob Helm's Riverside Roustabouts" (54)*

**Larry Helm, reeds** - [Down Home]

**Forrest Helmick, tpt** *(1957 Fresno CA) music teacher* - ldr Blue St

**Bill Helper, p** - Gem City

**Gordon Hembruff, reeds** *(1953 Toronto ONT) teacher* - Razzmajazz

**George Henas, d** - Silver Dollar-SAC

**"Colonel" John Henderson, tpt** - King Zulu; Mississippi; Newport Harbor

**Pete Henderson, d** *(1926 Newark NJ) drama teacher* - Hyperion

**Dee Hendricks, bass** *(1927 Denver CO) draftsman* - Capitol City; [Gramercy 6]; Jazz Beaux; Mardi Gras-SAC

**Al Hendrickson, g, v** *(1920 Eastland TX)* - Benny Goodman; Woody Herman; Matty Matlock; Ray Noble; Artie Shaw; Freddy Slack; studios

**Mike Henneman, bass** *(1956 Ladysmith WI)* - Lemon St

BOB HELM (with Turk Murphy, Bob Schulz) October 1979

TOMMY HEARN (with Tom Raftican) October 1980

**Carl Henriques, p** *doctor* - Hiz Honor; Swanee's

**Lorisue Henriques, d** - Swanee's; marr Carl Henriques

**John Herby, d** *(1970)* - Calif Express; son of Val Herby

**Val Herby, bjo, p** *teacher* - co-ldr Calif Express; [Good Time Levee]; symphony orchs

**Arthur "Skeets" Herfurt, reeds** *(1919 Denver CO)* - Benny Goodman; Jimmy Dorsey; Tommy Dorsey; Billy May; Glenn Miller; Red Nichols; studios; led own groups; to CA 39

**Brent Herhold, bass** *(1943 IL) music store owner* - Gem City

**Sam Hernandez, tpt** - Emperor Norton; 52nd St; La Honda

**Alan Herr, french horn** - Sugar Willie

**Jim Herrilson, bass** - Hiz Honor

**Jim Hession, p** *(Pasadena CA) teacher* - So Market St; ragtime exponent; duo concert work with his wife, with whom he merged talents while attending UCLA 68; Disneyland and much touring

    *BLAKE EBM6 "Eubie Blake Introducing Jim Hession" (c80); HS1 "The Odd Ecru-Colored JB" (79); TAM 1 "Eclectic Heritage" (79); =2 "Jazzapoppin"'*

**Martha Hession, v** *(San Diego CA) teacher* - marr Jim Hession

**Frank Heuser, bass** *(1947 Detroit MI)* - Orange Pealers

**Charley Hickerson, reeds** - Oregon

**Vince Hickey, d, v** - ldr Jazz Cardinals; Tom Kats; studied with Baby Dodds in NY

BOB HIGGINS May 1982

**Ethel Hiett, p** *(New York NY)* - ldr New Imperial

**Barbara Higbie, p** - Golden Age; combos

**Bob Higgins, tpt** *(1916 Kansas City MO)* - Marvin Ash; Hangover JB; Rosy McHargue; Elaine Mitchell; Ben Pollack; Jack Teagarden; Ted Vesely; led own groups

## BOB HIGGINS HANGOVER JAZZ BAND LA 1955-56

George Defebaugh, d; BOB HIGGINS, tpt; Fred Lent, p; Jay St John, cl; Warren Smith, tbn.

**Joyce Higgins, v** - High Society JB

**Ted Higgins, d** *(1938 Tekamah NB) sales* - Angel City; Jelly Roll Jazz Society; Note-ables

**Frank Highly, bass** - Yankee Air Pirates

## HIGH SIERRA JAZZ BAND Three Rivers 1976→

Nucleus and house band of the High Sierra Jazz Club and formed from JAZZBERRY JAM BAND. Their evangelistic fervor was a phenomenon, earning them a large, dedicated following at concerts and festivals throughout USA, Europe and Australia.

Charley Castro, d; Vic Kimzey, tbn; Bruce Huddleston, p; Stan Huddleston, bjo; Earl McKee, tu; AL SMITH, cor.

*CLAMBAKE C216 "Playin' Around" (81); = C217 "Jazzaffair" (81); = C218 "Jubilee By the Sea" (80 1 cut); = C220 "Make a Joyful Noise" (82); = C221 "A Slice of Jelly Roll" (83); = C222 "Family Album" (83); HSJB 771 "Over the Top" (77); = 772 "Back For Seconds" (80); SJS 27 "Jumpin' Jubilee Jazz" (81 1 cut)*

## HIGH SOCIETY FIVE Tucson AZ

MANNY TREUMANN, cor; others unknown.

## HIGH SOCIETY JAZZ BAND La Jolla 1979→

LARRY CHANNAVE, tpt; Bob Froeschle, sb; Gus Griffin, p; Don Loeffler, d; Rick Richardson, tbn; Jim Tabler, cl. ADD: Les Boynton, sb; Joyce Higgins, v.

**Fred Higuera, d** *(1909-1983 Oakland CA)* - Alexander's; Basin St Trio; La Honda; Bob Scobey

**Glenn Hildebrand, tpt, v** *(1930)* - org Crescent Bay; ldr Pepper

**Bill Hill, p** - Dixie Katz; ldr Sounds of Dixieland

**Walt Hill, reeds** *(1924 Rickreall OR) state hwy supervisor* - Oregon

**Rob Hilliard, p, reeds** *chemist* - Hume St; Royal Bourbon St

**Bruce Hilton, bass** - ldr Joyful Noise

**Paul Hilton, tpt** - Joyful Noise

**Earl "Fatha" Hines, p** *(1905-1983 Duquesne PA)* - Louis Armstrong; Benny Carter; Jimmie Noone (Apex); Jack Teagarden; led own groups; solo; shared a group with Muggsy Spanier. *Esquire* Silver Award winner 44; comp *My Monday Date, Rosetta*, others

*ATLANTIC 120 "Famous QRS Solos"; COLUMBIA CL2320 "Earl Hines Trio"; DECCA "Fatha Blows Best"; = DL9221 "South Side Swing"; = DL2202 "Hines Rhythm"; DELMARK DS212 "At Home"; EPIC 3223 "Oh, Fatha!"; = 3501 "Earl Hines Trio"; FANTASY 3217 "Fatha Plays Fats"; = 3283 "Hines Solos"; MUSE 2001 "Legendary Little Theater Concert of 1964" (85); OLYMPIC 7125 "The Essential Earl Hines" w/Muggsy Spanier*

## EARL HINES TRIO SF 1955-60

Sidemen over the years, in trios and larger groups, included Dizzy Gillespie, tpt; Benny Green, tbn; Jimmy Mundy, tsax; Charlie Parker, asax; Omer Simeon, cl; Trummy Young, tbn. As appeared at *Club Hangover*: Pops Foster, sb; EARL HINES, p; Darnell Howard, cl; Earl Watkins, d.

**Rod Hines, reeds** *(1933 San Francisco CA) music teacher* - Port City; Jimmy Dorsey orch; Tuleburg; symphony orchs; master's degree in music

**Allen Hinkle, reeds** - Rhythm Kings

**Myron Hinkle, bjo** *draftsman* - Hume St

**Bob Hinman, bass** *(1922 Elgin IL) financial planner* - And That's Jazz; Apex; Jack Buck; Delta Jazz Irreg ldr; Fulton St; Napa Valley; Phrisco

**Bob Hirsch, p** *(1937 Viroqua WI) college admin* - Fulton St; Clancy Hayes; Gene Mayl; Phrisco; Bob Scobey; recipient of 74 fellowship to study under Ralph Sutton
  *MEDIAWERKS 31402 "Bob Hirsch and His All-Stars; A Jazz Picnic" (76)*

**Luster Hite, d** - City of Industry; Faultless

## HIZ HONOR'S JAZZ BAND SAC 1981-84

Title alludes to Eissinger's position as a Municipal Court Judge.
Ben Barrow, g (81); John Dale, sb (81,84); ART EISSINGER, tbn; Abe Geban, d (81); Carl Henriques, p (-83); Dick Johnson, tpt (-83); Ted Thompson, cl/tsax (-83). ADD: Jack Baran, p (84); Ben Blakeman, bjo (82-83); John Carlson, sb (83); Ken Cave, tu (84); John Fratis, d (83-84); Red Hayes, bjo/g (84); Jim Herrilson, sb (82); Eddie LaDranke, tpt (84); Mike MacDonald, d (82); Paul Wusschmidt, tsax (84).

**Bill Hobart, tpt** *(Tacoma WA)* - Destiny City; Pete Kelly; Traffic Jammers

**Mike Hobbs, bjo** *(1942 Newport WALES) construction* - Razzamajazz

**Mike Hobi, tbn** *(Aberdeen WA) rehabilitation counselor* - Don Anderson; Blueblowers; ldr Shakey City; Uptown Lowdown

**Jim Hockings, tbn** - Bourbon St JB

**Robin "Bob" Hodes, tpt** - Great Pacific-SF

**Clark Hodge, tpt** *(1938 Buckeye AZ) mining engr* - Tri-City

**Frederick Hodges, p** *(1961)* - Churchill St; Royal Society

**Tom Hodges, tbn** *college student* - Sticks Strings

**Fred Hoeptner, p** - Excelsior; Impossible

**Henry Hoffman, reeds** - Hume St

**Henry Hogan, tpt** - Easy Winners

**Dexter "Deck" Hogin, tpt, tbn** - ldr Hogin's; Mudville

### HOGIN'S HEROES Modesto CA 1982→

House band of Modesto Dixieland Jazz Society.

Tom Castle, bjo; DECK HOGIN, tbn; Lynn Russell, sax; Ernie Ruud, p; Rich Simmons, d; Bill Smalley, cor; Manny Torado, sb.

**Bob Holder, reeds** *(Tacoma WA)* - Destiny City

**Mike Holland, tbn** - Newport Summit

**Wally Holmes, tpt** *(1928 New York NY) composer* - Freddie Slack; Yankee Wailers ldr; studios

WALLY HOLMES October 1985

**Dave Holo, bjo, cor, g** - Uptown Lowdown

**Jerry Holton, bjo** - Rhythm Kings

**Rick Holzgrafe, cor, tbn** *(1953 Oxnard CA) computer programmer* - Apex; Fink St; Milneburg; Silver Cornet

**Dean Honey, reeds** - ldr Goose Island; Reno Charlie; Resurrection; So Bay Zephyr

**Cuthbert "Red" Honore, bass** - Delta JB; Gutbucket

**Gideon Honore, p** - Roger Jamieson; Kid Ory

**Franklin "Slim" Hood, bjo, g** *(1910 Pueblo CO)* - ldr La Honda; big bands

**Steve Hope, tbn** - Monrovia; Newport Harbor; Dave Weirbach

**Dave Hopkins, bass, tpt** - Southside

**Joe Hopkins, reeds** *(1937)* - Cell Block 7 (TX); Churchill St

**Jim Hopperstad, bass** - Old Sacramento; Riverbank; Swanee's

**Ellis Horne, reeds** *(1920 San Francisco CA)* - Alexander's; Basin St Trio; [Delta Jazz Irreg]; [El Dorado-SJ]; Jelly Roll JB-SF; Bunk Johnson; Magnolia; Turk Murphy; Kid Ory; Polecats; Bob Scobey; Anson Weeks; Yerba Buena

**Max Horton, p, vib** - Jazz Formula; Note-ables

**Bob Hoskins, bass** - Polecats

**"Skoot" Hoskins, g** - Castle

**Dave Hostetler, reeds** - [Fink St]; Stomp Aces

## HOT FROGS JUMPIN' JAZZ BAND LA 1977→

Formed out of a late-night jam session at the Sacramento Jubilee, with roots in JELLY ROLL JAZZ SOCIETY. Incredible high energy brought them popularity on the festival circuit; toured extensively throughout USA and Europe.

Joe Ashworth, cl; Wally Craig, tbn; Lew Forrest, d (-82); Walt Greenawald, tu; Art Leon, bjo (-80,82-83); Gene Oster, p (-83); MIKE SILVERMAN, tpt. ADD: Janet Carroll, v (85→); Larry Kostka, d (82-83); Doug Mattocks, bjo (81,84→); Bob Mills, bjo (80); Paul Reid, p (83→); Joe Tenney, d (84→); Lou Tevis, v (alt).

*CLAMBAKE C218 "Jubilee By the Sea" (80 1 cut); RIBBIT 2195 "Really Cookin'" (78); =4382 "Hot Frogs Ride Again"; =4905 "On the Road"; =11705 "Hollywood" (84)*

## HOT JAZZ HOT SHOTS Vancouver BC 1983→

Formed from PHOENIX JAZZERS personnel to serve as a nucleus for Hot Jazz Society weekly jam sessions.

Jim Armstrong, tpt; Everett Atchison, sb; Gerry McLaughlin, d; Ian Menzies, tbn; Roy Reynolds, cl; Allison Taylor, p.

## HOT JAZZ STOMPERS South SF Bay 1977

*Granny's Attic SJ.*

Jeff Bender, p; Bill Carson, tbn; Dave Giampietro, cl; Ken Keeler, bjo; Phil Kirk, tpt; MIKE SWANSON, tu. ADD: Bill Armstrong, bjo.

**R. C. "Boots" Houlahan, tpt** *(1922 Seattle WA) masonry supply* - Rainier; ldr Rainy City

**Howard "Hub" Houtz, reeds** - Silver Stope

**Darnell Howard, reeds, viol** *(1895-1966 Chicago IL)* - Burt Bales; Doc Evans; Frisco Footwarmers ldr; W C Handy (viol); Coleman Hawkins; Fletcher Henderson; Earl Hines; James P Johnson; [Turk Murphy]; King Oliver; Kid Ory; Muggsy Spanier; led own groups. To CA 48, suffered stroke June 66, died 3 months later

**John Howard, reeds** *(1956)* - Black Diamond

**Phil Howe, reeds** *(1931 Sacramento CA)* - Basin St Trio; Great Pacific-SF; ldr Phrisco; [Donny McDonald]; Turk Murphy; [Nob Hill]; SF Swing Express; ldr Silver Dollar-SAC; Sinners; Sugar Willie; Tappers

**Jack Howell, p** - Turk Murphy

**Laird Howling, reeds** - Swipesy

**El Hubbard, tbn** *(1925 Pasadena CA)* - Emperor Norton

**Jim Hubbart, reeds** *journalist* - ldr Delta Rhythm Kings

**Bruce Huddleston, p** *(1939 Berkeley CA) printer* - High Sierra; Jazzberry; Monterey Bay Classic; degree in music; bro of Stan Huddleston, played as a duo since 54
  *SMST 6920 "The Huddleston Brothers"*

**Clark Huddleston, bjo** - Delta Rhythm Kings; El Dorado-LA; Impossible; Jelly Roll JB-LA; Mardi Gras-LA; Thee Saints

**Stan Huddleston, bjo** *(1937 Auburn WA) printer* - High Sierra

**Mark Hudson, tpt** *(1961 Minot ND)* - Lemon St

**Mike Hudson, tbn** - Camellia

**Crystal Huff, d** - Dixie Darlings; Dixie Floyd; Red Hot Peppers

**Morey Huff, p** *(1913 Grand Rapids MI)* - Nightblooming

**Wally Huff, tpt** - Resurrection

**Jeff Hughes, cor** - Rainier

**Charley Hull, reeds** *(1928 Bucklin MO) state prison adm* - Hangtown; Old Sacramento; Oregon; Riverbank

## HUME STREET PRESERVATION JAZZ BAND #405 Aberdeen WA 1982→

Formed from ROYAL BOURBON STREET, name and number refers to a red light district during the '20s and to a particularly famous house of ill repute.

Don Abrahamson, d (alt); Lorraine Alkire, bjo (-84); Rob Hilliard, cl/p; Greg Jones, cor; Bill McCaw, tpt; Terry McGarrah, p/wb (-84); Don Murphie, tbn; Bob Neisinger, d (alt); GARY NOEL, tu. ADD: Myron Hinkle, bjo (84→); Henry Hoffman, cl (83→); Walt Kerr, p (84→).

**Brad Humphries, bass** - Westside Feetwarmers

**Dick Hungerford, reeds** - Pier 100

**Alex Hunter, reeds** - City of Industry; New Bull Moose; Resurrection; So Bay

**Bill Hunter, p** *(1937 San Bernardino CA)* - John Best; Chicago 6; Mickey Finn; Jewel City; So Market St; solo; led own combos

**Clyde Hurley, tpt** *(1916 Ft Worth TX)* - Glenn Miller; Ben Pollack; Rampart St; Ted Vesely; studios; led own groups
  *KEY 633; CROWN CLP5045 "Clyde Hurley All-Stars"*

SKEETS HERFURT (with Don McDonald, Rex Allen) August 1974

JOHN INNES October 1980

**Jimmy Hurt, d** *(1922)* - Churchill St

**Gavin Hussey, bass, reeds** *(1931 Vancouver BC)* - Lance Harrison

**Dave Hutson, reeds** *(1938 Chicago IL)* - ldr Calif Ramblers; ldr Rhythm Kings; org New McKinney Cottonpickers (MI)

**Tom Hynes, bjo** - 32nd St

## HYPERION OUTFALL SERENADERS Manhattan Beach CA 1969→

Began as a 3-piece group, expanded to 6-10 as occasions dictated.

Syd Pattison, cl; BOB WHITE, cor; Dale van Scoyk, tbn (-85). ADD: John Carpenter, bjo; Dave Freeman, tu (75→); Fran Freeman, wbd (75→); Jack Freeman, tbn (75→); Jim Green, bjo (82→); Pete Henderson, d (78→); Bill Lamden, cl (80→); Don Lastra, bjo/tpt (75→); John Malone, d (77→); Jules Radinsky, tpt (78→); Don Ryckman, bjo (73→); Ross Siracusa, p (83→).

# I

**Mario Ibanez, tbn** - Blueblowers

**Alex Iles, tbn** - Rhythm Kings

**Allan Imbach, tbn** - Rosy McHargue

## IMPOSSIBLE JAZZ BAND LA 1958

Don Beam, d; Alan Crowne, tbn/tpt; Fred Hoeptner, p; Clark Huddleston, bjo; ART LEVIN, tu; Pete O'Leary, bjo; Tom Sharpsteen, cl.

*EPITAPH 3 (58)*

**Joe Ingram, tbn, tpt** - Abalone; Do-Do-Wah; Monterey Bay Stompers; Oregon; ldr Webfoot; co-fdr Monterey Bay Hot Jazz Society

**Mary Ingram, p** - Abalone; marr Joe Ingram

**John Innes, tbn** *(1913 Colorado Springs CO) display artist* - Jazzin' Babies

**Harry Ironmonger, reeds** - Original Inferior

**Doug Isaac, d** - 32nd St

**Moe Isaac, tbn** - Cider City

**Steve Isaacs, bass** - Rhythm Kings

**Gary Isbell, bjo** - MDJB

## ISLAND CITY JAZZ BAND Friday Harbor WA 1979→

Organized by Conrad and Skoog, ICJB was the host group for the San Juan Island Jazz Festival. Glossy, show band approach to jazz.

Don Anderson, tbn; Bill Bassen, cl/sax; Tom Bassen, p; Vern Conrad, d; Skip McDaniel, sb (83-); Gary Provonsha, tu (-83); TOM SKOOG, tpt; Lynda Travis, v.

*ICJB "Live At the Electric Company" (80); = "At Roche Harbor" (82); = "Bye-Bye Blues" (83)*

**Al Isley, tpt** - King Zulu

**Loren Iversen, d** *(1938 Willits CA) CYA team supervisor* - John Simon; ldr Tuleburg

# J

**Pete Jack, d** - ldr Bayside

**Dennis Jackman, bass** *(1940 Vincennes IN) truck fleet maintenance* - WFDJE&MKRB

**Bill Jackson, cor, tbn, tu** - Jamboree Hal; ldr Little Big Band; New Bull Moose; ldr Outcast

**Bob Jackson, tpt** *(1943 Iowa City IA) psychiatrist - Creole Sunshine*; ldr Grand Dominion; Great Excelsior; Lake Spanaway; Westside Feetwarmers

**Cliff Jackson, tbn** *(CA)* - Jimmy Dorsey; Harry James; Silver Stope

**Gene Jackson, reeds** - Resurrection

**Tony Jackson, d** - [Bay City]

**Jake Jacobsen, cor** - Do-Do-Wah

**Tom Jacobus, bass** *(1947 CA) teacher* - Chicago Ramblers; ldr Emerald; Stumptown; Uptown Lowdown

**Paul Jacqua, tpt** *(1958)* - Churchill St

**Chet Jaeger, cor** *(1924 Columbia MO) teacher* - ldr Nightblooming; co-fdr Society for the Preservation of Dixieland Jazz

**Janel Jaffee, viol** - Royal Society

**Ray Jahnigan, p** - Frisco JB

## JAMBOREE HAL'S JAZZ BAND LA c1977→

Norm Burnham, p; Lloyd Grafton, d; Ralph Harden, tpt; Hank McKee, bjo; Rod Ogle, tbn; HAL RUMENAPP, sb; Sandy Sandman, cl (-78). ADD: Jack Berka, cl (80); John Bishop, g (80); Richard Cruz, tpt (77,80); Wally Geil, d (78-79); Jim Hardesty, d; Roger Jamieson, tb (78-79); Jorge Mirkin, reeds (79); John Muchow, d (80); Lenny Paul, tpt (78-79); Mick Price, p (80); Mel Rapasarda, g (79); Vic Roberts, g (77); Jerry Rothschild, p (78-79); Bob Smith, tbn.

**Robbie James, p** - Dixie Rhythm Ramblers; Little Big Band

**Roger Jamieson, tbn** *(1932 San Fransisco CA) ABC investigator – Creole Sunshine*; Crescent Bay; Jamboree Hal; Jelly Roll JB-LA; Orange Blossom; Resurrection; Ken Scott; South Bay; Southern Stompers; Triple RRR; led own group

## ROGER JAMIESON AND HIS NEW ORLEANIANS LA 1969→

Named after first venue, New Orleans Hotel in Inglewood; subsequent casuals until *Jeanette's* Hermosa Beach (84), *Osko's* Long Beach (84→).

Andy Blakeney, tpt (-70,73,81,83-84); Ike Candioti, d (-69); Ed Garland, sb (-75); Ron Going, cl (-72); ROGER JAMIESON, tbn; Alton Purnell, p (-70). ADD: Benny Booker, sb

CHET JAEGER January 1979

(81); Bernard Carrere, sb (82→); Mike DeLay, tpt (74-79); Mike Baird, cl (73-75); Clora Bryant, tpt (84→); Bernard Carrere, sb (82→); Joe Darensbourg, cl (76-78); Lloyd Glenn, p (84-85); Gideon Honore, p (74-83); Vic Loring, bjo (84); Red Minor, d (83→); Bill Mitchell, p (71-73); Dolph Morris, sb (74,76,77,80); Syl Rice, d (70-82).

**Frank Jamison, p** - Chicago Ramblers

**Conrad Janis, tbn** *(1928 New York NY) actor* - ldr Beverly Hills; ldr Tailgate JB; led other groups

**Bonnie Janofsky, d** - Satin Dolls

**Greg Janusz, d** - Cypress

**Stanley Jarnolowez, bass** - Custer

**Les Jasper, tbn** - Easy Winners; Gold Standard

## JAZZ-A-MA-TASS JAZZ BAND Downey 1975, 1977-82

Organized by New Orleans Jazz Club of So California as that group's yearly representative band to the Sacramento Jubilees. Personnel varied considerably with each band and from the 81 version JAZZ GENERATION was formed.

Ross Brunett, tsax; Norm Burnham, p; Fabio Gerhardi, tbn; RALPH HARDEN, tpt (75,77,79); Hank McKee, bjo; Tom Raftican, d; Hal Rumenapp, sb; John Sheppard, cl. ADD: Larry Blair, bjo (77); Hal Blevins, tbn (77); Jack Booth, tbn (79); Vince Bosco, sb; George Carr, sb (78,80); BOB CHRISTY, sb (77,79); Ralph Craig, d (77,79); ART DAVIS, tpt

JILL JOHNSON
January 1979

(78,80); Bruce Gifford, cl (78,80,81); Hal Groody, bjo (80); Bill Grosvenor, p (77,79); Jack Keister, cl/sax (77,79); Ed Killops, tpt (81); Mark Kirby, tbn (81); Larry Kostka, d (81); Gil Kraus, p (78,80,81); Al Latour, tbn; Morey Levang, g (79); Parke Math, bjo; Don McGrath, tbn (78,80); Rich Parnell, d (78); Mel Rapasarda, g (81); Cully Reese, p; Bob Reitmeir, reeds (78,80); Joe Toomey, tpt; Jim Walling, d.

### JAZZ BEAUX Benecia CA 1978-84

Formed from members of PURPLE GANG.

Jack Baran, p; Ben Barrow, g (-81,83-84); LEONARD DIXON, cl; Dee Hendricks, d; Ed LaFranchi, tpt; Bob Lindfeldt, tbn; Ed Schmalz, tsax. ADD: Ben Blakeman, bjo (81-82); Dick Johnson, sb (82); Irv Lathrop, d (81); Jerry Ulrich, sb/tu (83).

### JAZZBERRY JAM BAND Three Rivers CA 1973-76

Forerunner of HIGH SIERRA JB.

Charlie Castro, d; Max Denning, viol; Don Franscioni, tpt (-74); Bruce Huddleston, p; Vic Kimzey, co/tbn; Earl McKee, sb/tu; LUEDER OHLWEIN, bjo; Doc Ropes, cl/ssax. ADD: Al Smith, cor (74-).

### JAZZBO NEW ORLEANS DIXIELAND BAND (IRA COBB'S) SD ?→

Alan Adams, tbn; Charlie Clark, p; IRA COBB, tpt; Ray Conseur, d; Chuck Coulter, tbn; Jim Eichel, tu; Len Goulis, cl; Howard Nielson, bjo; Ed Reed, cl. Also as four-piece combo: Adams; COBB; Nielson; Roger Twedt, tbn.

## JAZZ CARDINALS (VINCE HICKEY'S) SF 1973-79

Formed to play NOJCNC's Jazz Showcase, continued with personnel changes to play *The Baltic* Pt Richmond (c74-75), *Berkeley Square* Berkeley (c77-79), other Bay Area venues.

Jim Goodwin, cor (-79); Dick Hadlock, ssax; VINCE HICKEY, d/v; Ray Skjelbred, p (-74,77-78); Amos White, tpt (-73). ADD: Cyril Bennett, p (74-75); Gordon Bennett, sb (74); Byron Berry, tpt (74-75); Mike Duffy, sb (73-79); Ev Farey, cor (74); Alan Hall, p (77-79); Devon Harkins, p (74); Bob Neighbor, tpt (79); Hal Smith, d (78-79); John Smith, ssax (78). SUBS: Bill Carroll, sb; John Gill, bjo/d; Bob Helm, cl; P T Stanton, cor.

## JAZZ FORMULA LA 1982→

Fred Baumberger, g; Ike Candioti, d; DANNY DAVIS, vib; Frances Davis, sb; Don Dupree, reeds; Max Horton, p; Bill Myers, tpt; Bill Waters, tbn.

## JAZZ FORUM LA 1981-82

Big band Chicago flavor, re-formed into JAZZ FORMULA.

Fred Baumberger, g; Ike Candioti, d; Richard Cruz, tpt (81); DANNY DAVIS, vib; Brad Harrison, reeds (81); Dave Osborne, sb; Virginia Osborne, p; Bob Smith, tbn (81). ADD: Lance Buller, tpt (82); Francis Davis, sb; Charles May, tbn (82); Danny Snyder, tbn (82).

## JAZZ GENERATION LA 1982→

Formed from JAZZ-A-MA-TASS JB.

BRUCE GIFFORD, cl/sax; Russ Granger, tpt; Mark Kirby, tbn (-84); Gil Kraus, p (-84); Pete Perez, sb; Mel Rapasarda, bjo/g; Art Rodriguez, d (-84).

## JAZZIN' BABIES Sylmar CA 1976→

Originally named JAZZIN' BABIES BLUES BAND, but last part dropped in 79. Organized by Dolson from SMOGSVILLE SOCIETY ORCH, striving for a more traditional sound.

Jack Boppel, bjo (-79); DAVE DOLSON, ssax; Lew Forrest, d (-78); Jerry Green, p (-79); Walt Greenawald, tu (-78); John Innes, tbn; Dick Williams, cor (-81). ADD: Larry Fisher, d (78→); Parke Math, bjo (79→); Dick Miller, cor (81→); Don Romig, tu (78→); Larry Wilson, p (79→).

*CLAMBAKE C214 "Flying Without Wings" (80); MABEL "Flying With Spirit" (83)*

## JAZZIN' JUNIORS Sacramento 1981→

Formed as ORIGINAL SACRAMENTO JAZZIN' JUNIORS JUMPIN' JB, comprised of children aged 11-13 years; nucleus formed by tpt instructor Kurt Pearsall. Under the guidance of John Nelson, library was expanded to include arrangements from the swing era, as well. Most members participated in symphonic and other school music groups, regarding Jazzin' Juniors as their creative outlet.

Mark Allin, cl; Gene Berthelsen, dir; Maren Berthelsen, v; DAVID ETTERBEEK, tpt; Jon Etterbeek, tbn; Mike French, d; Kyle O'Brien, sax; (-84); Matt Perrine, tu/sb; Kelley Silvers, p. ADD: Joe Reardon, tpt (84).

*SJS 27 "Jumpin' Jubilee Jazz" (81 1 cut)*

## JAZZ INC LA 1974

Group organized for Sacramento Jubilee to represent Jazz Inc.

Frank Amoss, d; Chuck Anderson, tbn; JAKE PORTER, tpt; Charlie Romero, cl; Roger Snell, p; Dee Woolem, sb.

## JAZZ ME BLUES DIXIELAND BAND Fresno
TONY LALLO, d; others unknown.

## JAZZ MINORS Roseburg OR 1974→
Perhaps the most notable of the recent youth groups, beginning when members were in their early teens. After leaving school, the band went pro and were summer regulars from 79 at Disneyland.

Jon Brand, sb (-79); Mark Curry, sax (-79); Dale Dial, d (-84); Lori Moritz, p (-76); Brad Roth, bjo; RUSTY STIERS, tpt; Scott Wadsworth, tbn. ADD: John Allred, tbn (84); Tim Cline, p (76→); Matt Johnson, d (84→); Andy Martin, tbn (80-83); Eric Messerschmidt, tu (80→).

*JAZZ MINORS 1001 "USA Tour 1977" (77); TRIAD 902 "Cakewalkin' Babies" (75); =908 "The Jazz Minors" (76)*

## JAZZ OTTERS Monterey
DICK DOTTS, p; others unknown.

## JAZZ RAMBLERS (JEAN'S) LA c1971
Dick Broadie, cl; JEAN GWINN, p; Phil Gwinn, tbn; Ray Hall, d; Johnny Lucas, tpt; John Waterhouse, sb.

## JAZZ UNLIMITED Fresno 1984→
Bill Contente, tpt; Gene Lein, tbn; John Martin, reeds; Andy Prisco Jr, d; Eddie Ruud, p; MEL WARD, sb. ADD: Ralph Manfredo, p.

**Bill Jeffries, tbn** *(1926 Berkeley CA)* - Black Diamond

## JELLY ROLL JAZZ BAND (TED SHAFER'S) LA 1959-65, SF 1965-72
Shafer was one of many smitten with the sound of Lu Watters and his JRJB showed this. He formed a second group around Ronnei under this title (#2) with a more pure NO sound and had both bands going simultaneously (using bjo subs as necessary). Upon moving to SF, Shafer again formed two separate groups under the same title.

(LA): Mike Baird, cl; Tom Barnebey, cor (62-65); Pete Keir, tu; Dave Kennedy, tbn; Neil Kuhfuss, d; Jack Langlos, tpt; Don Martin, p (-60); TED SHAFER, bjo; Dick Shooshan, p (62-65); Ken Smith, cor (-62). (LA #2): Bob Allen, sb; Bert Grant, d; Clark Huddleston, bjo (alt); Roger Jamieson, tbn; Ray Ronnei, cor; Tom Sharpsteen, cl.

(SF): Burt Bales, p (65); Cyril Bennett, p (65); John Boland, cl (66); Edd Dickerman, tpt (66); Ev Farey, tpt (71); Squire Girsback, sb (66); Jim Goodwin, tpt (71); Bill Gould, p (66); Tony Landphere, tbn (66); Tom Moore, bjo (66); Bob Neighbor, tpt (70); Leon Oakley, cor (70); Walter Roberts, sb (66); Ray Skjelbred, p (71); Birch Smith, tpt (70); Karl Walterskirchen, bjo (66). (SF #2): Jim Cumming, sb; Bob Helm, cl/ssax; Ellis Horne, cl (69); Bill Maginnis, d; Bob Mielke, tbn; Ronnei; SHAFER.

*GHB 165 "Ted Shafer's Jelly Roll JB" (84); MMRC 101 "Ted Shafer's Jelly Roll JB, Vol 1" (81); =102 "do. Vol 2" (66); =104 "do. Vol 3" (67)*

## JELLY ROLL JAZZ SOCIETY LA 1975→
Came from SMOGVILLE SOCIETY ORCH after Dave Dolson left to form JAZZIN' BABIES. The group fractioned in 77 when Silverman formed HOT FROGS, and in later years featured

two separate bands under the title of JRJS, one led by Myers.

Joe Ashworth, cl; Wally Craig, tbn; John McConnell, sb; BILL MYERS, tpt; Gene Oster, p; BILL ROBERTS, d; Mike Silverman, tpt. ADD: Jerry Albert, tpt; Roy Bjanes, sb; Lance Buller, tbn; Reggie Dewar, tbn; Don Dupree, reeds; Ted Higgins, d; Dave Kennedy, tbn; Norm Logan, sb/tu; Rex Schull, bjo; Jack Wadsworth, tsax; Scotty Webster, p.

**Al Jenkins, tbn** *(1919 Newcastle PA)* - Blueblowers; Pete Daily; Doc Evans; Nightblooming

**Phil Jenkins, bass** - Bourbon St DJB

**Scott Jenkins, bass** - Good Time Levee

**Bob Jensen, tpt** - Mickey Finn; Platinum; San Diego DJB; Woodi's

**Marge Jensen, v** - Coos Bay

**Wilbur Jensen, tpt** - Emerald

**John Jestice, reeds** *(1916 Hamilton OH) ret USAF* - NOJB Hawaii

## JEWEL CITY JAZZ BAND La Jolla CA 1964-68

Title from the original name for La Jolla. *El Sombrero* (64-68).

Frank Chaddock, tpt; Bob Coblentz, cl (alt); Ed Halsey, d; Bill Hunter, p; Stan Kling, tu; Charlie Romero, cl (alt); Pete Spruance, tbn.

**John Jewett, reeds** - Dawn of Century; Kansas City; Thee Saints

**Pete Jochumson, cor** - Portland Rose

**Bill Johnson, p** - Old Sacramento

**Bob Johnson, p** - Castle

**Bob Johnson, bass** - Delta King; Fulton St; Riverbank

## BUNK JOHNSON'S JAZZ BAND SF 1943-45

Played a concert at SF's Geary Theater (Dec 43) under the name BUNK JOHNSON AND HIS HOT SEVEN, but changed title shortly after that. This and other concerts were under the aegis of SF Museum of Art, organized by Rudi Blesh to promote the art form of jazz.

Ed Garland, sb; BUNK JOHNSON, tpt; Kid Ory, tbn; Frank Palsey, g; Everett Walsh, d; Wade Whaley, cl; Buster Wilson, p. Subsequent groups under Johnson's leadership in SF (43-45): Burt Bales, p; Bill Dart, d; Clancy Hayes, bjo; Squire Girsback, tu; Ellis Horne, cl; JOHNSON; Pat Patton, bjo; Turk Murphy, tbn. ADD: Johnny Anderson, p (alt); Bill Bardin, tbn; Bob Helm, cl (44-45); George Lewis, cl (45).

*AMERICAN MUSIC (44); COLUMBIA CL829; GTJ 24, 37, 38; = L17, L12048 "Bunk Johnson's JB"; = L12024 "Lu Watters/Bunk Johnson" (53); JM 8-10 (42); RIV 1047 "Bunk Johnson and Kid Ory"*

**Burt Johnson, tbn** - Pete Daily

**Dave Johnson, tpt** - co-ldr Calif Express

**Dick Johnson, p** *(1923 Dartmouth MA) school supt* - Dixie Unltd

**Dick Johnson, tpt, reeds** *(1920 Oakland CA)* - Hiz Honor; Jazz Beaux; ldr Mardi Gras-SAC

**Ed Johnson, reeds** *(Chicago IL) military* - Desert City

**Ed Johnson, tpt** - Turk Murphy

**Eric Johnson, bass** - Dixie 6

**Feather Johnson, bass** - Dixie Belles

**Jill Johnson, p** - Riverbank; marr Roy Harper

**Jim Johnson, tbn** - Ponca City

**James P "Jimmy" Johnson, reeds** *(CANADA) postman* - 5 Guys Named Moe

**Manfred Johnson, bass** *(1929 Pierpont SD) environmental tech* - Capital; Dr Jon

**Mark Johnson, tpt** *(1963 Sacramento CA) micrographics tech* - ldr Bell St; Camellia; Jibboom St; Louisiana Purchase; Tuleburg

**Matt Johnson, d** - Jazz Minors

**Oliver "Dink" Johnson, pno, reeds** *(1892-1954 Biloxi MS)* - Freddy Keppard; Jelly Roll Morton; [Kid Ory]; solo pno. Cousin of Jelly Roll Morton; to CA 25; quit music in 45 to become restaurateur

  *AMERICAN MUSIC 515, 516 (45); = 523-526 (47)*

**Randy Johnson, bjo, g** - Great American; [Oakland A]; Powell St

**Stan Johnson, bass** - Gas Town; Carse Sneddon

**Tony Johnson, d** - [Delta Jazz Irreg]; Sinners

JUBILEE JAZZ BAND October 1985
L Hall, Clark, Gammon, J Hall

**William "Bunk" Johnson, tpt** *(1879-1949 New Orleans LA)* - Sidney Bechet; Buddy Bolden; led own groups, most notable of which were Bunk Johnson's JB, Bunk Johnson's Street Paraders, Original Superior Band (Baby Dodds, George Lewis, Jim Robinson, et al). Very little was known or recorded about this original jazzman until data were unearthed by historians Fred Ramsey Jr and William Russell in the late '30s, and he began playing anew on the West Coast in May 43 at age 64, with tours to CHI and NY, as well. Suffered paralyzing stroke in 48 which ended his brief comeback

**Kevin Johnston, bjo** - [Duwamish]; son of Ray Johnston

**Ray Johnston, bjo, p, tbn** - ldr Duwamish; Saints

**Betty Jones, p** - ldr Satin Dolls

**Burgher "Buddy" Jones, bass** - Abalone

**Dale Jones, bass** *(1902 Cedar County NB)* - Louis Armstrong; Charlie Teagarden; Jack Teagarden; led own groups in LA and Las Vegas

**Ernie Jones, tpt** - Toot Suite

**Greg Jones, cor** *photog* - Hume St; Royal Bourbon St

**Richard "Bunky" Jones, bass** *(UT)* - Harry James; Silver Stope; to CA c55

**Reginald Jones, bass** - Andy Blakeney

**Robert "Jonah" Jones, tpt** *(1908 Louisville KY)* - Lil Armstrong; Cab Calloway; Fletcher Henderson; Earl Hines; led own groups; became popular rec star in '50s and '60s with his glossy, muted trumpet styling

**Judy Jordan, p** - Coos Bay

**Stephen Joseph, d** *(1930 San Francisco CA) communications consultant* - Grand Dominion; Uptown Lowdown

**John Josephs, d** - Tailgate JB

## JOYFUL NOISE JAZZ BAND SF 1985→

Jeff Bender, p; Doug Franks, p; BRUCE HILTON, sb/tu; Paul Hilton, tpt; Bob Parker, tbn; Jerry Schimmel, bjo; Bill Slessinger, cl; Joe Staley, bjo.

## JUBILEE JAZZ BAND San Rafael 1969→

Formed and appeared under original names of BENGAL LANCERS and RACCOON STRAITS, before finalizing title in 71.

Milt Chambers, bjo (-74); Don Frolich, p (-77); Jackie Hall, v; LYNN HALL,p/tbn; Dick Randolph, cor (-79); Jack Reisner, sb/tu (-81); Hank Sharman, d (-74); Paul Widdess, cl/ssax (-75, 76→). ADD: Cal Abbott, cl/asax (75-76); Bill Armstrong, bjo (70-73); Tom Barnebey, p (85→); Tom Belton, d (76-79); Tom Buck, tpt (78-84); Don Bull, p (81-83); Tom Clark, sb/tu (81→); John Dodgshon, tpt (77-78); John Farkas, tbn (77-78); Bob Franklin, p (79-81); Jim Gammon, tpt (84→); Fay Golden, p (84-85); John Kinsel, d (79-82); Hugh O'Donnell, d (84→); John Potter, d (74-76); Brian Richardson, tbn (alt) (80→); Ray Skjelbred, p (81-83); Sharon Swenson, p (78-79); Rich Vose, bjo (78→); Ken Williams, d (82-84).

*JUBILEE 1 "The First Album" (82)*

**Art Juncker, p** *(1948)* - Churchill St

WARD KIMBALL (at recording of GTJ S10054), October 1969

# K

**Jerry Kaehele, tbn, tpt** *(1928 Columbus OH) deputy probation officer* - ldr Good Time Levee; ldr South Bay; fdr Sacramento New Orleans Hot Jazz Society; fdr Sacramento Traditional Jazz Society. Studied tpt under Mike DeLay

**Sherman Kang, reeds** - Rhythm Kings

## KANSAS CITY NIGHT OWLS LA 1958

Forerunner of THEE SAINTS; *Bali Bali* Palm Springs, Mayfair Hotel LA, casuals.
Pete Andreadis, d; K O Eckland, p; John Jewett, cl; Dave Kennedy, tbn; JACK LANGLOS, tpt.

**Ben Kantor, reeds** - Resurrection

**Morris "Sleepy" Kaplan, d** - Pete Daily

**Richard Karch, bass** - Camellia

**Jeff Karl, d** - Dixie Dissonants

**Art Katona, tbn** - Phoenix

**Hal Katzen, reeds** - Jazz-a-Ma-Tass

**Bob Kaufman, d** - Great American

**Brad Kay, p** *(1951 Los Angeles CA)* - Calif Ramblers; Rhythm Kings

**Tom Keats, g** - ldr Tom Kats

**Bruce Keck, bass** - Duwamish; Rainier

**Ron Keck, reeds** - [Mardi Gras-LA]; Unquenchables

**Don Keeler, p** *(1930)* - Bay City; Natural Gas; Original Inferior

**Jean Keeler, p, v** *(1938 Chicago IL)* - Devil Mtn; marr Ken Keeler

**Ken Keeler, bjo** *(1937 Danbury CT) airline pilot* - ldr Devil Mtn; Hot Jazz Stompers

**Bob Keely, bass** *(1935 Yuba City CA)* - Emperor Norton

**John "Jack" Keister, reeds** *(1929 Rockford IL) electrical engr* - Alligator; Bull Moose; Downey; Jazz-a-Ma-Tass; Orange Blossom; Orange Pealers; Triple RRR

**Lew Keizer, tpt** - Abalone; ldr Cider City

**John Keller, bass** - Do-Do-Wah

**Randy Keller, bass** *(1945 San Francisco CA) landscape architect* - Rainier; Uptown Lowdown

**Sheldon Keller, bass, bjo** - Beverly Hills

**Barbara Kelly, v** - Pete Lofthouse

**"Red" Kelly, bass** - Don Anderson

**Lorene Keltner, p** *(1916 Hot Springs AR)* - Dixieland Inc; marr Bill Burgess

**Bob Kennedy, reeds** - Dew Drop

**Dave Kennedy, tbn** *(1924 Hamilton OH)* - Dawn of Century; Down Home; Faultless; Good Time; Goose Island; Jelly Roll JB-LA; Jelly Roll Jazz Society; Kansas City; Mardi Gras-LA;

Resurrection; Southland; Thee Saints; Yankee Wailers

**Don Kennedy, bjo** - Muddy River

**Ken Kennedy, d** *cameraman, film production* - Desert City

**Ken Kennedy, p** - Dew Drop ldr

**Ward Kennedy, tbn** *prof of cardiology* - Ain't No Heaven

**Bob Kennerson, p** - City of Industry

**Tom Kenny, reeds** - Dr Mix; Swanee's

**Danny Kenyon, bass** - Elaine Mitchell

**Gregg Keplinger, d** - Great Excelsior

**Walt Kerr, p** *telephone co* - Hume St

**Peter Kershaw** *(1933 Yorkshire ENGLAND) construction* - Razzmajazz

**Ted Keyava, p** - Swanee's

**Bill Kick, tbn** *(1933 Everett WA) high school counselor* - Uptown Lowdown

**Willie Kiefer, bass, bjo, g** *(1954 Covington KY)* - Big Tiny Little

**Bill Kiehl, tbn** - King Zulu

**Vern Kiel, cor** *(Lima OH) civil engr* - Sammy Davis Jr; Desert City

**Pete Kier, bass** *(1922 San Diego CA)* - Beverly Hills; Crown City; [El Dorado-LA]; Faultless; Jelly Roll JB-LA; ldr Mardi Gras-LA; Resurrection; Smog City; Wilmington

**Becky Kilgore, g** - Rhythmakers; Wholly Cats

**Ed Killops, tpt** - Jazz-a-Ma-Tass

**Roland Kim, bass** - Newport Summit

**Ward Kimball, tbn** *(1914 Minneapolis MN) animator, producer* - Ambulance; ldr Firehouse 5 + 2; San Gabriel Vly Blueblowers

**Vic Kimzey, tbn** *(1919 Exeter CA) fire safety equipment* - High Sierra; Jazzberry

JERRY KAEHELE November 1985

Al Douglas

**Don Kinch, tpt, bass** *(1917 Kelso WA) stringed instrument repair* - Barney Bigard; Castle; ldr Conductors; Firehouse 5 + 2; Turk Murphy; [Ben Pollack]; Thee Saints; [Jack Teagarden]

**Patti (Bagan) Kinch, v** *(Harvey IL) viol shop mgr* - Conductors; marr Don Kinch

**Ernie King, tbn** *(1920 Edmonton Alba CANADA)* - ldr 5 Guys Named Moe

**Sally King, v** - Shakey City

**Steve King, g** - Angel City

**Tom King, tpt** *(Temple TX)* - ldr Capitol City; Easy Winners; Gas House; Gold Standard; Gramercy

## KING JAZZ BAND see CRESCENT BAY

## KING RIVERBOTTOM AND HIS BAY FLATS SJ 1974

Title came from orig KING RIVERBOTTOM JB, whose leader was responsible for Armstrong's interest in jazz. Elks Club Santa Clara (74).

Cal Abbott, cl; Steve Abrams, d; BILL ARMSTRONG, bjo; Jim Borkenhagen, cor; Norton Fredlund, p; Jim Klippert, tbn; John Scott, cor. ADD: Bill Bird, cl; Don Froelich, p; Lynn Hall, tbn; Dick Randolph, tpt; Jack Reisner, tu; Sam Shafer, d.

## KING RIVERBOTTOM JAZZ BAND SF Bay Area 1946-48

Robin Frost, p; Bob Golden, cor; Barry Phillips, sb; PETE PHILLIPS, tbn; Roland Working, cl.

## KING ZULU PARADERS (ED LEACH'S) LA 1967-82

Originally named ZULU STREET PARADERS.

Bob Dean, tbn; Jim Glitch, d; Tom Kubis, cl/ssax; ED LEACH, tbn; Charlie Martin, tpt; Jorge Mirkin, cl; Jim Ogden, tpt (-82); Bob Volland, p; Harvey Walker, g; Dee Woolem, sb. ADD: Frank Amoss, d (74-82); Chuck Bowers, sax (74); Hollis Bridwell, sax (77-78); Lonny Ferguson, tsax (74-77); Earl Griffiths, asax (74-82); John Henderson, tpt (74-82); Hal Groody, g (77); Al Isley, tpt (82); Bill Kiehl, tbn (82); Al Latour, tbn (78); John MacMullen, sax (77-82); Max Murray, sax (74-78); Walt Orth, sb (74-82); Bob Reitmeir, cl (82); Dave Rollin, tsax (82); Wayne Songer, tsax (82); Bob Smith, tbn (74); Bill Stumpp, tpt (74-78); Irv Williams, asax (74); Glen Woodmansee, tbn (77).

**John Kinsel, d** - Jubilee

**Lovell "Doc" Kinslow, bass** - Shakey City

**Greg Kiplinger, d** - Great Excelsior

**Paul Kipsey, d** - Grand Republic

**Mark Kirby, tbn** *(1954 Salinas CA)* - Jazz-a-Ma-Tass; Jazz Generation

**Phil Kirk, tpt** *(1936 Martinez CA) electronics* - Apex; Hot Jazz Stompers; ldr Prof Plum

**John Kitzmiller, bass** - Pearl Pacific; Woodi's

**Norman Klehm, tpt** - Barbary Coast; Polecats

**Manny Klein, tpt** *(1908 New York NY)* - Bauduc-Lamare; Red Nichols; Bob Scobey; Artie Shaw; Frankie Trambauer; studios; to CA 38; Jazz Forum "Jazzman Of the Year" 79

**George Kleinberg, p** - Blueblowers

**Stan Kling, bass, tbn** - Cottonmouth; Jewel City

**Jim Klippert, tbn** *(1941 Clarksburg WV) manufacturing mgr* - King Riverbottom; Magnolia; New Black Eagles (MA)

## KNIGHTS OF CAMELOT SF 1963-69
Title came from their venue, *Camelot Club.*
Bob Brennan, tbn; Jim Bodrero, tu; Don Bull, p; CHARLES EBERLE, cl; Tom Moore, bjo; Dave Rawson, tpt; Lee Valencia, bjo.

## KNIGHTS OF JAZZ North Hollywood 1957-58
*Beverly Cavern, Lark Club* LA.
ROY BREWER, tbn; K O Eckland, p; Don Kinch, cor; Bob McCracken, cl (-57); Gus van Camp, sb; unknown d. ADD: Jerry Fuller, cl (57); Tudie Garland, sb (58); Minor Hall, d (57-58); John Lane, cl (57); Del Ruark, bjo (57).

**George Knoblauch, bjo** *(1935 Omaha NB) window coverings* - co-ldr Black Diamond; Dixieland Synco

**Jack Knox, bjo, g** - Berkeley Rhythm; New Washboard RK; Phrisco Phunction; *SF Blues Serenders*

**John Knurr, d** - ldr Bell St; ldr Delta King

**Dick Kenton Knutson, tbn** *(1933 MI) security systems* - ldr Desert City; co-fdr Arizona Classic Jazz Society

**Glenn Koch, d** *(1913 CA)* - Salty Dogs (IL); Sons of Bix (IL); Stumptown; Swipesy

**Merle Koch, p** *(NB)* - Pete Fountain; ldr Silver Stope; solo; to CA 36, NV 61

**Ted Kohler, p** *(1921 Boston MA) PE teacher* - ldr Napa Valley; solo

**Harry Kooperstein, tpt** - New Bull Moose

**Loren Koravec, cor** - Chicago Ramblers

**Robert Korbelak, tpt** - Yankee Air Pirates

**Harold Koster, p** - Rose City JB

**Larry Kostka, d** - Hot Frogs; Jazz-a-Ma-Tass

**Dave Kraus, reeds** *(1960 Bronx NY)* - Lemon St

**Gil Kraus, p** *(1920 Yonkers NY)* - Dixie Jazz Bravos; Jazz-a-Ma-Tass; Jazz Generation

**Steve Kraus, tpt** *(1959 Bronx NY)* - Lemon St

**Rodger Kravel, d** - Yankee Air Pirates

**Ed Krenz, cor** *(1916 Seattle WA) music teacher* - Uptown Lowdown

**Sue Kroninger, v** *(1946 CA) club mgr* - Monterey Bay Classic; NO Syncopators

**Jerry Kronk, tbn** *(E St Louis MO)* - Warren Covington; Dixieland Stompers; Pete Kelly

**Lynn (Brown) Kronk, bjo** *(Seattle WA)* - Duwamish; Pete Kelly; marr Jerry Kronk

**Roger Krum, bass** *(1942 Fresno CA) rehabilitation administrator* - Fulton St

**Mark Krunosky, cor, reeds** - Chicago Ramblers

PHIL KIRK and BERT BARR October 1981

**George Kubis, d** - OC Dixiecats

**Tom Kubis, reeds** - King Zulu; ldr OC Dixiecats; Tailgate Ramblers; son of George Kubis

**Neil Kuhfuss, d** - Jelly Roll JB-LA

**Walt Kunnecke, reeds** - Fulton St; ldr Toot Suite

# L

**Jack Labbe, reeds** - Pete Kelly

**Norm Lacey, bjo** *(1903 Gladstone CO)* - WFDJE&MKRB

**John LaChapelle, bjo, g** *(1921 Orienta WI) music teacher* - Pete Candoli; Buddy DeFranco; Doc Severinsen; Tri-City; NBC staff orch

**Eddie La Dranke, tpt** - Hiz Honor

**Lee LaFaille, d** *(1932 Oakland CA) planning engr* - ldr Ponca City

**Ed LaFranchi, tpt** - Dr Mix; Jazz Beaux

## LA HONDA BANDITS La Honda (SF) CA 1977-78

Original lineup unknown. McNeal Breaux, sb; Duke d'Alessio, cl; Ted Gravance, d (77); Sam Hernandez, tpt; Fred Higuera, d (78); SLIM HOOD, g; Vern Olsen, tbn (77); Bob Strelitz, p; Howard Vandron, tbn (78).

NAPPY LAMARE (with Bob Haggart)  May 1977

**Myron La Hood, reeds** - Conductors; Rose City JB

**Eddy Lain** *(19—19—)* - ldr Bourbon St JB

## LAKESHORE SERENADERS Oakland 1978-79

Quartet formed to play at *The Serenader*, serving as a nucleus for jam musicians. John Gill, bjo; LEON OAKLEY, cor; Brian Nalepka, tu; Hal Smith, wb.

*SOS 1013 "New Orleans Joys" (82 w/Butch Thompson, p)*

## LAKE SPANAWAY JUG BAND Lake Spanaway WA 1959-61

Retitled HANGTOWN SYNCOPATORS in 60.

Mike Duffy, jug; Bob Jackson, tpt; BILL LOVY, g; Ray Skjelbred, acc/tbn; Pete Tedesco, jug.

**Lou Lalli, d** - Royal Dixie

**Tony Lallo, d** · Jazz Me Blues ldr; Raisin City

**Hilton Napoleon "Nappy" Lamare, bjo, g** *(1907 New Orleans LA)* - Marvin Ash; co-ldr Bauduc-Lamare group; Sharkey Bonano; Bob Crosby; Pete Daily; Joe Darensbourg; Monk Hazel; ldr Levee Loungers; Wingy Manone; co-ldr Riverboat Dandies; ldr Strawhat 7; led own groups; Jazz Forum "Jazzman Of the Year" 81

    *CAP 884, 1047, 10025, 15050, 15325; = T887 "Riverboat Dandies"; = T1198 "Two-Beat Generation"; FAIRMONT F105 "Rendezvous Ballroom Orchestra"*

**Bill Lamberton, p** - Platinum

**Bill Lamden, reeds** *(1946 San Diego CA) dentist* - Hyperion

**Dick Lammi, bjo, bass** *(1909-1969 Red Lodge MT)* - Barbary Coast; Great Pacific-SF; Turk Murphy; Polecats; Bob Scobey; *Washboard 5*; Yerba Buena

**Robin Lanbie, bass** - Camellia

**Gene Lancelle, tpt** - Camellia; ldr Dixieland Syncopators; ldr Happy Syncopators; Mudville; Swanee's

**Jo Lancelle, p** - Dixieland Syncopators; Happy Syncopators

**Ernie Landes, tbn** *(1935 CA) aeronautical engr* - Monterey Bay Classic; So Bay 7

**John Landes, tbn** - Camellia; Cats 'n' Jammers

**Tom Landino, bjo** - Gas House; Silver Dollar-SAC

**Tony Landphere, tbn** - Jelly Roll JB-SF

**Chester Lane, p** - Teddy Buckner

**John Lane, cl** - Knights

**Bill Langdon, p** - Dr Jon

**Darrell Langevin, bjo** *school principal* - Emerald City; Oregon

**Peter Langley** *(1935 Southhampton ENGLAND) electrician* - Razzmajazz

**Bill Langlois, bass** - Great American

**Harry "Jack" Langlos, tpt** *(1923-1976) psychologist* - Dawn of Century; ldr Kansas City; Jelly Roll JB-LA; ldr Thee Saints

**Alvin Larkin, bass** *(19—1978 Seattle WA) teacher* - Rainy City

**Dave Lario, bass** - Jack Sheedy; Joe Sullivan-SF

**Wayne Larsen, tpt** - Silicon

**Bob Larson, p** - UC Jazz

**Ron "Cork" Larson, bjo** *(1940 San Francisco CA) insurance* - Barrelhouse

**Barbara Lashley, v** - co-ldr Speakeasy
*SS 700 "How Long Has This Been Going On?" (83)*

**John Lasrieu, bass** - Feather Riverboat

## LAST CHANCE JAZZ BAND Camarillo CA 1981-83
DENNY BARNARD, bjo; others unknown.

**Don Lastra, bjo, tpt** *(1936 Santa Monica CA) policeman* - Hyperion

**Irv Lathrop, d** - Jazz Beaux

**Al Latour, tbn** - Jazz-a-Ma-Tass; King Zulu

**Al LaTourette, bjo** - Destiny; Duwamish; Pete Kelly

**John Laughlin, d** *(19—1981)* - Rainier

**Charlie Lavere, p** *(1910 Salina KS)* - ldr Chicago Loopers; Bob Crosby; Sextet From Hunger; Country Washburne; studios

RAY LEATHERWOOD
May 1980

**Bob Law, p** - Old Standard

**"Scotty" Lawson, p** - So Bay

**Dick Lazenby, bjo** - St Valentine

**Joe Lazzaro, tpt** *Colonel USAF* - Ponca City

**Ed Leach, tbn** - ldr King Zulu

**Geoff Leader, d** - Phoenix

**Donna Leah, v** - Carse Sneddon

**Ray Leatherwood, bass** *(1914 Itasca TX)* - Marvin Ash; Bauduc-Lamare; [Heinie Beau]; Les Brown; Tommy Dorsey; Bob Haggart; Rosy McHargue; Jack Teagarden; Joe Venuti; studios

**Jim Leavitt, bjo** - Silver Dollar-LA

**Max Leavitt, d** - Pier 23

**Sammy Lee, reeds** - Papa Celestin; Crown City; Roy Eldridge; Resurrection

**Walt Lee, d** *(1926 Alameda CA) sound engr* - Barrelhouse; Gutbucket

## LEGENDS OF JAZZ LA 1980-indef

Special performance and tour groups assembled by Martyn from some of the remaining original New Orleans jazzmen. Although personnel varied considerably, listing is representative.

Andy Blakeney, tpt; Joe Darensbourg, cl; Ed Garland, sb; BARRY MARTYN, d; Louis Nelson, tbn; Alton Purnell, p.

**Carol Leigh, v** *(1934 Redwood City CA)* - Chicago JB (IL); El Dorado-SJ; Jazz Missionaries; guest and combos

*EPITAPH 3 (2 cuts 63); GHB 88 "Wild Women Don't Have the Blues" w/Salty Dogs (75); = 167 "Go Back Where You Stayed Last Night" (84)*

**Jim Leigh, tbn** *(1930 San Francisco CA)* - Costa Del Oro; Bruce Dexter; El Dorado-SJ; Golden Gate Stompers

**Gene Lein, tbn** - Jazz Unltd; Royal Valley

**Gene Leis, g** *(1920 Wichita KS) publisher, teacher* - Ponca City

## LEMON STREET STOMPERS Fullerton CA 1981→

Youth groups organized and directed by Richard Cruz, music educator at Fullerton College; each one entered and became finalists in Southern Comfort JB competition, with the 81 band gaining first runner-up award.

1981-82: John Deemer, tpt; Mike Henneman, tu; Jim Mackin, d; Tim Moynahan, tbn; Larry Rousseve, bjo/g; Kurt Wahl, p; Penny Watson, ssax. 1982-83: Phil Erlich, d; Bob Heller, tbn; Henneman; Dave Kraus, ssax/tsax; Glen Nakahara, tpt; Rousseve; Wahl. 1983-84: Steve Alaniz, cl/ssax; D Kraus; Steve Kraus, tpt; Tricia McCarty, tbn; Jacque Paquette, bjo; Dan Price, sb/tu; Cheryl Savala, d. 1984-85: Russell Burt, reeds; Eugean Ermel, d; Bert Forbes, bjo; Mark Hudson, tpt; Tim Nitz, p; John Shideler, tu.

*JLFC1283 "Time for Dixie" (81)*

**Fred Lent, p** - Bob Higgins

**Art Leon, bjo** - Hot Frogs

**Jack Lesberg, bass** - Balboa JB

**Jon Lesch, p** - [Capital City]

**Dick Leupp, tbn** - Camellia

**Morris "Morey" Levang, bjo, g** *(1925 Bemidji MN) teamsters union* - ldr Dixie Rhythm Ramblers; Jazz-a-Ma-Tass; Merrymakers

## LEVEE LOUNGERS (NAPPY LAMARE'S) LA 1945-1949

Originally known as LOUISIANA LEVEE LOUNGERS. Much of the personnel shifted freely between several Bauduc and Lamare bands, especially those organized for recs, where band names were often created on the spot.

Ray Bauduc, d (-49); Budd Hatch, sb (-47); NAPPY LAMARE, g; Wingy Manone, tpt (45); Matty Matlock, cl (-48); Eddie Miller, cl/sax (-46); Stan Wrightsman, p (-47). ADD: Marvin Ash, p (47-); John Best, tpt (47-49); Ted Hammond, sb (49); Lou McGarity, tbn (47); John Plonsky, tpt (45-47); Doc Rando, cl/sax (46) Andy Secrest, tpt (49); Art Shapiro, sb (47-49); Zutty Singleton, d (49); Irv Verret, tbn (49); Country Washbourne sb/tu (49).

*CAP 10025 (45); = 15050, 15325 (47); = 884 (49); MERCURY 2071 (46)*

**Art Levin, bass** *(1925 Trenton NJ) zookeeper* - Blue 5; Dawn of Century; ldr Excelsior; ldr Impossible; Orange Blossom; Paradise; co-ldr Pepper; Resurrection; Unquenchables

**Blaise Levin, tpt** - Sticks Strings

**Henry "Hot Lips" Levine, tpt** *(1907 London ENGLAND)* - ldr Chamber Music Society of Lower Basin St on '40s radio show (NY); Original Dixieland JB (at age 15); Silver Stope; NBC staff orch; led own groups; to NV in '60s

*CAMDEN CAL321 "Chamber Music Society of Lower Basin St"; VIC 27304, 27829, 27831; = LPM1283 "Dixieland Jazz Band"*

**Jean Levinson, bass** *(Sarasota FL)* - Cats 'n' Jammers; Camellia; Delta King; Swanee's

**Terry Levitt, p** - Happy JB

**Dave Lewis, bass** *(1935 Columbus OH) manufacturer* - Natural Gas

**Don Lewis, bjo** - Cats 'n' Jammers

**Edna Lewis, reeds** - Dixieland Inc

**Elton Lewis, vib** - Capitol City

**Ernie Lewis, p** - Bob Scobey

## GEORGE LEWIS NEW ORLEANS BAND LA-SF

Although originated and based in NO, Lewis toured the West Coast extensively from 46-57, alternating principally between LA's *Beverly Cavern* and SF's *Club Hangover, Tin Angel,* but appearing in other venues and concerts with most of his original lineup, as well. Listing is representative.

Avery "Kid" Howard, tpt; GEORGE LEWIS, cl; Lawrence Marrero, tpt; Alcide "Slow Drag" Pavageau, sb; Alton Purnell, p; Jim Robinson, tbn; Joe Watkins, d. ADD: Buddy Burns, sb; Johnny Lucas (55); Albert V Walters, tpt (52).

**John Lewis, tpt** - Riverboat Ramblers

MEADE "LUX" LEWIS
undated, c1955

**Laurie Lewis, bass, viol** *(1950 Long Beach CA) viol shop owner* - Golden Age; Bob Neighbor

**Meade "Lux" Lewis, p** *(1905-1964 Louisville KY)* - solo boogie-woogie artist; many 78rpm recs; played clubs in LA and SF after moving to CA in 41. Teamed with Albert Ammons and Pete Johnson to form a piano trio in the late '30s with many recs as a result; appeared in film "New Orleans" (47). Killed in car crash while on tour in MN

 *ABC 164 "Out Of the Roaring '20s"; ATLANTIC 133 "Boogie-Woogie Interpretations"; DOWN HOME MGC7 "Yancey's Last Ride"; STINSON 25 "Meade Lux Lewis"; TOPS L1533 "Barrel House Piano"; VERVE MGV1006 "Cat House Piano"; =MGV1007 "Meade Lux Lewis"*

**Mel Lieberman, reeds** - Bearcats

**Owen Lienhard, bass** - Mickey Finn

**Abe Lincoln, tbn** *(1907 Lancaster PA)* - Ray Anthony; orig California Ramblers; Wild Bill Davison; Matty Matlock; Rampart St; Bob Scobey; Jack Teagarden; *Village Stompers*; Paul Whiteman; studios; to CA 40

**Bob Lindfeldt, tbn** - Jazz Beaux; Purple Gang

**Paul Lingle, p** *(1902-1962 Denver CO)* - Yerba Buena. Legendary pianist remembered best for his prolific solo work around the SF Bay area. *Paper Doll* SF (49), *Jug Club* Oakland (50-51); to HI 52 where he taught piano and led own combos up until his death

 *EUPH ESR1217 "Dance Of the Witch Hazels" (79); =ESR1220 "The Legend of Lingle" (80); GTJ 88 (52); =L13 "At the Piano" (53); =L12025 "They Tore My Playhouse Down" (1 side)*

**Ray Linn, tpt** *(1920 Chicago IL)* - ldr Chicago Stompers; Bob Crosby; Tommy Dorsey; Woody Herman; Artie Shaw; Lawrence Welk; led own groups; studios and rec

**Pete Lipman, d** - Little Big Band

**Dan Lipscomb, p** - Sausalito

**Mike Lipskin, p** *(Queens NY)* - solo; long-term at *Washington St Bar & Grill* SF
*BUSKIRK 001 "Harlem Stride Piano"*

**"Big Tiny" Little, bass, p, o** *(1930 Worthington MN)* - led own groups; solo

**Jay Little, d** - Royal Society

## LITTLE BIG BAND LA 1979→

Bob Christy, sb; Loren Helberg, cl; BILL JACKSON, cor; Robbie James, p (-80); Pete Lipman, d; Ray Lyon, bjo; Don McGrath, tbn. ADD: Norm Burnham, p (80-81).

## BIG TINY LITTLE JAZZ BAND NV

Details sketchy but recent group as appeared at 85 Sacramento Jubilee may be indicative.

Ed Easton, reeds; Dick Greene, tbn; Willie Kiefer, bjo; BIG TINY LITTLE, p; Dave Poe, reeds; Tom Saunders, cor; Danny Shannon, sb; Jack Sperling, d.

## LIVE STEAM Fresno 1983→

Harry Buyukian, tpt; DICK DOUTY, tu; Jay Fung, bjo; John Martin, cl/ssax; Bob McClung, p; Al Nersesian, d: Les Nunes, tbn; Bob Russell, cl/ssax. ADD: Vincent Moats, cl; Carl Schmitt, tbn.

**Joseph "Fud" Livingston, reeds** *(1906-1957 Charleston SC) arr* - orig Calif Ramblers; Jean Goldkette; Miff Mole; Ben Pollack; Paul Whiteman; Bob Zurke; studios; comp *Imagination, I'm Through With Love*, others

**Lila Lloyd, v** *(1930 San Francsico CA)* - Gem City; stage and tv comml work

**Rich Lockwood, reeds** - Riverbank

**Charley Lodice, d** - Barney Bigard; Pete Daily; Dukes of Dixieland; Pete Lofthouse; Wingy Manone; Jack Teagarden; Ted Vesely; studios

**Ray Loeckle, reeds** - Great American

**Don Loeffler, d** - High Society JB

**Pete Lofthouse, tbn** - led own groups

## PETE LOFTHOUSE AND HIS SECOND-STORY MEN Los Angeles c1965

Jackie Coon, cor; Bill Cooper, sb; Barbara Kelly, v; Charlie Lodice, d; PETE LOFTHOUSE, tbn; Jack Martin, ssax; Ron Rowe, p.

**Don Loftus, bass** - Coos Bay

**Bob Logan, tbn** - Blueblowers

**Chuck Logan, d** *(Los Angeles CA)* - 5 Guys Named Moe

**Norm Logan, bass** - Goose Island; Jelly Roll Jazz Society; Resurrection

**Tom Lommell, d** - Rosy McHargue; Platinum

**Bob Long, p** - Chicago 6

**Dave Loomis, tbn** - Uptown Lowdown

**Jerry Lopes, bass** *teacher* - Dixiecrats; River City; Sutterville; symphony orchs; master's degree in music

**Tom Lopes, bass** - Cats 'n' Jammers

**Dick Lopez, d** - Charlie's; Mickey Finn

**Shelly Lord-Howe, cor** - ldr Alligator; Triple RRR

**Vic Loring, bjo** *(1927 Lexington MA)* - British Connection; Condor; Down Home; Good Time; Jazz Missionaries; Mississippi; Orange Empire; Orange Pealers; Pepper; San Juan

**Hal Lotzenheimer, p** - solo

**Joe Loughmiller, d** *(19—1981)* - Great Excelsior

## LOUISIANA GENTS (PEPPY PRINCE'S) LA

Ed Barksdale, bjo/g; Hugh Bell, tpt; Henry Coker, tbn; Joe Comfort, sb; Leroy Lovett, p; George Orendorff, tpt; PEPPY PRINCE, d; Bobbie Smith, reeds.

## LOUISIANA LEVEE LOUNGERS see LEVEE LOUNGERS

**Leroy Lovett, p** - Louisiana Gents

**Bill Lovy, g** *(19—1969)* - Great Excelsior; ldr Lake Spanaway

**Jack Lowe, d** - Bob Mielke

**"Sonny" Lowe, g** - Mudville; Pier 100

**John Lowrey, g** *(1925 London ENGLAND)* - Conspiracy; Marin Jazz; Swing Fever

**Johnny Lucas, tpt, vib** *(1918 Minneapolis MN) writer* - ldr Blueblowers; Crown City; Firehouse 5 + 2; Jazz Ramblers; George Lewis; [Bob McCracken]; Old Standard; So Bay; [Jack Teagarden]; led own groups.

JOHNNY LUCAS October 1979

**Jerry Luck, tpt** - Silver Dollar-SAC

## LUCKY LADY JAZZ BAND Fresno 1980
RALPH MANFREDO, p; Al Nersesian, d; others unknown.

**Dick Luepp, bass** - Riverbank

**Gene Lundgren, bjo** *(1928 MN) tool & die maker* - Portland Rose; Rose City JB; Stumptown

**Jon Lundgren, d** *(1957 Los Angeles CA)* - Fullertowne

**Carl Lunsford, bjo** *(1934 Cincinnati OH)* - Dixieland Rhythm Kings (OH); Golden State; Turk Murphy; [Natural Gas]; Red Onion (NY); ldr Rhythm Wizards; led other combos

**Nellie Lutcher, p, v** *(1915 Lake Charles LA) AFM official* - solo and led own combos; long-term at Disneyland; many hit recs late '40s

**Barrie Luttge, bjo** *(1931 Providence RI) electronics engr* - And That's Jazz

**Gordon Lutz, tbn** - Monrovia

**Kedric "Ked" Lynch, p** *artist* - Newport Harbor

**Ray Lyon, bjo** - ldr Downey Dixie; Little Big Band; fdr Southeast Dixieland Jazz Inc

**Al Lyons, bjo** - Turk Murphy

**Bud Lyons, d** *(1917 Tacoma WA) sales mgr* - And That's Jazz

**Harry Lyons, bjo** - Cottonmouth


# M

**Jim MacDonald, d** - Firehouse 5 + 2

**Mike MacDonald, d** - Hiz Honor

**Eddie Macedo, bjo** - Easy Winners

**Norrie MacFarlane, tpt** - ldr Dixieland Express

**"Mac" MacGavran, p** - Southside

**Jerry MacKenzie, reeds** - Chicago Ramblers; Gold Standard; Grand Republic

**Chuck Mackey, tpt** - Chicago Loopers; ldr *Michigan Blvd*

**Jim Mackin, d** *(1957 Launschtuhl GERMANY)* - Lemon St

**John MacMullen, reeds** - King Zulu

**George Blake Maddox, cor** *(1933 Seattle WA) sales rep* - ldr Capital City; Portland Rose

**Bill Magellan, reeds** - Pier 100

**Bill Maginnis, d** *(1938 Yreka CA) music teacher* - Bay City Music Co; [Delta Jazz]; Jimmy Diamond; Golden Age; Jelly Roll JB-SF; Marin Jazz; Phrisco; Pier 23; Rose & Thistle; Speakeasy; Tappers; Norma Teagarden; symphony orchs

JOHN MARKHAM March 1977

## MAGNOLIA JAZZ BAND Stanford CA 1975→

Popular traditional group began as six-piece combo playing lounges in SJ and Palo Alto. Since 77, the nucleus has been a trio (cl/g/sb), expanding up to nine pieces for an occasion. Considerable touring of USA.

Cal Abbott, cl (-76); Bill Armstrong, bjo (-75); Jeff Hamilton, d; Jim Klippert, tbn; ROBBIE SCHLOSSER, sb/cor; Sharon Swenson, p (-75). ADD: Pete Allen, sb (alt 75→); Jeff Bender, p (75→); Jim Borkenhagen, tpt (75→); Jeff Buenz, g (alt); Bill Carter, cl (76→); Squire Girsback, sb (75-76); Marc Marcus, cl (75, alt 76→); Paul Mehling, g (78→); Bill Napier, cl (80→); Bill Newman, g (-80); Dan Ruedger, bjo (76-83); Karl Walterskirschen, bjo (75-76).

*GHB 171 "Magnolia JB with Art Hodes" (85); MAGNOLIA MJB78 "Live Recordings" (78); =MJB79 "Magnolia JB" (79); =MJB80 "On Tour" (81); SOS 1016 "Red Onion Blues" (81)*

**Bill Maher, tpt** - Downey Dixie

**Max Mahoney, bass** - Riverboat Ramblers

**Jim Maihack, bass, bjo, p, tbn** *(1935 Rock Island IL)* - Jim Beatty; [Capital City]; [Fulton St]; Golden State; Clyde McCoy; Turk Murphy; Oregon; Rhythm Wizards; ldr Rosie O'Grady (FL); SF Brass; Smokey Stover; ldr Tappers

**Marty Main, bass** *(1963 Mountain View CA) rec arts* - Devil Mtn; son of Pete Main

**Pete Main, reeds** *(1936 Redwood City CA) music teacher* - Devil Mtn

**John Malarkey, p** - Feather Riverboat

127

**Jack Malek, viol** *product dev* - Dawn of Century; symphony orchs

**Barry Mallagh, bass** *(1934 San Luis Obispo CA)* - Emperor Norton

**Clarke Mallery, reeds** *(1919 Los Angeles CA) animator* - Firehouse 5 + 2

**John Malone, d** *(1928 Los Angeles CA) financial adm* - Hyperion

**John Maloney, reeds** *(1921 Sayre PA)* - Emperor Norton

**Walt Malzahn, tbn** - Orange Pealers

**Ralph Manfredo, p** *AFM official* - Jazz Unltd; ldr Lucky Lady; ldr Royal Valley

**Jack Mangan, d, reeds** *(1925 San Francisco CA)* - co-org Do-It-Yourself; Churchill St; Emperor Norton; ldr Euphoria; Golden State; Prof Plum; Rose & Thistle

**Tommy Mann, reeds** - Dixie Rhythm Ramblers

**Joseph "Wingy" Manone (Mannone), tpt** *(1904-1982 New Orleans LA)* - Levee Loungers; NO Rhythm Kings; led own groups; wrote *Isle of Capri, Tailgate Ramble*, others. To CA c57, Las Vegas mid '60s. Appeared in film *Rhythm On the River* (40) and as frequent guest on Bing Crosby radio show. Subject of biography *Trumpet On the Wing* (Paul Vandervoort 48); auth *Tailgate Ramble, Tar Paper Stomp* (which later became *In the Mood*), others
   *DECCA DL8473 "Trumpet On the Wing"; RCA LPV563 "Wingy Manone"; RIV RLP1030*

## WINGY MANONE JAZZ BAND LA/SF

Listing is typical of SF group at *Clayton Club* SAC.

Zulu Ball, sb/tu; Wild Bill Early, p; Charley Lodice, d; WINGY MANONE, tpt; Bob Mielke, tbn; Bob Woods, cl.

**Frank Mansell, pno** *(1920 Edmonton ALBA)* - Lance Harrison

**John Marabuto, p** *comp* - Sweet & Hot

**Don Marchant, d** *(1921)* - Burt Bales; Bearcats; Estuary; Funky NOJB; Golden Age; Polecats

**Bob Marchessi, bass** - Pier 23

**Larry Marcus, p** - Rosy McHargue

**Marc Marcus, reeds** *(Pittsburgh PA) teacher* - Apex; Emperor Norton; Euphoria; Magnolia; Oakland Hot Babies. Out of music scene for several years due to serious injuries sustained in an auto accident

**Mike Marcus, bass** - Casa Bonita; son of Marc Marcus

## MARDI GRAS JAZZ BAND LA 1965-67

*The Honeybucket* Costa Mesa, *The Rumbleseat* Hermosa Beach.

Jim Adams, tpt; Gene Eidy, d; Rick Fay, cl/tsax (alt); Clark Huddleston, bjo; PETE KIER, tu; Dave Kennedy, tbn; Max Murray, cl/tsax (alt); Dusty Rhodes, p;. ADD as subs: Don Cox, d; Bob Duggan, bjo; Ron Keck, cl; Sy Rice, d; Pete van Oorschodt, cl.

## MARDI GRAS JAZZ BAND SAC 1983→

John Carlson, sb; Jack Gumbiner, p; Dee Hendricks, cl (-84); DICK JOHNSON, tpt/cl; Tony Rossi, tbn; Ed Schmalz, cl (84→); Jack Turner, d.

**Al Mariano, p** - Trumbo

**George Maribus, p** - Golden Age

**Mark Marin, bass** *(1961 Fresno CA) music teacher* - Blue St

## MARIN JAZZ Marin County CA 1977→

Originally named MARIN JAZZ QUARTET, known also as MARIN JAZZ & HOT TUB SOCIETY ORCHESTRA. *Mayflower Inn* San Rafael (77-83). Toured England 80.

Grace Ades, v (-78); Don Bennett, sb; JOHN DODGSHON, cor; John Lowrey, g (-78); Jim Putman, g; Brian Richardson, tbn; Ken Williams, d. ADD: Bunky Colman, cl (77); Ev Farey (77); Dick Hadlock (77, 80); Bill Maginnis, d (81); Jeff Sandford, c/sax (81); Wanda Stafford, v (78-).

**John Markham, d** *(1926 Oakland CA)* - Charlie Barnet; Benny Goodman; Billy May; Nob Hill; Red Norvo; ldr Sweet & Hot

**Fran Marois, v** *(1939-1983 Jennings LA)* - New Bull Moose; Outcast; marr George Marois; daughter of the Assuntos, of Dukes of Dixieland fame; served as Dukes' PR person

**George Marois, cor, tbn** *(1934 Boston MA) aeronautical engr* - ldr New Bull Moose; Outcast

**Mike Marois, bass** *(1961 Las Vegas NV) administrator* - New Bull Moose; Outcast; son of George and Fran Marois

**Mario "Marty" Marsala, tpt** *(1909-1975 Chicago IL)* - [Sidney Bechet]; Eddie Condon; Earl Hines; Joe Marsala; Miff Mole; Kid Ory; Tony Parenti; Rainy City; Bob Scobey; led own groups; to CA 53-64; bro of Joe Marsala

## MARTY MARSALA'S CHICAGO DIXIELAND BAND SF 1953-1959

Nucleus band at *Downbeat* SF (53), alternating with Miles Davis group, and adding traveling guest stars to lineups, such as Sidney Bechet. *Club Hangover, Easy Street, Kewpie Doll* throughout '50s and early '60s.

*(Downbeat)*: Bob Bates, sb (-54); Cus Cousineau, d; MARTY MARSALA, tpt; Skip Morr, tbn; Johnny Wittwer, p. ADD: Burt Bales, p; Vince Cattolica, cl; Bunky Colman, cl (56); Tiny Crump, p; Ernie Figueroa, sb; MARTY MARSALA, tpt; Bill Napier, cl; Pat Patton, sb; Tut Soper, p (54); others.

*JAZZ ARCHIVES JA44 "Jazz From California" w/Bechet (c80 1 side)*

**Ernie Marshall, bass** - Bathtub Gin

**Harry Marshall, d** - Pearly Band

**Andy Martin, tbn** - Jazz Minors

**Bruce Martin, p** *teacher* - Oregon

**Charlie Martin, tpt** - King Zulu

**Dave Martin, tpt** - Merrymakers

**Dick Martin, reeds** - Uptown Lowdown

**Don Martin, p, tbn** - Jelly Roll JB-LA; ldr Smog City

**Jack Martin, bjo** *(19—1984)* - Dixie Katz; Sutterville

**Jack Martin, reeds** - Pete Lofthouse; Pearly Band

DAVE McCARTNEY August 1982

**John Martin, reeds** *(1918 Wellston OH) teacher* - Blue St; Jazz Unltd; Stan Kenton; Live Steam; Royal Valley

**Willie Martinez, reeds** - Blueblowers; Pete Daily; Nightblooming

**Barry Martyn, d** *(1942 ENGLAND)* - org Legends of Jazz

**Bill Marvin, p** - Saints

**Paul Mascioli, d** - Dixieland Express

**Parke Math, bjo** *(1915 Buffalo NY) printing inks supply* - Jazz-a-Ma-Tass; Jazzin' Babies

**Jim Matheson, bass/bsax** *airline pilot* - French Quarter

**Brandon Mathews, tbn** - Toot Suite

**Bryn Mathieu, d** - Newport Summit

**Jack Mathis, tpt** - Abalone

**Julian "Matty" Matlock, reeds** *(1909-1978 Paducah KY) arr* - Louis Armstrong; Marvin Ash; Blueblowers; Hoagy Carmichael; Chicago Loopers; Bob Crosby; Bobby Hackett; Levee Loungers; *Michigan Blvd*; Red Nichols; ldr Paducah Patrol; Pete Kelly Big 7; Ben Pollack; ldr Rampart St; Jack Teagarden; led own groups; Jazz Forum "Jazzman Of the Year" 78
  *COLUMBIA CL690 "Pete Kelly's Blues"; MAYFAIR 9569 (TOPS L1569) "Dixieland"; WB 1262 "And They Called It Dixieland"*

**Steve Matthes, reeds** - Dr Jon

**Doug Mattocks, bjo** *(1950 Jacksonville NC)* - Hot Frogs

**Gene R. Maurice, cor** *(1926 Cincinnati OH) mechanical engr* - And That's Jazz ldr; Buena Vista; [Delta Jazz]; Gutbucket; Mud Flat

**Lennie Maxson, d** - Southside

**Billy May, tpt** *(1916 Pittsburgh PA) arr* - Charlie Barnet; Chicago Loopers (aka Billy May's DB on some recs); Glenn Miller; led own groups; studios; chiefly known for his arranging styles and film scoring

**Charles May, reeds** - Jazz Forum

**Karl May, bjo** *surgeon* - Ain't No Heaven

**Joe Mayer, bjo, g** - Silver Stope

**Greg Mazarian, bass** - Merrymakers

**Paul Mazlansky, tpt** - Beverly Hills

**John Mazzarella, d** *cardiologist* - Ain't No Heaven

**Bob McAllister, tbn** - Great Excelsior

**Kevin McCabe, bjo** - St Peter

**Joe McCaffrey, d** - Newport Harbor; Dave Weirbach

**Dave McCartney, bass** - Good Time Levee; ldr Hangtown; Riverbank

**Patricia McCarty, tbn** *(1964 Springfield MA)* - Lemon St

**Gardiner McCauley, bjo** - Bayside

**Bill McCaw, tpt** *banker* - Hume St; Royal Bourbon St

**Dale McClean, tbn** *bank loan officer* - Royal Bourbon St

**Bob McClung, p** - Live Steam

**Donna McClure, viol** *music teacher* - Dawn of Century

**Dick McComb, tpt** - Red Hot Peppers

**John McConnell, bass** - Jelly Roll Jazz Soc

**Al McCormick, bass** *(1927 San Francisco CA)* - Bob Scobey

**John McCormick, cor** *(1926 Huntington Beach CA)* - ldr Orange Pealers

**Mel McCoy, g** - Blueblowers

**Bob McCracken, reeds** *(1904-1972 Dallas TX)* - Louis Armstrong; Andy Blakeney; Pete Daily; Wild Bill Davison; Knights; Wingy Manone; Jimmy McPartland; Kid Ory; Ben Pollack; Tailgate Ramblers; Jack Teagarden; led own groups

**Arthur "Skip" McDaniel, bass, bjo, g** *(1946 Seattle WA)* - Great Excelsior; Island City

**Al McDearmon, p** *(1941 Palo Alto CA) computer programmer* - Euphonic; Euphoria; Natural Gas; Plum Forest; solo

**Donny McDonald, tpt** - Easy Winners; led own groups
  *20107 "Cooks For All the Cats"*

**Jim McDonald, tpt** - Sugar Willie

**Bill McFadden, d** - So Bay 7

**Terry McGarrah, p** *electrician* - Hume St

**Jane McGarrigle, p** - Golden Age

**John "Bucky" McGeoghegan, bass, p** - Bye Bye Blues; Cypress

**Don McGrath, tbn** - Jazz-a-Ma-Tass; Little Big Band

**Joe McHale, tpt** *(1962 Bakersfield CA) architect* - ldr Sticks Strings

BOB McCRACKEN
December 1967

AL McDEARMON
October 1979

**James "Rosy" McHargue, piano, reeds** *(1907 Danville IL)* - Chicago Loopers; Pete Daily; *Dixieboppers*; Benny Goodman; Peewee Hunt; Kay Kyser; Eddie Miller (Bob Cats); Red Nicholls; Joe Rushton; Ted Weems; led own groups; featured on '50s tv show *Dixie Showboat*; to LA 42. Jazz Forum "Jazzman Of the Year" 83. Nickname came from old song *When Rosie Racoola Dood the Hoola Ma Boola* he used to sing

## ROSY McHARGUE DIXIELAND JAZZ BAND LA 1954→

Many groups under this title, most recent of which was three-piece at *Sterling's* Santa Monica (74→), usually augmented by drop-in musicians; *Club Hangover* (50-55), *Zucca's* (58-66) and *Gwinn's West* Pasadena (67-70).

George Defebaugh, d (-53); Bob Higgins, tpt (-53); Ray Leatherwood, sb (-53); ROSY McHARGUE, cl/p/sax; Moe Schneider, tbn (-53); Earl Sturgis, p (-53). ADD: Jim Adams, tpt (67-77); Hugh Allison, d (67-74); George Ball, d (74→); Pud Brown, cor (55-56); Tom Thunen, cor (53-55); Lou Diamond, d (53-55); Bill Dods, p/tu (58-66); Robin Frost, g/p (56); Harry Hall, p (74-85); Allan Imbach, tbn (56); Tom Lommel, d (56); Larry Marcus, b (53-55); Burr Middleton, d; Dick Miller, cor (→); Max Murray, cl (67-74); Gene O'Neill, d (58-66); Bruce Paulson, p (85→); Spencer Quinn, bjo (58-66); Chuck Wheeler, tbn (67-74); Chuck Wilson, tbn (53-55).

*AUDIOPHILE 1330 "Jazz Potpourri #1"; CUSTOM FIDELITY CF1342 "Rosy McHargue and His Band"; FAIRMONT F109 "Rosy McHargue" (75); JM 334 "Dixieland Contrasts"; JUMP 28 (48)*

## *ROSY McHARGUE'S MEMPHIS FIVE* LA 1947

Traded rec titles with RUSHTON'S CALIFORNIA RAMBLERS.

Marvin Ash, p; Nick Cochrane, tpt; Brad Gowans, tbd; ROSY McHARGUE, cl; Joe Rushton, bsax; Graham Stevenson, d.

*JUMP 8, 13 (47)*

BOB MIELKE December 1979

## *ROSY McHARGUE'S RAGTIMERS* LA 1952
Ostensibly the *Hangover* band.
*JUMP J12 (74); TURNTABLE HF1*

**Earl McKee, bass , v** *(1931 Three Rivers CA) cattle rancher* - High Sierra; Jazzberry

**Hank McKee, bjo** *(1913 Rochester NY) real estate* - Jamboree Hal; Jazz-a-Ma-Tass; Milneburg; Orange Blossom; Orange Pealers; WFDJE&MKRB

**Jerry McKenzie, d** - Angel City

**Jerry McKenzie, bjo, reeds** - ldr Custer

**Chuck McKeon, tpt** - Powerhouse

**Craig McKinley, bjo** - Swipsey; son of John McKinley

**John McKinley, bjo** *(1936 Portland OR) music teacher* - Conductors; led own groups; understudy to Eddie Peabody

## **JOHN McKINLEY BAND** PTL 1982→

Jerry Heermans, p; Craig McKinley, bjo; JOHN McKINLEY, bjo; Bob Pettingill, tu; Chuck Simpson, cl; Lynn Teadtke, tpt; Joe Wimmer, cl/sax.

**Chuck McLain, tbn** *(1934 Fairfield IA) social worker* - Barrelhouse

**John "Gerry" McLaughlin, d** *(1940 Lethbridge ALBA) artist* - Grand Dominion; Hot Jazz Hot Shots; Phoenix

**Earnest McLean, bjo, g** - NO Creole Gumbo

**Dan McNiven, bjo** - So Bay 7

**Galen McReynolds, cl** - Shakey City

**Jack McVea, reeds** *(1914 Los Angeles CA)* - Benny Carter; Slim Gaillard; Lionel Hampton; JATP; ldr Royal St; led own groups

## **M D DIXIELAND JAZZ BAND** Fresno c1983

Lance Boyce, tpt; Skip Hadden, d; Gary Isbell, bjo; Jack Snauffer, tbn; AL TORRE, cl; Elmer Tuschoff, sb; Dick Whitten, tpt; Jimmy Woods, p.

**Bob Meek, reeds** *(1923 Waterbury CT) aerospace engr* -'Bye Bye Blues; Jazz Forum

**Paul Mehling, bjo, g** *(Pleasanton CA)* - Abalone; Cider City; Magnolia

**Pieter Meijers, reeds** *(1941 Oostkappelle NETHERLANDS) museum chemist* - Night-blooming

**Jack Meilahn, g** - Rhythmakers

**Frank Mencinger, bjo** - Yankee Air Pirates

**Iris Mencinger, bjo** - Yankee Air Pirates; marr Frank Mencinger

**Roger Mendez, d** - Dr Mix; Sugar Willie

**Ian Menzies, tbn** *(1932 Glasgow SCOTLAND) sales rep* - Hot Jazz Hot Shots; Phoenix; ldr Razzamajazz

## MERRYMAKERS LA 1978

Hal Blevins, tbn; Bob Gimber, cl; LLOYD GRAFTON, d; Morey Levang, g; Dave Martin, tpt; Greg Mazarian, sb; Ken Sands, p.

**Eric Messerschmidt, bass** - Jazz Minors

**Dave Metz, bjo** - Riverbank

**Frank Meyers, bass** - [Donnie McDonald]; Red Hot Peppers

**Larry Micheau, bjo** - Bathtub Gin

**Ian Michie, bass** *(1927 Kent ENGLAND) scientist* - Razzamajazz

## MICHIGAN BLVD GANG (MACKEY'S) LA 1947-48

Skippy Anderson, p; Richie Cornell, d; CHUCK MACKEY, tpt; Matty Matlock, cl; Floyd O'Brien, tbn; Artie Shapiro, sb.
*JUMP 10, 11 (47)*

**Burr Middleton, d** *(1941 Los Angeles CA)* - Pete Daily; Great Pacific-LA; Matty Matlock; Rosy McHargue

**Velma Middleton, v** *(1917-1961 St Louis MO)* - Louis Armstrong; combos

**Bob Mielke, tbn** *(1926 San Francisco)* - Burt Bales; Barbary Coast; ldr Bearcats; [Berkeley Rhythm]; Burp Hollow; Conspiracy; Estuary; Golden Age; Golden State; Jelly Roll JB-SF; Wingy Manone; Bob Neighbor; Oakland A; [Original Inferior]; [Phrisco]; Polecats; *SF Blues Serenaders*; Bob Scobey; Sinners; Muggsy Spanier; [Speakeasy]; Joe Sullivan; led own groups

## BOB MIELKE'S JAZZ BAND SF 1949

Bill Erickson, tpt; Jack Lowe, d; BOB MIELKE, tbn; Bill Napier; John Schuller, sb; Jerrold Stanton; unknown g.

**Kent Mikasa, tpt** *(1954)* - Churchill St; Glenn Miller orch; Port City; Royal Society

**Vera Miles, v** - [Bob Scobey]

**Bernie Miller, bass** - Pete Daily

**Bill Miller, tbn** - Dr Jon

**Dick Miller, cor** *(1936 New London WI) film producer/director* - Good Time; Jazzin' Babies; Rosy McHargue

**Earl Miller, reeds** - Cell Block; Dixieland Syncopators

**Eddie Miller, reeds** *(1911 New Orleans LA)* - Louis Armstrong; Marvin Ash; Bauduc-Lamare; [Heinie Beau]; Bob Crosby; Pete Fountain; Levee Loungers; Wingy Manone; Mound City Blueblowers; Red Nichols; Pete Kelly Big 7; Ben Pollack; Rampart St; Jack Teagarden; led own groups, a principal one of which was formed from Crosby Bob Cats (42); studios and rec. *Metronome* poll winner 39-40, *Down Beat* poll 40, Jazz Forum "Jazzman Of the Year" 81; comp *March of the Bob Cats*
    *BLUE ANGEL 509 "A Portrait of Eddie" (68); CAP 170, 10023, 10040, 40039; CORAL CRL757502 "With a Little Help From My Friend Pete Fountain"; JUMP 5, 16; TOPS L1571*

**Ken Miller, tbn** - Duwamish; Saints

ABE MOST May 1982                       EDDIE MILLER May 1979

**Paul Miller, g** - Jack Sheedy

**Ben Milliken, d** *(1916 St Louis MO)* - Milneburg; [Nightblooming]; Orange Pealers; Workingman

**Gary Milliken, reeds** - Apex

**Ralph Milling, bjo, g** *(Selma AL) insurance* - Desert City

**Bob Mills, bjo** - Hot Frogs

**"Dutch" Mills, reeds** - Blue Fox; Glen Gray; Ray Noble

## MILNEBURG CHAMBER ENSEMBLE LA 1976-78

Formed from WORKINGMAN'S 5 + 1, two years at Bellflower Eagles Club. Also NEW MILNEBURG CHAMBER ENSEMBLE after Cornell's death; evolved after breakup into GOOD TIME GROUP.

ZULU BALL, tu; CARL CORNELL, cor (-77); Dick Doner, tbn (-77); Harry Hall, p (-77); Ben Milliken, d (-78); Wayne Schmus, cl; ADD: Norm Burnham, p (77); Dan Comins, cor (77); Rick Holzgrafe, tbn (77-78); Hank McKee, bjo (77-78); Robbie Rhodes, p (77-78); Ted Thomas, cor (77-78); Dick Williams, cor (78); Larry Wright, p (78).

**Peter Milner, bjo** *teacher* - Tuleburg

**Johnny Mince (Muenzenberger), reeds** *(1912 Chicago Heights IL)* - Jimmy Dorsey; Tommy Dorsey; Glenn Miller; Ray Noble; studios; featured on Arthur Godfrey tv show in late '50s

**Jack Minger, tpt** *(1925 Los Angeles CA)* - Burt Bales; [Burp Hollow]; Casa Bonita; Golden Age; Kid Ory; Wally Rose; Jack Sheedy; owned *The Cellar* in SF (56).

**Chuck Minogue, d** - Tailgate Ramblers

**"Red" Minor (Minor Robinson), d** *(1920 Port Arthur TX)* - Roger Jamieson

**Ron Minshall, tbn** *(1935 Wallasey ENGLAND)* tv tech - Grand Dominion; Phoenix

**Jorge Mirkin, reeds** *(1924 Buenos Aires ARGENTINA) draftsman* - Fullertowne; Jamboree Hal; King Zulu

## MISS-BEHAVIN' JAZZ BAND Irvine CA 1985→

Chuck Anderson, tbn (alt); John Chessell, bjo; Dave Daniels, tbn (alt); Bill Mitchell, p; FRED MONTGOMERY, d; Mike Olson, cl/sax (-85); Bryan Shaw, tpt; Dan Zeilinger, tpt/tu. ADD: John Smith, ssax (85→).

## MISSISSIPPI MUDDERS Costa Mesa CA 1983-84

FRANK AMOSS, d; Leigh Downs, v; George Gibbs, tbn; John Henderson, tpt; Vic Loring, bjo; Jim Ogden, tu; Dave Rollin, sax; Wayne Songer, cl.

**Bill Mitchell, p** *(1924 Whittier CA) teacher, writer* - Back Bay; Bienville; [Billy Bachelors]; Bill Carter; Costa Del Oro; Crown City; Dixie Rhythm Ramblers; Down Home; El Dorado-LA; French Quarter; Roger Jamieson; Miss-Behavin'; Orange Blossom; co-fdr Maple Leaf Club

*ETHLYN 1750 "Ragtime Recycled" (71); EUPHONIC ESR1203 "Vintage Piano" (1 side 65); = ESR1225 "Echoes Of Chicago" (84)*

ELAINE MITCHELL (with Frank Haggerty) May 1975

**Elaine Mitchell, p, v** *(1922 Marquette NB)* - Angel City; solo; led own combos

## ELAINE MITCHELL AND HER ESCORTS LA 1981-84

Ed Anderson, tbn; Bob Higgins, tpt; Danny Kenyon, sb; ELAINE MITCHELL, p/v; Peppy Prince, d; Les Robinson, asax; Wayne Songer, cl.

**Gordon Mitchell, p, tbn** *(1912-1981 South Haven MI) engr supplies* - Angel City; ldr Crown City; ldr Resurrection; to CA 35; pres LA Astronomical Society

**Dick Mix, tbn** - ldr Dr Mix; Gas House; Sugar Willie; Trumbo

**Howard Miyata, bass, tbn** *(1956 Campbell CA) music teacher* - Monterey Bay Classic; NO Syncopators; Royal Society; Seaside Syncopators

**Vincent Moats, reeds** - Live Steam

## MONARCH JAZZ BAND LA 1985→

George Andrus, d; LANCE BULLER, tpt/tbn; Bill Cooper, sb; Andrew Fielding, p; Scotty Plummer, bjo; Jim Smale, tbn; Jeffrey Walker, cl.

**Paul Monat, cor** - Uptown Lowdown; Yankee Rhythm Kings (MA)

**Ron Monk, p** *(1939 Wenatchee WA) US Post Office* - Tri-City; solo

## MONROVIA OLD STYLE JAZZ BAND Monrovia CA 1983→

An offshoot of Probert's AMBULANCE CHASERS. Interesting is that several of the members came from rock and country groups to discover jazz more to their liking.

Wayne Allwine, d; Jack Faul, bjo; Ralph Hall, tu; Gordon Lutz, tbn; Joe Parker, cor; GEORGE PROBERT, reeds; Frank Thomas, p. ADD: Ham Carson, reeds; Sheryl Greenwood, v; Steve Hope, tbn; Garth Rodriguez, xyl.

**Dick Monsey, bjo, g** *(1933 Portland OR)* - Jim Beatty

**Bill Montague, reeds** *(Phoenix AZ)* - [Desert City]; Port City

**Bob Montalvo, tpt** - Powell St

## MONTEREY BAY CLASSIC JASS BAND Monterey 1974→

Originally named SOUTH BAY CLASSIC JB. Staging was unusual with stand-up brass and reeds in back, behind seated rhythm section.

Harry Campbell, bjo; Dave Cotter, bjo; Dick Eckhart, tu; FRANK GOULETTE, cor; Bruce Huddleston, p (-74); Ernie Landes, tbn; Louis Rale, cl (-79); Howard Miyata, tu (85→); Wally Trabing, d. ADD: Herb Buck, p; Bob Hanscom, p (85→); Dave Richoux, tu (83→); Earl Scheelar, cl (79→); Frank Tateosian, bjo.

## MONTEREY BAY STOMPERS Monterey 1977-78

NED BRUNDAGE, d; Jim DeNoon, sb/viol; Dick Dotts, p; John Fanning, vib; Joe Ingram, tpt; Al Ring, tbn; Bill Van den Burg, g.

**Dave Montgomery, tbn** - New Black Eagles (MA); Phoenix

**Fred Montgomery, d** *(1929 Pittsburgh PA) construction* - Dixie Rhythm Ramblers; ldr Miss-Behavin'

**Steve Montgomery, d** - Pete Kelly

**John Moore, bass, tbn** *(1941 San Francisco CA) photographer* - Golden Age; Oakland A; SF Brass; Tappers; Young Audiences

**Ron Moore, bass** *(1958 Castro Valley CA) cabinetmaker* - Rent Party; Sticks Strings

**Monette Moore, v** - Old Standard

**Sarah Moore, wb** *(1958 Concord CA)* - Rent Party; marr Ron Moore

**Tom Moore, bjo** - Jelly Roll JB-SF; Knights of Camelot

**Harry Mordecai, bjo** *(1918 San Francisco CA) electrician* - Alexander's; Turk Murphy; Yerba Buena

**Phil More, p** - Shakey City

**Rollie Morehouse, reeds** - Don Anderson; Great Excelsior; Uptown Lowdown

**Hal Moreno, p** *(1919 Palo Alto CA) computer tech* - Gem City

**Scott Moreno, d** - Riverboat Ramblers

**Al Morgan, bass** *(1908 New Orleans LA)* - Eddie Condon; Dixie Flyers; Fate Marable; Fats Waller

**Mark Morin, bass** - Blue St

**Lori Moritz, p** - Jazz Minors

**"Skip" Morr (Charles W Coolidge), tbn** *(1912-1962 Chicago IL)* - Charlie Barnet; [Sidney Bechet]; Wingy Manone; Marty Marsala; Artie Shaw; Muggsy Spanier; studios

**Adolphus "Dolph" Morris, bass** *(1915 Social Circle GA)* - Angel City; Blueblowers; Roger Jamieson; Legends of Jazz; Party Peppers; Royal Gardens; [Yankee Wailers]; Young Men From NO

**Steve Morris, d** *machinist* - Desert City

**Charles Morressey, cor** - Royal Society

**Henry "Benny" Morton, tbn** *(1907-1975 New York NY)* - Count Basie; Benny Carter; Wild Bill Davison; Edmond Hall; Fletcher Henderson; Ben Pollock; Joe Sullivan; Chick Webb; Teddy Wilson; World's Greatest JB; led own groups; spent considerable time on West Coast although principally an Eastern musician

**John Mosher, bass** - Benny Goodman; Nob Hill

**Edgar Mosley, d** *(1895-1962 Algiers LA)* - Papa Celestin; Bunk Johnson; orig Chris Kelly (NO); George Lewis; Old Standard; Resurrection; So Bay

**George Mosse, reeds** - Silver Stope; music major SMU

**Abe Most, reeds** *(1920 New York NY)* - Les Brown; Bob Crosby; Wild Bill Davison; Tommy Dorsey; [Bob Scobey]; World's Greatest JB; led own groups; studios
*ANNUNCIATA AR1051 "The Most"; LIBERTY 6004 "Mr Clarinet"*

## THE MOULDY FYGGES see CRESCENT BAY

**Monte Mountjoy, d** *(1912 Roundup MT)* - Banjo Kings; Blueblowers; Firehouse 5 + 2

**Al Moyle, tpt** - Aristocrats

**Johnny Moyle, tbn** - Aristocrats

**Tim Moynahan, tbn** - Lemon St

**Steve Mraz, tpt** - Side St

**John A Muchow, d** - Jamboree Hal

## MUDDY RIVER JAZZ BAND PTL

Jim Buchmann, cl; Jim Goodwin, cor; Don Kennedy, bjo; Ed Sabrowsky, bjo; Archie Thomas, tbn; Axel Tyle, d.

## MUD FLAT FIVE Berkeley 1950-1954

Predecessor of BUENA VISTA JB.

Joe Bithell, tu; HERB BUCK, p; Gene Maurice, cor; Dudley Stone, d; Al Villaire, ssax.

## MUDVILLE'S FINEST Stockton 1977-1979

Also titled MUDVILLE VALLEY CATS.

Joe Brown, p; Dave Geolecke, tpt (-77); Sonny Lowe, g (-77); ART NIELSEN, tsax (-78); BILL RENWICK, d (ldr 79); Brian Shanley, cl (-78); Buddy Walters, tbn; Ray Walters, sb (-78). ADD: Howie Berry, cl (79); Deck Hogin, tpt (79); Gene Lancelle, tpt (78); Hap Penny, sax (79); Jim Steffan, g (77-78); Bobby Travis, g (78); Ralph Webster, tpt; Russ Wray, sb (79).

**Bill Mulhern, p** *(1922 Oakland CA)* - Canal St

**Tom Mullinix, tpt** - Balboa JB

**Walter Murden, drums** - NO Creole Gumbo

**Don Murphie, tbn** *music teacher* - Hume St; Royal Bourbon St

**Bob Murphy, reeds** *(1936 Summit NJ) attorney* - Natural Gas

**Charles "Red" Murphy, g** *(1908-1981)* - Angel City; memorial annual scholarship in his name by Santa Clarita Dixieland Jazz Club

**Ken Murphy, d** - Dixiecrats

**Marge Murphy, v** *(1918 Chicago IL)* - Angel City

**Melvin "Turk" Murphy, tbn** *(1914 Palermo CA)* - Bunk Johnson; [Wingy Manone]; Benny Strickler; Yerba Buena; led own groups; prolific song comp and arr. Honored by SF Mayor Joseph Alioto proclaming 15 Mar 74 "Turk Murphy Day;" subject of comprehensive bio *Just For the Record* (Jim Goggin 82)

## TURK MURPHY JAZZ BAND SF 1948→

The original name BAY CITY STOMPERS was dropped on the advice of Les Koenig, owner of Good Time Jazz records, who felt that Murphy's name would be more recognizable. Featured in film *Good Neighbor Sam* (64); considerable radio and tv. Despite continual personnel turnover, typical of bands with such demanding schedules, Murphy managed to retain a fingerprint in the overall sound, due in the main to his rigid structuring of the basic group, which provided room for personal creativity, and by developing his own library of ensemble arrangements. Many subsequent jazz bands followed this approach, as they did that of the Yerba Buena JB, establishing credence in the "Lu Watters-Turk Murphy style" as a "West Coast" form of jazz. *Club Hangover* (49), *Round-Up* Albany (50), *Italian Village* (52-54), *Tin Angel* (54-58), *Easy Street* (58), *Earthquake McGoon's Evans Hotel* (60-61), *McGoon's Clay St* (61-78), *McGoon's Rathskellar* (78); *McGoon's Embarcadero* (78-82),

*McGoon's Pier 39* (82-84); Fairmont Hotel (84→). Toured extensively worldwide and became so much a part of the SF scene that *McGoon's* was included on tour-bus itineraries.

Burt Bales, p (-50); Bob Helm, cl (-50,51-55,59-65,72-81); Dick Lammi, tu/sb (-50,55-60); Harry Mordecai, bjo (50); TURK MURPHY, tbn; Bob Scobey, tpt (-50). ADD: Skippy Anderson, p (50); George Baker, bjo (61); Monte Ballou, bjo (54); Johnny Brent, d (51); George Bruns, tu/sb (50-51); Bill Carroll, tu (65→); Jack Carroll, tpt (60); Ernie Carson, tpt (61); Bill Carter, cl (55); Pete Clute, p (55-83); Al Conger, tu (57-58); Larry Conger, tpt (57-58); Freddie Crewes, tu; Jack Crook, cl (58,65-70); Bill Dart, d (52); Don Ewell, p (52); Doc Evans, cor (55); Ev Farey, tpt (54); John Gill, cl/ss (78), bjo (79→); Squire Girsback, tu/sb (50,63-65); Dick Hadlock, cl (58); Frank Haggerty, bjo (63-66); Clancy Hayes, bjo/v (52,65); Darnell Howard, cl (52); Phil Howe, c/ssax (70-72); Jack Howell, p (51); Ed Johnson, tpt (67); Don Kinch, tpt (50-53); Carl Lunsford, bjo (60,71-78); Jim Maihack, tu (69-71); Bill Napier, cl (50-51,57-58); Bill Newman, bjo/g (50); Bob Neighbor, tpt (63-64); Leon Oakley, cor (69-79); Pat Patton, bjo (50-52); Wally Rose, p (52-55); Bob Schulz, tpt (79→); Bob Short,tpt/tu (52-55,59-63); Ray Skjelbred, p (83→); Dick Speer, bjo (70); Jimmy Stanislaus, v (72-80); Smokey Stover, d (67-70); Stan Ward, d (51); Homer Welch, d (58); Thad Wilkerson, d (55-59,60); Harry Witczek, sb (57); Pat Yankee, v (57→); Lynn Zimmer, cl (83-85).

ABC 591 *"Clancy Hayes Live at McGoon's"* (66); ATLANTIC SD1613 *"Many Faces of Ragtime"* (72); COL CL546 *"When the Saints Go Marching In"* (53); = CL559 *"Jelly Roll Morton"* (53); = CL595 *"Barrelhouse Jazz"* (53); = CL650 (54); = CL793 *"New Orleans Festival"* (55); = CL927 (56); DC 2015 *"Live at Dawn Club, Vol 1"* (58); = 12018 *"do. Vol 2"*; = 12019 *"do. Vol 3"* (58); FAIRMONT F111 *"Live From the Cinegrill"* (50); = F112 *"do. Vol 2"* (50); GHB 91 *"In Concert, Vol 1"* (72); = 92 *"do. Vol 2"* (72); = 93 *"do. Vol 3"* (72); GTJ LP3 (53); = LP4 *"Turk Murphy's JB"* (49); = LP5 *"do. Vol 2"* (50); = LP7 *"do. Vol 3"* (50); = LP18 *"do. Vol 4"* (51); JAZZ & JAZZ YPRX2137 *"Chattanooga Stomp"*; = 6357903 *"Oz Turk"* (78); = 6437157 *"Ragged But Right"* (81); JM 31, 32 (47) (first recs); MMRC 105 *"Turk Murphy's JB"*; = 106 *"do. Vol 2"* (71); = 114 *"SF Jazz"* (84); MOTHERLODE M103 *"Turk Murphy's JB Vol 1"* (67); = M104 *"do. Vol 2"* (67); MPS G22097 *"Heidelberg"* (73); ROULETTE R25076 *"At the Roundtable"* (59); = R25088 *"Music for Wise Guys & Boosters"* (59); SONIC ARTS 14 *"Turk Murphy JB"* (79); VERVE MGV1013 *"Music For Losers"* (57); = MGV1015 *"Easy Street"* (58); = MGV8232 (57); SOLO S107 *"Turk Murphy's Frisco Band 58"* (58); VIC LPM2501 (61)

**Max Murray, reeds** - Blueblowers; Crown City; King Zulu; Mardi Gras-LA; Rosy McHargue

**Bill Myers, tpt** *(1923 Chattanooga TN) accountant* - Jazz Formula; Jelly Roll Jazz Society; Smogville

**Frank Myers, bass** - Easy Winners; Gold Standard; Old Sacramento

**Chuck Myrick, reeds** - Duwamish

## MYSTERY PACIFIC JAZZ BAND SF

Title used by Dick Hadlock for various bands employing most Bay Area jazzmen at one time or another, mainly for casual engagements.

TURK MURPHY JAZZ BAND October 1983

TURK MURPHY and PAT YANKEE May 1984

DEAN NELSON April 1980

JOHN NELSON (with Art Dragon, Gene O'Neill) Oct 1980

# N

**Glen Nakahara, tpt** *(1958 Garden Grove CA) student* - Lemon St

**Brian Nalepka, bass** - Lakeshore

## NAPA VALLEY JAZZ BAND Calistoga CA 1983→

Lori Catania, v; Jack Crook, reeds (-84); Bob Evans, tpt; Bob Hinman, sb; TED KOHLER, p; Bob Ohnhaus, tbn (-85); Bob Ulsh, d. ADD: Phil Smith, cl (84→).

**Bill Napier, reeds** *(1926 Asheville NC)* - Barbary Coast; [Bay City]; Bearcats; Jack Buck; Burp Hollow; Conspiracy; [Delta Jazz]; Dixieland Rhythm Kings (OH); Don Ewell (DC); Golden Age; Golden State; Magnolia; Wingy Manone; Marty Marsala; Turk Murphy; Oakland A; Kid Ory; Pier 23; Polecats; Powell St; Bob Scobey; Jack Sheedy; Joe Sullivan-SF; Young Audiences; led own groups. Serious injuries from an auto accident kept him out of playing late 64 to early 66

## BILL NAPIER TRIO SF 1948-69

Many groups were fronted by Napier, trios to quintets for the main, the first one playing at *Tin Angel*:

Bill Erickson, p; BILL NAPIER, cl; Bob Storm, d. ADD: Ken Peterson, sb (48).

**Bob Nash, bjo** - Camellia

## NATURAL GAS JAZZ BAND San Rafael CA 1970→

A group of professional men who successfully captured the Watters-Murphy style. Crumley assumed leadership 72. Steady at *Alvarado Inn* (76→); toured extensively, including Great Britain, Europe and Japan.

Earl Burgess, tbn (-71); PHIL CRUMLEY, cor (70→); Bill Finke, p (-73); Dave Lewis, tu (70→); Bob Murphy, cl/ssax (70→); BUD WEDEN, bjo (-72). ADD: Pete Deetken, bjo (72→); Bob Franklin, p (78-79); John Hartman, tbn (71-83); Don Keeler, p (78-79); Carl Lunsford, bjo (alt 85→); Al McDearmon, p (79→); Warren Perry, d (73→); Tom Small, tbn (83→); Jim Whiteside, p (73-78).

*CLAMBAKE C218 "Jubilee By the Sea" (80 1 cut); NATURAL GAS KQR141 "Natural Gas, Vol 1" (75); = KQR142 "do. Vol 2" (77); = KQR143 "Plays the San Francisco Jazz of Watters & Murphy"; = CR144 "Highlights of Juneau Centennial" (80); =JTS "With George Probert" (82); SJS 27 "Jumpin' Jubilee Jazz" (81 1 cut)*

## NATURALLY FERMENTED JAZZ BAND SF c1984

MARC MARCUS, cl; others unknown.

**Dick Neary, g** - Dr Mix

**Don Neely, reeds** *(1952 Fresno CA)* - Churchill St; ldr Royal Society; Seaside Syncopators

**Bob Neighbor, flug, tpt** *(1937 Oakland CA) graphic artist* - Bay City; Jack Buck; Golden Age; Golden Gate Rhythm Machine; Jazz Cardinals; Jelly Roll JB-SF; Turk Murphy; Oakland A; Phrisco; Tappers; Young Audiences; led own groups

## BOB NEIGHBOR JAZZ BAND SF 1979

Typical of several bands under this name in the '70s.

Dan Barrett, tbn; Dick Hadlock, cl; Jeff Hamilton, d; Laurie Lewis, sb; BOB NEIGHBOR, tpt; Dick Oxtot, bjo. ADD: Jim Cumming, sb.

**Jeff Neighbor, bass** *(1942 Grand Coulee WA)* - Barney Kessel; [Nob Hill]; Bill Watrous; Kai Winding

**Bob Neisinger, d** *head of college music dept* - Hume St

**Dean Nelson, tpt** *(1938 Portland OR) construction* - All-Army JB; ldr Fulton St; master's degree in music

**Don Nelson, reeds** - Great Pacific-LA

**John Nelson, p** - Gramercy 6

**John Nelson, viol** - Dixie Katz

**Richard "Cougar" Nelson, tbn** - Mickey Finn

**Louis Nelson, tbn** *(1903-19— New Orleans LA)* - Legends of Jazz; Preservation Hall (NO); orig Tuxedo Band (NO)

**Al Nersesian, d** *(1927 Detroit MI) sales mgr* - Bourbon St 5; Bob Crosby; Live Steam; Lucky Lady

**Sanford "Mick" Newbauer, tbn** *(1929)* - co-ldr Bay City; ldr Canal St; Great Pacific-SF

## NEW BAY CITY JAZZ BAND SF 1975

John Boland, cl; Lloyd Byassee, d; EV FAREY, cor; Don Keeler, p; Bob Neighbor, cor; Sanford Newbauer, tbn; Lee Valencia, bjo; Walt Yost, tu.

## NEW BULL MOOSE PARTY BAND LA ?→

Les Deutsch, p/tpt; Lew Forrest, d; Alex Hunter, cl; Harry Kooperstein, tpt; GEORGE MAROIS, cor; Fran Marois, v (-83); Mike Marois, tu. ADD: Charlie Aimo, tpt; John Bishop, g; Norm Burnham, p; Tom Ewing, d; Phil Gwinn, tbn; Bill Jackson, tbn; Kermit Welch, reeds.

**Herb Newell, reeds** - Feather Riverboat

## NEW IMPERIAL JAZZ EAGLES LA c1957-62

Wes Grant, tpt; ETHEL HIETT, p; others unknown.

**Bill Newman, bjo, g** - Abalone; Alexander's; Blueblowers; Dixie Flyers; Firehouse 5 + 2; Mel Henke; Magnolia; Matty Matlock; Turk Murphy; [Kid Ory]; Plum Forest

**Bill Newman, reeds** *construction supply* - Royal Bourbon St

**Bob Newman, reeds** *(1923 Tacoma WA) engr* - Fulton St

## NEW ORLEANS CREOLE GUMBO ZOUAVE LA 1982

Bob Allen, tpt; BUDDY BURNS, sb; Earnest McLean, bjo/g; Walter Murden, d; Jack Widmark, cl; George Williams, p; Burt Wilson, tbn.

## NEW ORLEANS HOUSE JB see FUNKY NOJB

BOB NEWMAN and SKEETS HERFURT May 1974

## NEW ORLEANS JAZZ BAND OF HAWAII Honolulu 1973→

"The only jazz band in the mid-Pacific area," according to Norris. When Trummy Young disbanded his All-Stars, which had been playing at Hilton Hawaiian since 66, Norris, Young's trumpet man, took over the group and renamed it. Played weekends at Hilton since 73, weeknights at Hyatt Regency Waikiki since 79.

Mark Hammond, bjo; John Jestice, cl/sax; JOHN NORRIS, cor; John Rasnur, d; Paul Reid, p (-74); Don Remine, tbn; Sydette Sakauye, v; Ed Shonk, sb; Ricardo Tolentino, p (74→); David Yap, sb (alt).

*WAIKIKI WJR6944 "Trappers" (81)*

## NEW ORLEANS RASCALS (BOB NEIGHBOR'S) SF c1968

Pete Berg, g; Vince Cattolica, cl; Ron Crotty, sb; Bob Mielke, tbn; BOB NEIGHBOR, tpt; Ben Randall, d; Jack Stewart, p.

## NEW ORLEANS SYNCOPATORS SJ 1985→

Bill Bardin, tbn; Sue Kroninger, v; Howard Miyata, tbn/tu; Earl Scheelar, cor/cl; Eric Siverson, cor/sax; Karl Walterskirchen, bjo.

## NEWPORT SUMMIT JAZZ BAND Newport Beach CA c1979

SCOTT CHAPMAN, p; Mike Holland, tbn; Roland Kim, sb; Bryn Mathieu, d; Teddy Ono, tpt; Frank Sano, d; Bryan Williams, cl/sax; Tom Zusag, bjo.

## NEW RAGTIME 3 + 2 + 1 see DR JON'S

**Les Newstrom, d** - Pier 100

**Lionel Newton, bass** - Oregon

## NEW WASHBOARD RHYTHM KINGS SF c1974

Pete Allen, sb; MANNY FUNK, wb; Dick Hadlock, cl; Jack Knox, g; Bert Noah, tsax; Ray Skjelbred, p; Larry Stein, tpt.

**Eric Nicoll, d** - Abalone

**Albert Nicholas, reeds** *(1900-1973 New Orleans LA)* - Andy Blakeney; Sidney Bechet; Jelly Roll Morton; King Oliver; Kid Ory; Luis Russell; [Bob Scobey]; to CA 49, France 53

**Wayne Nicholls, bjo, g** *(1947 San Jose CA) news photog* - Pismo; Rent Party; WFDJE&MKRB

**Ernest "Red" Nichols, cor** *(1905-1965 Ogden UT)* - led own groups (Charleston Chasers, Five Pennies, Redheads, etc); to CA 46. Subject of a "Hollywoodized" biographical film *The Five Pennies* (59), with Danny Kaye playing the part of Nichols, which accounted in part for a rebirth in his perdurable popularity. Also appeared as himself in *The Gene Krupa Story* (59)

## RED NICHOLS AND HIS FIVE PENNIES LA-SF 1945-65

Long-term engagements at *Club Morocco, Playroom* LA and *Club Hangover* SF, plus much touring both in the USA and overseas.

> *CAP; CORAL "Red Nichols and His Five Pennies"*

**Art Nielsen, reeds** *(19—1984)* - ldr Mudville

**Howard Nielson, bjo** - Jazzbo

## NIGHTBLOOMING JAZZMEN see CRESCENT BAY

## NIGHTBLOOMING JAZZMEN Claremont CA 1975→

House band for the Society for the Preservation of Dixieland Jazz, became immensely popular with their light and inventive approach to jazz. Much concert work and touring in USA and Europe.

George Anderson, cl (-79); Cliff Beard, p (-77); Charles Coulter, tbn (-78); Tommy Hearn, bjo; CHET JAEGER, cor; George Olson, sb; Tom Raftican, d. ADD: Kay Blanchard, cl

NIGHTBLOOMING JAZZMEN May 1980
Jenkins, Olson, Martinez, Jaeger, Huff, Hearn

(81-82); Dick Doner, tbn (79→); Morey Huff, p (77→); Al Jenkins, tbn (78-79); Willie Martinez, cl (79-81); Pieter Meijers, cl (82→).

*AMERITONE A1364 "More Bloomin' Jazz!" (80); CLAMBAKE C218 "Jubilee By the Sea" (80 1 cut); NBJ 2 "Sing Your Favorite Hymns" (81); =3 "And the Walls Came Tumbling Down" (82); =4 "And They Called It Dixieland" (83); =5 "Stars & Jazz Forever" (83); PHYLCO PA00132 "Tunes We Played In Sacramento" (77)*

**Gene Nilsen, reeds** - Sounds of Dixieland

**Tim Nitz, p** *(1966 Chicago IL) student* - Lemon St

**Dudley Nix, d** - Abalone

**Bert Noah, reeds** *(19—19—)* - Berkeley Rhythm; New Washboard RK; Phrisco; Rose & Thistle

**Don Noakes, bass, tbn** *(19—19—)* - Polecats; Yerba Buena

## NOB HILL GANG SF 1973→

Steady at Fairmont Hotel (76→).

George Butterfield, sb; Jerry Butzen, tbn (-85); Vince Cattolica, cl (-84); JIMMY DI-AMOND, p; Johnny Markham, d; Buddy Powers, tpt. ADD (frequent subs): Sammy Blank, tbn; Waldo Carter, tpt; Ernie Figueroa, tbn/tpt; Phil Howe, cl/ssax; John Mosher, sb; Jeff Neighbor, sb; Bob Schulz, tpt; Mike Starr, tbn.

*NHG "Nob Hill Gang" (74)*

**Chris Noel, bass** *(CANADA)* - 5 Guys Named Moe

**Ira Noel, p** - Riverboat Ramblers

**Garry Noel, bass** *asst store mgr* - ldr Hume St; ldr Royal Bourbon St

**Jimmy Noone Jr, reeds** - Cottonmouth; Creole Sunshine; son of legendary NO clarinetist

**Ray Nordahl, bass** *(1923 MT)* - Gem City

**Bob Noren, reeds** - Aristocrats

**John Noreyko, bass** *(1963 Chicago IL)* - Side St; symphony orchs

**Bob Norman** *teacher* - led own group

**Carla Normand (Neely), v** *(1953 St Louis MO)* - Royal Society; marr Don Neely

**Chris Norris, v** *(1953 Tacoma WA) prof of English Literature* - Cottonmouth; Golden Eagle; San Juan

**John Norris, cor** *(1916 Wallace WV) music teacher* - ldr NOJB Hawaii; Trummy Young

**Art Nortier, p** - Bay City; [Delta Jazz]; Original Inferior; Phrisco; Sinners

**Nile Norton, bass, d** *(1941 IL)* - [Gem]

## THE NOTE-ABLES LA 1984→

No leader since they stated "they do everything by committee."

Jim Bates, sb; Fred Baumberger, g; Don Dupree, reeds; Ted Higgins, d; Max Horton, p (-85); Joe Rucker, tpt; Bill Waters, tbn. ADD: Tom Tonyan, p (85→).

**Les Nunes, tbn** - Live Steam

**Ray Nutaitis, bass** *(1940 PA) realtor* - Desert City; symphony orchs

LEON OAKLEY and DAN COMINS October 1978

# O

**Patti Ann Oakes, v** - Platinum; marr Phil Oakes

**Phil Oakes, tbn** - ldr Platinum; Woodi's

## OAKLAND A's JAZZ BAND Oakland CA 1969→

Group formed to play for that baseball team's home games varied considerably over the years, dependent upon members who worked with other bands. Began as a quartet and expanded from that as was necessary.

Bob Helm, cl (-73); Bob Mielke, tbn; Bob Neighbor, tpt (-72,74→); Dick Oxtot, bjo. ADD: Squire Girsback, tu (70-71); Jim Goodwin, tpt (72-74); John Moore, tbn (71→); Bill Napier, cl (73→). SUBS: Bill Bardin, tbn; Norm Bates, tu; Ed Blanchard, tu; Peewee Claybrook, tsax; Ev Farey, tpt; Ernie Figueroa, tpt/tbn; Jack Frost, bjo; Dick Hadlock, cl; Randy Johnson, bjo; Buddy Powers, tpt; Brian Richardson, tbn; Jim Rothermel, cl; Ray Skjelbred, tbn; Mike Starr, tbn; Bob Stowell, tsax; Walt Yost, tu.

## OAKLAND HOT BABIES Oakland ?-1978

Disbanded when Vermazen organized CHRYSANTHEMUM.

Pete Allen, sb; Bill Bardin, tbn; Manny Funk, d; Dick Hadlock, sb; Al Hall, tbn; Marc Marcus, cl; BRUCE VERMAZEN, cor.

**Leon Oakley, cor** *(1940 Carbondale PA) electrical engr* - Jack Buck; [Delta Jazz]; ldr *Flaming Deuces*; Jelly Roll JB-SF; ldr *Lakeshore Serenaders*; Turk Murphy; Royal Society; So Frisco; Speakeasy

**James O'Banlon, tpt** - Swipsey

**Al Obidinski, bass** - Chet Baker; Stan Getz; Sweet & Hot

**James "Bunny" O'Brien, d** - Polecats

**Floyd O'Brien, tbn** *(1904 Chicago IL)* - Bob Cats; Chicago Loopers; Gene Krupa; Wingy Manone; *Michigan Blvd*; Jack Teagarden

**Ken O'Brien, tbn** *music teacher* - Calif Express; music degree at Stanford

**Kyle O'Brien, reeds** - Jazzin' Jrs

**Pat "Hotz" O'Casey, reeds** - Alexander's

**Alan O'Dea, bass** *(1947 Carmel CA)* - Abalone; Ernie Carson

**Dick O'Dette, d** *(Lansing MI) antique car restorer* - Desert City

**Hugh O'Donnell, d** *(1957 Oceanside CA)* - Jubilee

**Jim Oerman, d** - Bourbon St DJB

**Marilyn Ogburn, p** - Pete Kelly

**Jim Ogden, tpt, bass** - Dixie Katz; King Zulu; Mississippi

**Brian Ogilvie, reeds** - Phoenix; Westside Feetwarmers

**Rod Ogle, tbn** - Jamboree Hal

**Betty O'Hara, tbn, tpt** - Bob Crosby; ldr Maiden Voyage; Billy Vaughn

**Lueder Ohlwein, bjo** *(1937-1982 Gladbeck GERMANY) woodcarver* - ldr Jazzberry; [Royal Gardens]; *SF Blues Serenaders*; ldr Sunset Music; fdr High Sierra Jazz Club

**Bob Ohnhaus, tbn** *(1927 Kansas City MO) safety engr* - Rosy McHargue; Napa Valley; Pismo; WFDJE&MKRB

**Larry Okmin, reeds** - Charlie's; So Market St

**Phil Olander, bass** - Emperor Norton

**John Olbrich, bass, tbn** - Dr Mix; Sugar Willie

## OLD PUEBLO JAZZ BAND Tucson AZ
AL SAUNDERS; Manny Treumann, cor; others unknown.

## OLD SACRAMENTO JAZZ BAND SAC 1977-79
Re-formed into GOLD STANDARD MUSIC CO.
Jim Bartolotto, tpt (77,79); GEORGE BRUNO, reeds (77,79) ldr (77); Bob Cardoza, p (77); Frank Caughman, tbn (-78); Jim Hopperstad, sb/tu (77-78); PETE SALERNO, d (77-79) ldr (78-79). ADD: Joe Audino, p (79); Gene Berthelsen, cor (79); Pat Canosa, tpt (78); Charlie Hull, cl/tsax (78-79); Bill Johnson, p (78); Frank Myers, sb (79).

## OLD STANDARD JAZZ BAND LA 1960
*Green Bull* Hermosa Beach.
Bob Law, p; Johnny Lucas, tpt; Edgar Moseley, d; Monette Moore, v; Johnny St Cyr, bjo; Jim Sheldon, tbn; Jack Widmark, cl.

**Pete O'Leary, bjo** - Crescent Bay; Impossible

**Richard Olsen, reeds** - Powell St

LUEDER OHLWEIN May 1974

**Vern Olsen, tbn** - La Honda

**Barney Olson, tbn** - Oversextette

## DOC OLSON'S CONVICTION see COULSON FAMILY JB

**George Olson, bass** *(1924 Alhambra CA) law enforcement* - Nightblooming

**Mike Olson, reeds** *(1952 Santa Monica CA) piano tech* - co-org Miss-Behavin'

**Rudy Onderwyzer, tbn** - Crescent Bay; ldr King JB; co-ldr Pepper

**Pat O'Neal, tbn** *(1937 MI) auto sales* - Stumptown

**Peggy O'Neil, v** - Pete Kelly

**Gene O'Neill, d** *(1931 Philadelphia PA) phys ed* - Dixie Katz; Rosy McHargue; Thee Saints; Yankee Wailers

**Teddy Ono, tpt** - Newport Summit

**Jan Oosterhof, p** - Uptown Lowdown

### ORANGE BLOSSOM JAZZ BAND Orange Co 1981-85

Title changed in Nov 85 to PARADISE HOTEL JB to avoid confusion with Orange Pealers of the same area.

Dan Comins, cor (-81); Roger Jamieson, tbn (-82); Jack Keister, cl (-82) Hank McKee, bjo; Jerry Rothschild, p (-83); FRANK SANO, d; Paul Woltz, bsax (-84). ADD: Chuck Anderson, tbn (85 alt); Jeff Beaumonte, asax/bsax/cl (84-85); Dennis Gilmore, cor (84-85); Art Levin, tu (85); Bill Mitchell, p (84-85); Bill Rosenzweig, cor (82-83); Charlie Warren, bsax (84-85); Laurence Wright, asax (85 alt).

### ORANGE COUNTY DIXIECATS Santa Ana c1969

Jack Booth, tbn; Cecil Gregg, p; Hal Groody, bjo; George Kubis, d; TOM KUBIS, cl/ssax; Bill Stumpp, tpt; Lane Vifinkle, sb.

### ORANGE EMPIRE JAZZ BAND Costa Mesa CA 1971-73

Jim Bogan, cl; Mike Fay, sb; Vic Loring, bjo; Ron Ortmann, bjo; Eric Rosenau, tbn; KEN SMITH, cor. ADD: Ron Going, cl.

DON OWENS May 1976

**ORANGE PEALERS JAZZ BAND** Huntington Beach CA 1980→

Ed Dolby, d; Bob Hazen, tpt; Jack Keister, cl/sax; Walt Malzahn, tbn; JOHN McCORMICK, cor; Hank McKee, bjo (82-83); Ben Milliken, d (83-84); Fred Palm, tu; Ken Sands, p. ADD: Frank Heuser, tu; Vic Loring, bjo (83→); John Valle-Riestra, tbn; Dan Zeilinger, d (84→).
cass "Orange Pealers JB" (85)

**OREGON JAZZ BAND** Dixonville OR 1954→

Originally titled OREGON ALL-STARS, name change came in 58. Long-running group fluctuated from combo to big-band depending upon the occasion, personnel changed considerably with each one, with many members playing intermittently over a span of years.

BILL BORCHER, tpt; Phil Brandt, tbn (-83); Dave Gentry, sb (-64); Neil Hart, d; Charlie Hawkes, cl (-63); Walt Hill, sax; Bruce Martin, p (-57); Richard Synowski, g (-56). ADD: Charley Ahrens, sb/tu (70-83); Rex Allen, tbn (rec); Joe Audino, p (74-79); Bud Baird, p (80→); Jim Beatty, cl (84→); Ken Bielman, p (57-60); Dick Burley, tbn (83-84); Carl Butte, sb (82→); Ollie Fosback, cl/ssax (71-83); Charley Hickerson, cl (64-67); Darrell Langevin, bjo/g (56-68); Jim Maihack, tbn (85); Lionel Newton, sb (65-70); Vern Pinnock, bjo/g (69-83); Chuck Ruff, p (60-74); Brian Shanley, cl (68-70); Butch Schroeder, bjo (83→).

5 45rpms (59-63); OJB 1001 "Oregon JB" (63); = 1002 "One More Time" (64); = 1003 "Euphoric Dromomania" (66); = 1004 "Enjoy Yourself" (68); = 1005 "Why Don't We Do This More Often?" (70); = 1006 "Old Sacramento" (75); = 1007 "Saloon Serenade" (78); = 1008 "Hart Mountain" (82)

**George Orendorff, tpt** (1906 Antonina GA) - [Louis Armstrong]; Louisiana Gents; Ben Pollack; Resurrection

**ORIGINAL INFERIOR JAZZ BAND** SF 1953-64

Burp Hollow (58-64), Honeybucket (53-58), Sail'N (60). Personnel fluctuated considerably and listing reflects musicians of more permanency.

Fred Bjork, tbn (-59); Lloyd Byassee, d (-56); Pete Clute, p (-55); FRANK GOULETTE, cor; Harry Ironmonger, cl (53); Frank Tateosian, cl (53); unknown sb (53). ADD: Bill Bardin, tbn (61-62); John Boland, cl/ssax (58); Bob Burkhart, d (-58); Bill Carroll, tu (61-62); Fred Crewes, p (55-57) tu (58-64); Barry Durkee, bjo (59-61); Bob Hanscom, bjo (54); Ron Hanscom, bjo (55); Don Keeler, p (55); Tony Lanphier, p (60-64); Art Nortier, p (57-60); Earl Scheelar, cl (53-58,60-64); Jim Snyder, tbn (59); Ed Sprankle, bjo (61-62); Bob Twiss, bjo (55-59); Lee Valencia, bjo (62-64); Walt Yost, tu (53-58).

**Bobby Orlando, p** - ldr Bourbon St DJB

**Doug Orr, bass** - ldr Pete Kelly

**Mike Orth, p** (1962 Sacramento CA) - Sticks Strings

**Walt Orth, bass** - King Zulu

**Ron Ortmann, bjo, p** (1931 Santa Monica CA) - Chris Kelly; ldr Crescent Bay; [Roger Jamieson]; Orange Empire; Party Peppers; Pepper; Southern Stomers; So Frisco; Smog City; Wilmington

**Edward "Kid" Ory, bass, cor, reeds, tbn** (1886-1973 La Place LA) - Louis Armstrong; Barney Bigard; Bunk Johnson; King Oliver; led own groups, which included Armstrong, Sidney Bechet, Mutt Carey, Johnny Dodds, George Lewis, Jimmie Noone, Oliver and other

KID ORY September 1965

greats of jazz. Comp *Muskrat Ramble, Ory's Creole Trombone,* others. To CA 19-25, again in 29-66, HI 66. Appeared in films *New Orleans* (47), *Crossfire* (47) and *Benny Goodman Story* (55). Prolific rec artist with Armstrong, Morton, Oliver, Luis Russell, Ma Rainey. Retired from performing 33-42 to operate commercial chicken ranch, for good in 71

## KID ORY CREOLE BAND LA-SF 1944-71

Ory was one of the first to bring jazz to the West Coast (Jelly Roll Morton and King Oliver were the others), touring and playing LA and SF 20-25, again c30-33. After becoming active once again in 43, his group alternated principally between SF (*Blanco's, Club Hangover, Green Room, NO Swing Club, On The Levee, Venus,* others) and LA (*Beverly Cavern, 400 Club, Sardi's,* others), as well as concert tours.

Mutt Carey, tpt (-47); Ed Garland, sb; Minor Hall, d; Darnell Howard, cl (-45,47); Charley Lawrence, p (-46); KID ORY, tbn; Bud Scott, g (-49). ADD: Alvin Alcorn, tpt (54-55); Byron Berry, tpt (62-63); Andy Blakeney, tpt (47-49); Wellman Braud, sb (56); Harvey O Brooks, p (53-54); Joe Darensbourg, cl (45-46,48-51); Julian Davidson, g (56); Don Ewell, p (53-54); Squire Girsback, sb (48); Phil Gomez, cl (55-56); Cedric Haywood, p (63); Bob McCracken, cl (53); Jack Minger, tpt (48); Albert Nicholas, cl; Teddy Buckner, tpt (49-54); Bill Erickson, p (59); Lloyd Glenn, p (48-53); Pops Foster, sb; Bill Napier, cl (59); Bob Osibin, d (59); Reynard Perry, tpt; George Probert, ssax (49,54-55); Lionel Reason, p (56); Walter Roberts, sb (59); R C Smith, tpt (59); Johnny St Cyr, sb; Buster Wilson, p (44-46).

*CIRCLE S11 "This Is Jazz" (47); COL CL835 "Kid Ory"; = CL6145 "Kid Ory Dixie Band"; DC 12013 "Live At the Hangover, Vol 1"; = 12014 "do. Vol 4"; = 12016 "do. Vol 2"; = 12017 "do. Vol 3"; GTJ L12004 "Kid Ory Creole Band 1954" (54); = L12008 "do. 1955" (55); = L12016 "Legendary Kid Ory 1956" (56); = L12022 "Kid Ory Creole Band 1944-45" (57); SOUNDS 1208 "At Beverly Cavern"; VAULT 9006 "Live At Rendezvous Ballroom" (47); VERVE 1014; = 1017 "Plays W C Handy"; = 8233; = 8254; = 8456 "Storyville Nights"*

**Bob Osborne, reeds** - Ponca City

**Dave Osborne, bass** - Jazz Forum

**Virginia Osburn, p** *(1918 Assumption IL)* - Dixie Jazz Bravos; Jazz Forum

**Bob Osibin, d** *(1925-1969 Davis CA)* - Kid Ory; Joe Sullivan

**Gene Oster, p** *(Long Beach CA) aerospace engr* - Hot Frogs; Jelly Roll Jazz Soc

**Emmett O'Sullivan, reeds** - Camellia; Delta King; Dixie Dissonants; Dr Mix; Riverbank

## OUTCAST EIGHT LA 1978-79

Formed out of NEW BULL MOOSE, later changed title to LITTLE BIG BAND.
Charlie Aimo, tpt; Pete Andreadis, d (78); Norm Burnham, p (-79); BILL JACKSON, tu; Fran Marois, v; George Marois, tpt (78) tbn (79); Mike Marois, tu; John Valle, tbn (78); Dean Weprin, cl. ADD: Derek Thompson, d (79)

**Dave "Bud" Ovenall, flug, tpt** *(Burlington WA) prof of psychology* - Put Anderson; Pete Kelly

## OVERSEXTETTE Newport Beach CA 1979→

Art Bjork, d; Seaton Blanco, sb; JOE HART, bjo; Barney Olson, tbn; Al Rasmussen, tpt; Laurence Wright, cl (79).

## OVER THE HILL JAZZ BAND (TOM & JERRY'S) Bend OR 1984

Doug Bray, tbn; Curt Faulkner, d; Joanne Fox, p; TOM SHELDEN, cl; John Woodruff, sb; JERRY YANHA, cor.

DICK OXTOT May 1972

**Cal Owen, bjo** - Uptown Lowdown; Yankee Rhythm Kings (MA)

**Bill Owens, d** - Easy Winners

**Don Owens, p** - Blueblowers; Pete Daily; Jack Teagarden

**Dick Oxtot, bass, bjo, cor** *(1918 SC)* - Burt Bales; Bearcats; ldr Conspiracy; Dixieland Rhythm Kings (OH); Estuary; Funky NOJB; Golden Age ldr; Golden Gate Stompers; [Gutbucket]; Bob Neighbor; Oakland A; Polecats; Powell St; *SF Blues Serenaders*; Stone Age; Young Audiences; led other groups

# P

## PADUCAH PATROL LA 1955-indef

Generally same personnel as RAMPART ST PARADERS.

*WB BS1202 "Dixieland Story" (59); = BS1262 "And They Called It Dixieland" (59); = WS1280 "4-Button Jazz" (59)*

**Jim Painter, reeds** - Dr Mix; Sutterville; Swanee's

**Joe Pal, reeds** - Pearl Pacific

**Johnny Palif, reeds** - Aristocrats

**Fred Palm, bass** - Orange Pealers

**Jacque Paquette, bjo** - Lemon St

**Bob Parker, tbn** - Joyful Noise

**Doug Parker, bjo** - Crescent Bay; Dr Mix; Down Home; Goodtime Levee; Riverbank; Stomp Aces

**Doug Parker, p** - Lloyd Arntzen

**Joe Parker, cor, eb** *(1939 San Francisco CA) sound editor* - Ambulance; Monrovia; on eb, toured with Billy Daniels, Glen Campbell, Tina Turner, Righteous Bros

**John Parker, bass** - Capitol City

**John Parker, cor** *(1926 Evanston IL) tech writer* - Barrelhouse

**Graham Parkes** *(1942 Liverpool ENGLAND) engr* - Razzmajazz

**Rich Parnell, d** - Jazz-a-Ma-Tass

## PARTY PEPPERS LA 1981→

DAVE ALLISON, bjo; Ralph Diana, bjo; Dolph Morris, sb; Ron Ortmann, p; Walt Sereth, reeds; Ken Smith, tpt.

**Marissa Pasquale, tpt** - 32nd St

**Mike Passarelli, reeds** *(1911 San Jose CA) band dir* - Gem City

**Lin Patch, reeds** *(1953 Ft Belvoir VA) music teacher* - Royal Society

**Tito Patri, bjo** *(1934) landscape architect* - Bay City; Great Pacific-SF

**Syd Pattison, reeds** *(1928 Omaha NB) dentist* - Hyperion

PAT PATTON August 1965

**James "Pat" Patton, bjo, bass** *(1904-1976 Iola KS)* - Pete Daily; ldr Frisco JB; Bunk Johnson; Marty Marsala; Turk Murphy; Red Nichols; Rose & Thistle; Jack Sheedy; Ralph Sutton; Johnny Wittwer; Yerba Buena

**Bill Paul, p** - Westside Feetwarmers

**Ernie Paul (Gallego), d** *(1918 Lindsay CA) insurance* - Dixie Unltd

**Lenny Paul, tpt** - Jamboree Hal

**Bruce Paulson, p** - Burp Hollow; Rosy McHargue

**Don Paultha, bjo** - Mickey Finn; Silver Dollar-SAC

**Bill Pavia, reeds** - Castle; Rose City Stompers

**Bert Pearl, reeds** - Jack Sheedy

## PEARL PACIFIC JAZZ BAND Alpine CA

Charlie Clark, p; Ray Conseur, d; SAMMY DAULONG, tpt; Carl Evans, tsax; Carol Fehr, bjo; John Kitzmiller, tu/sb; Joe Pal, cl.

## PEARLY BAND Disneyland 1976

Jackie Coon, flug; Bill Cooper, sb; Harry Marshall, d; Jack Martin, cl; Charlie Romero, cl (alt); Ron Rowe, p.

**Ken Pearsall, p** - Camellia

**Kurt Pearsall, tpt** - Camellia; ldr Dixie Dissonants; org Jazzin' Jrs; Sutterville; Tuleburg

**Al Pease, reeds** - Dixieland Express

**Bob Pelland, p** *(1936 Mt Vernon WA) machinery mfr* - Grand Dominion; ldr Rainier; Uptown Lowdown

**Don Pellerin, reeds** *(1924 Long Beach CA) union official* - Abalone; ldr Bye Bye Blues; Cypress; Dixieland Inc; ldr Union St; president AFM Monterey Local 616

**Erdman "Ed" Penner, bass, bsax** *(1905-1956 Rosthern CANADA) artist, writer* - Firehouse 5 + 2

**"J. B." Penney, bjo** - Aristocrats

**Shirley Pennington, bass** - Dixie Rhythm Ramblers

**Harry "Hap" Penny, reeds** - Happy Syncopators; Mudville

**Pete Pepke, tbn** - Jim Beatty

**Fred Pepper, bjo** *(NETHERLANDS)* - ldr Red Hot Peppers

## PEPPER JASS BAND LA 1954-56

Orig ldr Hildebrand dropped out to form another group and Levin and Onderwyzer took over as co-ldrs. Title came from name on Onderwyzer's tbn; *Aldo's* W Hollywood (54-55), *Playhouse* Santa Monica.

Ralph Diana, bjo; GLENN HILDEBRAND, tpt/v (-55); ART LEVIN, tu; RUDY ONDERWYZER, tbn; Ron Ortmann, p (-55); Walt Sereth, cl; Lee Wedberg, d. ADD: Al Colter, tpt; Alan Crowne, tpt; Tom Sharpsteen, cl; Dick Shooshan, p (55-56).

*EPITAPH 1 "Cakewalking Babies" (2 cuts 55)*

**Hal Peppie, tpt** - Silver Dollar-LA

**Ray Perdomo, cor** *(1937 Havana CUBA) computer operator* - Triple RRR

**Oscar Perez, tpt** *(1926 Phoenix AZ) teen supervisor* - Dixie Unltd

**Pete Perez, bass** *(1934 Lancaster CA)* - Jazz Generation

**Matt Perrine, bass** - Jazzin' Jrs

**Renard Perry, tpt** *(1937 San Antonio TX)* - Custer; Gas House; Gold Standard; Gramercy; Kid Ory-SF; Silver Dollar-SAC

**Warren Perry, d** *(1930 San Francisco CA)* - Natural Gas

**Deborah Persellin, viol** *(1951) office worker* - Chrysanthemum

**Vince Pescatore, bass** - Downey

## PETE KELLY'S BAND SEA 1979-85

No relationship to PETE KELLY'S BIG 7.

Bill Bright, p (-80,82); Bill Hobart, tpt (-79); Lynn Kronk, bjo; Al LaTourette, bjo; Steve Montgomery, d (-80); Peggy O'Neil, v; DOUG ORR, sb. ADD: Jerry Kronk, tbn; Jack Labbe, reeds (80-82); Marilyn Ogburn, p (80-82); Dave Ovenall, tpt (79-85).

## PETE KELLY'S BIG SEVEN LA 1955-indef

From *Pete Kelly's Blues*, an ambitious film (WB 55) depicting the life and times of a jazz band in the midwest during the '20s. It is generally accepted that Pete Daily was the role model. While the film itself was not a dramatic milestone (it did earn actress Peggy Lee an Oscar nomination), the music under the direction of Cathcart was most memorable.

Dick Cathcart, tpt; Jud De Naut, sb; Nick Fatool, d; Matty Matlock, cl; Eddie Miller, sax; Moe Schneider, tbn; Ray Sherman, p; George van Eps, g. ADD (rec): Morty Corb, sb. 1985 Sacramento Jubilee: Cathcart; Mahlon Clark, cl; De Naut; Bob Havens, tbn; Miller; Dick Shanahan, d; Sherman; van Eps.

*WB WS1217 "Pete Kelly Lets His Hair Down" (59)*

**Dave Peters, d** - 52nd St

**Ralph Peters, g** *actor* - Ted Vesely; Vine St

**Eric Peterson, bass** *(1966 OR) student* - Dr Jon; Portland Rose; Stumptown

**Ernie Peterson Jr, tpt** - Barrelhouse

**Gary Peterson, p** *(1934 OR) consulting engr* - Portland Rose; ldr Stumptown

**"Hoot" Peterson, tbn** - Ponca City; Woody Herman

**Ken Peterson, bass** - El Dorado-LA; French Qtr; Bill Napier

**Steve Peterson, bjo** - Royal Society

**Bob Pettingill, bass** - John McKinley

**Elroy Pettyjohn, p** - Duwamish

**Barry Phillips, bass** - orig King Riverbottom; bro of Pete Phillips

**Bob Phillips, p** *(1936 Newton NJ)* - Abalone; Broadway show bands

**Bob Phillips, bass** *(1948 Honolulu HI) plumber* - Chrysanthemum

**George Phillips, tbn** - Castle

**Pete Phillips, tbn** - orig King Riverbottom

## PHOENIX JAZZERS Vancouver BC 1975→

Formed from the "ashes" of the LIONSGATE JB, thereby reference to the legendary bird, specializing in a British trad sound.

Everett Atchison, sb; MIKE COX, bjo/g; Gerry Green, cl (-83); Art Katona, tbn (76); Brian Ogilvie, asax/tsax (76); Al Willows, d (76). ADD: Jim Armstrong, cor (78→); Rod Borrie, tbn (76,78-79); Bob Claire, d (76); Geoff Leader, d (76); Gerry McLaughlin, d (79→); Ian Menzies, tbn (79-82); Ron Minshall, tbn (83→); Dave Montgomery, tbn (76-78); Roy Reynolds, cl (83→); Jim Rimmer, cor (76-78); Allister Taylor, p (82→); Mickey Walker, d (78-79).

*CVR1001 "Live At the Hot Jazz" (81); PH001 "Shout 'em, Aunt Tillie" (83); PH002 "Stomp Off, Let's Go" (84); Q110 "Some Like It Hot" (79); cass "Dreamin' the Hours away" (84); cass "Alligator Hop" (85)*

## PHRISCO PHUNCTION (PHIL HOWE'S) SF c1978→

Also titled PHABULOUS PHRISCO PHUNCTION.

Original lineup unknown. Rex Allen, tbn; Dave Black, d; Jim Cumming, sb; Devon Harkins, p; Bob Hinman, sb; Bob Hirsch, p (80-81); PHIL HOWE, cl/ssax; Jack Knox, g/bjo; Bill Maginnis, d; Bob Neighbor, tpt; Bert Noah, tsax; Art Nortier, p; Ken Plourde, sb; Doris Wayne, v.

*M&K 10011 "Swings Classic Jazz"*

ROY PIERCE January 1979

**Liston Pickering, d** - 5 Guys Named Moe
**Jack Pierce, bass** - Ponca City
**John Picardi, d** - Jim Beatty; Easy Winners; [Donnie McDonald]
**Roy Pierce, tbn** - Camellia; Hangtown; Riverbank

## PIER 23 JAZZ BAND SF 1956-77

*Pier 23* was a popular, long-running jazz haunt on the Embarcadero where Burt Bales held sway as solo pianist from 54-66. Additionally, there were many small combos formed under this name, some barely more than jam sessions, others more permanent groups made up in part of the following:

1963-68: Jimmy Carter, d; Ray Durand, sb; BILL ERICKSON, p; Wally Floyd, d; Bob Marchessi, sb; Bill Napier, cl. 1969-72: Cyril Bennett, p; Alex Colchak, d; Jim Cumming, sb; Floyd; Jim Goodwin, tpt; Devon Harkins, p; Max Leavitt, d; NAPIER; Ray Skjelbred, p; Jack Stewart, p. 1973-74: Harkins; Bill Maginnis, d; Napier; Jack Schafer, tpt.

## PIER 100 DIXIELAND JAZZ BAND Stockton 1980

Jim Bouska, tbn; Dick Hungerford, cl; Sonny Lowe, g; Bill Magellan, sax; Les Newstrom, d; BILL SMALLEY, cor; Chuck Soloman, tu.

161

**Bill Pietsch, d** - Delta Rhythm Kings

**DeVern Pinnock, bjo, g** *(1931 Portland OR) dentist* - Oregon; Pussyfoot

**David Pinto** - ldr Rhythm Kings

## PISMO EXPERIMENTAL JAZZ BAND Pismo Beach CA 1985→

Known as "PX," with attendant Roman numerals signifying particular groups, front lines varied around basic nucleus of WFDJE&MKRB rhythm section.

K O ECKLAND, p; Dennis Jackman, tu; Wayne Nicholls, bjo/g; Bob Vincent, d. ADD: Cal Abbott, cl/sax; Richard Cruz, tpt; Bob Ohnhaus, btpt/tbn.

**Mike Pittsley, tbn** - Capitol City; Delta King; Fulton St

## PLATINUM COAST JAZZ BAND SD

Bob Jensen, tpt; Bill Lamberton, p; Tom Lommell, d; Patti Ann Oakes, v; PHIL OAKES, tbn; Al Renzulli, cl; Curt Thompson, sb.

**John Plonsky, tpt** - Levee Loungers

**Ken Plourde, bass** - Phrisco

## PLUM FOREST JAZZ BAND Soquel CA 1974-75

DAVE BISHOW, sax/wb; Frank Goulette, cor; Al McDearmon, p; Bill Newman, bjo/g; Nile Norton, tu; others unknown.

THE POLECATS 1950
Eckland. Colman, Hoskins, Oxtot, O'Brien, Wood, Bissonette

**"Scotty" Plummer, bjo** - Dixie Katz; Monarch

**Ned Poffinbarger, bjo** *(1929 Burlington IA) sales* - Good Time Levee; [Riverbank]

**Dave Poe, bjo, reeds** *(1940 Birmingham AL)* - Big Tiny Little; led own groups

**Mike Polad, p** - Rhythmakers

## POLECATS (SOCIAL POLECATS) Berkeley 1950-52

Group organized by Eckland, disbanded when he moved to LA but Oxtot continued using the name as late as 60 for pick-up groups. Title contributed by Turk Murphy.

Bob Bissonnette, bjo; Bunky Colman, cl (-51); K O Eckland, p; Bob Hoskins, tu (-52); Bunny O'Brien, d (-51); Dick Oxtot, cor (-51); Howard Wood, tbn (-50). ADD: Ellis Horne, cl; Norman Klehm, tpt (51-52); Dick Lammi, sb (52); Don Marchant, d; (51); Bob Mielke, tbn (51-52); Bill Napier, cl (51-52); Don Noakes, tbn (50).

*CLAMBAKE 1-3 (50-51)*

**George Pollak, p** - Silver Stope; solo and show bands

**Ben Pollack, d** *(1903-1971 Chicago IL)* - Art Kassel; original NO Rhythm Kings; led own groups, most famous among which was the PICK-A-RIB BOYS, which he featured at his LA restaurant. Although a credible drummer, he was known more for his talent finding ability — alumni of his various groups dating from the mid '20s were Ray Bauduc, Irving Fazola, Benny Goodman, Harry James, Matty Matlock, Glenn Miller, Benny Morton, Freddie Slack, Muggsy Spanier, Jack Teagarden, Yank Lawson. Appeared in film *Benny Goodman Story* (55). Committed suicide in his Palm Springs home

## BEN POLLACK'S PICK-A-RIB BOYS LA 1950-c65

Lineups of those who played at Pollack's restaurant on Sunset Blvd in LA vary considerably. Listing is indicative of some long-term sidemen.

Barney Bigard, cl; Jerry Fuller, cl; Bob Higgins, tpt; BEN POLLACK, d; Charlie Teagarden, tpt; Jack Teagarden, tbn; Bobby van Eps, p; Ira Westley, sb.

*CAP; DISCOVERY; MODERN*

**Hugh Polley, tpt** *(1914 Red Lodge MT)* - Delta Rhythm Kings

## PONCA CITY JAZZ BAND Santa Maria CA 1978-81

LEE LAFAILLE, d; Joe Lazzaro, tpt (78,81); Bill Reid, p; Hoot Peterson, tbn (78); Bill Scott, cl (78-79); Jim Thompson, sb (78). ADD: Julie Cardoza, tbn (79); Joe Diamond, tpt (79-80); Marty Hagopian, sb (79); Jim Johnson, tbn (80-81); Gene Leis, g (81); Bob Osborne, cl/ssax (80-81); Jack Pierce, sb (78); Sonny Richter, g (79-80); Bob Swayze, sb (80-81).

*CLAMBAKE C218 "Jubilee By the Sea" (80 1 cut)*

**Joe Poppe, p** *(GERMANY) teacher* - 5 Guys Named Moe

## PORT CITY JAZZ BAND Stockton ?→

Original lineup unknown. Matt Brodie, cl; STEPHEN DRIVON, tbn; Ev Farey, tpt; Kent Mikasa, tpt; Bill Montague, cl; Bill Reinhart, cl; Mike Ross, tbn; Jim Rothermel, cl; Mark Schmid, bjo/p; Bob Stover, d; Roy Troglia, tpt; Stuart Zank, bjo.

### PORT COSTA YETI CHASERS SF 1977

Dan Barrett, tbn; Mike Duffy, sb; Jim Goodwin, tpt; Jeff Hamilton, d; RAY SKJELBRED, p; John Smith, ssax; P T Stanton, g.

*BR B4 "Jim Goodwin and Friends" (81 2 cuts); REALTIME RT22 "I've Got My Fingers Crossed" (77)*

**Jake Porter, tpt** - ldr Jazz Inc

**Kevin Porter, tbn** - Great American

### PORTLAND ROSE JAZZ BAND PTL 1977→

Original lineup unknown. Dick Barber, ssax; Bill Carter, tpt; Ted DesPlantes, tu; Norm Domreis, p; Hank Dougherty, bjo; Dick Fields, d; Jay Fleming, v; Bill Fletcher, d; Joe Gifford, tu; Leonard Harris, reeds; Pete Jochumson, cor; Gene Lundgren, bjo; Blake Maddox, cor; Eric Peterson, tu; Gary Peterson, p; BRADY ROBINSON, tbn; Paul Sabrowski, bjo; Bill Stauffer, tu; Marty Wright, tsax/cl.

**John Potter, d** - Jubilee

**Jake Powel, bjo, guit, reeds** - ldr Great Excelsior

### POWELL STREET JAZZ BAND SF 1974-75

Randy Johnson, bjo; Bob Montalvo, tpt (-75); Richard Olsen, cl/sax; Dick Oxtot, tu/sb. ADD: Bill Napier, cl (75).

**Bill Powell, reeds** - Bourbon St DJB

### POWERHOUSE SEVEN LA 1961

Comprised of personnel from North American Aircraft's Rocketdyne subsidiary.

Dick Duncan, bjo; Norton Fredlund, tbn; Walt Greenawald, tu; Tom Hall, d; Chuck McKeon, tpt; Don Reynolds, bjo; Scott Webster, p.

**Buddy Powers, tpt** - Woody Herman; Nob Hill; [Oakland A]; Sinners

**John Praiss, bass** - Workingman

**Naomi "Peewee" Preble, tbn** - Dixie Belles

**Dan Presley, bass** - Wholly Cats

**Dan Price, bass** - Lemon St

**William "Mick" Price, p** - Jamboree Hal

**Paul Price, p, viol *(1958)*** - Churchill St; Royal Society

**Preston "Peppy" Prince, d** - Joe Liggins Honeydrippers; ldr Louisiana Gents; Elaine Mitchell

### PEPPY PRINCE'S LOUISIANA GENTS see LOUISIANA GENTS

**Andy Prisco Jr, d** - Jazz Unltd; Royal Valley

**George Probert, reeds *(1927 Los Angeles CA)*** - Alexander's; ldr Ambulance; [Back Bay]; Firehouse 5 + 2; ldr Fine Time; [Gutbucket]; ldr Monrovia; [Natural Gas]; ldr Once or

GEORGE PROBERT October 1979

Twice; Kid Ory; Resurrection; Bob Scobey; [Tailgate Ramblers]; led own groups. Toured extensively in European performances, both as guest artist and with own groups

## PROFESSOR PLUM'S JAZZ Saratoga CA 1978→

Formed by members of APEX JB, popularity increased immensely, especially in the early '80s when they did much touring and festival work. Long-term at *Fargo's* Sunnyvale.

Cal Abbott, cl/ssax; Bob Burdick, bjo (-79); Bill Carson, tbn; PHIL KIRK, tpt; Mike Swanson, tu; Sharon Swenson, p (-79); Bill Todd, d (78-79). ADD: Bill Armstrong, bjo (79-81); Pat Dutrow, bjo (84→); Steve Hartwell, d (81-85); Jack Mangan, d (79-80); Jan Stiers, p (82→); Frank Tateosian, bjo (79); Bert Thompson, d (85→); Joanne Tobey, v (79-81); Steve Torrico, d (80-81); Karl Walterskirchen, bjo (81-84).

*CLAMBAKE C215 "Pickin' Plums" (80); = C218 "Jubilee By the Sea" (80 1 cut); PLUM PP001 "Live at Stockton" (81); = PP002 "After Hours" live at San Diego Jubilee (82); = PP003 "Tollgate Blues" (84)*

**Gary Provonsha, bass** *(19—1983)* - Island City; Uptown Lowdown. Killed flying his own plane from San Juan Island Festival

**Al Puderbaugh, p** - Castle

**Jimmy Pugh, reeds** - Silver Dollar-LA

## PURPLE GANG SAC 1978

Jack Baran, p; Ben Blakeman, bjo; Marvin Chappell, sb; LEONARD DIXON, cl; Al Frechette, tpt; Gene Frechette, d; Bob Lindfeldt, tbn; Ed Schmalz, sax.

**Alton Purnell, p** *(1911 New Orleans LA)* - Chris Kelly; Joe Darensbourg; Roger Jamieson; Bunk Johnson; Legends of Jazz; George Lewis; Silver Dollar-LA; Tuxedo; Young Men From NO

**Keith Purvis, d** - Destiny; Shakey City

165

JIMMY RIVERS January 1979

**PUSSYFOOT STOMPERS** PTL 1982→

Charlie Ahrens, tu; Ollie Fosback, cl; Vern Pinnock, bjo; Ted Van, d.

**Jim Putman, g** - Marin Jazz; Norma Teagarden

---

# Q

**Spencer Quinn, bjo** - Disneyland; Rosy McHargue; solo; led own groups; owned *The Hockshop* Hollywood
  *PIP 1907 "My Pick Is Quick"*
**Jim Quirk, cor** - Triple RRR

---

# R

**Jules Radinsky, tpt** *(1910 Denver CO) restaurant equip* - Hyperion
**Dave Radmore, bass** *(1927 Eugene OR) photog teacher* - Cell Block; Devil Mtn
**Tom Raftican, d** *(1924 Youngstown OH) sales* - Jazz-a-Ma-Tass; Nightblooming
**Bob Raggio, wb** - El Dorado-LA; So Frisco

## RAINIER JAZZ BAND Mt Vernon WA 1975→

Founded by Durkee upon moving from SAC. At his death in 80, he was replaced by Silberberg, and Pelland assumed leadership.

Jim Buettner, p (-75); BARRY DURKEE, bjo (ldr 75-80); Gordon Greimes, cl (-76); Stephen Joseph, d (75-76,84→); Bruce Keck, sb/tu (76-78); Tom Skoog, tpt (-76); Ken Wiley, tbn (-75). ADD: Al Barrows, tbn (76→); Larry Catlin, d (82-84); George Goldsberry, cl/ssax (78→); Boots Houlahan, tpt (78→; Jeff Hughes, cor (77-78); Randy Keller, tu (78→); John Laughlin, d (76-82); BOB PELLAND, p (75→); Ron Rustad, v (77→); Gene Silberberg, bjo (80→); Roy Whipple, cor (84→).
  *TLS 1218 "Back To Sacramento" (77); TRG T104 "Live At Mom's" (82)*

## RAINY CITY JAZZ BAND SEA 1946→

Group is still extant at this writing although public perfomances are rare, placing them in the category of the longest-lived jazz bands. Greimes assumed leadership in 49.

Dolph Bleiler, d (-50); GORDON GREIMES, cl; Boots Houlihan, tpt; Lowell Richards, tu (-50); JACK SHEEDY, tbn (-49); Barrie Vye, p (-60,64→). ADD: Perry Barth, d; Eddie Davis, d (60); Dave Driver, g (48-53); Bob Gilman, p (61-64); Alvin Larkin, tu (50-78); Marty Marsala, tpt (49-51); Murray Sennett, d (60→); Jim Wandesforde Jr, tbn (49→), Johnny Wittwer, p (60-61).
  *EXNER (47); = (49)*

**RAISIN CITY STOMPERS** Fresno 1982

Kevin Celey, tpt; Alice Deveau, p; Jay Fung, bjo; Don Hayworth, cl; Tony Lallo, d; DANNY TALBERT, tbn.

**Rich Rajewski, tpt** - Sausalito

**Louis Rale, reeds** - Monterey Bay Classic

**RAMPART STREET PARADERS** LA

Johnny Best, tpt; Nick Fatool, d; Clyde Hurley, tpt; Abe Lincoln, tbn; MATTY MATLOCK, cl; Eddie Miller, sax; Joe Rushton, bsax; George van Eps, g; Stan Wrightsman, p.

**"Oz" Ramsey, d** - Berkeley Rhythm; [Delta Jazz]; *SF Blues Serenaders*

**Ben Randall, d** - Bob Neighbor

**Keith Randles, d** - Cell Block

**Arthur "Doc" Rando, reeds** - Bob Crosby; Levee Loungers

**Dick Randolph, bass, cor** *(1936 Milwaukee WI) logistics planner* - Calif Ramblers; City of Industry; Emperor Norton; Jubilee; King Riverbottom; Resurrection; Rhythm Kings; Royal Society; Triple RRR

**Bob Rann, bass** *electronics* - So Frisco

**Mel Rapasarda, bjo, g** *(1923 Albany NY)* - Jamboree Hal; Jazz-a-Ma-Tass; Jazz Generation

**Frank Rasch, bass** - Yankee Air Pirates

RAY RONNEI
August 1966

**Rich Raskin, bass** - Chicago Ramblers

**Dennis Rasmussen, d** - Fulton St; Golden State; [Jelly Roll JB-SF]

**Al Rassmussen, tpt** - Oversextette

**John Rasnur, d** *(1941 Minneapolis MN)* - NOJB Hawaii

**Leon Ratsliff, reeds** - Bob Scobey

**Cliff Rawnsley, p** - Destiny City

**Dave Rawson, tpt** - Knights of Camelot

**Tim Ray, p** *(1962)* - Side St

## RAZZMAJAZZ Vancouver BC 1980→

Original lineup unknown. Larry Grant, tpt; Barry Gurney, d; Gordon Hembruff, cl; Mike Hobbs, bjo; Peter Kershaw; Peter Langley; IAN MENZIES, tbn; Ian Michie, p; Henk van der Heyden, cl/sax; Graham Parkes; Roy Styte; John Taylor; Casey Tolhurst, sb.

**Joey Reardon, tpt** - Jazzin' Jrs; Sizzlin' 7

**Lionel Reason, tpt** *(1906-19— New Orleans LA)* - King Oliver; Kid Ory

**Alton Redd, d** - Andy Blakeney; Young Men From NO

## RED PEPPERS see SOUTHERN STOMPERS

## RED HOT PEPPERS SAC 1982→

Named after Pepper's original band of that title in Holland, which was still extant at this writing. Played on *Delta King* riverboat under the title of King's Men (85).

Howard Berry, cl; Crystal Huff, d; Dick McComb, tpt; Frank Meyer, sb; FRED PEPPER, bjo; Sam Smith, tbn; Roger Snell; p. ADD: Joe Brown, p; Larry Salerno, d; Rich Selken, sb.

## RED PEPPER JAZZ BAND LA 1963

From PEPPER JB.

Frank Demond, tbn; RALPH DIANA, bjo; Mike Fay, sb; Ray Ronnei, cor; Walt Sereth, d; Tom Sharpsteen, cl; Dick Shooshan, p.

*EPITAPH 3 (1 cut 64)*

**Ed Reed, reeds** - Chicago 6; Jazzbo; ldr Memphis 5 (GA)

**Cully Reese, p** - Jazz-a-Ma-Tass

**Bill Reid, p** *(1942 Litchfield IL) optometrist* - Ponca City

**Paul Reid (Reinke), p, v** *(1936 Detroit MI) arr, comp* - Dixie Katz; Hot Frogs; Harry James; NOJB Hawaii

**Mike Reilly, d** - Cell Block

**Russ Reinberg, reeds** - Beverly Hills

**Bill Reinhart, reeds** - co-fdr Chicago 6; Port City; Tuleburg; co-fdr San Joaquin Dixieland Jazz Society; owned club *Jazz Ltd* in CHI for 25 years.

**Jack Reisner, bass** - Jubilee; King Riverbottom

**Bob Reitmeir, reeds** - Golden West; Jazz-a-Ma-Tass; King Zulu

**Don Remine, tbn** *(1933 Elizabeth NJ)* USAF - NOJB Hawaii

## RENO CHARLIE & THE SOUTH BAY RAMBLERS LA 1977

Bob Allen, sb; Chuck Austin, d; Allan Crowne, cor; Dean Honey, cl; ROGER SNELL, p; Burt Wilson, tbn.

**Ed Rentner, d** - Barrelhouse

## RENT PARTY STOMPERS San Luis Obispo CA 1985→

JEFF BEAUMONTE, cl; Shirley Beaumonte, bjo; Ron Moore, tu; Sarah Moore, wb; Wayne Nicholls, bjo; Rich Ward, tpt.

**Bill "Doc" Renwick, d** - ldr Mudville; co-fdr San Joaquin Dixieland Jazz Society.

**Al Renzelli, reeds** - Platinum

**Steve Resnick, bjo, d** *(1953 Los Angeles CA) printer* - [Down Home]; Fink St; Silver Cornet; Stomp Aces

## RESURRECTION BRASS BAND LA 1957→

NO-type street band originally assembled for Lutheran Hospital opening ceremonies and titled SOUTHERN CALIFORNIA HOT JAZZ SOCIETY MARCHING BAND, name changed c1973. Appeared at special functions and jubilees, notably Kid Ory's and Tudie Garland's funerals, Louis Armstrong's 70th birthday. Personnel varied greatly from year to year, so listings indicate no reference to years of association. Rieman assumed leadership in 81 upon Mitchell's death; Bourne ldr from 84.

Hugh Bell, Andy Blakeney, Norm Bowden, Dan Comins, Al Crowne, Leo Dejan, Mike DeLay, Dennis Gilmore, Wally Huff, George Orendorff, Dick Randolph, Rex Stewart, Bill Stumpp, Bob Young - cor/tpt; Dan Barrett, Lance Buller, Glenn Calkins, Phil Gwinn, Roger Jamieson, Dave Kennedy, GORDON MITCHELL, AL RIEMEN - tbn; Mike Baird, Polo Barnes, Heinie Beau, Barney Bigard, Joe Daresbourg, Ron Going, Dean Honey, Alex Hunter, Gene Jackson, Ben Kantor, Sammy Lee, George Probert, Les Robinson, Walt Sereth, Floyd Stone, Floyd Turnham, Jack Widmark - reeds; Benny Booker, Bernard Carerre, Ed Garland, Pete Keir, Art Levin, Norm Logan, Paul Woltz - sb/tu; Charlie Blackwell, Teddy Edwards, Bill Hadnott, David P Jackson Jr, Edgar Mosely, Syl Rice, Gene Washington, Gus Wright - d; DAVE BOURNE, tenor horn.

*GENTLE HEARTS GHR2014 "Resurrection Brass Band" (83)*

**Allan Reuss, g** *(1915 New York NY)* - Jimmy Dorsey; Benny Goodman; Harry James; Jack Teagarden; studio work; won *Down Beat* and *Metronome* polls 44

**Blake Reynolds, reeds** - Sextet From Hunger

**Don Reynolds, bjo** - Powerhouse

**John Reynolds, bjo** *(1953 Palo Alto CA)* - Calif Ramblers; [Down Home]

**Roy Reynolds, reeds** *(1929 Birmingham ENGLAND)* - Hot Jazz Hot Shots; Phoenix; led own group

**Robbie "Dusty" Rhodes, p, tbn** *(1934 San Jose CA) electronics engr* - [Ernie Carson]; Disneyland; Down Home; Mardi Gras-LA; Milneburg; Newport Harbor; Silver Cornet; So Frisco; solo; ragtime exponent; rec series of piano rolls for Play-Rite (81)

*EUPHONIC ESR1215 "Eight on the 88" w/Knocky Parker (77)*

BOB RINGWALD May 1977

## RHYTHMAKERS (HAL SMITH'S) PTL 1983→

Originally a rec band organized during Butch Thompson's West Coast tour, group continued appearances on a sporadic basis.

Mike Duffy, sb; Richard Hadlock, reeds; Becky Kilgore, bjo (-85); HAL SMITH, d; Butch Thompson, p (-83); Chris Tyle, tpt. ADD: Jack Meilahn, bjo (85→); Mike Polad, p (83→).

*JAZZOLOGY J136 "Hal Smith's Rhythmakers" (84)*

## RHYTHM KINGS LA 1984→

Large '30s-type band with varying personnel; listing indicates a reserve pool of players.

Mike Baird, asax; Glenn Calkins, tbn; Ham Carson, sb; Wayland Chester, bjo; Jeremy Cohen, viol; Richard Cruz, tpt; Buster Fitzpatrick, sb; Allen Hinkle, tsax; Jerry Holton, bjo; Dave Hutson, cl/asax; Alex Iles, tbn; Steve Isaacs, sb; Sherman Kang, asax; Brad Kay, p; DAVID PINTO, p; Dick Randolph, cor; Bill Schreiber, d; Bill Vogel, tpt; Robert Young, bsax.

## RHYTHM WIZARDS SF 1981→

Pete Clute, p; Bob Helm, cl; CARL LUNSFORD, bjo; Dave Rybski, tu. ADD: Jim Maihack, tbn (85→).

**Lloyd Rice, reeds** - Casa Bonita

**Sylvester "Syl" Rice, d** *(1905-1984 Oshkosh WI)* - Blueblowers; Roger Jamieson; Mardi Gras-LA; Resurrection

**Bill Richards, p, d** *(1937 Sacramento CA) structural engr* - ldr Boondockers; Golden State; Shakey's Inferior; ldr Sutterville

**David Richards, tpt** - Dixie 6

**Lowell Richards, bass** *(Seattle WA) journalist* - Rainy City

**Terrie Richards, v** - Sutterville

**Bob Richardson, tbn** *log scaler* - Oregon

**Brian Richardson, tbn** *(1933 Newcastle-on-Thyme ENGLAND)* - Cats 'n' Jammers; [Delta Jazz]; co-ldr Euphonic; Euphoria; 52nd St; Jubilee; Marin Jazz; [Oakland A]; orig ldr Rose & Thistle. To Canada 56, CA 61

**Rick Richardson, tbn** - High Society

**Dave Richoux, bass** *(1950 Omaha NB) product designer* - And That's Jazz; Churchill St; Monterey Bay Classic

**"Sonny" Richter, g** - Ponca City

**Ron Ridgewell, p** - Smogville

**Al Riemen (Riemenschneider), tbn** - Resurrection; Teddy Buckner

**Tom Riley, d** - Mardi Gras-LA

**Chuck Rimmer, bjo** - Alligator; Triple RRR

**Jim Rimmer, cor** - Apex; Phoenix Jazzers

**Al Ring, tbn** - Do-Do-Wah; Monterey Bay Stompers

**Bob Ringwald, bjo, p** *(1940 Sacramento CA)* - Boondockers; ldr Fulton St; ldr Great Pacific-LA; Sugar Willie; Tappers; solo
  *SJS 28 "Ringwald Rated R" (83)*

**Molly Ringwald, v** *(1969 Roseville CA) actress* - [Fulton St]; Great Pacific-LA; daughter of Bob Ringwald, began singing with when she was 3-1/2 years old; still sings occasionally but has made her mark in motion pictures
  *TAHOE R2899 "I Wanna Be Loved By You" (75)*

**Larry Risner, bjo** - Chicago Ramblers

## RIVERBANK BLUES BAND SAC 1973→

Held the singular record of being the only band to have performed at all Sacramento Jubilees.

ROY HARPER, d; Jill Johnson, p; Dave McCartney, sb (73,75-76); Emmett O'Sullivan, cl (-73); Roy Pierce, tbn (-80,83→); Fred Spitzer, tpt (-82); Dick Udell, tpt (-76). ADD: Denny Barnard, bjo (81→); Bob Bashor, tbn (81); Ben Blakeman, bjo (79); George Boyd, cl (74); Carl Cornell, cor (78); Leonard Dixon, cl (78-79); Norm Gary, cl (83→); Ira Greenstein, tpt/tbn (82→); Jim Hopperstead, tu/sb (83→); Charlie Hull, cl (80); Bob Johnson, sb (78-82); Rich Lockwood, cl (81-82); Dick Luepp, sb (74); Dave Metz, bjo (85→); Doug Parker, bjo (74-76); Joel Sandal, cor (77); Tom Schmidt, cl (76-77); Bill Tharp, tpt (79,82).

  *RH 1001 "Roy Harper's Riverbank Blues Band, Vol 1" (76)*

**RIVERBOAT DANDIES** see BAUDUC-LAMARE

**RIVERBOAT RAMBLERS Whittier CA 1985**

Group from Rio Hondo Community College was one of three finalists in 85 Southern Comfort national competition.

Steve Alaniz, cl; PAT ALEXANDER, tbn; John Lewis, tpt; Max Mahoney, tu; Scott Moreno, d; Ira Noel, p.

**RIVER CITY EXPRESS SAC 1975**

GEORGE BRUNO, tsax; Tom Gorin, p; Buddy Harpham, cl; Jerry Lopes, sb; John Skinner, tpt; Phil Stiers, cl (79-80); Cliff Swesey, d; Larry Tyrell, tbn.

**Jimmy Rivers, g** - Fulton St

## *RIVERSIDE ROUSTABOUTS (BOB HELM'S)* SF 1954

**Ev Farey, cor; BOB HELM, cl; Hank Ross, p; Bill Stanley, sb; Bob Thompson, wb.**

*RIV RLP2510 "Bob Helm's Riverside Roustabouts" (54)*

**Dave Robbins, tbn** *(1930 Vancouver BC)* - Lloyd Arntzen; Lance Harrison; Harry James; Solid Brass; Carse Sneddon

**Bill Roberts, d** *contractor* - ldr Jelly Roll Jazz Soc; Smogville

**Caughey Roberts, reeds** - Teddy Buckner; Fats Waller

CAUGHEY ROBERTS November 1966

WALLY ROSE May 1974

**Dick Roberts, bjo** *(19—1965)* - ldr Banjo Kings; Firehouse 5 + 2

**Joe Roberts, bjo** *(1925 Oakland CA) social worker* - Barrelhouse

**Vic Roberts, g** - Jamboree Hal

**Walter Roberts, bass** - Jelly Roll JB-SF; Kid Ory; Joe Sullivan

**Natalie Robin, reeds** - Dixie Belles

**Brady "Rip" Robinson, tbn** - ldr Portland Rose; Rose City JB

**Dick Robinson, d** *(IN)* - Desert City

**John Robinson, bjo, g** - Hangtown; Silver Dollar-SAC

**Les Robinson, reeds** - Elaine Mitchell; Resurrection

**Gene Roche, reeds** -Crown City

**Gil Rodin (aka Clark Randall), reeds** *(1906-1974 Chicago IL)* - Ray Bauduc; Bob Crosby; Ben Pollack; produced several tv series and specials on jazz during '60s and '70s

**Garth Rodriguez, xyl** - Monrovia

**Terry Rodriguez, p** - Golden Age

**Art Rodriquez, d** *(1952 Deming NM)* - Jazz Generation

**Terry Rogers, reeds** *physician* - ldr Ain't No Heaven

**Bill Rohr, tpt** - Bayside

**Dave Rollins, reeds** - King Zulu; Mississippi

**Bob Romans, cor** *(1932 Covington KY)* - ldr Cell Block; Headliners

**Charlie Romero, reeds** *(1937 Denver CO)* - ldr Balboa JB; Delta Ramblers; Dixie Katz; Doc Evans; Jazz Inc; [Jewel City]; Mickey Finn; Pearly Band; led own combos

**Don Romig, bass** *(1931 Pasadena CA) truck driver* - Jazzin' Babies; Southland

**Ray Ronnei, cor** *(1916 IA)* - Crescent Bay; El Dorado-LA; [Good Time Levee]; Jelly Roll JB-LA/SF; Tuxedo; So Frisco

**Ed "Doc" Ropes, reeds** *dentist- Jazzberry*

**Peggy Rose (Robertson), v** *(1925 South Bend IN)* - Dixie Unltd

**Wally Rose, p** *(1913 Oakland CA)* - Alexander's; Turk Murphy; Bob Scobey; *Washboard 5*; Yerba Buena; led own groups; solo. Extremely proficient exponent of ragtime, studied music at UC Berkeley, AA degree from Diablo Valley College

> *BLUEBIRD S12007 "On Piano"; COL CL2535 "Honky-Tonkin"; = C6260 "Ragtime Piano";*
> *= CL559 "Music of Jelly Roll Morton" w/Turk Murphy (53); DOWN HOME 2; GTJ 3, 25-28, 44 (50);*
> *= L12034 "Ragtime Classics"; JM 1, 7, 17; SOS 1057 "Wally Rose Revisited" (82); TRILON 222;*
> *WEST COAST 103, 107, 110, 112, 113, 116, 118, 120*

## *WALLY ROSE AND HIS DIXIELANDERS* SF 1950

Squire Girsback, sb; Ram Hall, d; WALLY ROSE, p.

## ROSE AND THISTLE JAZZ BAND SF 1960→

Founded by Brian Richardson and several other British expatriots at, and named for, the English pub on California Street where they played until 73, then to *Front Page* (originally *Dawn Club*). One of the oldest active jazz bands in the country.

Cyril Bennett, p (-69); Bill Maginnis, d; BRIAN RICHARDSON, tbn; Jack Wyard, cl (-69);

RESURRECTION BRASS BAND May 1980

others unremembered. ADD: BURT BALES, p (69→); Gordon Bennett, sb (69→); Bunky Colman, cl/arr (69-83); John Dodgshon, tpt (69→); Jack Mangan, d; Bert Noah, sax; Pat Patton, sb; Ed Sandoval, d; Bob Short, cor; Birch Smith, tpt; John Stringer, cl (83→); Ed Turner, bjo/g (69→).

   *SJS 20 "Burt Bales and Rose & Thistle JB" (83)*

### WALLY ROSE'S JAZZ BAND SF 1966-68

Formed while Rose was with Bob Scobey at *Tin Angel* to be Scobey's replacement band.

Norm Bates, sb; Jerry Butzen, tbn; Vince Cattolica, cl; Cuz Cousineau, d; Jack Minger, tpt; WALLY ROSE, p.

   *COL CL782 "Cakewalk to Lindy Hop" (67)*

### ROSE CITY JAZZ BAND Lake Oswego OR 1976-79

Portland Timbers (soccer team) band 76-77; various casuals in the PTL area.

MERYL CONGER, cor; Don Hunsicker, p; Myron LaHood, cl; Gene Lundgren, bjo/g; Rip Robinson, tbn; Bill Stauffer, tu; Chris Tyle, d.

### ROSE CITY STOMPERS PTL 1947

An offshoot of CASTLE JB.

Monte Ballou, g; George Bruns, tbn; Vince Dotson, cor; Bill Pavia, cl; Don Tooley, p; Axel Tyle, d; Hank Wales, sb.

**Bill Rosenzweig, cor** - Orange Blossom; Triple RRR

**Eric Rosenau, tbn** - Orange Empire; So Frisco

**Al Roset, reeds** *(19—1984)* - Headliners ldr; honored by Roset Memorial Scholarship Fund in support of youth bands in Fresno area

**Arnold Ross, p, tpt** *(1921 Boston MA)* arr - [Heinie Beau]; Beverly Hills; Harry James; JATP; studios; conductor, arr Bob Crosby tv show (54-56), Spike Jones tv show (57-58)
    *DISCOVERY DL2006; EMARCY MG26029 "Holiday In Piano"; NOCTURNE "Arnold Ross Trio"*

**Hank Ross, p** - *Riverside Roustabouts*

**Mike Ross, tbn** - Port City

**Tony Rossi, tbn** *(1926 New York NY)* - Mardi Gras-SAC; [Donny McDonald]; Sutterville

**Ray Roten, dms** - Dawn of Century

**Brad Roth, bjo** - Jazz Minors

**Jim Rothermel, reeds** - Golden Age; Golden Gate Rhythm; [Oakland A]; Port City

**Jerry Rothschild, p** *(1934 San Francisco CA)* - Fullertowne; Jamboree Hal; Orange Blossom; co-org/ldr Triple RRR

**Larry Rousseave, bjo, g** *(1956 Covina CA)* - Lemon St

**Ron Rowe, p** - Pete Lofthouse; Pearly Band

## ROYAL BOURBON STREET DIXIELAND BAND Aberdeen WA 1977-82

Formed from members of an Elks Club concert band. Renamed HUME STREET PRE-SERVATION JB #405 (cf).

Bob Boyer, cl (-78); Greg Jones, cor; Rich Daneker, d; Ray Davis, bjo; Rob Hilliard, cl/sax; Bill McCaw, tpt; Dale McClean, tbn (-78); Don Murphie, tbn; Bill Newman, sax (-82); GARRY NOEL, tu.

## ROYAL DIXIE JAZZ BAND Las Vegas 1973→

Started as house band and named for *Royal Inn Casino*, later to *Barbary Coast*.

CHUCK DIAMOND, tu; Jim Fitzgerald, tbn; Lou Lalli, d; Henry Levine, tpt; Joe Mayer, bjo; George Mosse, cl; George Pollak, p. ADD: Vinnie Tanno, tpt.
    *CONTRAST CRS2002 (81); RDJB 25687 "Bourbon St in Las Vegas" (75); = 29747 "Royal Dixie JB"*

## ROYAL GARDENS JAZZ BAND LA 1975-79

House band at *Old Chicago Gaslight* Newport Beach (75-76), then re-formed to play *The Depot* San Juan Capistrano (77-79). Sound was traditional, patterned after the Hot Five and New Orleans Footwarmers.

Mike Baird, cl (alt); STAN CHAPMAN, tbn; Dolph Morris, sb; Dick Shooshan, p; John Smith, cl/ssax (alt); Ken Smith, cor; Hal Smith, d. 1977: Dan Comins, cor; CHAPMAN; Leon Crabbe, bjo (alt); Mike Fay, sb; Leuder Ohlwein, bjo (alt); Walt Sereth, cl/ssax; Shooshan; Lee Wedberg, d.

## ROYAL SOCIETY JAZZ ORCHESTRA (DON NEELY'S) SJ 1976→

Originally ROYAL SOCIETY DANCE ORCH, changed to present name in mid-76. Featured authentic sounding jazz and dance band arrangements from the '20s and '30s.

Manny Alcantar, cor (-83); Jim Burlingame, p (-77); Ron Deeter, cl/asax (-84); Janel

Jaffee, viol (-77); Jay Little, d (-77); Howard Miyata, tbn (-83); Charles Morressey, cor (-77); DON NEELY, cl/sax; Lin Patch, cl, tsax; Steve Peterson, bjo (-76); Rick Siverson, tu/bsax (-79). ADD: Steve Apple, d (77→); John Benson, p (77-79); Tom Brozene, cor (77-84); Frank Davis, tpt (84→); Pat Dutrow, bjo (76-84); Frederick Hodges, p (82→); Kent Mikasa, tpt (80→); Carla Normand, v (82→); Dick Randolph, cor (77-79); Terry Russell, tbn (83-84); Jon Schermer, tbn (84→); Scott Sorkin, bjo (84→); Mark Warren, reeds (84→); Ray Webb, sb/tu (84→); Jeff Wells, tu (79-84).

*CLAMBAKE C218 "Jubilee By the Sea" (80 1 cut); MMRC 108 "Jazz of the Roaring '20s" (79); =109 "do. Vol 2" (81); =110 "Happy Feet" (82); =111 "Star Dust" (83)*

## ROYAL STREET BACHELORS Disneyland 1965-69

Strolling trio played in the French Quarter.
Herbert Gordy, sb; Harold Grant, bjo; JACK McVEA, cl.

## ROYAL VALLEY JASMEN Fresno ?→

Don Franzioni, tpt; Gene Lein, tbn; RALPH MANFREDO, p; John Martin, cl/ssax; Andy Prisco, d; Mel Ward, tu/sb.

**Del Ruark, bjo** - Knights

**Keith Rubrecht, bass, tbn** - Do-Do-Wah

**Joe Rucker, tpt** *(1920 Battle Creek MI)* - Note-ables

**Tom Rudy, bjo** *(1924 Chicago IL)* - Emperor Norton

**Dan Ruedger, bjo, p** *(1928-1984 San Jose CA) engr* - ldr El Dorado-LA/SF; Golden Eagle; Magnolia

**Chuck Ruff, p** *(1920 Pittsburgh PA) prof of English Literature* - Capital City; Doc Evans; Oregon

**Dave Ruffner, tbn** *(1952 Bakersfield CA) music teacher* - Blue Street; degrees in music

**Hal Rumenapp, bass** - ldr Jamboree Hal; Jazz-a-Ma-Tass

**Bret Runkle, d** - Great Pacific-SF

**Joe Runnels, d** *(1964)* - Blue Fox; Headliners

**Willard Rush, reeds** - Shakey City

**Joe Rushton, bsax, reeds** *(1907-1964 Evanston IL)* - Pete Daily; Chicago Loopers; *Dixieboppers*; Bud Freeman; Benny Goodman; Rosy McHargue; Jimmy McPartland; Rampart St; Red Nichols; led own groups; to CA 42

## *RUSHTON'S CALIFORNIA RAMBLERS* LA 1947

Almost the same as MCHARGUE'S MEMPHIS FIVE, a name trade-off for rec purposes.
Marvin Ash, p; Nick Cochrane, cor; Brad Gowans, tbn; Rosy McHargue, cl; JOE RUSHTON, bsax; Graham Stevenson, d.
*JUMP 19, 23, 31 (47)*

**Ben Russell, reeds** *(1926 Altus OK) dept store mgr* - WFDJE&MKRB

**Bob Russell, reeds** *(1947 Fresno CA) music teacher* - Bourbon St 5; Live Steam

**Bob Russell, tpt** - ldr Southland

**Lynn "Pete" Russell, reeds** - Hogin's

**Terry Russell, tbn** - Royal Society

**Irving "Babe" Russin, reeds** *(1911 Pitsburgh PA)* - orig Calif Ramblers; Jimmy Dorsey; Tommy Dorsey; Benny Goodman; Red Nichols; Ben Pollack; Jess Stacy; studios; to CA 46

**Sal Russo, p** - Do-Do-Wah

**Al Rustad, bass, reeds** *(1939 Tacoma WA) mechanical engr* - Ain't No Heaven; dir Cornucopia Concert Band

**Ron Rustad, reeds, v** *(1946 Tacoma WA) marine engr* - Rainier; bro of Al Rustad

**Eddie Ruud, p** - Hogin's; Jazz Unltd

**Bill Rutherford, p** - Camellia

**Gary Ryan (Soderer), bjo, p** - Abalone; Paddlewheelers; solo

**Dave Rybski, bass** - Camellia; Rhythm Wizards; ldr Sausalito

**Don Ryckman, bjo** *(1934 Pasadena CA) school adm* - Hyperion

RON RUSTAD c1983

# S

**Dale Saare, tbn** - Charlie's; So Market St

**Paul Sabrowski, bjo** - Muddy River; Portland Rose

**Dennis Sacco, d** - Fulton St

**Jesse Sailes, d** - Teddy Buckner

**Johnny St Cyr, bjo, g** *(1889-1966 New Orleans LA)* - Louis Armstrong; Paul Barbarin; Crown City; Fate Marable; Jelly Roll Morton; Old Standard; King Oliver; Kid Ory; So Bay; orig Tuxedo Band; ldr Young Men From NO; led own groups. Won *Record Changer* All-Star poll 51

   *SOUTHLAND 212 "Johnny St Cyr and His Hot 5"*

**Jay St John, reeds** - Bob Higgins; Jack Teagarden

## SAINT PETER STREET BAND SF 1985→

Trio named for street on which Preservation Hall in NO is located. McNeal Breaux, sb; DAVID GIAMPIETRO, cl; Kevin McCabe, bjo.

## THE SAINTS SEA 1958-61

Ed Bock, d (-60); Ernie Dalleske, tpt; DON GOE, sb; Frank Gulseth, cl; Ken Miller, tbn (58,60). ADD: Perry Barth, d (60-61); George Cuddy, tbn (58-59); Ray Johnston, tbn (59-61), p (59); Bill Marvin, p (59-61).

## THE SAINTS JB see CRESCENT BAY

## SAINT VALENTINE'S DAY MASSACRE Vancouver BC

LLOYD ARNTZEN, cl; Rod Borrie, tbn (alt); Charley Brown, d; Peter Clark, tpt; Dick Lazenby, bjo; Alf Sleid, tbn (alt); Casey Tolhurst, sb.

**Sydette Sakauye, v** *(1951 Honolulu HI)* - NOJB Hawaii

**Larry Salerno, d** - Custer; Hangtown; Red Hot Peppers; Toot Suite

**Pete Salerno, d** *(Sacramento CA)* - ldr Gold Standard; ldr Old Sacramento

**Duane Sammons, d** - Bathtub Gin

**Joel Sandal, cor** - Riverbank

**Beth Sanders, reeds** - Cell Block

**"Sandy" Sanders, bjo** - Oregon; Trumbo

**Jeff Sandford, reeds** - Marin Jazz

## SAN DIEGO DIXIELAND JAZZ BAND SD

Carol Andreen, v; PHIL ANDREEN, tbn; Charlie Clark, p; Ray Conseur, d; Carol Fehr, bjo; Bob Gobrecht, tu; Bobby Gordon, cl; Bob Jensen, tpt.

**Harold "Sandy" Sandman, reeds** - Jamboree Hal

Al Douglas

TOM SHARPSTEEN
November 1985

TOM SMALL June 1981

**Ed Sandoval, d** - Rose & Thistle

**Ken Sands, p** *(1913 Los Angeles CA)* - [Mardi Gras-LA]; Merrymakers; Orange Pealers

**"Sandy" Sandstrom, tpt** - Emperor Norton

## SAN FRANCISCO BLUES SERENADERS SF

Jim Cumming, sb; Jim Goodwin, cor; Bob Helm, cl; Jack Knox, g; Bob Mielke, tbn; Leuder Ohlwein, bjo; Dick Oxtot, bjo/v; Oz Ramsey, d; Ray Skjelbred, p; Karl Walterskirschen, bjo. *MMRC 107 "Lindbergh"*

## SAN FRANCISCO BRASS SF 1974-?

Resultant final name change for THE TAPPERS (cf) when they substituted for Turk Murphy at *Earthquake McGoon's.*

## SAN FRANCISCO SWING EXPRESS SF ?→

Rex Allen, tbn; Dave Black, d; Jerry Good, sb; Phil Howe, cl/ssax; Ed Wetteland, p. *"Birth of a Band" (85)*

## SAN JUAN JAZZ RASCALS Costa Mesa 1980-83

Original lineup unknown. Jeff Beaumonte, cl/sax; Preston Coleman, sb (83); Allan Crowne, tpt (83); Ralph Diana, bjo (81); Bob Finch, sb (80-81); Dennis Gilmore, cor; Ron Going, cl (82-83); Jim Green, bjo (80); Vic Loring, bjo; Chris Norris, v (83); Ken Smith, cor (80); JOHN VALLE, tbn; Gordon Wilson, p.

**Frank Sano, d** *(1935 Albany NY) police capt* - Newport Summit; ldr Orange Blossom; ldr Paradise Hotel

**Paul Sarmento, bass** - Gold Standard

**Ray Sasaki, tpt** - Bourbon St 5

**"Red" Sather, reeds** - Bourbon St JB

## SATIN DOLLS LA 1978

Kay Blanchard, reeds; Lynn Delmerico, tpt; Eunice Duroe, tbn; Bonnie Janofsky, d; BETTY JONES, p; Vi Wilson, sb.

**Al Saunders** - ldr Old Pueblo

**Tom Saunders, cor** *(1938 Detroit MI)* - Big Tiny Little; led own groups

**Richard Saunders, bass** - Great American

**Vince Saunders, bjo** *design engr* - Back Bay; ldr So Frisco; Tuxedo

## SAUSALITO STOMPERS SF 1977

Lee Dixon, cl; Ben Fuller, tbn; Dan Lipscomb, p; Rich Rajewski, tpt; DAVE RYBSKI, sb/tu; Fred Stall, d.

**Cheryl Savala, d** *(1965 Ishpeming MI)* - Lemon St

**Pat Scannell, bjo** *(1907 Hibbing MN) USC football scout* - WFDJE&MKRB

**Jack Schafer, tpt** *(19—1984)* - Pier 23

**Earl Scheelar, cor, reeds** *(1929 Tillamook OR) real estate* - Barrelhouse; ldr Funky NOJB; Gutbucket; Monterey Bay Classic; NO Syncopators; Original Inferior; Silicon Gulch; Stone Age; Sunset Stompers; owned *New Orleans House* Berkeley (65)

**John Schermer, tbn** *(1956)* - Royal Society

**Jerry Schimmel, bjo** - Joyful Noise

**Robbie Schlosser, bass, bjo, cor, tbn** *(1941 Los Angeles CA)* - ldr Magnolia

**Ed Schmalz, reeds** *(1923 ND) teacher* - Jazz Beaux; Mardi Gras-SAC; Purple Gang

**Mark Schmid, p** - Port City

**Tom Schmidt, reeds** - Riverbank; Trumbo

**Carl Schmitt, tbn** - Dew Drop; Live Steam

**Wayne Schmus, reeds** - Dixie Rhythm Ramblers; Milneburg; Workingman

**Don Schneider, tbn** *(1929 McCook NB) personnel mgmt* - WFDJE&MKRB

**Hank Schneider, bjo** - Swanee's

**Elmer "Moe" Schneider, tbn** *(1919 Bessie OK) accountant* - Bob Crosby; Pete Kelly Big 7; Matty Matlock; Rosy McHargue; Will Osborne; Ben Pollack; studios. Appeared in films *Pete Kelly's Blues* (55), *The Five Pennies* (59), *The Gene Krupa Story* (59)

**Mike Schooler, d** - Feather Riverboat

**Bill Schreiber, d** *(1958 Frostburg MD)* - Calif Ramblers; Rhythm Kings

**Bob Schroeder, reeds** *(1929 St Louis MO) electrician* - Desert City; Peewee Erwin; St Louis Ragtimers

**"Butch" Schroeder, bjo, g** *(1940 Chicago IL) bldg designer* - Oregon

**Dwight Schuelein, reeds** - Oregon

**Robert Schuh, d** *(1963 Ft Lauderdale FL)* - Side St

**Rex Schull, bjo** - Beverly Hills; Faultless; Goose Island; Jelly Roll Jazz Society

**John Schuller, bass** - Bob Mielke

**Bob Schulz, tpt** *(1938 Wonewoc WI)* - [Delta Jazz]; *John Gill*; [Nob Hill]; Turk Murphy

**Hugo Schulz, bass** *(1946 Chicago IL)* - Jim Beatty

**Stan Schuman, reeds** - Cypress

**Bob Scobey, tpt** *(1916-1963 Tucumcari NM)* - ldr Alexander's; Castle; Frisco Foot-warmers; [Darnell Howard]; Turk Murphy; Yerba Buena; led own groups. Subject of bio *'Til the Butcher Cut. Him Down* (Jan Scobey 76); biblio and discography *Bob Scobey* (Jim Goggin 77)

## *BOB SCOBEY JAZZ BAND* SF

Ostensibly same as BOB SCOBEY'S BAND.

*GTJ L9 "Bob Scobey JB"; VIC LPM 1344 "Beauty and the Beat"; = LPM 1448 "Swingin' On the Golden Gate"; RAGTIME RSLP5231 (60)*

## BOB SCOBEY'S BAND SF 1950-63

Once Scobey began his ALEXANDER'S JB upon the YBJB's demise, just where the trail of different titles for his simlilarly-staffed groups leads is too complicated to dwell upon here. Essentially, titles of BAND, FRISCO BAND, JAZZ BAND and even ORCHESTRA demand separation only by a serious discographer and it rests that the titles and personnel may well be evenly interchanged in the long run. In several instances, Scobey padded his touring (CHI-NY) and rec groups with regional musicians, so the listing here reflects an attempt to include primarily local sidemen of some tenure.

Jack Buck, tbn; Jesse Crump, p (55-56); Clancy Hayes, bjo/v (54-63); Fred Higuera, d; Bill Napier, cl (54-57,59-63); Hal McCormick, sb (55-57); Vera Miles, v; Dick Lammi, sb/tu (-54); Abe Lincoln, tbn; Matty Matlock, cl; Leon Ratsliff, cl; Elmer Schneider, tbn; Brian Shanley, cl; BOB SCOBEY, tpt; Bob Short, tu; Warren Smith, tbn; Frank Snow, tpt; Wayne Songer, cl; Phil Stephens, cl; Jack Sudmeier, tbn; Will Sudmeier, tbn; Ralph Sutton, p (56-57); Earl Watkins, d (54-57).

*DOWN HOME MGD1 "Bob Scobey's Band"; VERVE MGV1001, 1009 "Bourbon St"; = 1011 (57); VIC LPM1344 "Beauty and the Beat" (57); = LPM1473 "Bing With a Beat" w/Bing Crosby*

## BOB SCOBEY'S FRISCO BAND SF 1949-63

*Rancho Grande (53-54), Tin Angel (54), Storyville (56), Victor's & Roxie's (50-53), Zardi's LA, much touring. Also see ALEXANDER'S JB and notes above.*

Burt Bales, p; Jack Buck, tbn; Gordon Edwards, d (48-50,51); Clancy Hayes, bjo/v; George Probert, ssax; BOB SCOBEY, tpt. ADD: Dave Black, d; Jack Crook, cl; Jesse Crump, p; Squire Girsback, d; Fred Higuera, d; Darnell Howard, cl (50 rec); Dick Lammi, sb/tu; Bob Mielke, tbn; Albert Nicholas, cl (51 rec); Wally Rose, p; Bob Short, tu.

1954: Buck; Ernie Lewis, p; Hayes; Lammi (-55); Hal McCormick, sb; Bill Napier, cl; SCOBEY; Earl Watkins, d.

1957: Buck; Crump; Hayes; Higuera; McCormick; Vera Miles, v; SCOBEY.

*GTJ 60, 66, 71; = L12006 "Bob Scobey's Frisco Band" (55); = L12009 "Scobey and Clancy" (55); = L12023 "Direct From SF" (57); = L12032 "Scobey Story, Vol 1" (53); = L12033 "do. Vol 2" (53); = S7013 "Scobey & Clancy Raid the Juke Box" (58); JANSCO JLP6250 "Great Bob Scobey and His Frisco Band, Vol 1"; = JLP6252 "do. Vol 2"; VIC LPM2086 "Rompin' and Stompin'"*

**Arthur "Bud" Scott, bjo, g** *(1890-1949 New Orleans LA)* - Buddy Bolden; [Mutt Carey]; Jelly Roll Morton; Jimmy Noone; King Oliver; Kid Ory

**Bill Scott, reeds** - Ponca City

**John Scott, cor, tbn** - ldr Apex; Emperor Norton

**Ken Scott, d** - led own group; to England c77

## KEN SCOTT'S ALL-STARS Anaheim CA 1964-65

*Dixie Doodle Anaheim.*

Mike Baird, cl; Ed Garland, sb; Roger Jamieson, tbn; George Orendorff, tpt; Alton Purnell, p; KEN SCOTT, d.

**Tom Scott, tpt** - Headliners

**Bob Seaman, p** - Tailgate Ramblers

## SEASIDE SYNCOPATORS Santa Cruz c1979

Pat Dutrow, bjo; Howard Miyata, tu; Don Neely, ssax; Rick Siverson, cor; Steve Torrico, wb. ADD: Jerry Butzen, tbn.

**Bob Secor, p, tpt** - Great American

LOUIS ARMSTRONG and BOB SCOBEY c1950

BOB SCOBEY BAND c1961
Girsback, Bales, Buck, Dart,
Scobey, Crook

RAY SHERMAN May 1980

**Andy Secrest, tpt** *(1907-1977 Muncie IN) real estate* - Marvin Ash; Chicago Loopers; Levee Loungers; Frank Trambauer; Paul Whiteman; CBS/NBC staff orchs; to CA 32

**George Segal, bjo** *(1939 New York NY) actor* - Beverly Hills

**Joey Sellers, p, tbn** *(1962 Tempe AZ) composer, writer* - Side St

**Mark Sellman, tbn** - Swipsey Cakewalk

**Rich Selken, bass** - Red Hot Peppers

**Dennis Senff, d** *(1949 Portland OR)* - Over the Hill

**Les Senff, bass** *(1956 Petaluma CA)* - Over the Hill

**Murray Sennett, d** *(Seattle WA)* - Rainy City

**Dan Sensano, p** - Blue St

**Walt Sereth, reeds** *(1934 Brooklyn NY) word processing* - Blue 5; Condor; Costa Del Oro; Bruce Dexter; El Dorado-LA; Golden Eagle; Party Peppers; Pepper; Resurrection; Royal Gardens; Sunset Stompers

## SEXTET FROM HUNGER LA 1949-c1955

Richie Cornell, d; Charlie Lavere, tpt; Blake Reynolds, sax; Eddie Skrivanek, bjo; George Thow, tpt; Country Washburne, sb; Joe Yukl, tbn.

*MACGREGOR*

**Norm Shacker, tbn** - Crescent Bay

**Sam Shafer, d** - King Riverbottom

**Ted Shafer, bjo** *(1925 Rochester NY) record prod* - ldr Jelly Roll JB-LA/SF; producer of Merrymakers and Homespun labels

## TED SHAFER'S JELLY ROLL JB see JELLY ROLL JB

## SHAKEY CITY SEVEN SEA 1960-62

Formed when *Lake City Tavern* was remodeled and reopened as a Shakey's Pizza Parlor. Band was originally titled MIKE HOBI'S SHAKEY CITY SEVEN, then SHAKEY CITY SEVEN PLUS ONE with personnel changes.

Jack Caskey, tpt; Vern Conrad, d; Bob Gilman, p; Hap Harris, bjo; MIKE HOBI, tbn; Doc Kinslow, sb; Galen McReynolds, cl. 1962 (PLUS ONE): Don Anderson, tbn; Hal Champness, sb (alt); Caskey; Rollie Ellis, bjo; Sally King, v; Kinslow, sb (alt); McReynolds; Phil More, p; Keith Purvis, d; Willard Rush, sax.

*ESQUIRE 32194 (62); MORRISON 9384 (61)*

## SHAKEY'S INFERIOR FOUR SAC 1965

DUTCH DEUTSCH, cl; Dave Beeman, sb/tu; Barry Durkee, bjo; Bill Richards, d.

**Brian Shanley, reeds** *insurance* - Hangtown; Mudville; Oregon; Bob Scobey; Sutterville

**Danny Shannon, ebass** *(1929 Willoughby OH) welding instructor* - Les Brown; Desert City; Stan Kenton; Big Tiny Little

**Hank Sharman, d** - Jubilee

**Art Shapiro, bass** *(1916 Denver CO)* - Chicago Loopers; Benny Goodman; Bobby Hackett;

Nappy Lamare; Levee Loungers; Wingy Manone; *Michigan Blvd*, Paul Whiteman; studios; to CA 41

**Bill Sharp, tpt** *teacher* - Blue 5; Tuleburg

**Tom Sharpsteen, reeds** *(1926 Alameda CA)* - Crescent Bay; Crown City; El Dorado; Good Time Levee; co-ldr Impossible; Cornad Janis; Jelly Roll JB-LA; Pepper; Red Pepper; co-org Tailgate JB

*MAGNOLIA 210 "Tom Sharpsteen with New Orleans Rascals" (79)*

**Bryan Shaw, cor** *(1954 Newbury Port MA) sound rec* - Back Bay; Down Home; Fink St; Golden West; co-ldr Miss-Behavin'; Silver Cornet

**Jack Sheedy, tbn** *motion picture prod* - ldr Rainy City; led own groups

## JACK SHEEDY DIXIELAND JAZZ BAND SF 1949-53

Was first band into *Club Hangover* SF (49); later *Phone Booth, Persian Room, Edgewater Ballroom, Rendezvous Club.*

Norm Bates, sb; Bill Dart, d (-50); Jack Minger, tpt (-50); Bert Pearl, cl (-49); JACK SHEEDY, tbn; Johnny Wittwer, p (-50). ADD: Vernon Alley, sb; Bob Bates, sb; Vince Cattolica, cl (49-51); Cuz Cousineau, d (50); Paul Desmond, cl/sax (50-51); Carlos Duran, sb (50—); Bill Erickson, p (50—); Dave Lario, sb; Paul Miller, g; Bill Napier, cl (49,53); Pat Patton, bjo.

*CORONET 101, 102, 105, 106, 109, 110 (51)*

**Tom Shelden, reeds** *(1922 KS) piano tech* - co-ldr Over the Hill; Stumptown

**Jim Sheldon, tbn** *(1921 Cleveland OH) aerospace* - City of Industry; Delta Rhythm Kings; French Qtr; New Bull Moose; Old Standard

**Myron Shepler, bass** - Castle

DICK SHOOSHAN
October 1980

**John Sheppard, reeds** - Jazz-a-Ma-Tass

**Mike Sheppard, reeds** - Duwamish

**Brian Sherick, d** - British Connection

**Ray Sherman, p** *(1923 Chicago IL)* - [Heinie Beau]; Abe Most; Pete Kelly's Big 7; solo and studios

**Wayne Sherman, tbn** - Vine St

**Dick Sheurman, cor** - Castle

**Gerry Sheuster, tbn** *(1952 Salem OH) music instrument tech* - Dixie Unltd

**John Shideler, bass** *(1965 Pittsburg CA)* - Lemon St

**Georgia Shilling, p** - Dixie Belles

**Jimmy Shivnan, reeds** - Angel City

**Lin Shoemaker, bass** *(Carl Junction MO) tool designer* - Desert City

**Ed Shonk, bass** *(1933 Honolulu HI)* - NOJB Hawaii

**Dick Shooshan, p** *(1932 Pasadena CA) real estate* - Billy Bachelors; *Creole Sunshine*; [El Dorado-LA]; ldr Golden Eagle; Jelly Roll JB-LA; Pepper; Red Pepper; Royal Gardens; Sunset Stompers

**Bob Short, bass, tpt** *(1911-1976 Kirksville MO)* - Castle; [Berkeley Rhythm]; Great Pacific-SF; Turk Murphy; Rose & Thistle; Bob Scobey; Jack Teagarden; led own group. Killed in experimental airplane crash

**Tom Shove, p** - Custer; Gold Standard; Grand Republic

## SIDE STREET STRUTTERS Scottsdale AZ 1982→

Youth group from Arizona State University won 84 Southern Comfort Competition. Became regular performers during at Disneyland (summer 85).

Steve Mraz, tpt (-83); Joey Sellers, tbn; Rich Sparks, tu (-83); ROBERT VERDI, tsax; Vince Verdi Sr, d (-83); Vince Verdi, cl. ADD: John Noreyko, tu (83→); Tim Ray, p (84→); Rob Schuh, d (83→); Greg Wallace, tpt (83→).

*SEABROOK "Side St Strutters" (84)*

**Gene Silberberg, bjo** *(1940 New York NY) prof of economics* - Rainier; Uptown Lowdown

## SILICON GULCH JAZZ BAND Santa Clara CA 1980→

Pete Allen, sb; Ida Bithell, p; JOE BITHELL, d/tu; Ron Deeter, cl; Alan Hall, tbn; Wayne Larsen, tpt; Earl Scheelar, cl; Frank Tateosian, bjo.

**Ward Silloway, tbn** - Bob Crosby

**Frank Silva, reeds** - Cats 'n' Jammers; Easy Winners; Sutterville

**Lance Silva, tbn** - Headliners

## SILVER CORNET RAGTIME ORCHESTRA LA 1971-73

Specialized in orchestrated ragtime from orig manuscripts; played throughout CA.

Mike Arnold, cl; Dan Barrett, tbn; JEFF BEAUMONTE, tu; Rick Holzgrafe, cor; Steve Resnick, bjo; Robbie Rhodes, p; Bryan Shaw, cor; Hal Smith, d; Holly Ulyate, flute.

## SILVER DOLLAR JAZZ BAND (BURT WILSON'S) SAC 1955, 1961-63; LA 1966

Played *Shakey's* until Wilson was called for a tour of duty in the Army; re-formed upon his return. To all intents and purposes, this large Watters-type band was the beginnings of the jazz revival in SAC. *Shakey's* Hollywood (66), *Paddlewheeler* Orange (66).

1955: Jay Allen, tu; Jack Duke, p; Jim Hardesty, d; Phil Howe, cl; Jerry Luck, tpt; Don Paulthe, bjo; John Robinson, bjo; Joe Thomas, tpt; BURT WILSON, tbn. 1961: Dutch Deutsch, cl; George Henas, d; Tom Landino, bjo; Renard Perry, tpt; Roger Snell, p; WILSON. 1966: Teddy Edwards, d; Jim Leavitt, bjo/sb; Hal Peppi, tpt; Jimmy Pugh, cl/sax; Alton Purnell, p; WILSON.

**Mike Silverman, tpt** *(1943 Los Angeles CA) computers* - Beverly Hills; ldr Hot Frogs; Jelly Roll Jazz Society

**Kelly Silvers, p** - Jazzin' Jrs

**Keri Silvers, tbn** - Dixie Darlin's; UC Jazz

## SILVER STOPE JAZZ BAND (MERLE KOCH'S) Carson City NV 1961→

V J Bourgeois, d; Hub Houtz, cl; Cliff Jackson, tbn; Bunky Jones, sb; MERLE KOCH, p; John Thomas, cor.
    *JUMP J1211 "Silver Stope JB" (82)*

**Rich Simmons, d** *(1943 Miami OK) supply mgmt* - Axxidentals; Cell Block; Hogin's

**John Simon, bjo, g** - Cell Block; Tuleburg; led own orch

**Nancy Simon, v** - Traffic Jammers

**Wayne Simon, reeds, tpt** *(19—1981)* - Traffic Jammers

**Chuck Simpson, reeds** - John McKinley

**Steve Simpson, bjo** - ldr Workingman

## SINNERS (PAT YANKEE AND THE) SF 1962-64

Bob Bashor, tbn (-64); Bill Carroll, tu (-63); Ernie Carson, (-63); Bob Gilman, p; Phil Howe, cl; Tony Johnson, d; PAT YANKEE, v; Dave Weirbach, bjo. ADD: George Baker, bjo; Jack Crook, cl; Pops Foster, sb; Cedric Haywood, p (64); Bob Mielke, tbn (64); Art Nortier, p; Buddy Powers, tpt (63-64).

**Ross Siracusa, p** *(1943 Palermo SICILY) caterer* - Hyperion

**Eric "Rick" Siverson, bass, bsax, cor** *(1951) piano tech* - Churchill St; NO Syncopators; Royal Society; Seaside Syncopators

**John Skinner, tpt** - River City

**Ray Skjelbred, p, tbn** *(1940 Chicago IL)* - Bay City; ldr Berkeley Rhythm; Castle; *John Gill*; [Golden Age]; Golden State; co-ldr Great Excelsior; Richard Hadlock; Jelly Roll JB-SF; Jubilee; Lake Spanaway; Turk Murphy; New Washboard RK; [Oakland A]; Pier 23; ldr Port Costa; Rhythmakers; *SF Blues Serenaders*; co-ldr Speakeasy; solo. Studied with Johnny Wittwer
    *BR 2 "Ray Skjelbred" (74); EUPH ESR1223 "Chicago High Life" (83); SOS 1097 "Gin Mill Blues" (84)*

KEN SMITH October 1980

**Tom Skoog, tpt** *(1945 Seattle WA) commercial artist* - Island City ldr; Rainier

**Eddie Skrivanek, bjo** - Sextet From Hunger

**Ed Slauson, d** - British Connection; Dixie Jazz Bravos; Golden West; Jazz-a-Ma-Tass

**Al Sleid, tbn** - Dixieland Express; St Valentine

**Bill Slessinger, reeds** - Joyful Noise

**Bob Sloan, tbn** *(1932 Hollywood CA) restaurant owner* - Dixie Unltd

**Jim Smale, tbn** - Monarch

**Tom Small, tbn** *(1957 Palo Alto CA) lawyer* - Churchill St; Natural Gas

**Bill Smalley, cor** - Hogin; ldr Pier 100; Tuleburg

**Noel Smelser, tpt** - Sugar Willie; Sutterville

**Al Smith, cor** *(1938 Santa Ana CA) irrigation equipment mfr* - Delta King; Fulton St; Gas House; ldr High Sierra; Jazzberry

**Bill Smith, bass** - [Joe Sullivan-SF]

**Birch Smith, tpt** *(1926 Springfield IL)* - Dixieland Rhythm Kings (OH); co-ldr Euphonic; Euphoria; Great Pacific-SF; Jelly Roll JB-SF; [Turk Murphy]; Rose & Thistle; Salty Dogs (IL). Owned rec company (Windin' Ball) in CHI during '50s

**Bob Smith, tbn** *(1924 Sacramento CA)* - Dixie Jazz Bravos; Fullertowne; Jamboree Hal; Jazz Forum; King Zulu

**Bobbie Smith, reeds** - Louisiana Gents

**Brad Smith, bjo** - Uptown Lowdown

191

**Dave Smith, bass** - Frisco JB

**Eddie Smith, p, tpt** - Abalone; Dixiecrats; Frisco JB; Muggsy Spanier

**Gerri Smith, p** *(19—1985)* - Tuleburg

**Hal Smith, bass, d, wb** *(1953 Indianapolis IN)* - Conductors; ldr Down Home; Euphonic; Fink St; *Flaming Deuces*; Golden State; Hall Bros; Jazz Cardinals; Lakeshore; [Magnolia]; Royal Gardens; [Salty Dogs] (IL); [Ray Skjelbred]; ldr Rhythmakers; Silver Cornet; Sons of Bix (IL); So Frisco; Sunset Music; Wholly Cats; ldr Wilmington; led own groups
  *JAZZOLOGY J136 "Hal Smith's Rhythmakers" (84); SOS 1078 "Do What Ory Say" (Smith's Creole Sunshine Orch) (85)*

**Ian Smith, p** - Bathtub Gin

**John Smith, reeds** *(1941 Kansas City MO) purchasing agt* - Fine Time; [Firehouse 5 + 2]; Funky NOJB; [Jazz Cardinals]; Miss-Behavin'; Port Costa; [Royal Gardens]; Sunset Music; Tailgate Ramblers

**Ken Smith, cor** *(1928 San Francisco CA) aerospace engr* - Bienville; [Down Home]; Golden Eagle; Jelly Roll JB-LA; ldr Orange Empire; Party Peppers; Royal Gardens; San Juan Rascals

**Kirk Smith, d** - Westside Feetwarmers

**Phil Smith, reeds** - Napa Valley

**Reuben Smith, bass** - Calif Express

**Richard "R. C." Smith, cor** - Kid Ory; Tailgate JB

**Sal Smith, bass** *(1948 Seattle WA) music teacher* - Traffic Jammers; Uptown Lowdown

**Sam Smith, tbn** - Custer; Hangtown; Red Hot Peppers; Scottish Jazz Advocates

**Warren "Smitty" Smith, tbn** *(1908-75 Middlebourne WV)* - Andy Blakeney; Blueblowers; Bob Crosby; Pete Daily; Dixie Flyers; Bob Higgins; Nappy Lamare; Rosy McHargue; Red Nichols; Bob Scobey; Yerba Buena; to CA 45

## SMOG CITY JAZZ BAND LA 1958-60
*Handlebars, Friendship Cafe, Satellite*, other venues.
Mike Baird, cl; Ralph Diana, bjo; Don Martin, tbn; Ron Ortmann, p; Larry Stein, tpt.

## SMOG CITY STOMPERS LA 1965-66
*Nickelodeon Bar* on Wilshire Blvd.
Tom Barnebey, bjo, cor; Pete Kier, tu; Don Martin, bjo, p.

## SMOGVILLE SOCIETY ORCHESTRA LA 1974-76
Jack Boppel, bjo; Wally Craig, tbn; DAVE DOLSON, ssax; Walt Greenawald, tu; Ron Ridgewell, p; Bill Roberts, d; Bill Myers, tpt.

**Jack Snauffer, tbn** - MDJB

**Carse Sneddon, tpt** *(1928 Nanaimo BC)* - Lance Harrison; led own group

## CARSE SNEDDON JAZZ BAND Vancouver BC
Al Chappel, p; Lance Harrison, cl; Stan Johnson, sb; Donna Leah, v; Dave Robbins, tbn; CARSE SNEDDON, tpt; Mikey Walker, d.

**Roger Snell, p** - Cats 'n' Jammers; Gold Standard; Grand Republic; Jazz Inc; Red Hot Peppers; ldr Reno Charlie; Silver Dollar-SAC; ldr So Bay Zephyr

**Jim Snoke, bass, tbn** - Chicago Ramblers; Grand Republic; Trumbo All-Nite

**Frank Snow, tpt** - Bob Scobey

**Elmer Snowden, reeds** *(1900-1973 Baltimore MD)* - Eubie Blake; Duke Ellington; Turk Murphy; Lucky Roberts; led own groups; to CA 60-67

**Dan Snyder, tbn** *(1938 Marion OH) engr* - Angel City; Jazz Forum

**Jim Snyder, tbn** - So Frisco

**Bob Soder, p** - Toot Suite

**Chuck Solomon, bass** - Pier 100

**Charles Sonnanstine, cor** *cabinetmaker* - Dixieland Rhythm Kings (OH); ldr Great Pacific-SF; Red Onion (NY)

**Scott Sorkin, bjo** *(1962)* - Royal Society

**Wayne Songer, reeds** *(1913-1986 Ottumwa IA)* - Angel City; Phil Harris; King Zulu; Matty Matlock; Mississippi; Elaine Mitchell; Red Nichols; Bob Scobey; Joe Venuti; studios

**Cal Sorensen, tpt** - Dew Drop

## SOUNDS OF DIXIELAND SD 1977
John Best, tpt; Bill Coulson, tbn; Rod Cradit, cl; BILL HILL, p; Gene Nilsen, tsax.

## SOUTH BAY 7 + 1 1962-73 Sunnyvale CA
Formed from Lockheed personnel.
Marty Baldwin, tpt; Tom Downs, tu; Daryl Hosick, p; Ernie Landes, tbn; Bill McFadden, d; Dan McNiven, bjo; Bob Willwerth, cl; Bob Yates, bjo.

## SOUTH BAY CLASSIC JB see MONTEREY BAY CLASSIC JB

WARREN SMITH June 1966

JACK SPERLING May 1984      JESS STACY (with Jim Mathison) May 1975

## SOUTH BAY JAZZ BAND LA 1960-61

*Golden Nugget* El Segundo, *Green Bull* Hermosa Beach.

Alex Hunter, cl; Roger Jamieson, tbn; JERRY KAEHELE, tpt; Edgar Mosley, d; Gordon Wilson, p; Jimmy Wood, g. ADD: Scotty Lawson, p; Johnny Lucas, tpt; Johnny St Cyr, bjo; Jack Widmark, cl.

## SOUTH BAY ZEPHYR LA 1978

Bob Allen, sb; Ariana Attie, v; Ralph Craig, d; Al Crowne, cor; Hal Groody, bjo; Dean Honey, cl; ROGER SNELL, p; Burt Wilson, tbn.

## SOUTHERN STOMPERS LA 1960-61

Predominately casuals; Diana used same personnel to play *Jack's Bowery* Culver City under title of RED PEPPERS.

Bob Allen, sb; Mike Baird, cl; Ralph Diana, bjo; Roger Jamieson, tbn; Ron Ortmann, p; LARRY STEIN, cor.

## SOUTH FRISCO JAZZ BAND Costa Mesa 1965→

Inspired by the Watters-Murphy sound; first appeared at *The Honeybucket* Costa Mesa, subsequently *Pizza Palace* Huntington Beach (69); has since appeared worldwide. Original lineup unknown.

Mike Baird, cl (65→); Andy Blakeney, tpt (c71); Roy Brewer, tbn (69); Dan Comins, cor (71→); Leon Oakley, cor (79→); Ron Ortmann, p; Bob Raggio, wb (65→); Bob Rann, tu (65→); Robbie Rhodes, p (65→); Ray Ronnei, cor (65-?); Eric Rosenau, tbn (69); VINCE SAUNDERS, bjo; Jim Snyder, tbn (79→).

*MMRC 113 "San Francisco Jazz" (84); SFJB 21978 "Diggin' Clams" (Pismo Beach Jubilee 78); SOS 103 "Jones Law Blues" w/Bob Helm (85); =1027 "Live From Earthquake McGoon's" (82); =1035 "These Cats Are Diggin' Us!" (81); VAULT "Hot Tamale Man" (70)*

## SOUTHLAND SEVEN Arcadia CA 1960-64

Vinnie Armstrong, p; Tom Corth, cl; Leon Crabbe, bjo (-63); Dave Kennedy, tbn; Don Romig, tu; BOB RUSSELL, tpt.

## SOUTH MARKET STREET JAZZ BAND SD 1963-72

BILL DENDLE, bjo; Ken Donica, tu; Jerry Fenwick, tpt; Jim Hession, p; Larry Okmin, cl; Dale Saare, tbn; Ted Wolicki, d. ADD: Charlie Romero, cl.

## SOUTHSIDE JAZZ BAND LA c1965

Dave Hopkins, tpt/sb; Mac MacGavran, p; Lennie Maxson, d; Ken Watson, bjo/sb/viol.

**Ron Souza, tbn** - Dew Drop

**Brad Spangler, d** - Sticks Strings

**Francis "Muggsy" Spanier, cor** *(1906-1967 Chicago IL)* - Bob Crosby; Ted Lewis; Miff Mole; Ben Pollack; led own groups; lengthy engagement at SF's *Club Hangover* (57-59), other places in SF and LA. To CA c60

## MUGGSY SPANIER JAZZ BAND SF c1960

Sidemen varied considerably; billing shared with Earl Hines. Representative as appeared at *Club Hangover* in early '60s, briefly at *The Levee*.

Jimmy Archey tbn; Ernie Figueroa, tpt/tbn; Pops Foster, sb; Earl Hines, p; Darnell Howard, cl; Eddie Smith, tpt; MUGGSY SPANIER, cor; Earl Watkins, d. ADD: Bob Mielke, tbn (62); Joe Sullivan, p.

**Rich Sparks, bass** - Side St

**Neal Spaulding, p** - Bourbon St JB; Frisco JB

## SPEAKEASY JAZZ BAND (BARBARA LASHLEY'S) SF 1984→

A loosely-defined and various-sized group, beginning as a duo with Lashley and Skjelbred, subsequently expanding. Performed regularly throughout the Bay area, principally at Berkeley's *Shattuck Hotel.*

Dick Hadlock, reeds; BARBARA LASHLEY, v; Leon Oakley, cor; RAY SKJELBRED, p; Steve Strauss, sb; Tom Stamper, d. ADD: Devon Harkins, p; Bill Maginnis, d; Bob Mielke, tbn; Jack Stewart, p.

*SS 700 "How Long Has This Been Going On?" (83)*

**Susan Valliant Speer, v** *travel agent* - Uptown Lowdown

**Dick Speer, bjo** - Apex; Turk Murphy

**Jack Sperling, d** *(1922 Trenton NJ)* - [Heinie Beau]; Tex Beneke; Les Brown; [Morty Corb]; Dukes of Dixieland; Pete Fountain; Big Tiny Little; led own groups; studios and recs; to CA c50-60, c70

**Dick Spencer, tpt** - Yankee Air Pirates

**Don Spindler, reeds** - Dixiecrats

**Fred Spitzer, cor** *(1924)* - co-ldr Black Diamond; Riverbank

**Bill Spreter, bass** - Capitol City; Swanee's

**John Springer, d** - Sticks Strings

**Pete Spruance, tbn** - Jewel City

**Bruce Squires, tbn** - Blueblowers

**Jess Stacy, p** *(1904-19— Bird's Point MO)* - Blueblowers; Billy Butterfield; Eddie Condon; Bob Crosby; Tommy Dorsey; Benny Goodman; Harry James; Jack Teagarden; solo and led own groups. Won *Down Beat* polls 40-43, *Metronome* polls 40-41, 43. To CA 49. *Brown Derby, Ile de France* LA, *Club Hangover* SF; retired from performing 60-74

*ATLANTIC "Tribute to Benny Goodman"; BRUNSWICK BL54017 "Stacy Still Swings"; COL CL602 "Piano Music For Two"*

**Ron Stadtherr, reeds** *(1964 Minneapolis MN)* - Sticks Strings

**Wanda Stafford, v** - Marin

**Joe Staley, bjo** - Joyful Noise

**Fred Stall, d** - Sausalito

**Tom Stamper, d** - Richard Hadlock; Speakeasy

**Jimmy Stanislaus, v** *(1910 Oakland CA) prizefighter, fireman* - Turk Murphy

**Bill Stanley, bass** - *Riverside Roustabouts*

**Jerrold Stanton, p** - Barbary Coast; Bob Mielke; brother of P T Stanton

**Peter "P. T." Stanton, g, tpt** - Bearcats; Casa Bonita; Golden Gate Stompers; [Jazz Cardinals]; Port Costa; ldr Stone Age

**Lloyd Stark, p** - Casa Bonita

MIKE STARR October 1978

**Mike Starr, tbn** *(1933 Redwood Falls MN) commercial trailers* - [Delta Jazz]; Fulton St; Golden Gate Rhythm; [Nob Hill]; [Oakland A]; Tappers

**Bill Stauffer, bass** *(1945 Portland OR)* - Jim Beatty; Portland Rose; Rose City JB

**Jim Steffan, g** - Mudville

**Gary Stein, bass** - Dixie Dissonants

**Jeff Stein, tbn** - Alligator; co-org Triple RRR

**Larry Stein, tpt** - New Washboard RK; Smog City; ldr Southern Stompers

**Cheryl Stephens, v** *(1947 New York NY)* - Desert City; Jeff Woodhouse; led own combos
WHOOPEE JAZZ 2 "Shine" (83); "Lotus Blossom" (85)

**Haig Stephens, bass** - Bob Crosby

**Phil Stephens, bass** *(1907 Atlanta GA)* - Charlie Barnet; Pete Daily; Tommy Dorsey; David Rose; Bob Scobey; studios

**Lenny Stevens, reeds** - Bayside

**Phil Stevens, reeds** - Bob Scobey

**Alan Stevenson, p** - Ted Vesely

**Graham Stevenson, d** - Rosy McHargue; Joe Rushton

**Brian Stewart, g** - Westside Feetwarmers

**Bruce Stewart, tbn** - Devil Mtn

**Jack Stewart, p** - Golden State; Bob Neighbor; Pier 23; [Speakeasy]

**Rex Stewart, tpt** *(1907-1967 Philadelphia PA) radio program dir* - Benny Carter; Eddie Condon; Duke Ellington; Fletcher Henderson; McKinney Cotton Pickers; Resurrection; led own groups; to CA 59 where he became a disk jockey, wrote and lectured on jazz. Won *Metronome* poll 45; comp *Boy Meets Horn, Chatterbox*, others; auth *Jazz Masters of the '30s (MacMillan)*

**Winifred Stewart, bass** - Cottonmouth

## STICKS, STRINGS & HOT AIR San Luis Obispo 1980→

Formed at California Polytechnic University with direction and encouragement from Professor of Music emeritus George Beatie. Continued as an entity after members graduated.

Steve Bradbury, tu (-81); Brian Cardello, tbn (-83); Jeff Gamberutti, cl (-81); Blaise Levin, tpt (80); Brad Spangler, d (-83); Todd Temanson, bjo (-84). ADD: Tom Hodges, tbn (83→); JOE MCHALE, tpt (80-84); Ron Moore, tu (81→); Mike Orth, p (84→); John Springer, d (83→); Rod Stadtherr, ssax (81→).

**Jan Stiers, p** *(1933 Eugene OR)* - Desert City; Emerald City; Prof Plum; marr Phil Stiers

**Russell "Rusty" Stiers, tpt** *(1959 Springfield OR)* - ldr Jazz Minors; son of Phil & Jan Stiers

**Phil Stiers, reeds** *(1933 Eugene OR) electronics engr* - And That's Jazz; Black Diamond; Devil Mtn; Emerald City; River City

**Roger Stillman, bass** - Tailgate Ramblers

**Clemons "Jake" Stock, reeds** *(1910 Granville OH)* - ldr Abalone

**Grace Stock, p** *(1914-1979 Panama Canal)* - Abalone; marr Jake Stock

**Jackson Stock, tbn, tpt** *(1944 Monterey CA)* - Abalone; son of Jake Stock; degree at Berklee College of Music (MA)

**Ken Scott (Stoddard), d** - led own group

Al Douglas

RON STADTHERR
December 1985

## STOMP ACES (TED DES PLANTES') Pasadena 1971-72

*Handlebars Saloon* Pasadena.
Dan Barrett, tbn; TED DES PLANTES, p; Dave Hostetler, cl; Doug Parker, bjo; Steve
Resnick, d; Paul Woltz, bsax; Laurence Wright, sax.

**Bob Stone, bass** - Blueblowers

**Dave Stone, bass** - Angel City

**Dudley Stone, d** - Buena Vista; Mud Flat

**Floyd Stone, reeds** *(19—19—)* - Blueblowers; Crown City

## STONE AGE JAZZ BAND SF 1954-55

Pete Allen, sb; Bill Erickson, p; Frank Goudie, cl; P T STANTON, tpt; Dick Oxtot, bjo. ADD:
Bill Bardin, tbn; Peter Berg, g; Paul Boberg, bjo; Earl Scheelar, cl.

**Stan Stoneking, d** - Sutterville

**Bob Storm, d** - Bay City; Bill Napier

**Bob Storms, reeds** - ldr Bathtub Gin

**Norm Storms, tbn** - Bathtub Gin

**Stan Story, reeds** - Pete Daily; Ted Vesely

## STORYVILLE STOMPERS LA 1952, 1957

Original 52 lineup unknown, which Demond led; Bogan led 57 revival band:
JIM BOGAN, cl; Al Crowne, tpt; Frank Demond, tbn; Dick Dice, p; Mike Fay, sb; Hans
Neville, wbd; Jeremy Wire, bjo.
*TROPICANA (57)*

**Bob Stover, d** *music teacher* - Port City

**Harold "Smokey" Stover, d, mello** *(19—1974)* - Joe Sullivan-SF; Turk Murphy; Ted
Vesely; led own groups. Often confused with Robert Stover, who was no relation

**Robert "Smokey" Stover, tpt** *(1931 Conrad IA)* - ldr Original Fireman JB (NV); led other
groups during '60s and '70s, principally in Las Vegas, Reno and Lake Tahoe

**Kent Stow, bjo** - Canal St

**Bobby Stowell, reeds** - Basin St Trio; [Oakland A]

**Johnny Strangio, d** - Dixieland Syncopators

**Steve Strauss, bass** - Golden State; Gold Standard; Richard Hadlock; Speakeasy

**Newell Strayer, d** *(1931 Palo Alto CA)* - Bye Bye Blues; Cider City

**Bob Strelitz, p** - La Honda

**Benny Strickler, tpt** *(1917-1946 Fayetteville AR)* - Turk Murphy; Ben Pollack; Bob Wills;
Yerba Buena. Took over wartime version of YERBA BUENA JB in 42 for five months at *Dawn
Club* when most members left for military service
*GTJ 21, 22 (50)*

**John Stringer, reeds** *(1934 Liverpool ENGLAND) metallurgist* - Apex; Churchill St; ldr
52nd St; Rose & Thistle

**Bruce Stuart, tbn** *(1949 Concord CA) piano tech* - Devil Mtn

**Bill Stumpp, tpt** *music teacher* - King Zulu; OC Dixiecats; Resurrection; Tailgate Ramblers

## STUMPTOWN JAZZ PTL 1982→

Title came from pre-1845 name of Portland.

Meryl Conger, cor (-83); Jay Fleming, v; Leonard Harris, cl (-83); Glenn Koch, d; Gene Lundgren, bjo (-83); Pat O'Neal, tbn; Eric Peterson, tu (-83); GARY PETERSON, p. ADD: Harvey Brooks, cl (83-84); Van Crowell, cor (83-); Mark Curry, cl (84); Hank Dougherty, bjo (83→); Ollie Fosback, cl (84→); Tom Jacobus, tu (83-84); Tom Shelden, cl; Mark Vehrencamp, tu (84→).

*SJ-1 "Stumptown Jazz Live At the Quarry" (83)*

**Earl Sturgis, p** - Rosy McHargue

**Jim Stutz, bass** - Pete Daily

**Roy Styte** *(1962 Vancouver BC) student* - Razzmajazz

**Jack Sudmeier, tbn** - Bob Scobey

**Greg Sudmeier, d** - Great American

**Will Sudmeier, tbn** *(1929 Oakland CA)* - Ralph Flanagan; Tennessee Ernie Ford; Bob Scobey; ABC/CBS staff orchs; SF symphony

## SUGAR WILLIE AND THE TEN CUBES SAC 1965-?

WILLIE ERICKSON, p; Alan Herr, french horn; Phil Howe, reeds; Jim Maihack, tbn; Jim McDonald, tpt; Roger Mendez, d; Dick Mix, tbn; John Olbrich, sb/tu; Noel Smelser, tpt; Will Tallacksen, bjo. ADD: Bob Ringwald, p

**Dennis "Joe" Sullivan (O'Sullivan), p** *(1906-1971 Chicago IL)* - Louis Armstrong; Eddie Condon; Bob Crosby; Mound City Blue Blowers; Red Nichols; Muggsy Spanier; solo; led own groups. Intermission solo at *Club Hangover* (49-52,55-60) and *On The Levee* SF (61); *Trident* Sausalito (63). To CA 47; retired from performing c65. Comp *Little Rock Getaway, Gin Mill Blues*, others

*EPIC LN3295 "The Art of Jazz Piano"; PUMPKIN 112 "Gin Mill Blues" (84); RIV RLP12202 "New Solos by an Old Master" (53); SS 104 "Joe Sullivan at the Piano" (77); VERVE MGV1002 "Mr Piano Man" (54)*

## JOE SULLIVAN BAND SF c1950-61

Title embraced any number of combos which Sullivan formed occasionally from those listed (during his tenure as intermission pianist at *Club Hangover*) to fill in between appearances of featured jazz bands.

Pete Allen, sb; Byron Berry, tpt; Vince Cattolica, cl; Dave Lario, sb; Bob Mielke, tbn; Bill Napier, cl; Bob Osibin, d; Walter Roberts, sb; Bill Smith, sb; Smokey Stover, d; JOE SULLIVAN, p.

## SUPERIOR STOMPERS see BEARCATS

## SUNSET JAZZ BAND LA

BILL VOGEL, tpt; others unknown.

## SUNSET MUSIC COMPANY SF 1976-78

Formed from nucleus of BAY CITY JB by Ohlwein after leaving his JAZZBERRY JB; band played infrequently due to personnel being spread out all over the state. Played *Earthquake McGoon's* (76) as BAY CITY 6; Breda Jazz Festivals (77, 78).

Mike Baird, asax/cl (-78); Ev Farey, tpt (-78); Mike Fay, sb (-78); Bob Mielke, tbn (-77); LUEDER OHLWEIN, bjo; Hal Smith, d (-77). ADD: Norvin Armstrong, p (78); Bill Bardin, tbn (77); Dan Barrett, tbn (77-78); Jerry Butzen, tbn (77); Bill Carter, cl (78); Jim Goodwin, tpt (78); Jeff Hamilton, d (77-78); Jerry Kaehele, tbn (76); John Smith, ssax (78).

*SMC 79 "California Hot Jazz Beyond Category" (78)*

## SUNSET STOMPERS LA 1954-56

Original lineup unknown. Lou Allinger, p; Chris Clark, sb; Al Crowne, tpt; Roger de Laix, eg; Lorenzo Green, d; Earl Scheelar, cl; Walt Sereth, cl/wb; Dick Shooshan, p; Chuck Wilson, tbn.

**Dave Surtees, d** - Dixie Rhythm Ramblers

**Jan Sutherland, v** - [Chicago 6]; Custer; Gold Standard; Merseysippi (ENGLAND)

## SUTTERVILLE STOMPERS SAC 1976→

Bill Baker, sb (-79); Vince Bartels, d (-77); Dave Beeman, tbn (77); Jack Martin, bjo (-84); BILL RICHARDS, p; Frank Silva, cl (-83); Noel Smelser, tpt (-83); Terrie Richards, v. ADD: Kent Dunavent, tbn; Jerry Lopes, tu/sb (79→); Kurt Pearsall, tpt (83); Jim Painter, cl/sax (83); Tony Rossi, tbn (78-83); Brian Shanley, cl (84→); Stan Stoneking, d; Cliff Swesey, d (83→); Bill Tharp, tpt (83→); Lawry Yerby, d (78-83).

**Ralph Sutton, p (1922 Hamburg MO)** - primarily an East Coast musician, appeared freqently around West Coast as solo artist; Joe Schirmer; Bob Scobey; Jack Teagarden; World's Greatest JB; led own combos. To SF 49-64, then CO. Subject of bio *Piano Man* (James Schacter 75)

*AUDIOPHILE AP163 "Off the Cuff" (82); DECCA DL5498 "I Got Rhythm"; DOWN HOME 1003 "Ragtime Piano"; =MHD4 "Backroom Piano"; HARMONY HL7019 "Salute To Fats"; JM; OMEGA OSL51 "Jazz At the Olympics" (60); RIV RLP12211 "Ralph Sutton"; ROULETTE SR25232 "Ragtime USA"; VERVE V1004 "Ralph Sutton"*

## RALPH SUTTON TRIO SF 1949

Typical of many combos fronted by Sutton at *Club Hangover, Say When* 49-51. Albert Nicholas, cl; Pat Patton, sb; RALPH SUTTON, p.

**Hal Swan, tbn** - Capitol City; Gas House; ldr Swanee's

## SWANEE'S SWINGERS SAC 1978→

Wilda Baughn, p/v (-81); Howard Berg, reeds (-81); Bob Dodds, tpt (78); Stan Keyava, p (78); Hank Schneider, bjo; Bill Spreter, sb (78); HAL SWAN, tbn; Buddy Trumbo, d (-84). ADD: Alfred Frechette, tpt (79-80); Wes Grant, tpt (82-?); Carl Henriques, p (84); Lorisue Henriques, d (84); Jim Hopperstad, sb (79-83); Tom Kenny, cl (81); Gene Lancelle, tpt (80-82); Jean Levinson, tu (84): Jim Painter, cl (84); Ray Walters, tu (83).

**Mike Swanson, bass** *(1950 Sacramento CA) tool & die maker* - Apex; Euphonic; ldr Hot Jazz Stompers; Prof Plum; Sweet Molasses

MIKE SWANSON May 1985

**Bob Swayze, bass** *(1946 Newark NJ)* *trucking* - Ponca City

**Carolyn Swayze, v** *(1945 Chicago IL)* - Nob Hill; marr Jimmy Diamond

## SWEET AND HOT SF 1965-c78

Based on a group organized in 62 by Cattolica, featured a swing combo sound.

Jerry Butzen, tbn; Waldo Carter, tpt; Vince Cattolica, cl; Ernie Figueroa, tpt; John Marabuto, p; JOHN MARKHAM, d; Al Obidinski, sb. ADD: Herbie Steward, cl/asax.

*AMBIENCE 70301 "Sweet and Hot" (77); FAMOUS DOOR HL121 (77)*

**Sharon Swenson, p** *teacher* - Golden Age; Jubilee; Magnolia; Prof Plum

**Cliff Swesey, d** - Capitol City; Sid Catlett; River City; Sutterville

## SWIPSEY CAKEWALK RAGTIME BAND PTL 1979→

JOHN BENNETT, p; Laird Howling, cl; Glen Koch, d; Craig McKinley, bjo; James O'Banlon, tpt; Mark Sellman, tbn; Mark Vehrencamp, tu.

**Richard Synowski, g** - Oregon

# T

**Jim Tabler, reeds** - High Society

## TAILGATE JAZZ BAND LA 1949

Winners of *Record Changer* magazine competition 49; orig title CANAL ST STOMPERS.

Ralph Ball, tu; Bob Burns, bjo; Russ Gilman, p; CONRAD JANIS, tbn; John Josephs, d; Tom Sharpsteen, cl; R C Smith, cor.

*CIRCLE L404 (50); =R3006,R3007 (51); REC CHANGER CP1,CP2 (49)*

## TAILGATE RAMBLERS North Hollywood 1961-69

Nucleus formed from KNIGHTS OF JAZZ. *Storyville* Claremont (61-62), *Beverly Cavern* (63), *The Honeybucket* Costa Mesa (63).

Dick Braxhoofden, bjo; ROY BREWER, tbn; K O Eckland, p (-63); Rudy Eleff, tu (61-63); John Smith, ssax; Bill Stumpp, tpt; Walt Ventre, d (-68). ADD: Jimmy Grey cl; Tom Kubis, ssax; Bob McCracken, cl (69); Chuck Minogue, d (68→); Bob Seaman, p (63→); Roger Stillman, sb (63-); Gene Washington, d.

*VALON LPC504 "Tailgate Ramblers" (62)*

**Danny Talbert, bass, tbn, tpt** - org Blue Fox; Headliners; Raisin City

**Will Tallacksen, bjo** *(19—1968)* - Gas House; Sugar Willie

## TAPPERS (JIM MAIHACK'S) SF 1967-69, 1973-74

Became SAN FRANCISCO BRASS in 74.

Rex Allen, tbn (alt); Ev Farey, tpt; Phil Howe, cl/ssax; Bill Maginnis, d; JIM MAIHACK, bjo/tbn; John Moore, sb/tu; Bob Neighbor, tpt; Bob Ringwald, p; Mike Starr, tbn (alt); Norma Teagarden, p (alt).

**Bob Tarrant, bjo** - Dr Jon

**Frank Tateosian, bjo** *(1934 San Mateo CA) corporate counsel* - Monterey Bay Classic; Original Inferior; Prof Plum; Silicon

**Allister-Taylor, p** *(SCOTLAND)* - Hot Jazz Hot Shots; Phoenix

**Burt Taylor, tbn** - ldr Bienville

**Ed Taylor, p** *(1920 Camden NJ)* - ragtime exponent, band arr and comp

**Jack Taylor, d** - Conspiracy; Feather Riverboat

**John Taylor** *(1935 NEW ZEALAND) armored car driver* - Razzmajazz

**Joyce Taylor, bjo** *(Redwood City CA)* - Apex; [Delta Jazz]; led own groups

**Lynn Teadtke, tpt** - John McKinley

**Charlie Teagarden, tpt** *(1913 Vernon TX)* - Bob Crosby; Jimmy Dorsey; Red Nichols; Ben Pollack; Jack Teagarden; Cootie Williams; led own groups; to CA 40, Las Vegas c60. Bro of Jack Teagarden, thus nicknamed "Little T"

    *CAP T721 "This Is Teagarden"; CORAL "Little T"; =757438 "Great Hamp and Little T" w/Lionel Hampton; =757474 "Standing Room Only" w/Pete Fountain*

NORMA TEAGARDEN January 1976

**Norma Teagarden, p** *(1911 Vernon TX)* - Pete Daily; Bob Mielke; Matty Matlock; Ben Pollack; Tappers; Jack Teagarden; Ted Vesely; solo; All-Star groups worldwide; long-term at *Washington St Bar & Grill* (75→); toured and rec with bro Jack (43-46,52-55); to SF 57. Empress of Jazz Sacramento Jubilee 83

    *COMMODORE XFL14940 (44); DECCA 53*

**Weldon "Jack" Teagarden** *(1905-1964 Vernon TX)* - Louis Armstrong; [Chicago Loopers]; Eddie Condon; Ben Pollack; Paul Whiteman (incl "The Three Ts" with brother Charlie and Frankie Trambauer); led own groups; to CA mid-'40s. Won *Esquire* Gold Award 44, *Metronome* polls 37-41 and 45, *Playboy* All-Star Band poll 57-60. Bios *Jack Teagarden* (Smith & Guttridge 60) and *Jack Teagarden's Music* (Howard Waters 60)

    *BETHLEHEM 32 "Jazz Great"; CAP T721 "This Is Teagarden"; =T820 "Swing Low, Sweet Spirituals"; =T1095 "Big T's Dixieland Band"; =T1143 "Shades Of Night"; =T2076 "Tribute to Teagarden"; DECCA 8304 "Big T's Jazz"; =BL74540 "Golden Horn of Jack Teagarden" (55); COMMODORE XFL14940 "Big T and Mighty Max" (79); EPIC JSN6044 (3 vols) "King Of the Blues Trombone"; ROULETTE "Legendary Jack Teagarden"; =SR25243 "Portrait Of Mr T"; SOUNDS 1203 "Jack Teagarden"; SOUNDS OF SWING LP111 "It's Time For Teagarden"; TEAGARDEN 11221 "That Kid From Texas"; TOTEM 1001 "Teagarden & Trumbauer" (81); VERVE 8233 "At Newport"*

**Pete Tedesco, jug** - Lake Spanaway

**Todd Temanson, bjo** *(1961 La Mesa CA) architect* - Sticks Strings

**Ray Templin, d, pno** - Great Pacific-LA

**Joe Tenny, d** *(1936 Memphis TN)* - Hot Frogs

**Lou Tevis, v** - [Hot Frogs]

**Bill Tharp, tpt** - Dr Mix; Riverbank; Sutterville

## THEE SAINTS LA 1958-62

Retitled from KANSAS CITY NIGHT OWLS; *Guys & Dolls* West LA (60), *Handlebar* Sunset Strip (59); *Riviera* Palm Springs (58), *Rumbleseat, Why Not?* Hollywood (59-60).

Pete Andreadis, d (-61); K O Eckland, p; John Jewett, cl (-62); Dave Kennedy, tbn; JACK LANGLOS, tpt. ADD: Zulu Ball, tu (60); Jimmy Gray, cl (62); Don Kinch, sb (62); Gene O'Neill, d (59-61); Walt Ventre, d (61→).

**Jerrie Thill, d** - Dixie Belles

## 32nd STREET JAZZ BAND LA 1982→

Comprised of musicians at USC School of Music.

MIKE ANGELOS, tu; Ron Davis, bjo; Tom Evans, cl; Doug Isaac, d; Marissa Pasquale, tpt; Gil Zimmerman, tbn. ADD: Tom Hynes, bjo.

**Archie Thomas, tbn** *(1903 SD)* - Jim Beatty; Muddy River

**Charles "Chuck" Thomas, reeds** *(1917 St Louis MO)* - Angel City; Teddy Buckner

**Frank Thomas, p** *(1912 Santa Monica CA) animation dir* - Ambulance; Banjo Kings; Firehouse 5 + 2; Monrovia. Auth *Disney Animation; the Illusion Of Life*

**John Thomas, cor** *(FL)* - Salt City 6 (NY); Silver Dollar-SAC; Silver Stope

**Mark Thomas, bass** - Cats 'n' Jammers

**Ted Thomas, cor, d** *(1951 Glendale CA) filmmaker* - British Connection; Fink St; Milneburg

ROY TROGLIA November 1981

**Thomas "Tat" Thomas, reeds** - Happy JB; ldr Wilmington

**Bert Thompson, d** *(1931 Dundee SCOTLAND) prof of English* - And That's Jazz; Prof Plum; to CA 76

**Bob Thompson, wb** - *Riverside Roustabouts*

**Curt Thompson, bass** - Platinum

**Derek Thompson, d** - Outcast

**Jim Thompson, bass** *(1924 Springfield MO) optometrist* - Ponca City

**Jim Thompson, d** *(1944 Horton KS) electrical engr* - Tri-City

**Ralph Thompson, bjo, g** - Gas House

**Ted Thompson, reeds** - Easy Winners; Hiz Honor

**John Thornbrue, bjo** *heavy equipment mech* - Oregon

**George Thow, tpt** *(1908 Cleveland OH)* - Jimmy Dorsey; Isham Jones; Sextet From Hunger; Jack Teagarden; Lawrence Welk; to CA c36

**Jan Threlkeld, tbn** - Triple RRR

**Freddie Throop, d** - Goose Island

**Tommy Thunen, cor** - Rosy McHargue

## TOM & JERRY OVER THE HILL JB see OVER THE HILL JB

**Al Tobey, bass** - 52nd St

**Joanne Tobey (Burnett), v** *(1946 Los Angeles CA)* - Prof Plum; combos

**Bill Todd, d** - Prof Plum

**Steve Todd, tbn** - Dr Jon

**Ricardo Tolentino, p** *(Cavite City PI) USN bandleader* - NOJB Hawaii

**"Casey" Tolhurst, bass** *(1955 Vancouver BC) draftsman* - Razzmajazz; St Valentine

**Tom Tonyan, p** *(1951 St Cloud MN)* - Note-ables

**Don Tooley, p** - Castle; Rose City Stompers

**Joe Toomey, tpt** - Jazz-a-Ma-Tass

## TOOT SUITE Shingle Springs CA 1985

Steve Comber, sb; John Doolitle, sax; Byron Graff, sax; Ernie Jones, tpt; WALT KUNNECKE, cl; Brandon Mathews, tbn; Larry Salerno, d; Bob Soder, p.

**Manny Torado, bass** - Hogin's

**Wayne Torkelson, bass, tbn** *(1941 Aberdeen WA)* - And That's Jazz; Uptown Lowdown

**Al Torre, reeds** - ldr MDJB

**Steve Torrico, d, wb** - Prof Plum; Seaside Syncopators

**Wally Trabing, d** *(1921 Kingsburg CA) journalist* - Monterey Bay Classic; symphony orchs

## TRAFFIC JAMMERS Tacoma WA 1979-82

Gary Aleshire, tbn; Bill Blackson, d; Jimmy Buettner, p; Virgil Harwood, cl/sax; Bill Hobart, cor; Nancy Simon, v; WAYNE SIMON, tpt/reeds; Sal Smith, tu/sb.

**Edouard "Dutch" Trautwein, p** *(1933 Amsterdam NETHERLANDS) airline pilot* - [Tri-City]

**Bobby Travis, g** - Mudville

**Lynda Travis, v** *(1945 Seattle WA)* - Island City

**Dee Trent, bjo** - Alligator

**Manny Treumann, cor** *(1921-1984)* - ldr Bourbon St JB; ldr High Society 5; Old Pueblo

## TRI-CITY JAZZ BAND Kennewick WA 1980→

Started as DIXIELAND FIVE, changed to proclaim geographical location of Kennewick, Pasco and Richland.

John Boland, cl; MIKE COATES, tbn; Mary Lou Gnoza, v; Clark Hodge, tpt; John LaChapelle, bjo/g; Ron Monk, p; Jim Thompson, d; Dutch Trautwein, p (alt); Mac Wright, tu.

**Peter Trill, p** - Lloyd Arntzen

## TRIPLE RRR JAZZ BAND LA 1979-81

John Bishop, g (-79); Les Deutsch, tu (-80); Wally Geil, d; Jack Keister, cl (-81); Ray Perdomo, tpt (-80); Jim Quirk, tpt (-79); JERRY ROTHSCHILD, p; Jeff Stein, tbn (-80). ADD: Glenn Calkins, tbn (80-81); Jim Collins, bjo (79); Roger Jamieson, tbn (80-81); Shelly Lord-Howe, tpt (79-80); Dick Randolph, cor (80-81); Chuck Rimmer, bjo (79-81); Bill Rosenzweig, cor (80-81); Jan Threlkeld, cl (81); Bob Young, bsax (80-81).

**Al Trobbe, p** *(1921 San Francisco CA) paper supplier* - Gramercy; led own big bands

**Roy Troglia, tpt** - Port City

**Joe Trubic, bass** *(1920 Chicago IL)* - Emperor Norton

**Buddy Trumbo, d** - Easy Winners; Swanee's; led own groups

## TRUMBO'S ALL-NITE ALL-STARS SAC c1976

Al Mariano, p; Dick Mix, tbn; Sandy Sanders, bjo; Tom Schmidt, cl; Jim Snoke, sb; BUDDY TRUMBO, d.

**Tom Tucker, p** - Gold Standard

## TULEBURG JAZZ BAND Stockton 1978→

House band of San Joaquin Dixieland Jazz Society, formed out of four-piece John Simon Orch; Iversen assumed leadership when name was changed. Group was very active in concert and festival circuits.

Paul Boore, sax; LOREN IVERSEN, d/tpt; JOHN SIMON, bjo/g (78); Gerri Smith, p (-83). ADD: Dannie Balser p/tpt/v (83→); Jim Bouska, tbn (79-80); Tom Dutart, tu (80→); Chuck Eastman, bjo/tpt (81→); Bob Edson, tbn (80→); Truett Guthrey, bjo (79); Rod Hines, cl/ssax (79-85); Mark Johnson, tpt (83→); Peter Milner, bjo (80-81); Kurt Piersall, tpt (83); Bill Reinhart, cl (79-80); Bill Sharp, tpt (80-83); Bill Smalley, tpt (79-80).

**Bill Tull, reeds** *(1940 CA)* - Chrysanthemum

**Floyd Turnham, reeds** - Resurrection

**Ed Turner, bjo, g** *(1934) rancher* - [Bay City]; Fulton St; Rose & Thistle

**Jack Turner, d** *(1919 ENGLAND)* - Mardi Gras-SAC

**Jim Turner, p** *(1954 Los Angeles CA) music and talent dir* - Great Pacific-LA

**Elmer Tuschoff, bass** - Dew Drop; MDJB

## TUXEDO JAZZ BAND LA 1972-73

Steady 5 nights a week at *Club New Orleans*, dressed in real tuxedos; also known as Salutation Tuxedo JB.

Andy Blakeney, tpt; Frank Demond, tbn; Teddy Edwards, d; Mike Fay, sb; Ed Garland, sb (alt); RON GOING, cl; Alton Purnell, p; Vince Saunders, bjo.

**Roger Twedt, tbn** - Jazzbo

**Axel Tyle, d** *(1912-1981 Copenhagen DENMARK) electronics engr* - Castle; Conductors; Muddy River; Rose City Stompers

**Chris Tyle, d, tpt** *(1955 Vancouver WA) insurance* - Jim Beatty; Castle; Conductors; [Great Excelsior]; [Turk Murphy]; Rainier; Rhythmakers; Rose City JB; co-ldr Wholly Cats; led own groups; son of Axel Tyle

**Larry Tyrell, tbn** - River City

# U

## UC JAZZ HUNGRY SIX Berkeley 1983-84

Phil Antonaides, d (-84); JOHN BOSKOVICH JR, cl/sax; Tom Butke, tbn (-84); Ron Divincenzi, sb (-84); Pat Ellison, tpt; Bob Larson, p. ADD: Keri Silvers, tbn (84); Peter Washington, sb (84); Stephen White, d (84).

ED TURNER
February 1973

UPTOWN LOWDOWN JAZZ BAND October 1982
Goodrich, Kuenz, Barr, Loomis, Joseph, Brown, Vehrencamp, Sparks

**Dick Udell, tpt** Riverbank

**Brad Ullrich, reeds** Wholly Cats

**Jerry Ulrich, bass** Jazz Beaux

**Bob Ulsh, d** Jack Buck; Delta JB; Napa Valley

## UNION STREET JAZZ BAND Watsonville CA
DON PELLERIN, cl; others unknown.

## THE UNQUENCHABLES Los Angeles 1964
Mike Crane, d; John Finley, tpt; Ronnie Keck, cl; Art Levin, tu; John Robbins, bjo; JIM SAWYER, tbn.

## UPTOWN LOWDOWN JAZZ BAND SEA 1972→
Began as a pizza parlor group limited to five pieces, developed a strong style influenced by Barr's SF area upbringing, where he "grew up" in *Earthquake McGoon's* to the sounds of Turk Murphy. The two-cornet front line was adopted in 80. Despite discipline of arrangements, the ULJB's personality showed through. The group toured extensively both nationally and abroad.

BERT BARR, cor; Howard Gilbert, d (-73); Mike Hobi, tbn (-73,82); Dick Martin, cl (-73); Johnny Wittwer, p (-73). ADD: Tom Avants, sb (74); Bert Bertram, tbn (78-79); Dave Brown, bjo (83→); Bob Dunn, p (75-76); George Goldsberry, cl/ssax (75-79); John Goodrich, cl/ssax (81→); Roger Haapenen, tbn (74); Dave Holo, bjo/g (78-79) cor (80-81); Tom Jacobus, tu (78-81); Stephen Joseph, d (73-84); Randy Keller, tu (76-77); Bill Kick, tbn (83→); Ed Krenz, cor (83→); Dave Loomis, tbn (79-81); Paul Monat, cor (82); Rollie Morehouse, cl/ssax (79-81); Jan Oosterhof, p (73-75); Cal Owen, bjo (82); Bob Pelland, p (76-77); Gary Provonsha, sb/tu (75-77); Gene Silberberg, bjo/g (74-76); Brad Smith, bjo (77); Sal Smith, tu (83→); Rose Marie Sparks (Barr), p (77→); Susan Valliant Speer, v (74-80); Wayne Torkelson, tb (73,79); Mark Vehrencamp, tu (82,84); Gary Walker, tu (73); Ken Wiley, tbn (75-78); Jeff Woistman, bjo (79-81); Paul Woltz, bsax/tu (84→).

*CLAMBAKE C218 "Jubilee By the Sea" (80 1 cut); GHB 149 "Uptown Lowdown JB" (79); =159 "Hauling Ash" (80); HLR 5253 "Live in Japan" (82); SOS 1030 "In Colonial York, PA" (81); ULJB 101 "Uptown Lowdown JB, Vol 1" (75); =202 "do. Vol 2" (77); =303 "do. Vol 3" (78); = cass "Midwest Tour" (84)*

# V

**Lee Valencia, bjo** *(1929 San Francisco CA) player piano restoration* - Bay City; Great Pacific-SF; Knights of Camelot; Original Inferior

**Jim Valentine, reeds** - Grand Republic

**Rico Vallese, cor** - Chicago Loopers

**John Valley (Valle-Riestra), tbn** *(1934 Beverly Hills CA) sales* - Condor; Orange Pealers; Outcast; ldr San Juan Rascals

GEORGE VAN EPS
May 1976

**VALLEY JAZZ BAND** Walnut Creek CA 1965
details unknown.

**Ted Van, d** *auto parts* - Pussyfoot

**Gus van Camp, bass** - *Dixieboppers*; Knights of Jazz

**Bill Van den Burg, bass, g** - Monterey Bay Stompers

**Henk van der Hayden, reeds** *(1923 Leiden NETHERLANDS) gardener* - Razzamajazz

**Howard Vandron, tbn** - La Honda

**Bobby van Eps, p** - Ben Pollack

**George van Eps, g** *(1913 Plainfield NJ) sound engr* - Chicago Loopers; Benny Goodman; Ray Noble; Pete Kelly's Big 7; Ben Pollack; Rampart St; Paul Weston; studios. Won *Metronome* poll 37; appeared in film *Pete Kelly's Blues* (55)

**Vern van Lone, bjo** - Feather Riverboat

**George Vann, d** - Dixie Flyers

**Eric van Nice, reeds** - Calif Express; Cottonmouth

**Pete van Oorschodt, reeds** - Mardi Gras-LA

**Dale van Scoyk, tbn** *(1946 Dayton OH)* - Hyperion

**Johnny Varro, p** *(1935 Brooklyn NY)* - [Heinie Beau]; Wild Bill Davison; Dukes of Dixieland; Eddie Condon; Bobby Hackett; Phil Napoleon; solo and combos
  *MG MJ101 "Street of Dreams" w/Eddie Miller (82); "Roots of Jazz" w/Chuck Hedges (85)*

**Jack Vastine, bjo** - Bay City

**Spencer Vaughn bjo** - Excelsior

**Mike Vax, flug, tpt** - Jimmy Dorsey; Dukes of Dixieland; ldr Great American; Stan Kenton; Glenn Miller

**Mark Vehrencamp, bass** *(1953 Glendale CA) teacher* - Stumptown; Swipsey Cakewalk; Uptown Lowdown

**Walt Ventre, d** *(19—1968)* - French Qtr; Thee Saints; Tailgate Ramblers

**Giuseppe "Joe" Venuti, viol** *(1898-1978 Lecco, Italy)* - [Chicago Loopers]; Jean Gold-kette; Eddie Lang (Lang-Venuti groups); Red McKenzie; Red Nichols; Adrian Rollini; Paul Whiteman; led own groups; studios; guest appearances; to CA 43, SEA 63. Numerous recs 26-76; appeared in film *Five Pennies* (59)

**Robert Verdi, reeds** *(1961 Ossining NY) music teacher* - ldr Side St

**Vince Verdi, reeds** *(1958 Ossining NY) shop teacher* - Side St

**Vince Verdi Sr, d** *(Ossining NY) shop teacher* - Side St; father of Robert and Vince Jr; fdr Side St Strutters

**Bruce Vermazen, cor** *(1940 IA) prof of psychology* - ldr Chrysanthemum; Churchill St; Emperor Norton; ldr Oakland Hot Babies

**Irvin "Cajun" Verret, tbn** *(1906 Alexandria LA)* - Marvin Ash; Blueblowers; Levee Loungers; Wingy Manone; studios

**Ted Vesely, tbn** - Benny Goodman; Fred Waring; Ben Pollack; led own groups

## TED VESELY DIXIELAND BAND LA 1948-indef

1948 *(Beverly Cavern)*: Lee Countryman, p; Ralph Harden, tpt; Bob Higgins, tpt; Stan Story, cl; Smokey Stover, d; TED VESELY, tbn. 1950: Morty Corb, sb; Harden; Charlie Lodice, d; Ralph Peters, g; Alan Stevenson, p; VESELY, tbn; Bill Wood, cl.

*TOMTOM (49)*

**Lane Vifinkle, bass** - OC Dixiecats

**Al Villaire, reeds** *(1929 Honolulu HI) physicist* - And That's Jazz; Buena Vista; Gutbucket; Mud Flat

**Bob Vincent (Blacquiere), d** *(1933 Summerside, Prince Edward Isl CANADA) tv pro-duction* - PX; WFDJE&MKRB; org Jubilee By the Sea

## VINE STREET RAMBLERS LA 1947-49

Referred to by Owes as "McHargue's Farm Club" band; *Ja-Da Room* (48).

Lee Countryman, p (alt); Jack Doerr, cl; Joe Felix, p (alt); CLYDE OWES, tpt; Ralph Peters, bjo/tu; Jimmy Pratt, d; Wayne Sherman, tbn.

**Bill Vogel, tpt** *(1940 Chicago IL) teacher* - Beverly Hills; Calif Ramblers; Down Home; Rhythm Kings; ldr Sunset JB

**Bob Volland, p** - King Zulu

**Rich Vose, bjo** *(1938 Liverpool ENGLAND) chemical engr* - Jubilee

**William S Barrie Vye, p** *(Seattle WA) electrical contractor* - Rainy City

LU WATTERS 1949

LU WATTERS, BOB SCOBEY, TURK MURPHY c1946

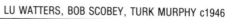

JACK WADSWORTH 1983

# W

**Jack Wadsworth, bsax, reeds** *(1930 Hollywood CA) music ed* - Ambulance; Great Pacific-LA; Jelly Roll Jazz Society

**Scott Wadsworth, tbn** - Jazz Minors

**Henk Wagner, bjo, d** *(1934 Amsterdam NETHERLANDS) mattress mfr* - Apex; 52nd St; Magnolia; to BC 58, CA 64

**Kurt Wahl, p** *(1957 Santa Maria CA)* - Lemon St

**Vic Wahlmeir, bjo** - Pepper

**Harvey Wainapel, reeds** - Great American

**Jerry Walcott, tbn** - Capitol City; Easy Winners; Gas House; Gramercy

**Hank Wales, bass** - Castle; Rose City Stompers

**Dick Walker, d** - Duwamish

**Gary Walker, bass** - Uptown Lowdown

**George Walker, d** - [Sidney Bechet]; Dr Mix; [Gas House]

**Harvey Walker, g** - King Zulu

**Jeffrey Walker, reeds** - Angel City; Dixieland Delinq; Monarch

**Mickey Walker, d** *realtor* - Phoenix; Carse Sneddon

**Maurey Walker, bjo** - Excelsior

**Greg Wallace, tpt** *(1962 Joliet IL)* - Side St

**Wally Wallace, bass** - Desert City

**Jack Waller, d** - Aristocrats

**Jim Walling, d** - Jazz-a-Ma-Tass

**John Walling, bass** *(1956)* - Churchill St

**"Buddy" Walters, tbn** - Happy Sync; Mudville

**Ray Walters, bass** - Dixieland Sync; Happy Sync; Mudville; Swanee's; co-fdr San Joaquin Dixieland Jazz Society

**Karl Walterskirchen, bjo** *(1935 Missoula MT)* *engr* - Euphonic; Euphoria; Funky NOJB; Jellyroll JB-LA; Magnolia; NO Syncopators; Prof Plum; *SF Blues Serenaders*

**James Wandesforde Jr, tbn** *(Seattle WA)* *commercial artist* - Rainy City

**Mel Ward, bass** *(1923 Fresno CA)* - ldr Jazz Unltd; Royal Valley

**Rich Ward, tpt** - Rent Party

**Stan Ward, d** - Turk Murphy

**Bob Wardlaw, reeds** *(Pima AZ)* *materiels planner* - Desert City

**Charley Warren, bass, bsax** *(1952 Orange CA)* - Fink St; Orange Blossom

**Mark Warren, reeds** *(1952)* *accountant* - Royal Society

## *WASHBOARD FIVE* SF 1950

Bill Dart, d; CLANCY HAYES, bjo/v; Bob Helm, cl; Dick Lammi, bjo; Wally Rose, p.
*DOWN HOME 11-14 (50; rec at Hambone Kelly's*; uncredited on wbd is Turk Murphy.)

**Joe "Country" Washburne, bass** *(1904-1974 Houston TX)* - Marvin Ash; Chicago Loopers; Pete Daily; Spike Jones; Levee Loungers; Sextet From Hunger; Ted Weems; comp *Oh, Mona, One Dozen Roses*, others

**Gene Washington, d** *(1925 Savannah GA)* - Blueblowers; Teddy Buckner; Crown City; Lucky Millinder; [Nightblooming]; Resurrection; Tailgate Ramblers

**Peter Washington, bass** - UC Jazz

**Bill Waters, tpt** *(1925 Centralia IL)* *psychologist* - Jazz Formula; Jelly Roll JB; Jelly Roll Jazz Society; Note-ables

**Rick Waters, reeds** - Norma Teagarden

**John Waterhouse, bass** - Jazz Ramblers

**Earl Watkins, d** *(1920 San Francisco CA)* *real estate* - Earl Hines; Bob Scobey; Muggsy Spanier; led own groups

**Barney Watson, tbn** *(19—1960)* - Abalone

**Ken Watson, bass, bjo, viol** - Southside

**Penny Watson, reeds** *(1961 Lynnwood CA)* - Lemon St

**Scott Watson, bass** *(CANADA)* - 5 Guys Named Moe

**Lucius "Lu" Watters, tpt** *(1911 Santa Cruz CA) gemologist* - ldr Yerba Buena; retired from music on New Year's Day 51; performed only once after that, at Bodega Bay benefit 63

## LU WATTERS' YERBA BUENA JB see YERBA BUENA JB

**Les Wayne, bjo** *(Palo Alto CA)* - Magnolia

**Russ Weathers, bass** - Blueblowers; City of Industry

**Ray Webb, bass** *(1956)* - Royal Society

**Al Weber, percussion** *(1925 Cleveland OH) safe deposit vaults* - Fine Time

**Howard Weber, d** - Dew Drop

**"Blackie" Webster, bass** - Castle

**Ralph Webster, tpt** - Mudville

**Scott Webster, p** *aerospace* - Goose Island; Jelly Roll Jazz Society; Powerhouse

**Lee Wedberg, d** - Blue 5; Bruce Dexter; Condor; Cottonmouth; Crescent Bay; Golden Eagle; Pepper; Royal Gardens

**"Bud" Weden, bjo** - ldr Natural Gas

**Dan Weinstein, tbn, viol** *(1954 Los Angeles CA)* - Calif Ramblers

**Dave Weirbach, bjo, reeds** *(1931 Los Angeles CA)* - Jim Beatty; [Conductors]; [Turk Murphy]; ldr Newport Harbor; Sinners; led own groups; owned jazz club *23 Skid Row* Redondo Beach early '60s

## DAVE WEIRBACH JAZZ BAND see NEWPORT HARBOR

**Jim Weiss, reeds** - ldr Dixie 6

**Tim Weiss, tbn** - Dixie 6; bro of Jim Weiss

**Sid Weiss, bass** *(1914 Schenectady NY)* - Eddie Condon; Benny Goodman; Wingy Manone; Artie Shaw; Ralph Sutton; studios; to CA 54

**Homer Welch, d** *(1912 Portland OR) radio production* - Castle; Turk Murphy

**Kermit Welch, reeds** - New Bull Moose

## LAWRENCE WELK DIXIELAND BAND LA 1961-82

Few realize that Welk began his career in the Midwest with a small jazz group and was popular therein before switching to the dance circuit. Although more known for his "champagne" dance music, notable was the band-within-a-band featured on his long-lived West Coast tv show, which, although rigidly structured, had some credible jazz poking through all the bubbles, with talented jazzmen like Dick Cathcart, tpt; Mahlon Clark, cl; Henry Cuesta, cl; Pete Fountain, cl; Bob Havens, tbn; Buddy Hayes, sb; Peanuts Hucko, cl; Ray Linn, tpt; Big Tiny Little, p; George Thow, tpt.

*DOT DLP3317 "Lawrence In Dixieland"*

**Billy Wells, bjo** - ldr Billy Bachelors

**Jeff Wells, bass** *(1959) industrial x-ray tech* - Churchill St; Royal Society

**Marion Wells, tpt** - Dixie Belles

**Dean Weprin, reeds** - Outcast

**"Frosty" West, cor** - ldr Coos Bay

**Ira Westley, bass** *(1923 Cooperstown ND)* - Ben Pollack; Dixie Jazz Bravos; [Firehouse 5 + 2]; Jack Teagarden; Yankee Wailers

## WESTSIDE FEETWARMERS Vancouver BC 1976-81

ROD BORRIE, tbn; Brad Humphries, sb/tu; Bob Jackson, tpt; Brian Ogilvie, cl/tsax; Bill Paul, p; Kirk Smith, d; Brian Stewart, g.

**Ed Wetteland, p** - Bay City; SF Swing Express; solo; won SF Symphony competition at age 14

**Robin Wetterau, p** *(1930 Woodstock NY)* - Dixieland Rhythm Kings (OH); Easy Winners (FL); co-ldr Great Pacific-SF; Red Onion (NY); solo; led own groups. Comp *Chelsea On Down*, others

**Aaron Wheeler, tbn** - Chicago Ramblers

**Chuck Wheeler, tbn** - Rosy McHargue

**Roy Whipple, cor** *(1922 Spokane WA)* - Rainier

**Amos White, tpt** *(1889-1980 Kingstree SC)* - Papa Celestin; Jazz Cardinals; Fate Marable; led own groups

**Bob White, cor** *(1927 St Louis MO) sales* - ldr Hyperion

**John White, p, vib** - Benny Goodman; Jack Teagarden

**Steven White, d** - UC Jazz

**John Whited, d** - Dixie Katz

**Jim Whiteside, p** - Natural Gas

**Dick Whitten, tpt** - MDJB

## WHOLLY CATS PTL c1984

Becky Kilgore, g/v; Dan Presley, sb; Hal Smith, d; CHRIS TYLE, tpt; Brad Ullrich, reeds.

**Paul Widdess, reeds** *(1935 Los Angeles CA) clothing retailer* - Emperor Norton; Jubilee

**Larry Widener, d** *(1962 Seattle WA) music teacher* - Blue St

**Jack Widmark, reeds** - City of Industry; Faultless; Old Standard; NO Creole Gumbo; Resurrection; So Bay

**Al Wied, bass** - Destiny

**Peggy Wied, v** - Destiny

**Paul Wiegand, tbn** - *Dixieboppers*

**Jack Wieks, bjo** *(1936 Portland OR)* - And That's Jazz

**Linda Wiggins, p** - Golden Age

## WILDA'S EASY WINNERS see EASY WINNERS

KEN WILLIAMS (with Don Bennett) October 1980

**Blaine Wikjord, d** *(1943 Vancouver BC)* - Gas Town; Lance Harrison

**Johnny Wilder, bjo, p** - Cell Block

**Ken Wiley, tbn** *teacher* - Great Excelsior; Rainier; Uptown Lowdown

**Bryan Williams, reeds** - Newport Summit

**Dick Williams, cor** *(1939 Los Angeles CA) sales mgr* - Desert City; [High Sierra]; Jazzin' Babies; Milneburg; WFDJE&MKRB

**Dick Williams, p** - Woodi

**George Williams, p** - NO Creole Gumbo

**Ken Williams, d** *(1930 Oakland CA) drum store owner* - Burt Bales; Jubilee; Marin Jazz; Marty Marsala; Eddie Miller; Ralph Sutton; Norma Teagarden

**Irv Williams, reeds** - King Zulu

**Ray Williams, tpt** - Dixie Rhythm Ramblers

**"Woodi" Williams, reeds** - ldr Woodi's

**Dave Willis, d** - Coos Bay

**Al Willows, d** *stagehand* - Phoenix

**Bob Willwerth, reeds** - South Bay 7

**Thad Wilkerson (Vandon), d** - Turk Murphy

**Randy Wilkinson, d** - Bay City

## WILMINGTON'S GREATEST JAZZ BAND Wilmington CA 1972-73

Vinnie Armstrong, p (alt); Dan Comins, cor; Pete Kier, tu (alt); Ron Ortman, p (alt); Hal Smith, d; TAT THOMAS, cl; Laurence Wright, bjo/tu.

**Albert "Buster" Wilson, p** *(1897-1949 Atlanta GA)* - Lionel Hampton; Kid Ory

**Bud Wilson, tbn** - Pete Daily

**Burt Wilson, p, tbn** *(1933 Stockton CA) advertising exec* - Gas House; Goose Island; NO Creole Gumbo; Reno Charlie; ldr Silver Dollar-LA/SAC; So Bay Zephyr

**Chuck Wilson, tbn** - Rosy McHargue; Sunset Stompers

**Gordon Wilson, p** - ldr Condor; ldr Cottonmouth; San Juan; So Bay

**Larry Wilson, p** *(1934 Santa Ana CA) construction engr* - Jazzin' Babies

**Vi Wilson, bass** - Satin Dolls

**Joe Wimmer, reeds** - John McKinley

**Jeremy Wire, bjo** - Storyville Stompers

**Bill Wise, reeds** - Camellia

**Harry Witczek, bass** - Turk Murphy

**Bob Witham, d** - Gutbucket

**Johnny Wittwer, p** - Don Anderson; [Sidney Bechet]; Marty Marsala; Bill Napier; Rainy City; Jack Sheedy; Jack Teagarden; Uptown Lowdown; Yerba Buena; ragtime exponent; solo, intermission at *Hambone Kelly's* (c50)

## JOHNNY WITTWER TRIO

Several combos under this title, first listing was a SEA group (47); second as appeared at SF's *Club Hangover* (49).
Joe Darensbourg, cl; Ram Hall, d; JOHNNY WITTWER, p.
Marty Marsala, tpt; Pat Patton, sb; WITTWER.
*JM 18-20 (47); EXNER 2*

**Jeff Woistman, bjo** - Uptown Lowdown

**Al Wold, p** - Gas Town; Rainbow

**Tad Wolicki, d** - Crown City; So Market St; Woodi

**Paul Woltz, bjo, bass, reeds** *(1950 Hollywood CA) instrument repair* - Back Bay; Down Home; Fink St; Golden Eagle; Happy JB; Orange Blossom; Resurrection; Stomp Aces; Uptown Lowdown

**Randy Woltz, d, p** *(1952 Hollywood CA)* - Dixie Kings; [Fink St]; Happy JB; bro of Paul Woltz

**Susan Wong, viol** *(1960 CA)* - Chrysanthemum

**Bill Wood, clar** *(1920 San Francisco CA)* - Blueblowers; Eddie Condon; Red Nichols; Ted Vesely; Yankee Wailers

**Howard Wood, d** - Polecats

**Jimmy Wood, g** - So Bay

**Ken Wood, p** - Cats 'n' Jammers

## WOODI'S REBEL ROUSERS SD

Bob Jensen, tpt; John Kitzmiller, tu; Phil Oakes, tbn; Dick Williams, p; WOODI WILLIAMS, cl; Tad Wolicki, d.

AMOS WHITE February 1972

**William Woodman, tbn** - Andy Blakeney; Teddy Buckner

**Glen Woodmansee, tbn** - King Zulu

**John Woodruff, bass** - Over the Hill

**Bob Woods, reeds** - Wingy Manone

**Jimmy Woods, p** - MDJB

**Dee Woolem, bass** - ldr Dixie Katz; Jazz Inc; King Zulu

**Roland Working, reeds** *(1930-1957 CHINA)* - Costa Del Oro; El Dorado-SJ; orig King Riverbottom

## WORKINGMAN'S 5 + 2 LA 1976

Formed to play SAC Jubilee; origins of MILNEBERG CHAMBER ENSEMBLE.

Zulu Ball, tu; Dick Broadie, cl; Carl Cornell, tpt; Dick Doner, tbn; Harry Hall, p; Ben Milliken, d; STEVE SIMPSON, bjo.

## WORLD FAMOUS DESOLATION JAZZ ENSEMBLE & MESS KIT RE-PAIR BATTALION (WFDJE&MKRB) Pismo Beach 1977-85

House band of Basin Street Regulars (CCHJS), with irreverent attitude towards music, stressed entertainment and outlandish humor. One of first to instigate popular concept of jazz on cruise boats (LA-Mexico 81). Rhythm section was basis for PISMO EXPERIMENTAL JB.

Charlie Bonner, tpt (-78); Derek Brown, tu (-77); Dave Caparone, tbn (-84); K O ECKLAND, p; Norm Lacey, bjo (-77); Ben Russell, cl; Bob Vincent, d. ADD: Denny Barnard, bjo (78-79); Richard Cruz, tpt (85-); Marty Frazier, cor (78-85); Dennis Jackman, tu (77-); Hank McKee, bjo (79-81); Wayne Nicholls, bjo (80-); Bob Ohnhaus, tbn (85-); Pat Scannell, bjo (77-78); Don Schneider, tbn (84-85); Dick Williams, cor (78).

*CLAMBAKE C213 "Live & In Choler" (78); = C218 "Jubilee By the Sea" w/Joe Darensbourg (80 1 cut)*

**Russ Wray, bass** - Mudville

**Dave Wright, bass** *(1948 Oakland CA) sales* - Dixie Jazz Bravos; Fullertowne

**Gus Wright, d** - Resurrection

**C. M. "Mack" Wright, bass** *(1937 Fresno CA) nuclear plant* - Tri-City; symphony orchs

**Laurence Wright, cor, d, p, reeds** *(1950 Los Angeles CA) filmmaker* - co-ldr Back Bay; British Connection; Down Home; co-ldr Fink St; Happy JB; Milneburg; Oversextette; Paradise Hotel; So Frisco; Stomp Aces; Wilmington

**Stan Wrightsman, p** *(1910-1975 Gotebo OK)* - Claire Austin; Ray Bauduc; Hoagy Carmichael; Bob Crosby; Levee Loungers; Matty Matlock; Eddie Miller; Ben Pollack; Rampart St; studios; solo; to CA 33

**Paul Wusschmidt, reeds** - Hiz Honor

**Jack Wyard, reeds** - Rose & Thistle

**John Wyatt, p** - Headliners

·

# Y

**Jerry Yanha, tbn** *(1936 Larimore ND) teacher* - co-ldr Over the Hill

**Pat (Weigum) Yankee, v** *(1929 Lodi CA)* - Turk Murphy; ldr Sinners

## YANKEE AIR PIRATES SD ?→

DOM ADDARIO, tpt; Marie Addario, bjo; Janed Casady, p; George Harris, bjo; Frank Highly, tu; Robert Korbelak, tpt; Frank Mencinger, bjo; Iris Mencinger, bjo; Frank Rasch, perc; Dick Spencer, tpt. ADD: Chuck Coulter, tbn; Rodger Kravel, d.

*"Yankee Air Pirates"*

## PAT YANKEE AND THE SINNERS see SINNERS

YERBA BUENA JAZZ BAND 1946
Lammi, Hi Gates, Dart, Scobey, Ellis Horne, Watters, Rose

YERBA BUENA JAZZ BAND, Hambone Kelly's 1949
Patton, Don Noakes, Watters, Hayes, Dart, Helm, Rose, Lammi

## YANKEE WAILERS LA 1983→

Vinnie Armstrong, p; WALLY HOLMES, tpt; Dave Kennedy, tbn; Gene O'Neill, d; Ira Westley, sb/tu; Bill Wood, cl. ADD: Dolph Morris, sb (alt).

**David Yap, bass** - [NOJB Hawaii]

**Hironobu Yashikawa, reeds** - Fink St

**Bob Yates, bjo** - So Bay 7

## YERBA BUENA JAZZ BAND (LU WATTERS') SF 1939-42, 1946-50

Starting out life as DAWN CLUB JAZZ BAND, the original name of the settlement now called San Francisco was quickly adopted instead. Began as a jam group at Berkeley's *Big Bear* (38), played *Dawn Club* (39-42,46-47). Leadership was taken over for five months at the start of WW2 by Benny Strickler after many of the musicians went into the service, then Watters re-formed most of the original group at *Hambone Kelly's* in 47. This was their home until New Year's Day 51, when Watters announced his retirement. Despite its relatively short active lifespan, the YBJB had as much influence on jazz, in particular the sound of jazz, as any other band in history. Lest this be construed as a reckless statement taking into consideration the ODJB, Armstrong, Morton and other early groups, when size of audience is considered, the reach and effect of the YBJB could only be described as enormous. The band also served as a physical nucleus for many other groups, some still extant at this writing, the most notable alumnus being Turk Murphy. Interesting is that such a group would gain such popularity in an era and location somewhat devoid of jazz aficionados and for this single reason the YBJB would be accurately described as being the *force majeur* in starting a new cycle, the second resurgence of jazz. The ripples on San Francisco Bay would quickly spread around the world.

1939: Squire Girsback, tu (-40); Bob Helm, cl (-40,46-50); Paul Lingle, p; Turk Murphy, tbn (-41,46-49); Pat Patton, bjo; Bob Scobey, tpt (-42,46-49); LU WATTERS, tpt (-42,46-50). ADD: BENNY STRICKLER, tpt (42).

1946: Bill Dart, d (40-42,46-50); Helm; Dick Lammi, sb/tu (46-50); Harry Mordecai, bjo; Murphy; Wally Rose, p (46-50); Scobey; WATTERS. ADD: Burt Bales, p; Jack Buck, tbn (49); Clancy Hayes, bjo/v; Don Noakes, tbn (50); Russ Bennett, bjo; Warren Smith, tbn (49); Johnny Wittwer, p (49-50).

*DC DH12011 "Lu Watters' YBJB"; DOWN HOME 1-6 (49-50); FAIRMONT 101 "Lu Watters and His YBJB Live From the Dawn Club" (73); =108 "Louie and Lu" (74 one side); GTJ EP1011 (53); =L12001 "Lu Watters' YBJB, Vol 1" (54); =L12002 "do. Vol 2" (54); =L12003 "do. Vol 3" (54); =L12007 "Lu Watters' YBJB" (55); =L12024 "Lu Watters/Bunk Johnson" (53); HOMESPUN H101 "Lu Watters' YBJB"; =H102 "do. Vol 2" (73); =H103 "do. Vol 3" (73); =H104 "do. Vol 4" (73); =H105 "do. Vol 5" (73); =H106 "do. Vol 6" (73); =H107 "Air Shots From the Dawn Club 1941" (79); JM 1-7, 13-15 (41-42), 108 (41); MERCURY 103 (50); =10025, 11026, 10057, 11065, 11077, 11081; =MGC503 "Lu Watters and His YBJB" (50); =MGC510 "do. Vol 2"; WEST COAST 101-111, 115-120 (46-47)*

**Lawry Yerby, d** - Sutterville

**Walt Yoder, bass** *(1914 Hutchinson KS)* - Bob Crosby; Woody Herman; Matty Matlock; Red Nichols; Ben Pollack; studios

**Walter Yost, bass** *(1926)* - Bay City; Golden Age; Great Pacific-SF; [Oakland A]; Original Inferior

**Bill Young, d** - Golden Gate Stompers

**Dick Young, d** *(1917 Brooklyn NY) realtor* - Dixie Unltd

**James "Trummy" Young, tbn** *(1912-1984 Savannah GA)* - Louis Armstrong; CBS orch; Benny Goodman; Earl Hines; JATP; Jimmy Lunceford; led own groups; to HI 47-52, CA 52-64, HI 64-70, CA 70-75, HI 75

**Robert Young, bsax, org, tpt** *(1948 Wheeling WV) teacher* - Calif Ramblers; Golden Eagle; Rhythm Kings; Triple RRR; colleague American Guild of Organists

## YOUNG AUDIENCES SF c1980

Group performed at Bay Area schools, bringing the sounds of traditional jazz in educational programs; made up from the nucleus of Ev Farey, tpt; Bob Helm, cl; John Moore, sb/tbn; Bill Napier, cl; Bob Neighbor, tpt; Dick Oxtot, bjo.

## YOUNG MEN FROM NEW ORLEANS Disneyland 1960-1968

Popular group played Disneyland throughout the summer seasons; St Cyr was original leader, Darensbourg next in 66 upon St Cyr's death, finally Brooks when Darensbourg left in 68 to lead own group.

Andy Blakeney, tpt (60); HARVEY O BROOKS, p; JOE DARENSBOURG, cl (-61,66-68); Dolph Morris, sb (-65); Alton Redd, d; JOHNNY ST CYR, bjo (-66). ADD: Polo Barnes, cl; Barney Bigard, cl (62); Bernard Carerre, sb (65-); Mike DeLay, tpt (61-69); Ed Garland, sb (65-67).

**Joe Yukl, tbn** *(1909 New York NY)* - Chicago Loopers; Jimmy Dorsey; Ben Pollack; Sextet From Hunger; studios; to CA 39. Coached Jimmy Stewart for his lead role in *The Glenn Miller Story* (53)

# Z

**Stuart Zank, bjo** - Blue Fox; Headliners; Port City

**Rubin "Zeke" Zarchy, tpt** - *(1915 New York NY)* Bob Crosby; Tommy Dorsey; Benny Goodman; Great Pacific-LA; studios

**Dan Zeilinger, bass, tpt** - *(1954 Omaha NB) arr* Golden West; Miss-Behavin'; Orange Pealers

**Lynn Zimmer, bjo, reeds** - *(1956 Kansas City KS)* Turk Murphy

**Dick Zimmerman, p** - *magician* co-ldr Dawn of Century; solo; ragtime exponent

**Gil Zimmerman, tbn** - 32nd St

**Vasile Znaco, tpt** - Headliners

## ZULU STREET PARADERS see KING ZULU PARADERS

**Tom Zusag, bjo** - Newport Summit

# YOUTH GROUPS

Perpetuation and future performance of American jazz rests entirely on the shoulders of the young, and those youth groups presently active throughout the nation represent a large part of the well of talent. It is from these bands, many experimental in nature, many organized as single-purpose — like some of those appearing at Sacramento Jubilees — or merely to fulfill scholastic requirements, that exciting new talent will appear. A majority will quickly pass into oblivion after the final school bell but a few groups will remain in existence and join the roster of active jazzmen in the tradition of SIDE ST STRUTTERS, LEMON ST STOMPERS, STICKS STRINGS & HOT AIR, JAZZ MINORS, et al.

Individual musicians, attracted by the creativity and uniqueness in jazz or influenced by personal or parental exposure, will suddenly appear at jam sessions and be cautiously welcomed by their seniors. It has all happened before; it is the matrix of history. Despite a wide chasm between contemporary music and traditional jazz, the inherent quality of the music will always attract that special breed of cat. Within the next decade, many of those names listed below will be regarded in the same light as the Mielkes, McHargues, Proberts and Carys of today.

## BELL STREET HOUSEWRECKERS SAC 1980-81

Dir: Bill Wise. Bill Bua, sax; Wayne Fiori, d; Jill Haney, p; Mark Johnson, tpt; Larry McKibben, cl; Mark Reibson, tu; Rob Shane, tbn. (Title traced back to 74 with John Knurr as dir.)

## BOBCAT JAZZ BAND Roseville CA

Dir: Jack Hensen. Melanie Boisa, sax; Dyne Eifertsen, tbn; Ryan Glasgow, cl; Aaron Ivey, tpt; Kim Johnson, p; Todd Peters, perc; Kris Richards, sb; Gregg Shopes, perc.

## CAPITAL TRANSIT JAZZ SAC 1983

John Berby, bjo/d; Eun-Jie Kahn, p; Laura Merrifield, sax; Isaac Parsons, sb/tu; Jeremy Pasternak, tbn; Michelle Sabin, cl/sax; Julie Wilson, tpt.

## DIXIE DARLINGS SAC 1983-85

Betty Adams, tbn (84-85); BOBBIE BOGGS, p (83-85); Sheri Buckles, sax (83-85); Kris Guensler, cl (84-85); Linda Herd, tpt (83); Crystal Huff, d (83-85); Elana Morgan, v (85); Diana Newcomb, tu (83-85); Stephanie Short, tpt (85); Keri Silvers, tbn (83); Sue West, tpt (84).

## DIXIE FLOYD BLUES BAND SAC 1982-83

Formerly ROYAL CREEK BEAVERS.
Dir Les Lehr. DAN BISIAR, tpt; Bonnie Boggs, p; Brandt Braswell, tpt; Crystal Huff, d; Jeff McAlpine, tbn; Bruce Nye, tu; Tony Schneider, reeds; Vic Walker, sax.

## DIXIEKATS SEA 1982→

Dir. Ray Johnston. Max Dimoff, tu; Lance Eggers, cl; Brian Fischer, d; Karl Johnston, tbn; Ken Johnston, cor; Melanie Malla, p.

## DIXIELAND DELINQUENTS Whittier CA 1980-82

John Anagnostou, d; John Aranda, tpt; PATRICK ARANDA, tbn; Nolan Gasser, p; Mark Malone, tu; Scott Mummpert, cl (-82); Jeff Silas, tsax (-81); Jeff Walker, cl (81-82).

## EL CAMINO HIGH SCHOOL JAZZ BAND SAC 1981

Dir: Steve Foster. Warren Astleford, sb; Scott Benton, tsax; Mark Doctor, cl; Clark Jewell, d; Pat Kelly, tbn; Jim Pantages, tpt.

## FOUR HITS & A MISS Lake County CA 1981-82

Andy Bailey, tpt; Joe Duri, tbn; Ken Kugelman, p; Polly Morine, cl/sax; Bill Sneed, p.

## JAZZMATICIANS SAC 1983

Steve Colter, tbn; Dave Kohlker, cl; Roy Merlino, tpt; Jim Ryan, sb; Kirt Shearer, p; Mike Ward, d.

## JIBBOOM STREET GANG SAC 1982

Bill Bua, cl/tsax; Glen Cunningham, d; Mark Johnson, tpt; Scott Lindfelt, tbn; Mark Reibson, tu; Kurt Shear, p.

## LA SIERRA HIGH SCHOOL JAZZ BAND SAC 1982

Bob Arnold, cl; Heather Boyer, tsax; Linda Campfield, v; Don Faller, tpt; Matt Iskra, tu; Brett Jackson, d; Steve Loveall, tbn; Derek Radulski, p.

## LOUISIANA PURCHASE SAC 1982

John Boskovich, sax; Larry McKibben, cl; Roy Merlino, tpt; Keri Silvers, tbn.

## QUARRY CATS Rocklin CA 1985

Nicole Barenchi, v; MATT BRADBERRY, tpt; Mark Foust, cl; James Franks, tbn; Erik Hoagland, sax; Nicki McCracken, p; Al Mendoza, d; Darrin O'Connor, d; Sean Ryan, p/tpt; Keith Simpson, tpt; David Wasley, sb/tu.

## REEDLEY RIVER RATS Reedley CA 1985

Stephanie Borjorquez, cl; Randy Collin, tpt; Julius Din, tu; Craig Linder, tbn; Derek Nishimoto, vib; John Saucedo, sax; BURL WALTER JR, d.

## RIO AMERICANO RIVER RATS SAC 1981-83

John Boskovich, tsax; Danielle Darracq, cl; Randy Doyle, d; Miles Erlich, tpt; Keith Farley, tbn; Rita Frink, sb; Scott Russell, bjo; Cynthia Whitcomb, p.

## ROYAL CREEK BEAVERS SAC 1981-82

Dir: Les Lehr. Bonnie Boggs, p (82); Victoria Calderone, tsax (81); Joanie Clark, tsax (81); Gerald Ford, bjo; Bob Hayes, d; Linda Herd, tpt; Dahlyan Johnson, cl (82); Dave Johnson, tbn (81); Karen Kronquist, cl (81); Tom Ledbetter, tpt (81); Randy Newey, p (81); Bruce Nye, tu; Betty Powell, cl; Tom Schneider, tsax (82).

## ROYAL GARDEN JAZZ BAND Chico CA 1984

From SIX HITS & A MISS.

Andy Bailey, tpt; Ken Kugelman, p; Polly Morine, reeds; Rich Powell, d; Greg Richardson, tu; Ken Taylor, tbn.

## SACRAMENTO JAZZ JUBILEE MESSENGERS SAC 1981

Joe Gilman, p; Scott Gordon, d; Larry Mooney, tbn; Svetozar Necak, sb; Kurt Pearsall, tpt; Terrie Richards, v; John Spivack, g; Kent Sylvester, ssax; Bill Tharp, tpt.

## STJS SCHOLARSHIP JAZZ BAND SAC 1985

Sponsored by Sacramento Traditional Jazz Society.

Blair Chenoweth, cl; Dennis Kurima, sax; David Morton, tbn; Diane Pyle, sax; Mike Rice, tpt; PASQUALE SALERNO, d; Huey Todd, p.

## SIX HITS & A MISS REVISED Chico CA 1983

From FOUR HITS & A MISS, recently retitled ROYAL GARDEN JB.

Rudy Anderson, tu; Andy Bailey, tpt; Dan Betschart, sax; Joe Duri, tbn; Ken Kugelman, p; Polly Morine, cl/asax; Rich Powell, d; Greg Richardson, tu (84); Ken Taylor, tbn (84).

## SIZZLIN' SEVEN SAC 1984-85

Dir: Val Herby. Bill Dauphinais, d; Maria Denney, tsax; Melissa Haisten, p; Nancy Herby, sb; Peter Lehmann, cl; JOE REARDON, tpt; Jordan Stockton, tbn.

## SWEET MOLASSES SJ 1977

Joe Earl, tbn; Chris Finelli, p; Dave Giampietro, cl; Mike Swanson, tu; Jim Wagner, d; Skip Wagner, tpt.

# ADDENDA

**Bob Aguilera, reeds** - Newport Harbor

**Howard Alden, bjo** - Golden West

**Lou Allinger, p** - Blue 5; Sunset Stompers

**Marty Baldwin, tpt** - So Bay 7

**Shirley Beaumonte, bjo** *(1952 Nyack NY)* - Rent Party

### BILLY AND THE BACHELORS LA 1965-70
Palmer Casey, bjo; Frank Demond, tbn; Bill Mitchell, p (alt); Dick Shooshan, p; John Smith, ssax; BILLY WELLS, bjo; others unknown.

### THE BLUE FIVE LA 1954
Lou Allinger, p; Al Colter, tpt; Art Levin, tu; Walt Sereth, cl; Bill Sharp, sb; Lee Wedberg, d.

**Earl Boyle, reeds** - Newport Harbor

### BILL CARTER'S JAZZ BAND LA 1956
Buddy Burns, sb; BILL CARTER, cl; Frank Demond, tbn; Bruce Dexter, tpt; Bill Mitchell, p; Lee Wedberg, d.

**Palmer Casey, bjo** - Billy Bachelors

**Ed Chapin, cl** *physician* - Bienville

**Chris Clark, bass** - Sunset Stompers

### COSTA DEL ORO JAZZ BAND LA1950-56
Ralph Ball, tu; Bruce Dexter, tpt; Ed Durant, bjo; Russ Gilman, p/tbn; Ellen Hertel, p; JIM LEIGH, tbn (-54); Roland Working, cl (-53). ADD: BILL CARTER, cl (53-56); Bill Hawley, bjo.

**Mike Crain, d** - Unquenchables

**Roger deLaix, bjo** - Sunset Stompers

### BRUCE DEXTER'S JAZZ BAND LA 1956
Buddy Burns, sb; Frank Demond, tbn; BRUCE DEXTER, tpt; Russ Gilman, p; Jim Leigh, tbn; Walt Sereth, cl; Lee Wedberg, d.

### DIXIE TRAVELERS LA 1965
Jack Booth, tbn; Bill Garner, sb; Jim Hammerton, cl; Charlie Lookabill, d; Duane Moyers, bjo; KEN SOUTHWORTH, p; Dick Williams, cor.

**Jack Doerr, reeds** - Vine St

**Ed Durant, bjo** - Costa Del Oro

**Joe Felix, p** - Vine St

228

RANDY KELLER 1973

## *JOHN GILL'S ORIGINAL SUNSET FIVE* SF 1985

JOHN GILL, d/v; Ray Skjelbred, p; Bob Schulz, cor; Mike Starr, tbn; Lynn Zimmer, cl.
*SOS 1094 "I Lost My Heart In Dixie Land" (85)*

## GOLDEN GATE RHYTHM MACHINE SF 1985→

SCOTT ANTHONY, bjo; Jack Frost, sb; Bob Neighbor, tpt; Jim Rothermel, cl; Mike Starr, tbn.

## GOLDEN WEST SNYCOPATORS Huntington Beach CA 1981

Winners of 81 Southern Comfort Collegiate JB Competition, representing Golden West College.

Howard Alsen, bjo; Dan Barrett, tbn; Mark Curry, cl; Denny Hardwick, bjo/g; Bill Liston, tsax; Bob Reitmeier, asax; Bryan Shaw, tpt; Ed Slauson, d; Dan Zeilinger, tu.
*"Like a Dixieland Band" (81)*

**Lorenzo Green, d** - Sunset Stompers

**Chuck Greening, bass** *aerospace engr* - Bienville

**Jim Hammerton, reeds** - Dixie Travelers

229

**Denny Hardwick, bjo, g** - Golden West

**Bill Hawley, bjo** - Costa Del Oro

**Ellen Hertel, p** - Costa Del Oro

**Elmer Hess, bass** - Dixie Rhythm Ramblers

**Daryl Hosick, p** - So Bay 7

**Don Hunsicker, p** *music store owner* - Rose City JB

## THE JAZZ MISSIONARIES LA 1963

Also called SKIFFLE 5; *Keg & /*Redondo Beach.
AL CROWNE, tpt; Frank Demond, tbn; Mike Fay, sb; Carol Leigh, v; Vic Loring, bjo; Walt
Sereth, cl; Dick Shooshan, p.
*EPITAPH 3 (4 cuts 63)*

**Robin King, bass** - Newport Harbor

**Bill Liston, reeds** - Golden West

**Charlie Lookabill, d** - Dixie Travelers

**Duane Moyers, bjo** - Dixie Travelers

## NEWPORT HARBOR JAZZ BAND Newport Beach CA 1956-59

*Honeybucket* Costa Mesa (56-58); *Speakeasy Club* Venice (58-59).
Bob Aguilera, cl (-57); John Henderson, tpt (-58); Steve Hope, tbn; Ked Lynch, p (-57);
Robin King, tu; Joe McCaffrey, d; DAVE WEIRBACH, bjo. ADD: John Boland, cl (58-59); Earl
Boyle, cl (57-58); Ernie Carson, tpt (58-59); Russ Gilman, p (58-59); Robbie Rhodes, p
(57-58).

**Clyde Owes, tpt** *(1925 Chicago IL) fine artist* - ldr Vine St

## PARADISE HOTEL JAZZ BAND see ORANGE BLOSSOM

**Jimmy Pratt, d** - Vine St

**John Robbins, bjo** - Unquenchables

**Jim Sawyer, tbn** - ldr Unquenchables

**Stan Soroken, tpt** *(1940 Los Angeles CA)* - Bye Bye Boys; big bands; led own groups

**Ken Southworth, p** - ldr Dixie Travelers

## STRAWHATTERS LA c1950

One of many titles Lamare used for his groups playing in Hollywood.
Pud Brown, reeds; Brad Gowans, tbn; NAPPY LAMARE, bjo/g; Stu Pletcher, tpt; Zutty
Singleton, d.

# THE ORGANIZATIONS

Backbone of the jazz movement, jazz societies were responsible for the perpetuation of the art, for exposing and supporting new bands, for underwriting jubilees and concerts, for bringing people together socially under a common banner. As is typical with all organizations, although membership figures may be impressively large, the burden of maintenance and operation usually rested on the shoulders of a handful of stalwarts and because of their efforts, the music thrived and the Clubs grew.

Indicative of the appeal of jazz is that once a jazz club was conceived, it usually flourished — there were few failures — and there was something like 150 active traditional jazz clubs in the USA by 1985.

**AMERICA'S FINEST CITY DIXIELAND JAZZ SOCIETY (1982)** P.O. Box 82776, San Diego CA 92138. MEMBERS: 800. PPs: 83-84 John Dehler; 85 Alan Adams (pro tem). PUBL: *Jazz Rambler*. Founded by Phil Andreen and John Dehler. Incorporation pending. Bimonthly concerts and dances presented at various locations. Hosted annual Great American Dixieland Jazz Festival.

**ARIZONA CLASSIC JAZZ SOCIETY (1985)** 3344 North 56 Street, Phoenix AZ 85051. MEMBERS: 150. PPs: Board of Directors. PUBL: *Arizona Classic Jazz*. Founded by Dick Knutson and Jeff Woodhouse. Originated from a chartered bus trip to San Diego Jazz Festival in Nov 1984. Monthly sessions planned. House Band: Desert City 6.

**BASIN STREET REGULARS (CENTRAL COAST HOT JAZZ SOCIETY) (1977)** P.O. Box 1193, San Luis Obispo CA 93406. MEMBERS: 1200. PPs: 77 Mort Berman, 78 Dave Watson, 79 Jeanne Scaief, 80-81 Ben Russell, 82 O. P. Chase, 83 Pat Russell, 84 Al Davis, 85 Jack Goddard. PUBL: *Offbeat*. SCHOLARSHIP: two awarded each year to area musicians who demonstrated an interest and proficiency in traditional jazz. Founded by Bob Connolly and K. O. Eckland. Incorporated 1978. Monthly sessions at Pismo Beach Veterans Hall drew audiences of 300-400. House Band: World Famous Desolation Jazz Ensemble & Mess Kit Repair Battalion (-85). Hosted annual Jubilee By the Sea in Pismo Beach, as well as yearly picnic and New Year's Eve costume dance. Associate Member UJSC.

**CENTRAL CALIFORNIA TRADITIONAL JAZZ SOCIETY (1981)** 139 West Olive, Fresno CA 93786. MEMBERS: 800. PPs: 81-83 Woody Laughnan, 84-85 Vern Constantin. PUBL: *Jazz*. Founded by Woody Laughnan. Fractioned into FRESNO DIXIELAND SOCIETY in 1984. Monthly sessions at Fresno Elks Lodge. Hosted annual Hanford Dixieland Jazz Revival.

**DIXIELAND JAZZ SOCIETY OF SAN DIEGO COUNTY** Details unknown.

**FEATHER RIVER JAZZ SOCIETY (1983)** P.O. Box 677, Graeagle CA 96102. MEMBERS: 200. PPs: 84-85 Don Fleming. PUBL: *Dixieland Jazz Notes*. SCHOLARSHIP: two annually at College of Pacific for deserving music students. Founded by Julie Cardoza, Don Fleming and Herb Newell. Monthly sessions eight times a year in Graeagle. House Band: Feather Riverboat Jazz Band.

**FRESNO DIXIELAND SOCIETY (1984) P.O. Box 16399, Fresno CA 93755.** MEMBERS: 350. PPs: 84-85 Don Kessler. PUBL: *Dixieland Gazette*. Founded by Don Kessler and Woody Laughnan as a spinoff group from CENTRAL CALIFORNIA TRADITIONAL JAZZ SOCIETY due to policy disagreements with members of the board of directors. The two, along with 12 other CCTJS members, formed the new Society. Monthly sessions at Hacienda Inn. House Band: Blue Street Jazz Band. Non-profit status applied for; scholarships planned. Hosted annual Fresno Mardi Gras and other events.

**GRAYS HARBOR TRADITIONAL JAZZ SOCIETY (19-) P.O. Box 646, Aberdeen WA 98520.**

**HIGH SIERRA JAZZ CLUB (1973) P.O. Box 712, Three Rivers CA 93271.** MEMBERS: 450. PPs: 73-75 Lueder Ohlwein, 76-78 Chet Crain, 79 Vic Kimzey, 80 Sam Ragan, 81 Earl McKee, 82 Rusty Crain, 83 Stan Huddleston, 84-85 Sue Mills. PUBL: *Jazzomania*. Founded by Lueder Ohlwein; originally SIERRA TRADITIONAL JAZZ CLUB. Incorporated 1978. A hard core nucleus kept jazz thriving in the scenic mountain town not much greater in population than the jazz Club membership. Monthly sessions at Veterans Hall included a potluck dinner and featured High Sierra Jazz Band as house band, usually in concert with a guest group. Hosted annual Jazzaffair. Associate Member UJSC.

THE NATURAL GAS JAZZ BAND October 1979

**HONOLULU HOT JAZZ SOCIETY (1984) P.O. Box 22862, Honolulu HI 96822.** PPs: 84 Don Sharp. PUBL: *Dr Jazz*.

**HOT JAZZ SOCIETY (1973) 2120 Main Street, Vancouver BC Canada V5T 3C5.** MEMBERS: 2500. PPs: years unstated, Barry Bonner, Martin Hatfield, Glen Page, Dave Todd, Jerry Wineberg, 85 Bruce McRae. PUBL: *Hot Sheet*. Founded by Lloyd Arntzen and Dave Todd to honor Louis Armstrong upon his death. Incorporated 1975. Club had its own venue with dance floor and bar, open five to six nights per week featuring various forms of jazz and big band music. House band: Phoenix Jazzers. Hosted annual Vancouver Dixieland Jazz Festival.

**INLAND EMPIRE JAZZ CLUB (1984)** Monthly sessions at Fontana Elks Lodge.

**JAZZ FORUM (1977) P.O. Box 2351, Encino CA 91343.** MEMBERS: 450. PPs: 77-79 Chuck Conklin; 80 Norm Albert; 81-82 Paul Lenart; 83 Chuck Conklin; 84 Elaine Mitchell; 85 Marge Murphy. PUBL: *Jazz Forum*. SCHOLARSHIP: four awarded since 1980. Founded by Chuck Conklin, Tom and Kathy Walsh. Incorporated 1977. Allied with AFM Local 47 to further the performance of jazz. Monthly sessions at Hacienda Hotel in El Segundo. Presenters of annual "Jazzman of the Year" award for outstanding contributions to the art form: 78 Matty Matlock; 79 Manny Klein; 80 Wild Bill Davison; 81 Nappy Lamare and Eddie Miller; 82 Joe Darensbourg; 83 Pete Daily and Rosy McHargue, 84 unknown, 85 Heinie Beau. Sponsored annual Fall Festival for benefit of scholarship fund. Member UJCSC.

**JAZZ INCORPORATED (1968) 13171 Cedar St, Westminster CA 92683.** MEMBERS: 275. PPs: (years unstated) Herb Hunt, Roy Brewer, Bill Stumpp, Dee Woolem, Bert Griffin, Lloyd Grafton, Fred Palm, Morrie Levang, Fred Montgomery. PUBL: *Sessions*. Founded by Phil McMahon. Incorporated 1968, benevolence Musicians' Wives Club Local 7. Monthly sessions at West Anaheim Moose Lodge. Member UJCSC.

**MAPLE LEAF CLUB (1967) 5560 West 62nd St, Los Angeles CA 90056.** PPs: 84 Dick Zimmerman. PUBL: *The Rag Times*. Founded by Dave Bourne, Albert Huerta, Chuck McClure, Bill Mitchell and Dick Zimmerman to perpetuate classic ragtime and to present bi-monthly concerts specializing in that form of jazz at Variety Arts Center in downtown LA.

**MODESTO DIXIELAND JAZZ SOCIETY (1982) 2813 Richmond Ct, Modesto CA 95350.** MEMBERS: 600. PPs: 82-84 unstated, 85 Tommy Gulindo. PUBL: *Modesto Jazette*. Incorporated 1982. House band: Hogin's Heroes. Monthly sessions, location unstated.

**MONTEREY BAY HOT JAZZ SOCIETY (1975) P.O. Box 1872, Salinas CA 93902.** MEMBERS: 450. PPs: 75 John Fanning, 76 Barney Laiolo, 77 Joe Ingram, 78 Charley Pond, 79 Ned Brundage, 80 Ina Dow, 81 Tom Maddern, 82 Bill Burgess, 83 Don Pellerin, 84 Doug Curtis, 85 Pat O'Malley. PUBL: *Hot Notes*. Founded by John Fanning and Joe Ingram. Monthly sessions at Monterey Elks Lodge. Hosted annual Dixieland Monterey.

**NEW ORLEANS JAZZ CLUB OF CALIFORNIA (1963-indef) P.O. Box 1225, Kerrville TX 78028.** PUBL: *Jazzologist*. Founded by Bill Bacin, patterned after a concept of Doc Souchon (NO), and formed in Southern California. Dissolved as an entity upon his move to Texas, where it continued in titular form there.

**NEW ORLEANS JAZZ CLUB OF NORTHERN CALIFORNIA (1965) P.O. Box 27232, San Francisco CA 94127.** MEMBERS: 700. PPs: 65-72 Marshall Peterson; 72-77 David Walker, 78-79 Steve Manhard, 80-81 Ed Lawless, 82-83 Janella Fleming, 84-85 Fred Zaft. PUBL: *NOJC News*. Founded by Marshall Peterson in Santa Rosa, who amassed some 50 jazz fans to form the Club in 1965; staged sessions at various commercial locations and Grange Hall until 1969, when Club was re-established in SF. Predating was HOT MUSIC SOCIETY OF SAN FRANCISCO, which folded in 1941. Incorporated 1966. Monthly sessions at various locations; annual picnics at Marin Art & Garden Center. Hosted annual jazz concerts at Armstrong Grove on Russian River until 1975 and Jazz On San Francisco Bay cruises from 1966-77. Hosted annual San Francisco Jazz Showcase from 1972.

**NEW ORLEANS JAZZ CLUB OF SOUTHERN CALIFORNIA (1968) P.O. Box 15212, Long Beach CA 90815.** MEMBERS: 300. PPs: 68-69 Bill Grosvenor, 70 Dee Woolem, 71 John Sheppard, 72 Jim Hardesty, 72 John Sheppard, 73-75 Hal Rumenapp, 76 Bill Balendonck, 77-78 Norm Burnham, 79-80 Bob Christy, 81-82 Don Barnett, 83-84 Larry Baker, 85 Norm Burnham. PUBL: *Intermission*. Roots lie in original NEW ORLEANS JAZZ CLUB OF

CALIFORNIA. Incorporated 1968. Monthly sessions at Los Amigos Country Club in Downey. House Band: Jazz-a-Ma-Tass, later Jazz Generation. Sponsored annual Catalina Dixieland Jamboree. Member UJCSC.

**OREGON CITY TRADITIONAL JAZZ SOCIETY (1975) P.O. Box 214, Oregon City OR 97045.** PPs: 75-84 unstated, 84 Jo Simms, 85 Chuck Kelly. PUBL: *OCTJS Newsletter*. Founded by Bill and Corinne Bertrand. Monthly sessions at Oregon City Elks Lodge.

**PALM SPRINGS JAZZ SOCIETY (19-) P.O. Box 8442, Palm Springs CA 92262.** PPs: 84 Dick Broadie.

**PHOENIX HOT JAZZ SOCIETY** Never extant as such but rather a listing in the Phoenix telephone book as an information center for jazz aficionados.

**POOR ANGEL HOT JAZZ SOCIETY (1972) 5719 Bertrand Ave, Encino CA 91316.** PPs: Bob Taber. PUBL: newsletter. Founded by Marvin Ash and Bob Taber as a labor of love, patterned after Doc McPherson's Blue Angel Jazz Club, and was unincorporated. Hosted invitational all-star concerts six times a year, the first ones at *Sky Trails* in Van Nuys, later at Pasadena Eagles Lodge.

**PUGET SOUND TRADITIONAL JAZZ SOCIETY (1975) 610 17th Avenue East, Seattle WA 98112.** MEMBERS: 600. PPs: 75-77 Barry Durkee, 77-81 Tom Rippey, 82-83 Mamie Russell, 84 Jim Walker. PUBL: *Jazz Soundings*. Founded by Barry Durkee. Chartered 1975, had ten monthly sessions and an annual New Year's Eve dance. House Bands: Great Excelsior, Rainier and Uptown Lowdown.

**SACRAMENTO NEW ORLEANS HOT JAZZ SOCIETY (1972-1975)** Founded by Jerry Kaehele, featured traditional style jazz. Monthly sessions at various locations until club was disbanded.

**SACRAMENTO TRADITIONAL JAZZ SOCIETY (1968) P.O. Box 15604, Sacramento CA 95813.** MEMBERS: 3700. PPs: 68 Jerry Kaehele, 69 Bill Richards, 70 Chuck McKay, 71 Free Hafer, 72 David Beeman, 73 Ozzie Belmore, 74 Joe Mickleson, 75 Jack Weaver, 76-77 Hank Lawson, 78 Dutch Deutsch, 79 Bill Richards, 80 Ted Tripp, 81-82 Chuck Mason, 83-84 Jack Martin, 85 Ruth Rainwater. PUBL: *And All That Jazz*, formerly *Jazz Club Notes*. SCHOLARSHIP: Since 80, some 30 scholarships have been awarded to young people to further studies in music. Founded by Jerry Kaehele with Bill Borcher, Jack Burke, Roy Harper. First meeting drew 68 persons at Orangevale Grange Hall, subsequent monthly sessions at Elks Club attracted 600. Hosted annual Sacramento Dixieland Jubilee and Mini-Jubilee.

**SAN FRANCISCO TRADITIONAL JAZZ FOUNDATION (1980) P.O. Box 433, San Leandro CA 94577.** Non-profit organization established by James P Goggin as a repository for jazz-related material to be featured in a proposed jazz museum. Dedicated to research, preserve and exhibit Bay Area jazz memorabilia, recordings and historical data.

**SAN JOAQUIN DIXIELAND JAZZ SOCIETY (1978) P.O. Box 9339, Stockton CA 95208.** MEMBERS: 750. PPs: 79-80 Vince Marino, 81-82 Art Nielsen, 83-84 Bob Romans, 85 Buddy Walter. PUBL: *Delta Rag*, formerly *SJDJS*. Founded by Tom Castles, Otis Edmondson, Ed Huntington, Vince Marino, Bill Reinhart, William Renwick and Ray Walters. Incorporated 1979. Staged first monthly session at Stockton Elks Lodge Feb 1979 and remained there ever since. Hosted annual Jazz On the Waterfront (Stockton Dixieland Jubilee).

**SAN JUAN ISLAND GOODTIME CLASSIC JAZZ ASSOCIATION (1972) P.O. Box 1379, Friday Harbor WA 98250.** MEMBERS: 200. PPs: 72-79 unstated, 80-81 Gary Provonsha, 82 Nate Benedict, 83 Charmaine Provonsha, 84 Ronn Everman, 85 Debbie Emery. PUBL:

Umbrella parade for the HIGH SIERRA JAZZ BAND

*Jazzsession.* Founded by Gary Provonsha, club supported and subsidized Island City Jazz Band. Hosted annual San Juan Island Dixieland Jazz Festival.

**SANTA BARBARA DIXIELAND JAZZ SOCIETY (1965) P.O. Box 626, Santa Barbara CA 93116.** MEMBERS: 150. PPs: 65-82 Chuck Shaefer, 82-85 Nancy Jent. PUBL: *Dixie Doodles.* Non-profit association founded by Chuck and Leone Shaefer. House band: Aristocrats. Monthly sessions at Goleta Elks Lodge. Associate Member UJCSC.

**SANTA CLARITA DIXIELAND JAZZ CLUB (1979) P.O. Box 2331, Newhall CA 91351.** MEMBERS: 275. PPs: 79 Board of Directors (Wally Craig, pres), 80 Regi Byette, 81 John Cornelius, 82 Jim Smith, 83 Peggy Bisset, 84 Ray Masters, 85 John Cornelius. PUBL: newsletter. SCHOLARSHIP: Annual Red Murphy Memorial Scholarship Award. Founded by Wally Craig and Russ Bissett. Incorporated 1980 within the areas of Valencia, Newhall, Saugus and Canyon Country. First session Jun 1979 with a group fronted by Pete Daily. Sessions monthly at Newhall-Saugus Elks Lodge. Member UJCSC.

**SEATTLE JAZZ SOCIETY** Evolved into WASHINGTON JAZZ SOCIETY, which supported modern jazz, and which was the organization some members broke away from to form PUGET SOUND TRADITIONAL JAZZ SOCIETY.

**SOCIETY FOR THE PRESERVATION OF DIXIELAND JAZZ (1961) 636 Alamosa Drive, Claremont CA 91711.** MEMBERS: 400. PPs: 61 Ted Sharpe, 62 Pete Turner, 63 Guy Bussell, 64 Ward Popenoe, 65 John Beals, 66-67 Chet Jaeger, 68 Carl Cornell, 69 George Anderson, 70 Ernie Grindle, 71 Scot Nicholson, 72 Neil Shumaker, 73 Charles Coulter, 74 Beverly Mayfield, 75 George Olson, 76 Jack Stewart, 77 Tom Raftican, 78 Hal Blevins, 79-80 Chet Jaeger, 81 Rosalie Blevins, 82-83 Morey Huff, 84-85 Wayne Sefton. PUBL: *Dixie Flyer.* SCHOLARSHIP: available for young musicians in the area. Founded by John Beals, Chet Jaeger and Allan Peck. Incorporated 1966. First meetings at *Storyville*, thereafter at a succession of locations, finally growing to two sessions each month, alternating between Riverside Moose Lodge and Azusa Elks Lodge. House Band: Nightblooming Jazzmen. Member UJCSC.

**SOUTH BAY NEW ORLEANS JAZZ CLUB (1962) 5018 Arvada St, Torrance CA 90503.**
PPs: 62-62 Larry Marvin, 63-74 Ron Going, 75-76 William Meyer, 77 Hal Newman, 78 Roger Snell, 79 Jack Widmark, 80 Stuart Keesling, 81 Ben Benson, 82 Stuart Keesling, 83-84 Howard Beard, 85 George Marois. PUBL: *Blue Note*. SCHOLARSHIP: available for students interested in the study and perpetuation of American music (presumably jazz). Founded by several musicians at Redondo Beach's *The Keg and I*. Incorporated 1981. Had sister jazz club in Tokyo's Waseda University, which sent a touring jazz group to visit in 1981. Monthly sessions at Hawthorne Elks Lodge. Member UJCSC.

**SOUTH BAY TRADITIONAL JAZZ SOCIETY (1971) P.O. Box 1547, Pacifica CA 94044.** MEMBERS: 675. PPs: 71 Board of Directors, 72 Hugo Mateus, 73 Ted Zuur, 74 Art Cesena, 75 Roy Butler, 76 Art Cesena, 77-78 Pat Ault, 79 Art Cesena, 80 Lenore Martin, 81 Garret Bouma, 82-83 Bob Allenby, 84-85 Frank McTiernan; 86 Pat Patrick. PUBL: *South Bay Beat*. Founded by Hugo Mateus, Pat Mateus and Ted Zuur; developed from an idea conceived during lunch at a restaurant in SJ. Incorporated 1977. First session May 1971 at *Bold Knight* in Sunnyvale. Hosted Annual Spring Fling.

**SOUTHEAST DIXIELAND JAZZ, INC (1984) P.O. Box 1012, Downey CA 90091.**
MEMBERS: 250. PPs: 84 Ray Lyon. PUBL: *The Chord*. Founded by Ray Lyon. Initial meeting Jan 1984 drew some 400 aficionados and monthly sessions continued thereafter at Rio Hondo Country Club in Downey.

**SOUTHERN CALIFORNIA HOT JAZZ SOCIETY (1949) 1016 West Santa Cruz St, San Pedro CA 90731.** PPs: 49-83 unstated, 82-84 Alice Widmark, 85 John Bishop. PUBL: *Fanfare*. Incorporated 1962. Monthly sessions at Maywood-Bell American Legion Hall. Member UJCSC.

**SOUTHERN OREGON TRADITIONAL JAZZ SOCIETY (1981) P.O. Box 1001, Ashland OR 97520.** MEMBERS: 1100. PPs: 81-83 unstated, 84 Don Tingle. PUBL: newsletter. SCHOLARSHIP: available. Incorporated 1981. First session was sparsely attended, but membership and support grew steadily. In Sept 1982, monthly session format was changed to that of a concert, with featured guests like Johnny Guarnieri, Eddie Miller, Abe Most and Henry Cuesta, among other notables, as well as participating area musicians.

**TRADITIONAL JAZZ SOCIETY OF OREGON (19-) P.O. Box 7432, Eugene OR 97401.**
PPs: 84 Dick Hickenbottom, 85 Mike Blagaich, others unstated. PUBL: newsletter. Monthly sessions at Emerald Valley Forest Inn in Creswell. Hosted annual Emerald Valley Dixieland Jazz Jubilee.

**TRI-CITIES TRADITIONAL JAZZ SOCIETY (1983) 207 West Columbia Drive, Kennewick WA 99336.** MEMBERS: 300. PPs: 83-85 Marian Overturf. PUBL: *Tri-Jazz*. Founded by Marion Overturf with Bill and Corinne Bertrand. Incorporated 1984 after beginning as an impromptu picnic in Overturf's back yard. Being in a remote area of Oregon, the principal problem was attracting performing musicians, but they have had many noteable jazzmen as guests since Mike Vax's Great American Jazz Band appeared at their first session Sept 1983. Monthly sessions at Rivershore Motor Inn in Richland. House Band: Tri-City Jazz Band.

**UNITED JAZZ CLUBS OF SOUTHERN CALIFORNIA (1984)** A congress of non-profit jazz organizations in Southern California banded together for mutual benefit. Member Clubs: Jazz Forum; Jazz Incorporated; New Orleans Jazz Club of Southern California; Santa Clarita Jazz Club; Society for the Preservation of Dixieland Jazz; South Bay New Orleans Jazz Club; Southern California Hot Jazz Society; Valley Dixieland Jazz Club. Associate Clubs: Basin Street Regulars (CCHJS); High Sierra Jazz Club; Santa Barbara Dixieland Jazz Society. PP: 85 Morey Levang.

**VALLEY DIXIELAND JAZZ CLUB** (1969) **5658 Winnetka Ave, Woodland Hills CA 91367.** MEMBERS: 400. PPs: 69-70 Walt Greenawald, 71 Dave Dolson, 72 Joe Hook, 73 Bill Myers, 74 Ron Ridgewell, 75 Gus Willmorth, 76 Joe Robertson, 77 Mike Silverman, 78 Cliff Wunschel, 79 Dan Snyder, 80 Margaret Teagarden, 81 Mike Silverman, 82 Dan Grant, 83 Margaret Teagarden, 84 Dan Grant, 85 Margaret Teagarden. PUBL: *Dixie Beat*. Founded by Dick Duncan, Dave Dolson, Walt Greenawald, Joe Hook, Les Shepard and Gus Willmorth. Incorporated 1969. Monthly sessions at Canoga Park Knights of Columbus Hall. Member UJCSC.

**VIRGINIA CITY JAZZ SOCIETY** (19-) **P.O. Box 423, Virginia City NV 89440.**

**WILLAMETTE VALLEY JAZZ SOCIETY** (1985) **P.O. Box 307, Albany OR 97321.** PPs 85 Jon Balschweid. PUBL: newsletter.

Stern Grove, San Francisco, 1983
PRESERVATION HALL JAZZ BAND concert

237

Mrs R L ''Jeff'' White

# THE CELEBRATIONS

"Everybody wants to get in the act," Jimmy Durante claimed. This was apparent, entering the '80s, by the proliferation of jazz features almost anywhere there was a spot big enough to hold a hundred bodies. Where one was once hard pressed to find a single jazz band playing at some fairly convenient location, the bandwagons and showcases grew to immense proportions. Hardly a fair-weathered weekend went by that any thirst for jazz could not be slaked.

As with the blossoming of jazz clubs throughout the nation, celebrations took shape to provide arenas where aficionados could hear dozens of jazz bands for comparatively little expense. Early on, the Bull-Norman concerts at LA's Shrine Auditorium set the pattern for those to follow. Along the way there were historic gatherings like the early mixed-bag Monterey Jazz Festivals, where trad jazz musicians were stirred into a curious melange with progressive musicians... the boisterous Dixielands at Disneyland... the 1970 Louis Armstrong birthday gala at the Shrine with its SRO crowd... the city-sponsored Hollywood Bowl presentations... the Stern Grove concerts in SF. These kept the spirit alive and well through the low part of the cycle. However, the flower really came into blossom on Memorial Day 1974 with the initial Sacramento affair, which paved the way for a new generation of true jazz celebrations.

Generally, the festivals were non-commercial, jazz club oriented and maintained, staffed by willing, often harried, volunteers and staged with impressive professionalism. Several were fund-raising campaigns or publicity devices. All had their share of surprises.

For some aspirants jazz brought unexpected rewards, while for others it represented a fizzle. Reasons for the sporadic, hit-and-miss success rate of jazz festivals are anybody's guess — some were damned by weather, location, conflicting schedules, an on and on. One bright idea flashed in the pan because it was scheduled on Mother's Day, while another, tried as an offhand venture, is in its ninth successful year. Sacramento, Pismo Beach, San Juan Island, Nugget Casino and Disneyland have all scored notable successes despite respective onuses of being too hot, too cold, too out-of-the-way, too commercial and too expensive.

Many so-called jamborees and jazz festivals were not as big as they might appear in first light, sometimes featuring only two or three bands on a Sunday afternoon, and many were not devotedly altruistic in conception. Some were billed under the banners of "Dixiland" and "Cool Jazz Festival" by entrepreneurs somewhat uncertain about the spelling and temperature of their subject matter. Not that there wasn't musical merit in any or all of these, but a line had to be drawn somewhere for inclusion here.

Acknowledgement of the following special events is by virtue of their being among the more recognized celebrations. As known, after the years are shown the dates, approximate attendance, featured bands, and the chairmen or festival chargés:

## CAPITOLA JAZZ JAMBOREE Capitola CA

Conceived and implemented by "Travelin' Dan" Westerman and his hypothetical group, the Society for the Preservation Of Ragtime and Tradjazz — SPORT. Event took place at several venues in the town's business district. Attendances are unknown since admissions were for the most part free.

**1982 - 7 Aug** Churchill; Hangtown; Monterey Bay; Prof Plum; Silicon; Tuleburg; WFDJE&MKRB.

**1983 - 6-7 Aug** And That's Jazz; Devil Mtn; Dixieland Inc; 52 St; Hangtown; Jubilee; Monterey Bay; Natural Gas; Prof Plum; Rascals Ragtime; Riverbank; Swing & Sway; Tuleburg.

**1984 - 4 Aug** And That's Jazz; Breakloose 6; Calif Express; Churchill; Del Rey Dos; Hot Blues & Jazz; Jubilee; Monterey Bay; Rascals Ragtime; Take 2.

## CATALINA ISLAND DIXIELAND JAMBOREE Avalon CA

Conceived by Hal Rumenapp and hosted annually by the New Orleans Jazz Club of Southern California.

**1972-81** unknown.

**1982 - 24 Jul** Jamboree Hal; Nightblooming Jazzmen; WFDJE&MKRB

**1983** unknown.

**1984 - 21 Jul** Chicago 6; Dixie RR; Fullertowne; Hyperion; Jazz Formula; Jazz Gen; Men of Note.

**1985 - 27 Jul** Angel; Fullertowne; Hyperion; Jazz Formula; Jazz Gen; WFDJE&MKRB.

## DIXIELAND AT DISNEYLAND Buena Park CA

A classic showcase of stars made this one- and two-day annual event an immediate hit, bringing crowds of jazz lovers into the park. It could be said that all future jazz festivals would be based upon the principles of Dixieland at Disneyland. Here was one of precious few places at that time where the attraction of massed bands with one admission charge was available, and in an environment most unique. Why this program was dropped, or at least not revived as the popularity of jazz again grew during the seventies, remains a mystery.

**1960-65** unknown.

**1966** Louis Armstrong; Crosby Bob Cats; Firehouse 5; Turk Murphy; Doc Souchon; Young Men From NO.

**1967** Louis Armstrong; Teddy Buckner; Eddie Condon; Firehouse 5; Doc Souchon; Young Men From NO.

**1968** Teddy Buckner; Dukes of Dixieland; Mickey Finn; Firehouse 5; Pete Lofthouse 2nd Story Men; Santo Pecora; Turk Murphy; SCHJC Marching Band; So Market St; Young Men From NO.

**1969 - 10-11 May** Louis Armstrong; Dukes of Dixieland; Firehouse 5; Clancy Hayes; Barbara Kelly; LA All-Stars (dir Bill Bacin, Bigard, Cary, Garland, Havens, Manone, Pollack, Purnell); Turk Murphy; Pawn Ticket & Hockshop 4 (youth); Wally Rose; So Market St; Sugar Willie.

## DIXIELAND JUBILEE Shrine Auditorium, Los Angeles CA

Outstanding productions by entrepreneurs Gene Norman and Frank Bull catered to the public's demand for "show time" in jazz, and featured most of the giants of jazz at one time or another. It would be proper to describe these stellar functions as the very beginning of showcasing traditional jazz. Bull had the "America Dances" radio show on KFWB in the late forties and early fifties, which managed to get in a fair share of hot jazz; Norman did likewise on KLAC. Attendances for all events were capacity, about 7000.

**1948 - 5 Oct** Louis Armstrong All-Stars; Chicagoans; Eddie Condon; Wild Bill Davison; Wingy Manone; Kid Ory; Ted Vesely DJB.

**1949 - 7 Oct** Castle; Chicago Loopers; Crosby Bob Cats (E Miller's); Chicagoans; Firehouse 5; Red Nichols; Kid Ory; Muggsy Spanier/Ed Freeman Band.

**1950 - 6 Oct** Castle; Curbstone Cops; Chicagoans; Firehouse 5; Pollack Pick-a-Rib; Sextet From Hunger; Sharkey Bonano Kings of Dixieland; Ted Vesely.

**1951 - 5 Oct** Bjo Kings; Bob Crosby Band; Chicagoans; Firehouse 5; Pete Kelly Big 7; Rosy McHargue Ragtimers; Turk Murphy; Kid Ory; Sextet From Hunger; guest Jack Teagarden.

**1952 - 10 Oct** Chicagoans; Nick Fatool's Friends; George Lewis NO Band; McHargue Ragtimers; Scobey Frisco Band; J Teagarden Orch; Sextet From Hunger; guest Frank Trambauer.

## DIXIELAND MONTEREY Monterey CA

First one under this title, separated from Monterey Jazz Festival which had included trad jazz in token form, began under the direction of Don Lewis but failed to gain needed support for yearly continuance.

**1969 - 10-11 May** Louis Armstrong; Dukes of Dixieland; Firehouse 5; Clancy Hayes; Phil Howe Festival Band; Barbara Kelly; LA All-Stars (dir Bacin, Bigard, Cary, Garland, Havens, Manone, Pollack, Purnell); Turk Murphy; Pawn Ticket & Hockshop 4 (youth); Wally Rose; So Market St JB; Sugar Willie.

A second try, under the title MONTEREY DIXIELAND JAZZ FESTIVAL, was underwritten by the County Fair Board because of insurance problems; none was held in 1981. In 1982 Monterey Bay Hot Jazz Society assumed sponsorship, retitled it and moved events to the Doubletree Hotel and the waterfront and downtown business districts.

**1980 - 22-24 Aug** Apex; Beal Racquette Club 5; Desert City; Dixie Katz; Dixieland Inc; Fulton; Golden State; Gramercy; Hangtown; Jazzin' Babies; Monterey Bay; Natural Gas; Oregon; Prof Plum; Royal Society; WFDJE&MKRB. Chair: Joe Ingram.

**1982 - 5-7 Mar** Abalone; Apple Knockers; Desert City; Dixieland Inc; Do-Do-Wah; Fulton; Gem; High Sierra; Monterey Bay; Natural Gas; Nightblooming; Royal Society; Prof Plum; Tuleburg; WFDJE&MKRB; Your Father's Moustache (CO). Chair: Joe Ingram.

**1983 - 4-6 Mar** Abalone; Bruhner's All-Stars (SWEDEN); Desert City; Dixieland Inc; Do-Do-Wah; Fulton; Gem; Gramercy; High Sierra; Monterey Bay; Nightblooming; Port City; Prof Plum; Royal Society; WFDJE&MKRB; Your Father's Moustache (CO). Chair: Allen Caldiera.

**1984 - 2-4 Mar** Chicago 6; Devil Mtn; Dixieland Inc; Dixie 6; Do-Do-Wah; Fulton; Gem; Hangtown; High Sierra; Monterey Bay; Nightblooming; Prof Plum; Rascals Ragtime; Tuleburg; WFDKE&MKRB; Your Father's Moustache (CO); guest stars. Chair: Bill Burgess.

**1985 - 8-10 Mar** Do-Do-Wah; Fulton; Great American; High Sierra; Nightblooming; Royal Society; WFDJE&MKRB. Chair: Bill Burgess.

## GREAT AMERICAN DIXIELAND JAZZ FESTIVAL San Diego CA

Conceived by Phil Andreen. Originally privately funded and titled the HOLIDAY BOWL DIXIELAND JAZZ FESTIVAL because of its concurrency with the annual football bowl game, switched to the present tributary title in 1982 with sponsorship from that date by the America's Finest City Dixieland Jazz Society and backing by Great American First Savings Bank. Despite all the rampant humility, the annual event has grown in popularity partly because of an ideal location providing convenient access to all stages — everything takes place in the Town & Country and Hanalei Hotel complexes.

**1980 - 18-21 Dec - 500** Coulson; Desert City; Dixie Katz; Gem; Great Pacific; High Sierra; Jazzbo; Jazzin' Babies; Natural Gas; Nightblooming; Royal Society; San Diego Hysterical Bjo Society; Yankee Air; All-Star group; guest Fred Finn. Chair: Phil Andreen.

**1981 - 17-20 Dec - 1000** - Chicago 6; Desert City; Dixie Belles; Dixie Katz; Doc Olson; El Jebel (CO); Gem; High Sierra; High Society; Hot Frogs; Jazzbo; Natural Gas; New Bull Moose; Nightblooming; Oregon; Jazzin' Jrs; Rosie O'Grady (FL); San Diego DJB; San Diego HBS; WFDJE&MKRB; Yankee Air; guests Henry Cuesta, Phil Harris. Chair: Phil Andreen.

**1982 - 26-28 Nov - 3000** Alamo City (TX); Best All-Stars; Charlie's; Chicago 6; Cottonmouth; Daulong & Notes; Desert City; Dixie Katz; Gem; Golden Eagle; High Sierra; High Society JB; Island City; Jazzbo; Jazz Forum; Jazzin' Babies; Jazzin' Jrs; Nightblooming; Oregon; Prof Plum; San Diego DJB; San Diego HBS; Summit Ridge (CO); Sutterville; Woodi's; Yankee Air; guests Henry Cuesta, Tommy Newsom. Chair: John Dehler.

**1983 - 25-27 Nov - 7500** - Alamo City (TX); Best All-Stars; Buck Creek (VA); Charley's GTB; Chicago 6; Cottonmouth; Desert City; Fulton; Golden Eagle; Great American; Great Pacific; High Sierra; High Society; Hot Cotton (TN); Hot Frogs; Island City; Jazzbo; Jazzin' Babies; Jazzin' Jrs; Mississippi

Mudders; Natural Gas; NOJB Hawaii; Nightblooming; Oregon; Pearl Pac; Platinum Coast; Royal Society; San Diego DJB; San Diego HBS; So Frisco; Summit Ridge (CO); Sutterville; Uptown Lowdown; Woodi's; Yankee Air; guests Henry Cuesta, Maxine Sullivan. Chair: John Dehler.

**1984 - 23-25 Nov - 9000** Alamo City (TX); Black Diamond; Buck Creek (VA); Chicago 6; Cottonmouth; Crown City; Desert City; Dixie 6; Golden Eagle; High Sierra; High Society; Hot Cotton (TN); Hot Frogs; Island City; Jazzbo; Jazzin' Babies; Natural Gas; New Black Eagle (MA); Nightblooming; Prof Plum; San Diego HBS; So Frisco; Summit Ridge (CO); Uptown Lowdown; Yankee Air; guests John Best; Henry Cuesta. Chair: John Dehler.

**1985 - 29 Nov-1 Dec** Alamo City (TX); Black Diamond; Buck Creek (VA); Chicago 6; Cottonmouth; Desert City; Fulton; Golden Eagle; Great Pacific; High Sierra; High Society; Hot Cotton (TN); Hot Frogs; Hysterical DBS; Island City; Jazzin' Babies; Jazzbo; Natural Gas; Nightblooming; Prof Plum; St Louis Ragtimers (MO); San Diego HBS; Sons of Bix (CO); So Frisco; Summit Ridge (CO); Uptown Lowdown; Yankee Air; guests Henry Cuesta; Maxine Sullivan. Chair: Bob and Mary Solsbak.

## HANFORD JAZZ REVIVAL Hanford CA

Sponsored by the Central California Traditional Jazz Society and presented on the renovated city hall grounds.

**1983 - 16 Oct** Chicago 6; High Sierra; WFDJE&MKRB; others unknown.

**1984 - 20-21 Oct** Blue St; Chicago 6; Harding JB; High Sierra; Hogin's; Live Steam; MDJB; Nightblooming; Part Time; Royal Valley; Show Boat; Tuleburg; 7 other local groups. Chair: Vern Constantin.

**1985 - 14-15 Sep** Black Diamond; Chicago 6; Custer; Dew Drop; High Sierra; Hogin's; Live Steam; MDJB; Monterey Bay; River Rats; Royal Valley; Southtown Strummers; Statesmen Big Band; Tuleburg. Chair: Vern Constantin.

## JAZZAFFAIR Three Rivers CA

Sponsored by the High Sierra Jazz Club. Roots of the popular festival went back to Feb 73 when HSJC staged a one-band version (Jazzberry Jam Band) and the 1983 Jazzaffair was dubbed "the tenth annual." Audiences were necessarily limited due to lack of accommodations.

**1980 - 12-13 Apr - 1000** High Sierra; Jazzin' Babies; Nightblooming; Prof Plum; Riverbank; So Frisco; WFDJE&MKRB. Chair: Sam Ragan.

**1981 - 4-5 Apr - 1100** High Sierra; Jazzin' Babies; Monterey Bay; Natural Gas; Nightblooming; Prof Plum; Riverbank; So Frisco; WFDJE&MKRB. Chair: Sue Mills.

**1982 - 2-4 Apr - 1150** Desert City; Fulton; High Sierra; Hot Frogs; Nightblooming; Prof Plum; So Frisco; WFDJE&MKRB. Chair: Rusty Crain.

**1983 - 8-10 Apr - 1200** Desert City; Fulton; High Sierra; Natural Gas; Nightblooming; Prof Plum; WFDJE&MKRB. Chair: Sue Mills.

Wayne Nicholls

HIGH SIERRA JAZZ BAND, 1980 Jubilee By the Sea

**1984 - 13-15 Apr - 1300** Chicago 6; Fulton; High Sierra; Fullertowne; Gramercy; Natural Gas; Nightblooming; Prof Plum; Tuleburg. Chair: Sue Mills.

**1985 - 12-14 Apr - 1400** Chicago 6; Fulton; Golden Eagle; Gramercy; High Sierra; Island City; Natural Gas; Nightblooming; Prof Plum; WFDJE&MKRB. Chair: Sue Mills.

**1986 - 11-13 Apr - 1500** Black Diamond; Buck Creek (DC); Fulton; High Sierra; Natural Gas; Nightblooming; Prof Plum; PX.III; Tule Basin. Chair: Sam Ragan.

## JAZZ ON THE WATERFRONT Stockton CA

Sponsored by the San Joaquin Dixieland Jazz Society in the second year of their existence. Originally staged in downtown Stockton, the annual festival was finally located along the canal and the title changed in 1984 from the Stockton Dixieland Jubilee. The first one barely made expenses but succeeding ones proved increasingly successful.

**1980 - 20-21 Sep** Dixie Sync; Euphonic; Gem; Golden State; Gramercy; Fulton; Hangtown; High Sierra; Magnolia; Monterey Bay; Mudville; Pier 100; Port City; Prof Plum; Purple Gang; Riverbank; Tuleburg. Chair: Vince Marino.

**1981 - 3-4 Oct** Churchill; Dixie Kings; Fulton; Gem; Golden State; Happy Sync; Headliners; High Sierra; Jazz Beaux; Mudville; Natural Gas; Pier 100; Port City; Prof Plum; Sutterville; Tuleburg; Vax NOJB; WFDJE&MKRB. Chair: Art Nielson.

**1982 - 2-3 Oct - 2500** Black Diamond; Cell Block; Dixie Kings; Fulton; Happy Sync; High Sierra; Hot Frogs; Jazzin' Babies; Jazzin' Jrs; Mudville; Natural Gas; Oakland A; President's Men; Prof Plum; River Town; Swingaires; Tuleburg; Vax All-Stars. Chair: Steve Drivon, Bill Reinhart, Bob Stover.

**1983 - 1-2 Oct - 4000** And That's Jazz; Black Diamond; Cell Block; Fulton; Gem; Gold Standard; Hangtown; Happy Sync; Headliners; High Sierra; Jazz Beaux; Jazzin' Jrs; Jubilee; Monterey Bay; Natural Gas; Nightblooming; Prof Plum; Raisin; Red Hot Peppers; Royal Society; Swingaires; Tuleburg; Mike Vax JB; WFDJE&MKRB. Chair: Art Nielson, Bettelou Young.

**1984 - 28-30 Sep - 5000** B# Axxidentals; Black Diamond; Devil Mtn; Cell Block; Churchill; Fulton; Gold Standard; Gramercy; Hangtown; Happy Suncopators; High Sierra; Hogin's; Jubilee; Monterey Bay; Turk Murphy; Napa Valley; Natural Gas; Nightblooming; Prof Plum; Red Hot Peppers; So Frisco; Sutterville; Tuleburg. Chair: Shane Keven, Bill Reinhart.

**1985 - 27-29 Sep** Black Diamond; Calif Express; Desert City; Fulton; Golden Eagle; High Sierra; Turk Murphy; Natural Gas; others unknown. Chair: Marge Nielsen.

## JUBILEE BY THE SEA Pismo Beach CA

Sponsored by the Basin Street Regulars (Central Coast Hot Jazz Society). It was an ambitious plan, proposed by Bob Vincent, for a jazz club still wet behind the ears but it came out in the black and headed a steady string of Jubilees By the Sea ("Dixieland" was dropped after 81). In fact, the first was so successful that it was decided to append the "First Annual" title to all future events. Consistent popularity of the events was due to the littoral setting and to the fact that the number of admission badges were held to a minimum, keeping a "family" feeling to the weekend celebration.

**1977 - 28-30 Oct - 1000** Angel; Apex; DJE&MKRB; Fulton; High Sierra; Milneburg; Ponca City; Turk Murphy. Grand Jubilator: Pete Daily (in absentia). Chair: Bob Connolly.

**1978 - 27-29 Oct - 1500** Angel; Apex; Desert City; DJE&MKRB; Fink; Golden State; High Sierra; Jazzin' Babies; Natural Gas; Fulton; So Frisco; Swingin' 40s; guest Joe Darensbourg. Chair: Joe Darensbourg. Chair: Bob Connolly.

**1979 - 26-28 Oct - 1900** Apex; Blueblowers; DJE&MKRB; Fine Time; Fulton; High Sierra; Jazzin' Babies; Monterey Bay; Natural Gas; Nightblooming; Prof Plum; So Frisco; Swingin' 40s; Turk Murphy; Uptown Lowdown. Grand Jubilators: Ed & Dottie Lawless. Chair: Bob Newton.

**1980 - 24-26 Oct - 2000** Apex; Dixie Katz; Golden Eagle; Hangtown; High Sierra; Hot Frogs; Natural Gas; Nightblooming; Ponca City; Prof Plum; Royal Society; So Frisco; Swingin' 40s; Tuleburg; Uptown Lowdown; WFDJE&MKRB. Grand Jubilators: Chet & Thelma Crain. Chair: Jack Graham, Harold Guess.

**1981 - 23-25 Oct - 2000** Cal Poly JB; Camellia; Churchill St; Desert City; Great Pacific; Good Time Levee; High Sierra; Jazz Beaux; Jazzin' Babies; Jubilee; Monterey Bay; Nightblooming; Oregon; Port City;

Prof Plum; Rose & Thistle; Royal Society; So Frisco; Tuleburg; WFDJE&MKRB. Grand Jubilator: Pete Daily. Chair: Harold Guess.

**1982 - 29-31 Oct - 2000** Chicago 6; Desert City; Fulton; Golden Eagle; Hangtown; High Sierra; Jazz Gen; Jazzin' Babies; Lemon; Monterey Bay; Natural Gas; Nightblooming; Port City; Prof Plum; Uptown Lowdown; WFDJE&MKRB; guest Jerry Fuller. Chair: Roy Schmidt.

**1983 - 28-30 Oct - 2466** Black Diamond; British Conn; Chicago 6; Desert City; Darensbourg All-Stars; Fulton; Golden Eagle; Gramercy; Great Pacific; High Sierra; Jazzin' Babies; Monterey Bay; Nightblooming; Prof Plum; Rose & Thistle; Sticks Strings; Turk Murphy; WFDJE&MKRB; Yankee Wailers. Chair: Frank Exter.

**1984 - 26-28 Oct - 2140** Abalone; Angel; 52 St; Fullertowne; Fulton; High Sierra; Live Steam; Natural Gas; Orange Blossom; Prof Plum; Side St; Sticks Strings; Tuleburg; WFDJE&MKRB; Yankee Wailers. Chair: Frank Exter.

**1985 - 25-27 Oct - 2250** Abalone; And That's Jazz; Desert City; Fulton; Gramercy; Hangtown; High Sierra; Hot Cotton (TN); Hot Frogs; Jubilee; Monterey Bay; Natural Gas; Nightblooming; Prof Plum; WFDJE&MKRB; Yankee Wailers. Chair: Pat Russell.

## LOS ANGELES CLASSIC JAZZ FESTIVAL Los Angeles CA

Sponsored by United Jazz Clubs of Southern California and staged at the Marriott Hotel at LAX. The concept was forwarded by Chuck Conklin and Dan Grant to Morey Levang, president of UJCSC. The event, most ambitious in scope, proved to be an artistic success but a financial disaster, and a second one was planned using other methods of funding.

**1984 - 1-4 Sep - 12000** Angel; Banu Gibson Hot Jazz Orch (LA); Bev Hills; Buck Creek (VA); Chicago 6; City Industry; Dixie Katz; Dixie RR; Fulton; Golden Eagle; Goose Isl; Great Pacific; Jazz Formula; Hot Frogs; Jazz Gen; Jazzin' Babies; Monrovia; Natural Gas; New Rhythm Kings; Prof Plum; Side St; Sons of Bix (CO); So Frisco; Summit Ridge (CO); Sutterville; Uptown Lowdown; Yankee Wailers; individual artists. Chair: Chuck Conklin.

**1985 - 30 Aug-2 Sep -** Alamo City (TX); Angel; Bev Hills; Climax (CANADA); Dapogny Chicago JB (IL); Fullertowne; Fulton; Banu Gibson (LA); Golden Eagle; Great Pacific; Hot Cotton (TN); Island City; Chris Kelly; Jazz Formula; Jazzin' Babies; Liggins' Honeydrippers; Miss-Behavin'; Monrovia; Resurrection; Rhythm Kings; So Frisco; Yankee Wailers; individal artists. Chair: Chuck Conklin.

## NUGGET JAZZ FESTIVAL Sparks NV

A commercial project by John Ascuaga, owner of the Nugget Casino. No chairpersons as such, but festival was under the aegis of publicity director Art Long, who felt it was an opportunity to promote the Nugget "and have some fun at the same time."

**1983 - 26-28 Aug - 1242** Desert City; Fulton; Hot Frogs; Island City; Jazzin' Babies; Jazzin' Jrs; Jazz Minors; Silver Stope; Sutterville; Vax All-Stars.

**1984 - 24-26 Aug - 3000** Abalone; Fulton; Great American; High Sierra; Hot Frogs; Island City; Jazzin' Jrs; New Reformation (MI); Prof Plum; Rosie O'Grady (FL).

**1985 - 23-25 Aug** Firehouse (NM); Great American; High Sierra; Hot Frogs; New Reformation (MI); Phoenix; Prof Plum; Rosie O'Grady (FL); Stumptown; Sutterville.

## PISMO BEACH MARDI GRAS JAZZ FESTIVAL Pismo Beach CA

With the disappearance of the famed Pismo clam from overdigging plus an influx of clam-hungry otters, the city fathers agonized over increasingly sagging attendance at the once-popular annual Pismo Clam Festival. With jazz so successful at the Jubilee By the Sea, they decided to give that a try, eschewing references to clams and stressing the Mardi Gras theme. The first one, while not exactly a resounding success due to management problems and an underabundance of promotion, was still enough so to ensure continuance and it gained popularity.

**1980 - 16-17 Feb - 500** DJE&MKRB; Dixieland Inc; Fink; Hot Frogs; Jazzin' Babies; Magnolia; Nightblooming; Swingin' 40s. Chair: Bob Newton.

**1981 - 28 Feb-1 Mar - 600** Desert City; DJE&MKRB; Hangtown; High Sierra; Hot Frogs; Prof Plum; So Frisco; Swingin' 40s. Chair: Bob Newton.

1982 - 25-27 Feb - 700 Desert City; Grand Republic; Hot Frogs; Jazzin' Babies; Port City; So Frisco; Swingin' 40s; Tuleburg; WFDJE&MKRB. Chair: Bob Newton.

1983 - 25-27 Feb - 900 British Conn; Chicago 6; Desert City; Fulton; Gramercy; Hangtown; Jazzin' Babies; Sticks Strings; Tuleburg; WFDJE&MKRB. Chair: Richard Kvidt.

1984 - 18-19 Feb - 1200 British Conn; Chicago 6; Desert City; Fulton; Gramercy; Hangtown; Jazzin' Babies; Sticks Strings; Tuleburg; WFDJE&MKRB. Chair: Hardy Hearn.

1985 - 16-17 Feb - 1300 Chicago 6; Fullertowne; Fulton; Golden Eagle; Gramercy; Great Pacific; Jazzin' Babies; Nightblooming; Nighthawks; Orange Blossom; Sticks Strings; WFDJE&MKRB. Chair: Hardy Hearn.

## QUEEN MARY JAZZ FESTIVAL Long Beach CA.

1979 - 26-28 Oct Angel; Bev Hills; DJE&MKRB; Fulton; Hot Frogs; Louisiana Gents; New Bull Moose; Nightblooming; guest artists.

1980-82 unknown.

## SACRAMENTO DIXIELAND JUBILEE Sacramento CA

It was Bill Borcher's idea that jazz would ideally be featured in a festival form in the Old Sacramento area as restoration was begun. As well as drafting original blueprints, he served as Jubilee Chairman since the first one and watched his volunteer staff grow from a handful to more than 2500. Truly, this could be called the granddaddy of the new wave of jubilees since so many of the other current ones are based upon its winning tactics. The first ones were contained within Old Sacramento, but as crowds grew larger each year, the boundaries were set further out. Later Jubilees encompassed so much more area removed from the original environs that a fleet of municipal buses became necessary to transport the masses of jazz lovers.

1974 - 24-27 May - 510 Capitol City; Delta King Derelicts; Emerald; Euphoria; Fulton; Gas House; R Hodes JB; Hot Jazz All-Stars; Jazzberry; King Zulu; Legends Jazz; Turk Murphy; Oregon; Phrisco; Riverbank; SF Brass; Smogville; SPDJ All-Stars; Sugar Willie.

1975 - 23-26 May - 1275 Abalone; Act of Providence; American Museum of Jazz; Angel; Bourbon St; Capitol City; Collie Rhythm Aces (ENGLAND); Delta Jazz; Emerald; Fulton; Gas House; Jazz-a-Ma-Tass; Jazzberry; Jazz Inc All-Stars; Jazz Minors; King Zulu; Magnolia; New Bay City; NOJC All-Stars; Oregon; Queen City (CO); Riverbank; River City Expr; Smogville; SPDJ All-Stars; Sugar Willie.

1976 - 28-31 May - 4000 Abalone; Angel; Balboa; Beatty JB; Big Broadcast; Bourbon St; Camellia; Capitol City; Chicagoans; Climax (CAN); Conductors; Delta Jazz; Easy Winners; Emerald; Euphoria; Fulton; Gas House; Great Excelsior; Jamboree Hal; Jazz-a-Ma-Tass; Jazzberry; Jazz Minors; Jubilee; King Zulu; Magnolia; Mudville; Natural Gas; Nightblooming; Oregon; Queen City (CO); Rainier; Riverbank; Rose City; Rosie O'Grady (FL); Smogville; So Bay NOJB; Sutterville; Trumbo's All-Nite; Uptown Lowdown; Vancouver All-Stars.

1977 - 27-30 May - 6200 Abalone; Angel; Apex; Aristocrats; Beatty JB; Bruno Big Band; Camellia; Chicagoans; Climax (CAN); Conductors; Cottonmouth; Desert City; Dr Mix; Easy Winners; Emerald; Euphoria; Fulton; Gas House; Golden Age; Grand Republic; Happy JB (TX); High Sierra; Jamboree Hal; Jazz-a-Ma-Tass; Jazz Minors; Jazzin' Babies; Jellyroll; Jubilee; King Zulu; Magnolia; Mudville; Natural Gas; New Black Eagle (MA); New Milneburg; Nightblooming; Old Sacto; Oregon; Phoenix; Platte River (CO); Portland Rose; Prof Plum; Queen City (CO); Rainier; Reno Charlie; Resurrection; Riverbank; Rosie O'Grady (FL); Royal Society; Sutterville; Uptown Lowdown; Westside Feetwarmers. Grand Jubilator: Shakey Johnson.

1978 - 26-29 May - 14000 Alamo City (TX); Angel; Apex; Aristocrats; Beatty JB; DKE&MKRB; Blueblowers; Camellia; Capitol City; Churchill; Climax; Cottonmouth; Coulson; Cypress; Desert City; Dixiecats; Dixieland Saints; Dr Mix; Easy Winners; Euphonic; Fulton; Gem; Golden State; Good Time Levee; Grand Republic; Great Excelsior; Happy JB; High Sierra; Hot Frogs; Jamboree Hal; Jazz-a-Ma-Tass; Jazz Minors; Jazzin' Babies; Jellyroll; Jubilee; King Zulu; La Honda; Magnolia; Merrymakers; Monterey Bay; Mudville; Natural Gas; New Black Eagle (MA); New Milneburg; NOJB Hawaii; Nightblooming; Old Sacto; Oregon; Outcast 8; Pearl St; Platte River (CO); Ponca City; Port City; Portland Rose; Queen City (CO); Rainier; Resurrection; Riverbank; Rosie O'Grady (FL); Royal Society; Salt Creek (WY);

1974 Sacramento Jubilee

San Francisco JB (AUSTRALIA); Satin Dolls; Sausalito; So Bay NOJB; Summit Ridge (CO); Sunset Music; Sutterville; Swanee's; Uptown Lowdown; Westside Feetwarmers; Yankee RK. Grand Jubilator: Benson Curtis.

**1979 - 25-28 May - 16000** Alamo (TX); Aristocrats; Bev Hills; Blueblowers; J Buck JB; Camellia; Capitol City; Churchill; Cider; Climax (CAN); Condor; Coulson Family; Desert City; Dixieland Saints (JAPAN); Dr Mix; El Jebel (CO); Euphonic; Fine Time; Fink; Fulton; Gem; Good Time Levee; Gramercy; Grand Republic; Great Excelsior; Hart Society Sync; High Sierra; Hot Frogs; Jamboree Hal; Jazz Band Ball (POLAND); Jazzin' Babies; Jazz Inc All-Stars; Jazz-a-Ma-Tazz; Jazz Minors; Jubilee; Louisiana Gents; Merseysippi JB (ENGLAND); Monterey Bay; Mudville; Natural Gas; New Black Eagle (MA); New Bull Moose; NOJB Hawaii; Nightblooming; Old Sacramento; Oregon; Pearl St; Phoenix; Platte River (CO); Ponca City; Port City; Portland Rose; Prof Plum; Queen City (CO); Rainier; Resurrection; Riverbank; Rosie O'Grady (FL); Royal Society; Salt Creek (WY); So Bay; Sutterville; Swanee's; Traffic Jammers; Uptown Lowdown; WFDJE&MKRB; Yankee RK. Grand Jubilator: Vince Marino.

**1980 - 23-26 May - 17500** Alamo (TX); Angel; Apex; Aristocrats; Bev Hills; Big Daddy Dixiecats (CAN); J Buck JB; Camellia; Cats 'n' Jammers; Churchill; Coos Bay; Coulson; Desert City; Dixie RR; Dixie Katz; Dixieland Delinquents; Dixieland Inc; Dr Mix; El Jebel (CO); Euphonic; Faultless; Fulton; Gas Town; Gem; Gold Standard; Golden State; Gramercy; Grand Republic; Hangtown; Hot Frogs; Jamboree Hal; Jazz-a-Ma-Tazz; Jazz Band Ball (POLAND); Jazz Minors; Jazzin' Babies; Jubilee; Magnolia; Marin; Merseysippi (ENGLAND); Monterey Bay; Natural Gas; New Bull Moose; NOJB Hawaii; Nightblooming; Oregon; Papa Bue Viking JB (DENMARK); Phoenix; Pink Elephant Serenaders (NETHERLANDS); Platte River (CO); Ponca City; Portland Rose; Prof Plum; Purple Gang; Queen City (CO); Rainier; Resurrection; Riverbank; Rosie O'Grady (FL); Royal Society; St Louis Ragtimers (MO); Salt Creek (WY); San Juan Rascals; Scottish Society Sync (SCOTLAND); Sons of Bix (CO); So Frisco; Sutterville; Swanee's; Thai Internationals (THAILAND); Traffic Jammers; Tuleburg; Uptown Lowdown; Watergate 7 + 1 (FRANCE); Wolverine (MI); WFDJE&MKRB; Yankee RK. Grand Jubilator: Joe Darensbourg.

**1981 - 22-25 May - 22000** Alamo (TX); Allotria (AUSTRIA); Apex; Aristocrats; Big Daddy Dixiecats (CAN); Blue Note 7 (AUSTRIA); Buck Creek (VA); Jack Buck JB; Camellia; Cats 'n' Jammers; Churchill; Climax (CAN); Coos Bay; Crescent City; Desert City; Dixie Katz; Dixie Delinquents; Dixie Inc; Dixie RR; Dr

246

Mix; El Jebel (CO); Fulton; Gem; Gold Standard; Golden Eagle; Golden State; Gramercy; Grand Republic; Great Pacific; Hangtown; Heritage JB (MA); High Sierra; NOJB Hawaii; Hot Frogs; Island City; Jazz Band Ball (POLAND); Jazz Beaux; Jazz Forum; Jazz-Ma-Tazz; Jazz Minors; Jazzin' Babies; Jubilee; Little Big Band; Magnolia; Marin; Merseysippi (ENGLAND); Natural Gas; New Black Eagle (MA); New Bull Moose; NO Rascals (JAPAN); Nightblooming; Oregon; Papa Bue Viking JB (DENMARK); Phoenix; Platte River (CO); Ponca City; Port City; Portland Rose; Prof Plum; Queen City (CO); Rainier; Resurrection; Riverbank; Rosie O'Grady (FL); Royal Society; San Juan Rascals; Scat Cats (NETHERLANDS); Scottish Jazz Advocates (SCOTLAND); So Frisco; Sutterville; Swanee's; Peoria JB (SWEDEN); Traffic Jammers; Triple RRR; Tuleburg; Uptown Lowdown; Watergate 7 + 1 (FRANCE); Water St Tavern Band (WI); WFDJE&MKRB. Grand Jubilator: Pete Daily.

**1982 - 28-21 May - 26900** Abalone; Alamo (TX); Allotria (AUSTRIA); Australian JB (AUSTRALIA); Benko JB (HUNGARY); Big Daddy Dixiecats (CAN); Bourbon St (FL); Bruno Band; Buck Creek (VA); Cakewalkin' JB (OH); Camellia; Cats 'n' Jammers; Chicago 6; Churchill; Climax (CAN); Desert City; Dixie Belles; Dixie Jazz Bravos; Dixie Jazz Gen; Dixie Delinquents; Dixie RR; Downtown Dixie Tigers (FINLAND); 4 Hits & Miss; Frankenfield All-Stars (PA); Fullerton College; Gem; Golden Eagle; Goose Isl; Gramercy; Grand Republic; Great Pacific; Hangtown; Headliners; Heritage (MA); High Sierra; High Society; Hiz Honor; Hot Frogs; Island City; Jazz Band Ball (POLAND); Jazz Beaux; Jazz Forum; Jazzin' Babies; Jazz Jrs; Jazz Powerhouse (AUSTRALIA); Jibboom; Jubilee; King Zulu; La Sierra; Little Big Band; Louisiana Purchase; Magnolia; Merseysippi (ENGLAND); Monterey Bay; Natural Gas; New Black Eagle (MA); New Bull Moose; NO Creole Gumbo; Nightblooming; North Water St (WI); Orange Pealers; Oregon; Phoenix; Platte (CO) River; Port City; Portland Rose; Prof Plum; Queen City (CO); Rainier; Resurrection; Riverbank; River Rats; Rose & Thistle; Rosie O'Grady (FL); Royal Creek; Royal Society; Salty Dogs (CT); Scat Cats (NETHERLANDS); Scottish Jazz Advocates (SCOTLAND); Seatown 7 (GERMANY); Silver Stope; Sons of Bix (CO); So Frisco; Sticks Strings; Summit Ridge (CO); Sveriges JB (SWEDEN); Swanee's; Swingaires; Timbuktu + 5 (CO); Tuleburg; Uptown Lowdown; Your Father's Moustache (CO). Grand Jubilator: "Papa" Jac Assunto.

**1983 - 27-30 May - 38500** Alamo (TX); Pete Allen JB (ENGLAND); Allotria (AUSTRIA); And That's Jazz; Angel; Benko (HUNGARY); Black Diamond; Bourbon St; Bruno Band; Buck Creek (VA); Cakewalkin' (OH); Camellia; Cats 'n' Jammers; Chicago 6; Capital Transit; Churchill; Civilized Tribe (OK); Climax (CAN); Coos Bay; Crow's Australian JB (AUSTRALIA); Cullum's Happy JB (TX); Dapogny's Chicago JB (MI); Desert City; Dixie Darlin's; Dixie Floyd; Dixie Jazz Bravos; Dixie Katz; Dixie RR; Dixieland All-Stars (E GERMANY); Dixie Inc; Goldie Jazz Expr (FL); Frankenfield All-Stars (PA); Fulton; Gem; Gentleman Jim Jazz Barons (CAN); Gold Standard; Gramercy; Grand Republic; Great Pacific; Hangtown; Helsinki (FINLAND); High Sierra; High Society; Hiz Honor; Hot Antic (FRANCE); Hot Cotton (LA); Hot Frogs; Island City; Jazz Band Ball (POLAND); Jazz Beaux; Jazz Gen; Jazzin' Babies; Jazzin' Jrs; Jazzmaticians; Jubilee; Lemon; Little Big Band; Little Bit of Dixie (IL); Lone Star (TX); Milano Jazz Gang (ITALY); Natural Gas; New Black Eagle (MA); New Bull Moose; NOJB Hawaii; New Reformation; Nightblooming; Oregon; Phrisco; Phoenix; Port City; Portland Rose; Queen City (CO); Rainier; Red Rose (IL); Resurrection; Rio Americano; Riverbank; Rosie O'Grady (FL); San Bernardino Vly College; San Diego; San Juan Rascals; Scottish Jazz Advocates (SCOTLAND); Silver Stope; 6 Hits & Miss; Sons of Bix (CO); So Frisco; Sticks Strings; Stumptown; Summit Ridge (CO); Sutterville; Sveriges (SWEDEN); Swanee's; Swingaires; UC Jazz; Uptown Lowdown; Watergate 7 + 1 (FRANCE); Wolverine (MI); WFDJE&MKRB; Yankee Wailers. Grand Jubilator: Norma Teagarden.

**1984 - 25-28 May - 38200** Abalone; Alamo (TX); Pete Allen JB (ENGLAND); Allotria (GERMANY); Banu Gibson (LA); Black Diamond; Blue St; Bourbon St (FL); Bruno Band; Calif Express; Camellia; Cats 'n' Jammers; Chicago Northwest; Chicago 6; Crosby Bob Cats; Chysanthemum; City Industry; Climax (CAN); Coos Bay; Desert City; Destiny; Devil Mtn; Dixie Darlin's; Dixie Katz; Dixie All-Stars (GERMANY); Dixie Expr; Dixie Inc; Feather Riverboat; 52 St; Fenix (ARGENTINA); Firehouse (NM); Flathead Stompers (MT); Frankenfield All-Stars (PA); Front St Wanderers; Fullertowne; Fulton; Gem; Gold Standard; Goose Isl; Great Pacific; Gramercy; Goldie Jazz Expr (FL); Hangtown; High Sierra; Hiz Honor; Hot Cotton (TN); Hot Frogs; Jazzbo; Jazz Band Ball (POLAND); Jazz Formula; Jazz Gen; Jazzin' Babies; Jazzin' Jrs; Jazz Minors; Jelly Roll Stompers; Jubilee; Lemon; Louisiana Purchase; Mardi Gras; McDonald's All-City Band; Mississippi Mudders; Monterey Bay; Turk Murphy; Napa Valley; Natural Gas; New Melbourne (AUSTRALIA); NOJB Hawaii; New Reformation (MI); New Yankee RK; Nightblooming; Oregon; Pacific Expr;

1985 Sacramento Jubilee

Phoenix; Platte River (CO); Portland Rose; Prima's Witnesses; Prof Plum; Red Hot Peppers; Rent Party Revellers; Riverbank; Rio Americano; Rosie O'Grady (FL); Royal Garden; Royal Society; Scottish Jazz Advocates (SCOTLAND); Side St; Sizzlin' 7; Smokey & Bearcats; So Frisco; South Jazzband; Sticks Strings; Stumptown; Summit Ridge (CO); Sutterville; Sveriges (SWEDEN); Swanee's; Swingaires; Tuleburg; UC Jazz; Uptown Lowdown.

**1985 - 24-27 May - 40000** Allotria (GERMANY); Back Room Gang; Bathtub Gin; Benko (HUNGARY); Big Tiny Little JB; Black Diamond; Blue St; Bobcat JB; Bruno Band; Calif Express; Cats 'n' Jammers; Chicago 6; Chrysanthemum; Coos Bay; Cuesta Royal Swing Quartet; Desert City; Destiny; Devil Mtn; Dixie Darlin's; Dixie Katz; Dixie Expr; Dr Jazz Companie (GERMANY); Dr Jon; Feather Riverboat; Fenix (ARGENTINA); Firehouse (NM); Flathead Stompers (MT); Flower St JB (GERMANY); Frankenfield All-Stars (PA); Fulton; Gem; Banu Gibson (LA); Goldie Jazz Expr (FL); Gold Standard; Gramercy; Great American; Great Pacific; Hangtown; High Sierra; Hot Antic (FRANCE); Hot Cotton (TN); Hot Frogs; Irish All-Stars (IRELAND); Jazz Band Ball (POLAND); Jazzin' Babies; Jazzin' Jrs; Lloyd Jones Western JB; Pete Kelly's Big 7; Kowloon Honkers (HONG KONG); Las Vegas; Lemon; Liggins' Honeydrippers; Big Tiny Little; Live Steam; Mardi Gras; McDonald's All-City DB; Merseysippi (ENGLAND); Metropolitan JB (CZECHOSLOVKIA); Milano Jazz Gang (ITALY); Miss-Behavin'; Monrovia; Most Jazz Sextet; Natural Gas; New Bull Moose; New Melbourne (AUSTRALIA); NOJB Hawaii; Nightblooming; Oregon; Paco Gatsby (GUATEMALA); Phoenix; Polcer Condon Gang (NY); Port City; Portland Rose; Prima's Witnesses (NV); Prof Plum; Quarry Cats; Rainier; Red Rose Ragtime Band (IL); Reedley River Rats; Resurrection; Alvino Rey & King Sisters; Riverbank; Riverboat Ramblers; Rosie O'Grady (FL); STJS Scholarship Band; Scottish Society Sync (SCOTLAND); 6 Friars & Monk (WI); Sizzlin' 7; Smokey & Bearcats (TX); Some Like It Hot (FRANCE); So Frisco; Sticks Strings; Summit Ridge (CO); Sutterville; Swingaires; N Teagarden & Friends; 32 St; Toots Suite; Tri-City; Tuleburg; UC Jazz; Yankee Wailers; Your Father's Moustache (CO). Grand Jubilator: Floyd & Lucille Levin.

## SACRAMENTO MINI-JUBILEE Sacramento CA

Staged in conjunction with an annual gathering of jazz club representatives from around California, event was dropped in 1983.

**1976 (Roseville) - 8 Feb** W Baughn & Friends; Capitol City; Fulton; Gas House; Hendricks Big Band; Jazzberry; Oregon; Riverbank; Trumbo's All-Nite.

**1977 (Cal-Expo) - 26 Jan** Camellia; Fulton; Gas House; High Sierra; Jazz Minors; Natural Gas; Old Sacramento; Platte River (CO); Riverbank; Sutterville.

**1978 (Old SAC) - 22 Jan** Apex; Camellia; Coulson; DJE&MKRB; Dr Mix; Droop's Dixie Dignitaries; Easy Winners; Fulton; Golden State; Grand Republic; High Sierra; Hot Frogs; Jubilee; Mudville; Natural Gas; New Milneburg; Turk Murphy; Old Sacramento; Riverbank; Sutterville.

**1979 (Old SAC) - 14 Jan** Apex; Camellia; DJE&MKRB; Droop's; Gramercy; High Sierra; Hot Frogs; Jazz Minors; Milneburg; Riverbank; Old Sacramento; Sutterville.

**1980 (Roseville)** Cats 'n' Jammers; Desert City; Dixie Delinquents; Dixieland Inc; Fulton; Gramercy; High Sierra; Natural Gas; Oregon; Riverbank; Royal Society; So Frisco; Swanee's; Tuleburg.

**1981 (Roseville) - 18 Jan** Camellia; Cats 'n' Jammers; Dr Mix; Gramercy; Golden State; Gold Standard; Grand Republic; High Sierra; Hangtown; Hot Frogs; Port City; Riverbank; Sutterville; Swanee's.

**1982 (Roseville) - 17 Jan** Cats 'n' Jammers; Fulton; Gramercy; Grand Republic; Hangtown; Headliners; High Sierra; Jazz Beaux; Jazzin' Jrs; Louisiana Purchase; Natural Gas; Nightblooming; Port City; Prof Plum; Riverbank; Rose & Thistle; So Frisco; Sutterville; Swanee's; Tuleburg; Vax NOJB.

## SAN FRANCISCO JAZZ SHOWCASE San Francisco CA

Originally titled SAN FRANCISCO TRADITIONAL JAZZ JAMBOREE, this was changed to Showcase by Dottie Lawless in 1979 when it was suggested that the name "Jamboree" sounded too Boy Scoutish. Parent theme behind the festival was the old NO "rent party." Sponsored by New Orleans Jazz Club of Northern California, the first one was held at Holiday Inn in Point Richmond, the second at Jack Tar Hotel in SF, all subsequent ones at *Bimbo's* in SF. This was the brainchild of Marshall Peterson and Dave Walker.

**1972 - 20 Feb - 300** Bandleader's Band; Golden Age; Great Excelsior; Vince Hickey JB; Pier 23; Rose & Thistle; SAC Swing Expr; Scheelar & Friends. Chair: Dave Walker.

**1973 - 25 Feb - 450** Bow & Bell; Judith Durham & Her Jazzmen; Funky NOJB; Golden Age; Great Excelsior; Jazz Cardinals; Rose & Thistle; Tappers; N Teagarden Jazzmen.

**1974 - 17 Feb - 500** Delta; Euphoria; Funky NOJB; Golden Age; Jazz Cardinals; King Riverbottom; Tappers; Monterey Bay; New Washboard RK; Phrisco. Chair: Tom Buck.

**1975 - 23 Feb - 550** Berkeley Rhythm; J Buck JB; Euphoria; Funky NOJB; Golden Age; Jazz Cardinals; King Riverbottom; New Bay City; Oakland A; Phrisco; Pier 23 Cats; Stone Age; Jack Teagarden Memorial JB. Chair: Tom Buck.

**1976 - 15 Feb - 550** Berkeley Rhythm; J Buck JB; Euphoria; Funky NOJB; Golden Age; Jubilee; Magnolia; Natural Gas; SF Jazz All-Stars; Stone Age.

**1977 - 20 Feb - 600** Apex; Delta Jazz Irreg; Euphoria; Golden Age; Jubilee; Magnolia; Natural Gas; Jazz-a-Ma-Tass.

**1978 - 19 Feb - 600** Apex; Euphonic; Golden Age; Jubilee; Magnolia; Natural Gas; New Magnolia; NOJC Breda. Chair: Mike Gerba.

**1979 - 18 Feb - 700** Apex; J Buck JB; Euphonic; Golden Age; Golden State; Jazz Cardinals; Kyoto Hot Cats; Tom Kats; Magnolia; Natural Gas; Prof Plum; N Teagarden & Friends. Chair: Ev Farey.

**1980 - 17 Feb - 750** And That's Jazz; J Buck JB; Casa Bonita; Churchill; Euphonic; Marin; Natural Gas; N Teagarden & Friends; Prof Plum; Royal Society; SF Swing Expr; Tom Kats. Chair: Ev Farey.

**1981 - 15 Feb - 700** And That's Jazz; Apex; J Buck JB; Chrysanthemum; Churchill; Golden State; Jubilee; Magnolia; Natural Gas; Royal Society; Silicon. Chair: Robbie Schlosser.

**1982 - 21 Feb - 700** Apex; Jack Buck JB; Churchill; Golden Age; Golden State; Jubilee; Magnolia; Natural Gas; Prof Plum; Rose & Thistle; Royal Society. Chair: Bill Armstrong and Bunky Colman.

**1983 - 20 Feb - 750** And That's Jazz; Chrysanthemum; Devil Mtn; 52 St; Golden Age; Jubilee; Magnolia; Napa Valley; Natural Gas; Neighbor JB; Prof Plum; Rose & Thistle; Royal Society. Chair: Lynn Hall.

**1984 - 19 Feb - 750** Black Diamond; Chrysanthemum; Devil Mtn; 52 St; Golden Age; Jubilee; Monterey Bay; Turk Murphy; Napa Valley; Natural Gas; Oakland A; Prof Plum; Norma Teagarden & Friends. Chair: Lynn Hall.

**1985 - 17 Feb - 730** And That's Jazz; Black Diamond; J Buck JB; T Buck JB; Churchill; Devil Mtn; Jubilee; Napa Valley; Natural Gas; Nob Hill; Rose & Thistle; Silicon; Norma Teagarden. Chair: Rod Roberts.

## SAN JUAN ISLAND DIXIELAND JAZZ FESTIVAL Friday Harbor WA

Sponsored by San Juan Island Goodtime Classic Jazz Association, this popular annual celebration was the brainchild of Gary Provonsha. The scenic town was a natural location, although hard pressed to handle the increasing influx of jazz lovers who swarmed onto the island in planes and boats, the only access from the mainland.

**1980 - 25-27 Jul - 1900** unknown.

**1981 - 24-25 Jul - 3600** Dixie Expr; Great Excelsior; Kitsilano Kat Kickers; Natural Gas; Phoenix; Prof Plum; Rainier; Royal Bourbon St; Uptown Lowdown; WFDJE&MKRB; four combos.

**1982 - 23-25 Jul - 4300** unknown.

**1983 - 21-24 Jul - 6000** unknown.

**1984 - 27-29 Jul - 6300** Buck Creek (VA); Dixie Expr; Excelsior; High Sierra; Great American; Old School Band; Phoenix; Rainier; Stumptown; Summit Ridge (CO); Uptown Lowdown.

**1985 - 26-28 Jul** Alamo (TX); Dixieland Expr; Fulton; Grand Dominion; Great Excelsior; Hot Antic (FRANCE); Island City; Jazzin' Jrs; New Black Eagles (MA); Phoenix; Pussyfoot; Rainier; Uptown Lowdown.

## SANTA ROSA DIXIELAND JAZZ BENEFIT Santa Rosa CA

Presented annually by United Cerebral Palsy agency as a fundraising benefit, the concept by board member Marty Powell. Marshall Peterson acted as Music Director since 1982, and the idea proved successful from the first.

**1980 - 17 Aug - 1072** And That's Jazz; Gold Standard; Hangtown; Norman DB; Natural Gas; Southtown Strummers; Tuleburg.

**1981 - 23 Aug - 1135** Jubilee; Natural Gas; Norman DJB; Port City; Riverbank; Rose & Thistle; Tuleburg; local groups.

PROFESSOR PLUM at Bimbo's Jazz Showcase 1983

**1982 - 22 Aug - 1568** Appleknockers; Port Chicago JB; Hangtown; Natural Gas; Norman DJB; Port City; Prof Plum; Tuleburg; local groups.

**1983 - 27-28 Aug - 1941** And That's Jazz; Appleknockers; Churchill; Norman DJB; Emperor Norton; Golden State; Good Time Levee; Jubilee; Monterey Bay; Napa Valley; Port Chicago JB; Wally Rose; Rose & Thistle; Tuleburg; local groups.

**1984 - 25-26 Aug - 1916** Appleknockers; Black Diamond; Golden Age; Good Time Levee; Jubilee; Napa Valley; Natural Gas; Norman DJB; Port Chicago; Rose & Thistle; Riverbank; Tuleburg; local groups.

**1985 - 24-25 Aug** And That's Jazz; Black Diamond; Good Time Levee; Jazz Salvation Co; Jubilee; Magnolia; Napa Valley; Natural Gas; Southtown Strummers; Tagawa Bjo Band; Tuleburg; guest Jan Sutherland.

## SEATTLE DIXIELAND FESTIVAL Seattle WA

Sponsors 1983: Senior Center of West Seattle; 1984: Senior Center, *West Seattle Herald* and Wien Air Alaska; 1985: Senior Center, *Herald* and radio KIXI.

**1983 - 17 Sep** - Capitol City; Cornucopia Concert Band; Destiny; Dixiekats; Duwamish; Foremost JB; Great Excelsior; Hume St; Jet City JB; Mulberry St JB; Ragtime $3 + 2 + 1$; Rainier; Seattle Bjo Band; Tri-City; Uptown Lowdown.

**1984 - 22-23 Jun** - Ain't No Heaven; Cornucopia; Destiny; Dixiekats; Dr Jon; Duwamish; Island City; Phoenix; Platte River (CO); Rainier; Seattle Bjo Band; Stumptown; Tri-City; Uptown Lowdown.

**1985 - 21-22 Jun** - Ain't No Heaven; Bathtub Gin; Cornucopia; Dixiekats; Duwamish; Great Excelsior; Hume St; Rainier; Seattle Bjo Band; Stumptown; Uptown Lowdown. Chair: Marlene Miller.

## SPRING FLING San Jose CA

Conceived and implemented by Ted Zuur in January 1980 and sponsored by South Bay Traditional Jazz Club, the first event was a financial success, that quite unusual in itself, despite financial shenanigans by hired bartenders and waitresses. Staged at *Bold Knight* in Sunnyvale until 1985, then SJ Cultural Center.

**1980 - 3 May - 390** And That's Jazz; Apex; Churchill; Gem; Magnolia; Monterey Bay; Prof Plum; Royal Society.

**1981 - 9 May - 428** Churchill; Coy Orch; Gem; Jubilee; Kelie's Bayside Jazz; Magnolia; Monday's Blues; Prof Plum; Royal Society; Seaside Sync; Silicon; Tagawa Bjo Band. Chair: Janet Bouma.

**1982 - 8 May - 434** Churchill; Coy Orch; Cupertino HS JB; Dixie Hot Shots; Gem; Isle City; Magnolia; Prof Plum; Royal Society; Silicon; guest Rex Allen. Chair: Janet Bouma.

**1983 - 14 May - 411** And That's Jazz; Churchill; Coy Orch; Devil Mtn; 52 St; Prof Plum; Monterey Bay; Silicon; So County Dixie Expr; Tuleburg. Chair: Joan Bryning.

**1984 - 12 May - 743** And That's Jazz; Black Diamond; Churchill; Devil Mtn; Jubilee; Leratones; Magnolia; Monterey Bay; Silicon; Tuleburg. Chair: Terry Hartwell.

**1985 - 18 May - 443** And That's Jazz; Black Diamond; Calif Express; Churchill; Devil Mtn; 52 St; Joyful Noise; Jubilee; Prof Plum; Magnolia; Monterey Bay; Silicon; Tuleburg. Chair: Jeanne Dale, Stuart Leaf, Ted Zuur.

## STOCKTON DIXIELAND JUBILEE see JAZZ ON THE WATERFRONT

## TERRIFVIC JAZZ PARTY Victoria BC

Originally VICTORIA DIXIELAND JAZZ PARTY, changed to new title in 1985.

**1983-84** unknown.

**1985 - 25-28 Apr** Big Daddy Dixiecats; Buck Creek (VA); Climax (CAN); Dixie Expr; Garden City; High Sierra; Hot Frogs; Island City; Natural Gas; Phoenix; Prof Plum; Rainier; So Frisco; Stumptown; Tri-City.

## TIBURON JAZZ FESTIVAL Tiburon CA

Conceived by Tom Belton and John Dodgshon, sponsored by New Orleans Jazz Club of Northern California in league with Tiburon's Chamber of Commerce and Fine Arts Commission. Attendance is anybody's guess since no badges were sold and admission to the clubs was free, revenue was derived from clubs and advertising, plus one concert for which tickets were sold, and there was no army of volunteers — the whole thing was run by only three people. 1984 offered a limited program due to reconstruction of Tiburon business district, 1985 was cancelled completely.

**1980 - 18-19 Apr** Fulton; Golden State; Jazz Cardinals; Jubilee; Marin; Natural Gas; Prof Plum; SF Swing Expr.

**1981 - 30 Apr-1 May** Churchill; Jubilee; Golden Age; Golden State; Hangtown; Bob Hirsch Trio; Jubilee; Magnolia; Marin; Natural Gas; Phrisco; Prof Plum; Norma Teagarden; Rose & Thistle; Sutterville; Swing Fever.

**1982 - 30 Apr-1 May** Garvin Bushnell; Churchill; Delta Jazz; Golden Age; Golden State; Hangtown; Jubilee; Mike Lipskin; Magnolia; Monterey Bay; Natural Gas; Rose & Thistle; Swing Fever; Norma Teagarden.

**1983 - 29-30 Apr** Wild Bill Davison; 52 St; Fulton; Golden State; Jubilee; Lunceford's Rhythm Wizards; Monterey Bay; Natural Gas; Prof Plum; Rose & Thistle; Silicon; Speakeasy Band; Swing Fever.

**1984 - 16 Jun** Golden State; Rose & Thistle; SF Swing Expr.

## VANCOUVER JAZZ FESTIVAL Vancouver BC

Records for 1974-1980 festivals were unavailable. Chair for 1981-85 was Witt Mueller.

**1981** Clark All-Stars; Great Excelsior; Kitsilano Kat Kickers; Harrison DJB; Phoenix; Rainier; Reynolds Quartet; St Valentine; Uptown Lowdown.

**1982** Arntzen Classic JB; Big Daddy Dixiecrats; Dixie Flyers; Dixieland Expr; Harrison DJB; Island City; Phoenix; Rainier; Razzmajazz; Roberts JB.

**1983** Capital City; Dixieland Expr; Harrison DJB; Oregon; Rainbow; Rainier; Phoenix; Stumptown; guest Jan Sutherland.

**1984 - 9-11 Nov** Coos Bay; Dixieland Expr; 5 Guys Named Moe; Harrison DJB; Oregon; Oriental Rooftop; Phoenix; Razzmajazz; Rainbow; Rainier; Reynolds Quartet; Young Quartet; guests Monty Sunshine, Jan Sutherland.

**1985 - 8-11 Nov** Arntzen JB; Capital City; 5 Guys; Grand Dominion; Great Excelsior; Harrison DJB; Phoenix; Rainier; Razzmajazz; Reynolds JB; Sneddon JB; guest Jim Beatty.

## VICTORIA DIXIELAND JAZZ PARTY see TERRIFVIC JAZZ PARTY

Others of note, on a less grand scale or which were lacking in requested information, were **EMERALD VALLEY DIXIELAND JAZZ JUBILEE** Creswell OR; **FLYING LADY JAZZ FESTIVAL** Morgan Hill CA; **GREAT NORTHERN JAZZ FESTIVAL** Paradise CA; **JAZZAFAIR** Del Mar CA; **OREGON DIXIELAND JUBILEE**; **OVERLAND DAYS JAZZ FESTIVAL** Temecula CA; **RAIN OR SHINE JAZZ FESTIVAL** Aberdeen WA; **VIRGINIA CITY CARNIVAL OF JAZZ** Virginia City NV.

1978 Jubilee By the Sea

All-Star group for Camarillo, October 1966
Wayne Songer, Bill Cooper, Stan Wrightsman,
Dr Louis Nash, Jackie Coon, Nick Fatool, Moe Schneider

## Those Fabulous Camarillo Concerts

They're the ones nobody heard about and couldn't attend, except under rather exacting conditions, and they featured some of the world's greatest jazz stars. They took place in the small town of Camarillo, California, during the mid '60s, and those exacting conditions were that you had to be a patient at Camarillo State Hospital! Think of sitting back in Hagerty Auditorium and what it must have been like at one of these All-Star Sunday Sessions:

27 Jun 1965: Harry Babasin, sb; Gene Bolen, cl; Nick Fatool, d; Bob Higgins, tpt; Moe Schneider, tbn; Stan Wrightsman, p.

25 Jul 1965: Fatool; Higgins; Gordon Jenkins, vib; Matty Matlock, cl; Eddie Miller, tsax; Wrightsman; Walt Yoder.

24 Oct 1965: Fatool; Higgins; Jenkins; Ray Leatherwood, sb; Jay St John, cl; Schneider; Wrightsman.

29 Aug 1965: Marvin Ash, p; Higgins; Charlie Lodice, d; St John; Warren Smith, tbn; Yoder.

24 Sep 1965: Tiny Berg, cl; Higgins; Lodice; Don Owens, p; Pat Patton, bjo, sb; Smith.

5 Dec 1965: Ash; Bolen; Charley Estes, d; Higgins; Leatherwood; Abe Lincoln, tbn.

And so it went, until 26 May 1968, with performing jazzmen like Bill Campbell, p; Dick Cary, pno/tpt; Dick Cathcart, tpt; Mahlon Clarke, cl; Jackie Coon, tpt; Bill Cooper, tu/sb; George Defebaugh, d; Lou Diamond, d; Bob Havens, tbn; Nappy Lamare, bjo; Artie Lyons, cl; Bob McCracken, cl; Bob Pring, tbn; Wayne Songer, cl; Cliff Swesey, d. Jazz rears its happy head in the most unlikely places!

# FAMILY ALBUM

DAVE LEWIS October 1979

TURK MURPHY October 1979

FRED HIGUERA May 1977

During a period of years, a jazz player learns about his audiences, sifts the chaff from the wheat, finds out who is pseudo and who is elite. He appreciates them all, of course, as they fill a chair in the nightclub, since an empty house means "Kiss your two-week option good-bye."

The elites are who make it all worth the while. This musician recalls with pleasure and fondness Paul de Revere at the old *Bluebird Cavern* leaving his table to sit on the edge of the little bandstand, hunched under Polo Barnes' clarinet every time he played "High Society," slipping him a dollar bill for it. In fact, *any* clarinetist got a dollar bill from Paul for "High Society."

Also with fondness and pleasure a gaggle of girls — Helen Shope, Kay Cavanaugh, Loa Smith, MaryAnne Morgan and her mother, Merle — who, around 1950, used to troop from the *Royal Room* down to *Sardi's*, and stops in between, when Hollywood Boulevard was chock-a-block with jazz saloons. The five of them made for a happy roomful — the world's first groupies! MaryAnne sat in on vocals, a very pretty and recordable songstress, and Helen, a couple of years later, became Mrs Joe Darensbourg.

There were John and Jane Waterhouse, who had a Jazz Oktoberfest at their home for eight years, and Joe and Elsa Thompson, who have had Fourth of July fuctions at theirs for 25! There were Adrian and Diane Tucker... Adrian was instrumental in getting Dink Johnson, Jelly Roll's cousin, recorded. All are aficionados — elite ones.

There was the studio arranger who used to come into *Astor's* in North Hollywood. When the band didn't know a tune he had shyly requested, he'd go home and write out a sketch of it and bring it back in a half an hour! There were the blues-loving Ladniers every week at the *Green Bull*, Tony Navarro's Hermosa Beach beer bar. They knew the band didn't take to beer all that much and discreetly provided a stash of VO in the side alley for intermissions.

There are hundreds and hundeds of memorable, elite fans one recalls with great enjoyment over 40 years and it's a shame they all can't be spotted here for all the world to know. They were all the important half of show business and, without them, it would be comparable to singing in the shower... marvelous, *wonderful* singing, but who is there to hear it?                                                                      *— Johnny Lucas*


In August 1973, a party was held for Richard Krause in Berkeley featuring all those musicians he had been close to. This friend of jazz and its musicians was dying of cancer, and Manny Funk arranged for the party in his back yard. Two months later, Krause died, but the memorial gatherings continued each year at Funk's home until, because of damage from a fire during 1978, it ws moved to Walnut Creek. In 1985, it was held indoors for the first time at Oakland's *Iron Gate Inn*.

They were unusual parties, generally lasting two days, with no money, no publicity, no star billings, no other reason than to celebrate the memory of a close friend. Although organized

(right) COUGAR NELSON May 1975
(below) JOYCE TAYLOR c1980
(bottom) BOB McCRACKEN,
WILD BILL DAVISON and
BOB HAVENS June 1966

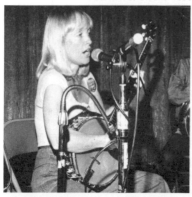

groups appeared — Berkeley Rhythm, Magnolia, Oakland A's Swingers, and such — the groups were usually pickups with a predesignated leader like Burt Bales, Ev Farey, Leon Oakley. Styles ran the gamut from Preservation Hall to even some Western Swing and guests like Marty Grosz and Bob Greene showed up. Everyone was the guest of Richard Krause.

*— Hal Smith*


The Resurrection Brass Band was first known as the SCHJS Marching Band. Art Levin was the first person I knew in the band and he indicated that the only way to get into it was if somebody died or left. However, Gordon Mitchell wanted to expand the band for appearances at the Disneyland Jubilees and, with Art's recommendation... and no audition... I was in. Imagine the thrill of marching alongside Barney Bigard, Joe Darensbourg and Tudie Garland on bass drum. Perhaps two of the most rewarding recollections for me were meeting Louis Armstrong at LAX when he flew in for his 70th birthday party, and playing for Kid Ory's funeral. I'll never forget slowly marching up that hill to the gravesite, strictly dirge-style, with English drummer Barry Martyn joining us that day. He did a great job on New Orleans second-line drumming and keeping the band together.    *— Dave Bourne*


During the early '60s, jazz was still very much alive and kicking in the West, although perhaps not so much as a decade earlier. Around the Southland one could find many weekend oases even in the heyday of rock 'n' roll: Teddy Buckner at *The Chariot Room* in Anaheim; Firehouse 5 + 2, Jack McVea trio, Young Men From New Orleans, and occasionally Buckner, at Disneyland; Bob McCracken at *Zucca's* and Delta Rhythm Kings at *The Jolly Coachman* in Pasadena; Red Nichols at *The Zebra Room* on Wilshire; Dean Honey at *Dino's* in Garden Grove; Nappy Lamare at *Shakey's* in Santa Monica; Hal Peppie and Warren Smith at *Beverly Cavern*; Rosy McHargue at *Reuben E Lee* in Newport Beach; Charlie Lodice and Rick Fay at *The Clouds* in Sylmar; Thee Saints at *The Gaslight Club* on La Cienega; Pete Daily at *The White Way Inn* in the Valley; Ernie Carson at Marineland; Ethel Hiett Trio at *The Sportsman* in La Mirada; Gene Palmer at *Chico's* in Lynwood; Jelly Roll JB at *McGee's* in Westwood; French Quarter JB plus John Finley Trio at *The Honeybucket* and Alton Purnell trio at *The Gables* in Orange County; Bill Dods at *Gatsby's* up in Santa Barbara.

Besides these groups, there were steady solo appearances by Marvin Ash, Dave Bourne, Johnny Guarnieri, Elaine Mitchell and other pianists, and just about every *Shakey's* in the area supported at least a jazz trio. It was like a Jubilee every weekend, only you had to do a bit of driving.    *— Don Ellison*


After several weeks of rehearsal, the band (YBJB) reopened this March first (1946) at the *Dawn Club* on Annie Street, just off Market in the center of San Francisco. The *Dawn Club* had been redecorated for the occasion; with its big dance floor and large seating capacity it provides the ideal setting for Lu's music. Also, it is one of the nicest, neatest looking and most efficiently run clubs I have ever seen.

The opening night was really unforgettable. A tremendous crowd was present to welcome back the band and around nine o'clock, when they had played for less than an hour, there were over 900 people in the place. The doors had to be closed in accordance with fire

FIREHOUSE FIVE PLUS TWO, Disneyland July 1965
Eckland, Newman, Probert, Forrest, Alguire, Kimball

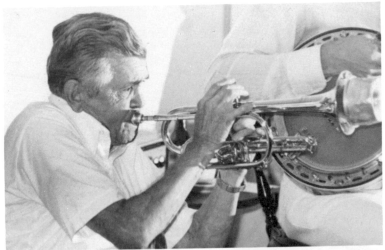

PETE DAILY October 1978

PETE AND LOIS DAILY October 1984

regulations and several hundred people had to be turned back. I had fortunately arrived early and for four hours listened in amazement to one of the most powerful bands in the history of jazz.
— *Nesuhi Ertegun*
*from an article in Clef, May 1946*

I found Bunky Colman in the University of California band's rehearsal room, hunkered down behind the last row of lockers, running scales on his clarinet. He had been pointed out to me when I stuck my head in the door to inquire if there might be a reedman interested in joining the Polecats I was forming back in 1950. He certainly didn't look much like a jazzman — shy, bespectacled, soft-spoken — but he showed interest, and that was enough for me. He hung in there valiantly for the better part of two years, the star of my modest aggregation, never complaining or admitting that it had to be somewhat of an uphill battle to stay in the limited general area of what the rest of us were playing. Woody, Bob, Bunnie, Biz and I were really first-timers, limping through stock jazz tunes in our best three-chord fashion; only Oxtot had any real talent, although even he was a bit green at that time. But Bunky hung in there and managed to enjoy it all. He was that kind of a guy.

Shyness was such that we could never convince him to lift his clarinet any higher than waist-level. At our recording sessions at KRE in Berkeley, we had to set him in a chair on top of a table so that his horn would mate with a mike.

He was blessed with an instinctive ear for picking up on what everybody was doing and an ability to come in always at the right time, with the right notes. And there was an unquenchable seasoning of humor in his playing, something that often surprised even him. He was pure joy to play along with. Ask anyone whose life had been graced with his presence.

My own best personal remembrance of Bunky is when he showed up at the musicians' check-in room at the 1981 Pismo Jubilee By the Sea wearing his old, striped Polecat band shirt. He had saved it 30 years for just such a moment. He was that kind of guy. — *KOE*

It occurs to me that for many people in Southern California the only source of jazz was from Benson Curtis' and Frank Bull's "Strictly From Dixie" radio shows, which Benson later carried on solo. Listening to them provided a real education as Benson always listed all the performers, the year of the recording and, generally, the composer of each tune. Choice of material was always the best, and I'm sure that the regrets I had when the show finally went off the air were shared by many.
— *Dave Bourne*

While serving as ship's surgeon on the *SS Monterey*, I met Dr Louis Nash and his wife, who caught the "jazz bug" from me and who helped me spend our stopover time in Australia catching all the jazz venues we could.

On returning to California, we became active members in the NOJCSC at the Anaheim Moose Club. When Louis' duties as medical director and superintendent of Camarillo State Hospital became more demanding, rather than driving to LA, he came up with the idea of having concerts at the hospital and asked me to implement the idea.

The idea for Jazz on a Sunday Afternoon, as we called it, stemmed from a similar soiree in New Orleans, and our first one in June 1965, fronted by Bob Higgins, was a rousing success.

FAY GOLDEN
February 1984

FRANK GOULETTE,
ERNIE LANDES
October 1985

Al Douglas

Patients packed the auditorium and many showed evidence of response for the first time since they came to the hospital. It was reported later that they slept better, were less agitated and restless, so we considered jazz music to be psychiatric therapy. We always supplied a bit of food and libation to compensate the musicians for their efforts, but they said their thanks came from the smiles on the patients' faces.　　　　　*— Dr Ed Lawless*


In September 1960, Paul Affeldt released the first issue of *Jazz Report* magazine, which he had volunteered to take over from Bob Koester of Chicago. It became a family affair, printed on an old mimeograph machine in his home — Paul's wife, Pat, did the artwork and his three youngsters, Vicky Jean, Scott and Butch, tackled the collating and stapling.

Devoted to trad jazz, ragtime and the blues, the magazine continued for over 20 years, a labor of love on Paul's part. It operated on a shoestring as Paul, a young postman with a family to tend to, wasn't exactly affluent.

By the end of 1961, he had inaugurated his own record label, realizing a long-held ambition. *Euphonic* was designed to be devoted to piano, Paul's special passion, and his first release featued rare items by ragtime pioneer Brun Campbell and Dink Johnson, Jelly Roll Morton's brother-in-law. This was the beginning of a catalog that was to later include Paul Lingle, Burt Bales, Dave Jasen, Neville Dickie, Art Hodes, Pete Johnson, Albert Ammons, Meade "Lux" Lewis, Charlie Thompson and several more "professors."

In 1961, I submitted some unsolicited copy to *Jazz Report* by mail, which led to an exchange of letters with Paul and a trip to Ventura to meet him and his family. It was the beginning of a long friendship that continues to this day.

Paul reluctantly suspended the magazine a couple of years ago but continues to build his *Euphonic* catalog, which features music — let's face it — of such limited commercial appeal that only a quixotic crusader would choose to handle it. Paul Affeldt is a real champion of traditional jazz. We owe him a lot.　　　　　*—Bill Mitchell*
*ex-associate editor, Jazz Report*


It was 3 July 1970 and the Shrine auditorium was filled to overflowing with fans, friends and wellwishers who came to honor the greatest name in jazz on the occasion of his 70th birthday. It was Louis Armstrong's night of nights and the same might well be said of the jazz aficionados, as well, for they would witness an array of jazz artists and bands the likes of which would never be seen or heard again.

Musically, the evening's activities featured a prelude by Barry Martyn's Band (Legends of Jazz), followed by a recreation of the Riverboat Band (Roy Brewer, Joe Darensbourg, Mike DeLay, Ed Garland, Sammy Lee, Alton Purnell, Alton Redd); a recreation of King Oliver's Creole JB (Andy Blakeney, Bill Hadnott, Matty Matlock, Bill Mitcheil, George Orendorff, Syl Rice, Warren Smith); a recreation of Louis' Hot Five (Teddy Buckner, Art Edwards, John Ewing, Chester Lane, Nappy Lamare, Caughey Roberts, Jesse Sailes); the All-Stars (Ray Brown, Doc Evans, Lloyd Glenn, Bob Havens, Charlie Lodice, Max Murray, Maxim Saury); the Ambassador Satch Band (Louis Bellson, Barney Bigard, Red Callender, Benny Carter, Tyree Glenn, Clark Terry, Ray Sherman); plus Joe Bushkin, Claude Luter, Joe Marsala, Bob McCracken and Sarah Vaughn in featured spots. Masters of Ceremonies were Hoagy Carmichael and Benson Curtis, sponsorship by the Association of Southern California Jazz Clubs.
　　　　　*— KOE*

TURK MURPHY JAZZ BAND May 1974
Stanislaus, Helm, Carroll, Oakley, Lunsford, Murphy, Clute

BILL MITCHELL
October 1985

CLAIRE AUSTIN August 1971

BURT BALES February 1981

JOHN SMITH, CLARK
HUDDLESTON, GEORGE
PROBERT mid-1960s

TONY JOHNSON
April 1977

One night early in 1971, the Alcoholic Beverages Commission stormed into the *Handlebars* and told all the underaged kids in the Stomp Aces they'd have to quit playing and clear out. Poor Doug (Parker) and Ted (Des Plantes) had to finish out the whole evening by themselves. After that, Ted used people like Ron Going, Pete Kier, Pete van Oorschot, Vinnie Armstrong, Glenn Calkins...                                                  — *Laurence Wright*


California... I can think of few better places to grow up in if you love jazz. Though La Jolla was hardly an epicenter of jazz activity, Los Angeles was an easy drive away, thanks to willing parents. There were great bands to hear and plenty of Sunday afternoon jazz clubs at which to learn how to play (and how not to play).

I drifted to the SF Bay Area after an unproductive year in Portland in 1978. Almost immediately I was working regularly with Ev Farey's Golden State JB, and lucked out in casuals and subs with Jazz Cardinals, Magnolia, Golden Age, Euphonic and others. I enjoyed listening to Bay Area groups, as well as playing with some of them. Jeff Hamilton and John Gill taught me a lot about the music, and I had a lot to learn. The legendary Fred Higuera was still playing strong at 70 — I still get a chill up and down my spine when I remember hearing him with Phil Howe and Devon Harkins at Oakland's Leamington Hotel — and I always enjoyed Vince Hickey playing drums in his wonderful Baby Dodds-patterned way. That group was my favorite Bay Area band. The instrumentation, repertoire and overall sound of his Jazz Cardinals was the main influence when I formed the Rhythmakers in 1983. My memories of the Bay Area are all happy ones.

I gave Portland two more shots and they were fun while they lasted — there aren't many nicer cities to live in but it was a constant uphill battle to work at music for a living there. Before the lure of the Midwest beckoned me, I at least got to play some *quality* music in those West Coast venues.                                                              — *Hal Smith*


I came to Hollywood in 1942, intending to go into defense work, and headed for Lockheed, which had office on Vine. While crossing the street, I was offered a playing job right there — the musicians were all gone in the war — and my first steady job was with Eddie Miller, doing movie work. I went on the road with him with Crosby, then I was with Kay Kyser from 1943 to 1947.

I played my first job with Red Nichols at the *Morocco*. Then I met Pete Daily on the street, who said he was going to make a record and wanted me to join him. Remember, there was hardly any jazz at all — it really started up in San Francisco. So I did the Sunset records with his Chicagoans. After that, things began opening up a bit more.

When Red left L.A., I went with Peewee Hunt over at the Palladium — I was still with Kyser at the time, doing radio shows — then when Peewee left town, I didn't want to go, so I went with Pete Daily into the *Brass Rail* in Glendale for a couple of weeks. Then we got booked at the *Hangover Club*, and I'll tell you nobody was more surprised than I when after two weeks it was standing room only. And it stayed like that for the year we were there.

We went into what later became *Sardi's*, but I left the Daily in early 1949 to play with Nicholls at the *Hangover* for about a year, then over to *Sardi's* again. In 1950 I formed my own band and went into the *Hangover*.

Now at that time, there was a lot going on — down the street on Vine at *Mike Lyman's* there was Red Nichols, around the corner at *Sardi's* Nappy Lamare had his group, Daily was at the *Royal Room*, at the *Beverly Cavern* was Ben Pollack, Kid Ory at the *400 Club* on 8th

BILL NAPIER February 1976

DON KINCH at Malibu Jam c1962

Street, out in Glendale there was Ted Vesely with Ralph Harden on trumpet, it was really something. Then there was Teagarden and others in and out of the area. I stayed at the *Hangover* until it closed in 1955, except for a few months when I formed another group to play Vegas and some other jobs — that was the second band I came back into the *Hangover* with.

The Memphis Five was just a recording group, while I was still with Daily, and the name was Clive Acker's idea, after the original '20s group.

When the *Hangover* folded, we went into the *400 Club* for a while, then to *Zucca's* after Nichols left — he recommended us. That was from 1958 to 1966. In the early '70s, I switched to piano for four years, first at *Reuben E Lee* in Newport with Spencer Quinn for a year and a half, then solo at the *Tower Room* (now *Monty's* in Westwood), and *Gwinn's West* in Pasadena, where I played piano during the week and had a band on weekends. After that, I started in 1974 at *Sterling's* with a trio and we're still going strong after eleven years.

*— Rosy McHargue*

Satisfaction is the major value I place on all my Southern California jazz experience. From a period when *le jazz hot* was just about dead in the area until I moved my jazz activities to Texas, my personal involvement resulted in many inner-warming speculations and accomplishments.

It took several months of thinking and planning before unveiling the New Orleans Jazz Club of California, and from 1963 through 1968, the NOJCC was perhaps the most highly recognized and acclaimed jazz club in the world, serving as a role model for others to follow. Two to four musicians received a paycheck of some sorts at every monthly meeting — a first. And would you believe that the most consistent winner — checks were by lottery — was Warren Smith? Also interesting is that Richard Carpenter (of *the* Carpenters) was a winner once... probably got his first pro paycheck from NOJCC.

We introduced and assisted youngsters like Tom Kubis, Jim Hession, Ted des Plantes, and the South Market Street Jazz Band, and supported many then-unknown jazzmen like Bill Allred, Mike Silverman, Charlie Bornemann, and others. As far as I know, we were the first jazz club ever to not only spotlight two or three feature bands every meeting, but to roust night club owners to come out and hear them. We even got jazz writers and critics to show up and dig — Ian Whitcomb, Ruth Ashton, Digby Diehl, Leonard Feather, et al.

Other satisfactions came in getting jazz records into juvenile homes and orphanages, and arranging for jazz bands to play at them. And in bringing the famous Kenny Ball Jazzmen over from England for three concerts, and in reuniting Pete Daily's Chicagoans. Perhaps most satisfying above all was putting together the NOJCC All-Stars for the sole Monterey Dixieland Jazz Festival in 1968, who surpassed plain satisfaction — they were splendiferous! Rave reviews came one after another, and one such came when Phil Elwood, who was master of ceremonies, reviewed us over the microphone in most glorifying terms. For years, a hallmark of a jazzman's history was playing in Ben Pollack's band... now, forever, I can tell how Ben Pollack played in *my* band!

*— Bill Bacin*

The El Dorado more or less ceased to exist after Ruedger went to Ohio — his regular job took him there — and Jim and Carol Leigh went to Mexico. Bill Carroll joined Turk; Carter

Sacramento All-Stars May 1974
John Smith, Bob Mielke, Dick
Cary, Bill Napier, Barney Bigard,
Dick Oxtot, Jim Cumming

RALPH SUTTON
May 1978

went to the Middle East. That left Pete Fay and myself and we never re-formed the band. Danny subsequently returned to Los Angeles from Ohio and started a new band there, which he also call the El Dorado. This was the band with Ray Ronnei, Sereth, Crown and Mike Fay which burned up the L.A. area.

Rowland Working died tragically by drowning near Tracy. He must have been about 28 or so. He played in a style similar to Bob Helm. In fact, Helm would sometimes come to the old *Kerosene Club* and sit in and when the two of them traded fours, you could hardly tell them apart. They used to do a duet on "Perdido Street Blues" that would make chills run down your spine.

Next to go was Pete Fay, who committed suicide. He was going through a divorce when everything got to be too much, I guess. Danny eventually left L.A. for Grass Valley. I was able to coax him out of musical retirement there to join the Magonila in '78, I think. We became very close friends during those years with Robbie's band on tour and around the Bay Area. Then he died of a heart attack in March 1984.

As Bill Carroll said to me, these guys will always be remembered for their contributions to the jazz scene. — *Jim Borkenhagen*

Perhaps the most visible (and visual) band was the Firehouse 5 + 2 with their bright red fireman's shirts and white helmets, an idea of Ward Kimball's when his group, then the San Gabriel Valley Blueblowers, was scheduled to play a horseless carriage trip to San Diego. The final name arose out of an occasion at the *Club 47* in the San Fernando Valley where musicians sat in with Zutty Singleton's group. There an unknown, slightly boozy patron, upon eyeing the original band uniform of red shirts, said: "Y'know what? You guys look like a bunch of firemen. You look like the firehouse five..." and Kimball immediately adopted the name, tacking on the "Plus Two" for scenic effect. The name, the costumes and the siren became an instant trademark, so much so that many other jazz groups seized upon the idea, adding a "plus" number to their titles and dressing accordingly. — *KOE*

The world has changed for no one more than the musician. They now have drum machines and bass machines, synthesizers you program instead of playing. The music depends on what you can plug in. Where you once found a trio, you'll now find a one-man electronic wizard producing his digital sounds. Still, there'll always be jazz musicians around who will go anywhere to play just for the joy of it. — *Norma Teagarden*

In the fall of 1957, I joined Dave Weirbach's Newport Harbor Jazz Band and celebrated my 19th birthday playing at the infamous *Honeybucket* in Costa Mesa, telling the audience I was 22. That was a great joint... low gunny-sack ceiling, smoke like ocean fog. Marines would come up from Camp Pendleton and collide with college boys from Orange Coast College. When a fight started, as it almost always did, the manager would gently steer them out into the parking lot and call the cops only if it became necessary. Only a few years ago, the Costa Mesa city fathers rejected another club in the district with "Oh, no... we're not going to have another *Honeybucket* in this town!"

Ernie Carson was still in the Marines then and would sit in with us, often still in his colorful dress uniform. When he was discharged, he replaced "Colonel" John Henderson on

JIM MAIHACK May 1973

DIXIE FLYERS c1960
Brooks, Vann, Darensbourg, DeLay, W Smith, Morgan

cornet. In the summer of 1958, we opened at Pacific Ocean Park in Venice, next to Lawrence Welk's Aragon Ballroom. During the day we marched and played for acts like the Seal Circus, and at night we played a speakeasy built almost below the pier. The keytops of the brand-new piano fell within three months, it was so humid! — **Rob Rhodes**

Early in 1960, Burt Bales was hit by a car and had to undergo a lot of expensive medical treatment. It seemed that every musician in town was pulling for him, so I approached several club owners and bandleaders about putting together a benefit night to help cover some of those hospital bills. The response was immediate and heartwarming, and it says something about why San Francisco musicians preferred to stay near home as much as possible.

For just one dollar, a ticket-holder could wander from *Pier 23* to *On the Levee* to the *Jazz Cellar* to the *Kewpie Doll* — all of whom kicked in a large chunk of their profits that evening — and hear Kid Ory's Creole Band, Bob Mielke's Bearcats, the El Dorado and Great Pacific Jazz Bands, Muggsy Spanier's and Marty Marsala's groups, Dick Oxtot's Polecats and Wally Rose's band.

The newspapers helped to promote the affair and every club overflowed with fans, musicians and well-wishers. The next day, I took a check for $2000 — an impressive amount in 1960 — to Burt at the hospital. San Francisco's closely-knit jazz family had come through. And so did Burt. — **Richard Hadlock**

It's true I had carte blanche with the Watters band. I must say that was an exception. Lu was a man with an idea and he clung to it until the end of the Yerba Buena days. He looked at each performance of the music as if it were a tapestry, each part or thread contributing to the whole.

Lu said, "Play a lot of piano." He knew I was timid, so he encouraged me to play out. He always wrote a beautiful bass line to build on but the main thrust in the Watters band was ensemble playing. The sound was *awsome*, a veritable juggernaut! That's why he wanted me to play rich. Both musicians and audiences were caught up in it.

Watters was shy, too, but a powerful player. I imagine Oliver's two-trumpet band had some of that same feeling. Lu had a huge collection of Oliver-Armstrong records and I took to that music like a duck to water. It was Watters who got me to play ragtime, you know. — **Wally Rose**
*from an interview by Jean Keeler*

I moved from Oklahoma City to Long Beach in 1942, where my brothers, Charles and Cub, were stationed after enlisting in the Air Corps' Ferry Command. Jack decided to make his headquarters there, too, and for the first time in many years, the Teagardens were all in the same town.

After playing with Jack's band during the war — mostly military bases — I rejoined him in 1952 at the old *Royal Room* in Hollywood. Ray Bauduc was on the drums, Charles on the trumpet, Bob McCracken on clarinet and Kas Malone on string bass. It was really a great feeling to be together since we were such a close family and Jack and Charles were such great musicians. Cub was, too, but he dropped out of music to go into business.

273

PEANUTS HUCKO
May 1977

BUNKY COLMAN
May 1980

I've been lucky about working steadily. I've been at the *Washington Square Bar & Grill* for almost 11 years and so many fine players have worked there. Lou Levy comes up from LA frequently, and one of my very favorite pianists in this area is Don Haas. I worked several festivals with Rex Allen, a fine trombonist, and played in LA recently with Betty O'Hara, one of the few women horn players I know. She is wonderful.

In 43 years of performing in California, I couldn't possibly name the musicians I have met and known, loved and admired, but it has been a ball. Thank goodness, it isn't over yet.

— *Norma Teagarden*


A little-known fact about Ken "Scott" Stoddard is that he was responsible for bringing Tudie Garland out of retirement. We happened to be sitting around one evening, discussing the whereabouts of various musicians. I dug up the phone number of Tudie and Ken called him several times, trying to convince him to bring his bass to some session or jazz club meeting. He didn't want to be bothered at first but Ken persisted and, finally, one day got him to play. This was a historic event as Tudie then went on to play for almost another 20 years!

— *Roger Jamieson*


By the late '50s, Burt Bales had become a reliable tourist attraction at *Pier 23* on San Francisco's waterfront. The old shacklike building, with outdoor plumbing, seemed as earthy and indestructable as Burt himself. It was a joy to sit at the bar and watch the sparkling bay while listening to a capsule history of jazz piano.

Musicians of every stripe gathered nightly, trying their wings or polishing their skills. Marty Marsala, Ernie Figueroa, Muggsy Spanier and Darnell Howard were among those who would drop in to jam. Take this good company, add Burt's blunt criticism or gruff praise and you get a master class for young musicians. Burt was patient with beginners, but firm with anyone who came to show off rather than to play. In short, he was a real professor.

— *Richard Hadlock*


The 1975 Sacramento Festival was their second but it was the first for everyone in the nine-piece Magnolia Jazz Band. Our first performance was Friday night at the big concert site, following Teddy Wilson's All-Stars, and we were scared stiff! Guest artists were assigned to play with certain bands at certain times and, for that opener, we had Cougar Nelson and George Probert. With their help, we managed to get through it alive and were on top of the world.

How I did it, I don't know, but I somehow survived the rest of the Memorial Day weekend without sleep and in a condition that would warm the heart of any bar owner. I loved every note I heard and missed damn few of them.

Then the big thrill came on our final set at the *Union*. There was an SRO audience and we had a good set, with some of the Max Collie band joining us. As was often the case with the Magnolia, our last number, "Cakewalking Babies," went on for ten minutes. We normally played sitting down, but we stood up for the last chorus and so did the audience, clapping and cheering and carrying on for quite a while after we had finished. That last chorus and that audience was one nobody in the band will ever forget. There wasn't a dry eye on the stage. I doubt that I'll ever have a bigger musical thrill.

— *Cal Abbott*

SANFORD NEWBAUER April 1973

AUD ALEXANDER and his Alexander's Ragtime Band 1924

1985 Pismo Jubilee "Megamess" - Bob Ohnhaus, Lynn Hall, Dick Knutson, Phil Crumley, Richard Cruz, Wayne Nicholls, Cal Abbott, Ben Russell, unknown tpt, Danny Davis

JEFF WALKER
October 1985

YOUNG MEN FROM
NEW ORLEANS 1966
Redd, Carrere,
Darensbourg, DeLay

DAVE KENNEDY
October 1985

In 1982, actor George Segal put together a jazz band to tour Israeli hospitals and soldiers' rest centers after their invasion of Lebanon and I was fortunate to be included, along with Lloyd Byassee, Pat Gogerty, Walt Greenawald, Art Leon, Mike Silverman and Dan Weinstein. On our first night we were invited to play a live radio show at the Tel Aviv Hilton — the first time the band had played together. The show was similar to Merv Griffin's or Johnny Carson's format and the host, who began with an interview with George, had the most gutteral Israeli accent I'd ever heard.

"So tell me, Mr Segal, is this your first time in Israel?" he asked. George politely answered, "Yes," to which the host retorted, "Nu, so vat took you so long?" That line has remained a mainstay with the group ever since. Whenever the guys in that band see each other, it's, "Nu, so vat took you so long?"

Then, right after our debut on radio, we ended up backstage in a three-hour jam session with Itzhak Perlman on violin and Zubin Mehta on drums! So went our introduction to Israel.                                                             — *Dave Dolson*

In 1949, when Good Time Jazz began operations, there were four traditional jazz bands on the West Coast, each one in its own way unusual, to say the least. In Los Angeles, Kid Ory had made a remarkable comeback with his Creole Jazz Band, and the newly organized and spectacularly popular Firehouse Five Plus Two were also livening things up. The group which began the worldwide traditional revival of the '40s, Lu Watters' Yerba Buena Jazz Band, with Turk Murphy and Bob Scobey, were at *Hambone Kelly's* across the bay from San Francisco. And in Portland was the talented group of jazz lovers, *amateurs de jazz*, as the French say, who called themselves the Castle Jazz Band.

These groups, despite their many differences, had several things in common: they believed in the New Orleans style of ensemble improvisation; they used the repertoire of tunes developed by King Oliver, Jelly Roll Morton and, in Ory's case by himself, plus ragtime classics; and they were characterized by a happy, spontaneous, "good time" feeling.

— *Lester Koenig (1958)*
*founder of Good Time Jazz Record Co*

Just what is Trad Jazz? I don't know for sure, but I do know that this form of American music is responsible for more amateur musicians continuing to play than any other form.

Whenever I run into one of my "kids" (some are in their fifties now), our "remember whens" always turn to those shared enjoyable musical experiences. This is true whether they are professional musicians, architects, Arabian horse breeders, taxi drivers, engineers or whatever. This unique American experience provides a rare opportunity for self-expression in a relaxed and friendly atmosphere. And yet, good jazz is highly disciplined. The possibility for error in a 32-bar chorus with a jazz sextette playing eight notes to the bar is 1,536! And we expect it to be in tune, too. Wow!                           — *George Beatie*
*Professor Emeritus, Music,*
*California Polytechnic State University*

The luster of Hollywood and Vine today retains no semblance of its post-war glory. That famed intersection was only a few feet east of *Sardi's*, a cavernous club nestled behind several stores where Nappy Lamare's Strawhatters entertained nightly. The *Club Morocco* was a block away on Vine. Frankie Laine attracted the customers but Carl Fisher's piano

VESS BETHEL
January 1966

JAZZIN' BABIES August 1985
Miller, Math, Dolson, Fisher,
Rosy McHargue

delighted the jazz fans. A few years later, it became *Kid Ory's*, which promptly folded and became a Thrifty Drugs store.

Crossing Sunset a few blocks away, you could hear Rosy McHargue's Ragtimers in the *Club Hangover*, now a monolithic office building. That tiny club was home for many jazz fans of the late '40s and early '50s; the smoke was thick but the music was lively and Marvin Ash's intermission piano kept the customers happy. Even the dusty moose over the bar had a perennial smile. *Mike Lyman's* across the street was where Red Nichols and his Five Pennies were the attraction, where Joe Rushton was a fixture. Because of some long-forgotten disagreement, Joe and Red never spoke to each other, but played beautifully together. Invariably, after an exquisite solo, Joe would disassemble his huge horn, cursing a faulty mouthpiece or a loose pad, but he always managed to get it back together in time for the final chorus.

A few blocks down on Vine Street, on a corner now the parking lot of the musicians' union, was Louis Prima's *Jitterbug House*. From time to time his illustrious sidemen included Matty Matlock, Eddie Miller and Ray Bauduc. A most popular club on Vine was *Billy Berg's*, where we had an opportunity to hear the local debut of Louis Armstrong's All-Stars, with Bigard, Catlett, Hines, Shaw and Teagarden. The cover charge was steep and the drinks watered but Satchmo was at the peak of his powers and SRO was the format there every night.

Back on Hollywood Blvd, the *Royal Room* featured the George Lewis Band from New Orleans. Across the street at *The Jade*, Kid Ory's Creole Band played their first engagement after those historic appearances on Orson Welles' Mercury Theater radio series. The clarinet chair was occupied initially by Jimmy Noone, then by Darnell Howard and Joe Darensbourg. Papa Mutt Carey blew that soulful, muted trumpet. Ory had the reatest rhythm section: Buster Wilson, Ed Garland, Bud Scott and Minor "Ram" Hall. Later, the Ory band, with Andy Blakeney on trumpet, moved to the *Beverly Cavern*, where we spent many wonderful evenings listening to those great musicians.

A short ride over Cahuenga Pass, in the San Fernando Valley, a huge bank now stands on Ventura Blvd where *The Astor* was once a regular locale for Pete Daily's Chicagoans. Another Valley bistro, *Club 47* (named after the musicians' union), hosted nightly jam sessions. Eventually, Zutty Singleton became the house drummer and occasionally cooked his famous red beans and rice for enthusiastic customers.

Unfortunately, none of the clubs exists today and so few of the fine musicians are still alive. It was truly a golden era that has left many warm memories with me.

*— Floyd Levin*

WILD BILL DAVISON May 1975

EARL McKEE (minus tuba and cowboy hat) November 1973

# REFERENCE

**Collector's Jazz** John S Wilson (1958 J B Lippincott)

**The Complete Encyclopedia of Popular Music and Jazz 1900-50** Roger D Kinkle (four vols 1974 Arlington)

**Hear Me Talkin' To Ya** Nat Hentoff & Nat Shapiro (1955 Holt Reinhart & Winston, reprint 1966 Dover)

**Jazz Directory** Dave Carey & Albert McCarthy (1955)

**Jazz: New Orleans 1885-1963** Samuel B Charters (1963 Oak Publications)

**The Jazz Story** Dave Dexter Jr (1964 Prentice-Hall)

**Just For the Record** Jim Goggin (1982 SF Traditional Jazz Foundation)

**New Orleans Jazz** Al Rose & Edmond Souchon (1967 LSU Press)

**Pictorial History Of Jazz** Bill Grauer & Orrin Keepnews (1966 Crown)

**The Real Jazz Old and New** Stephen Longstreet (1956 Louisiana State University)

**TJ Today** quarterly publication; Box 533, Watsonville CA 95077

**Who's Who In Jazz** John Chilton (1972 Chilton, rev 1979 Time Life)

For those who are curious about production details, the entire book was created on an Apple IIe computer, using an Applewriter word processing program, with a resultant 530,000 character count. Codified type commands were added to the copy and the data then sent via modem to a Merganthaler Linotype digital typesetter at Tintype Graphic Arts in San Luis Obispo, California. Primary typeface is Garamond Book Condensed. Time of involvement from conception of the idea to the first hard copy was 16 months.